A GAELIC LEXICON FOR

Finnegans Wake

A GAELIC LEXICON FOR
Finnegans Wake
AND GLOSSARY
FOR JOYCE'S OTHER WORKS

by Brendan O Hehir

University of California Press

BERKELEY AND LOS ANGELES 1967

UNIVERSITY OF CALIFORNIA PRESS
BERKELEY AND LOS ANGELES, CALIFORNIA
CAMBRIDGE UNIVERSITY PRESS
LONDON, ENGLAND

© 1967 BY THE REGENTS OF THE UNIVERSITY OF CALIFORNIA
LIBRARY OF CONGRESS CATALOG CARD NUMBER: 67-29785

PRINTED IN THE UNITED STATES OF AMERICA

FOR
Norman Shumway, M.D., and his colleagues, and A. A. Bolomey, M.D.

Preface

To attempt such a Lexicon as this of the Gaelic or Irish in *Finnegans Wake* probably seems today, even in the abstract, less derisory a task than it might have seemed a decade ago. The actual extent of the present list may occasion some surprise, but certainly not so much as it would have when the fashion still was to assume that Joyce knew little or no Irish. Partly Joyce himself is to blame for the prevalence of that assumption, for he intimates in *A Portrait of the Artist as a Young Man* that Stephen Dedalus dropped the Irish course in which he had enrolled after only one lesson. Taking fiction for fact, readers were content in the comfortable belief that the Gaelic in *Finnegans Wake* could not amount to more than a smattering—more perhaps than of Basque or Albanian, but not a great deal more. The belief was all the more comfortable in that Irish is a difficult language with a thorny orthography and opaque even to the most polyglot of ordinary readers.

That old assumption has more recently been not so much shattered as slowly dissipated. More and more snippets of Irish have been dredged up, by one reader or another, from here and there in *Finnegans Wake*. Above all, the undesigned revelations of Stanislaus Joyce have shown that his brother left Ireland with a better initial knowledge of the language of his ancestors than anyone had previously supposed. The Irish lessons James Joyce submitted to, for instance, lasted sporadically for about two years rather than the single session Stephen Dedalus undertook: with Joyce's linguistic flair even a desultory attention for so long would have given him at least a modest competence in Irish. Stanislaus shows also that he and his brother shared a penchant for etymologizing the names of the places where they lived—Glengarriff Road, for instance, and Clontarf. He provides, too, some pleasant vignettes of the Reverend Patrick S. Dinneen, Professor of Irish at the National University in Dublin while Joyce was a student there. Dinneen published in 1904 the first edition of what has since been recognized (especially since the second edition of 1927) as the standard modern dictionary of Irish. Father

Dinneen arrives offstage during the library episode in *Ulysses*, and among the books Joyce left in his Paris apartment was an abridged edition of Dinneen's dictionary. To complement Dinneen, Joyce's collection also included E. E. Fournier d'Albe's *English-Irish Dictionary*. One is additionally free to speculate upon how much some of Joyce's young companions who came out from Ireland in the Paris days were able to feed him of whatever bits of Irish he wished.

The penchant for etymologizing place-names persists in *Finnegans Wake* ("Meadow of Honey" [076.04], "brow of a hazelwood, pool in the dark" [135.13–14]), and has therefore constrained this Lexicon to etymologize all Irish place-names in *Finnegans Wake*, whether or not their relevance is apparent. Likewise Joyce not infrequently etymologizes personal and family names (see, for instance, 140.02), forcing upon the Lexicon a like etymologizing of all Irish personal names in *Finnegans Wake*. It has already been observed (for example, in Mrs. Glasheen's *Second Census*) that Joyce employs the name "Mahon" or "Mahan" in the direct light of his awareness that it represents Irish *mathghamhain*, "bear." Sometimes etymologizing names in *Finnegans Wake* reveals a surprising applicability in the context, often enough it reveals nothing at all that I, at any rate, can see. But perseverance has its rewards, and perhaps the most joyous of these comes in the etymologization of one conjunction of personal name and place-name: "Dorsan from Dunshanagan" (417.31). Sometimes a sudden flash will illuminate the use Joyce is making of an underlying meaning; sometimes no flash comes and the etymologizing of names remains a dry pedantic exercise. But a lexicographer is not called upon to decide the relevance of what he records. I have therefore endeavored to reveal the meaning of whatsoever Irish I have been able to find in *Finnegans Wake* so that more sensitive readers will have, I trust, all the materials available on which to deploy their perceptions.

Undoubtedly many items in this Lexicon will prove ultimately irrelevant or useless, but their inclusion requires no apology. Likewise it would be vain to apologize for the inadvertent omissions, which I am sure must be many. Each day that this Lexicon has been in my hands I have found something to add to it; each time I go again over the text of *Finnegans Wake* I find some new and seemingly obvious bit of Irish I had not seen before. That the process will stop now that the lists are no longer in my hands seems an empty hope.

Another task beyond the scope of the present work which this Lexicon should nevertheless facilitate, is that of determining exactly how much Irish Joyce knew. As a preliminary to that task, for whoever may undertake it, a few brief observations may be made:

1. A hasty spot check of this Lexicon against David Hayman's edition of the *First-Draft Version of Finnegans Wake* leaves the impression that most of the Irish was superadded after the first draft. This presumably indicates that the Irish did not flow spontaneously to Joyce's pen, but had to be worked up deliberately.

2. In his "Scribbledehobble" notebook for *Finnegans Wake* (edited by Thomas Connolly) Joyce included a longish list of the languages employed in the book. The first three in order are English, Irish, Norse. The order of these languages corresponds exactly to the vocabulary content they have contributed to modern Irish vernaculars, and the possibility is worth exploring that Joyce intended the languages of *Finnegans Wake* to bulk in the book in relative volume directly proportionate to this order. The considerable amount of Irish revealed by this present Lexicon may support this hypothesis.

3. Joyce's spelling habits in Irish may provide a clue to the source or sources from which he drew his knowledge of the language. The test is provided by the spelling of the vowel sound in these doublets: Seumas/Séamus, Beurla/Béarla, reul/réal. All three words are found in *Finnegans Wake*, and Joyce invariably opts for the -eu- spelling even though both Dinneen's and Fournier d'Albe's dictionaries use -éa-, which is also by far the more common (although *reul*, "sixpenny piece," is the spelling on Irish coins).

It should not be supposed that Joyce was a profound Gaelic scholar. With a number of sharp and surprising exceptions, the Gaelic displayed in *Finnegans Wake* is of an elementary and commonplace character. Often too the grammar is faulty, and one would wish it possible to ascertain if Joyce was cognizant of his solecisms. But here subtle discrimination would be called for: how much evidence does *Finnegans Wake* provide that Joyce was this century's master of both idiomatic and recherché English prose? On occasion, moreover, he attains authentic Joycean virtuosity exclusively within the medium of Irish, as when, at 042.11–12 ("seinn fion, seinn fion's araun"), he saturates a nationalist slogan with public-house revelry. He had at any rate the eyes and minds of some of his younger Irish friends to help him, and scarcely any authority used in verifying the Irish for the present Lexicon was not also available to Joyce: Dinneen,

Woulfe on personal names, P. W. Joyce's *Irish Names of Places* (mentioned in "Gas from a Burner").

Joyce's use of Gaelic materials, like his use of most other classes of materials, was eclectic and often secondhand. His sources were common handbooks, common source books, common tradition, frequently of infrascholarly authority and outmoded or exploded by recent research. Yet since utility for his ends constituted all the authority Joyce sought, it would be blind pedantry to attempt to "correct" either him or his sources. But although readers of *Finnegans Wake* will scarcely require the disclaimer, at least *pro forma* it should be stated that the present work does not and cannot pretend to be an infallible guide to Irish history or Celtic lexicography. Its sole intent is to serve as a Gaelic vade mecum for readers of *Finnegans Wake*, and *Finnegans Wake* is the universe of its discourse. In any crux, therefore, Joyce's most probable source *ipso facto* carries the weightiest authority. Consequently Joycean readers will readily grasp the fact that a shaky etymology offered by P. W. Joyce is infinitely more authoritative than all the topographical-onomastic researches of more learned academicians (and an etymology invented *ad hoc* by James Joyce outweighs all the law and the prophets). Likewise it would be fatuous to attempt to discriminate to any degree fact from fiction in the traditional stories about historical and pseudohistorical persons that Joyce deals with.

Although few readers are likely to run aground on shoals such as those, one further reef needs a warning marker. Although the present is no place for a general discussion of the Irish language, some remarks may be in order to clarify certain apparent anomalies in the Glossary of this Lexicon which an acute reader may spot, though the reasons for them will be patent enough to any Gaelicist. History has precluded the formation for Irish either of a rigid standard orthography or of a single dominant dialect. Additionally, the phonemes of Irish, though more numerous than those of English, seem often individually to embrace a broader range of phonetic values than is usual in English. In Irish, for instance, there is frequently no phonemic distinction between the sounds of v and w; it is largely custom, dialect, or even choice on the part of a speaker that determines the occurrence of one pronunciation rather than the other. Consequently Irish words have rarely a single "proper" pronunciation, and the reader of this Lexicon should therefore understand that inconsistencies he may find in the spelling and pronunciation of ostensibly the same word in different occurrences are not necessarily inadvertent. As to the spelling, I have in general adhered to the older spelling of Irish—that prevalent during Joyce's lifetime and that in which Dinneen's dictionary is printed —rather than the reformed spelling promulgated in 1948. My sporadic use of the new spelling is perhaps essentially irrational, but I never use it where the written appearance of the word was obviously in Joyce's mind; *siúl*, for instance, as against the former *siubhal*, seems warranted by Joyce's purely phonetic "shool" and "shule" (*suil* in *Ulysses*).

The tricolumnar format of this Lexicon has been adopted both as the most rational approach to the glossing of the Irish in *Finnegans Wake* and also to conform as closely as possible to a common pattern for all similar projected lexicons, most especially that of the companion work, Helmut Bonheim's *German Lexicon*. Occasionally, however, three columns have been too procrustean a bed for unwieldy information and matter that would require a multifold repetition or endless cross-referencing. In such cases a compromise has been effected, and the columnar entry directs the reader to one or more of a series of Supplementary Notes arranged alphabetically at the end of the Glossary. Three Additional Notes at the end supply some further more general information.

Because the main glossary for *Finnegans Wake* is followed by a glossary of the Gaelic words and phrases in all the rest of Joyce's works (excepting only the fragmentary *Stephen Hero*), this book might fairly claim to be *A Gaelic Lexicon to All of Joyce*. Nevertheless the number of glosses required by all the other works combined is only about three hundred, so that the value of the glosses is that of sporadic illumination of local obscurities in the texts. For *Finnegans Wake* the glosses are vital to the elucidation of the whole work.

The more important authorities consulted in compiling this Lexicon are listed separately in the Bibliography. A number of Irish place-names I have checked the etymologies of myself, on the ground in Ireland. Others have been provided by my uncle, Brendan Lennon, of Dublin (and at the moment, of Central Butte, Saskatchewan). I should also like to thank Éamonn de hÓir, Oifigeach Sinsearach Logainmeacha, of An Coimisiún Logainmeacha, for help with some difficult place-name derivations. Also an immense debt remains outstanding to my friend Professor Vivian Mercier who kindly read over the manuscript and pointed out some glaring omissions and errors; the remaining flaws, however, must be attributed to myself alone.

In this place also some special recognition should be made of the inestimable help in any such project as the present that is afforded by Clive Hart's *Concordance to Finnegans Wake*; without that work compiling and cross-checking any lexicon to *Finnegans Wake* would be a task almost insuperable. I should also like to express gratitude for encouragement in my task extended by Clive Hart, Fritz Senn, Helmut Bonheim, David Hayman, and other Joyceans, and by my friend and colleague Professor Ralph Rader, of the English Department at Berkeley, and by Robert Zachary, Los Angeles editor of the University of California Press. And last but most of all I must thank my wife, Diana Farnham O Hehir, for early help in compiling materials, and for her patience and her impatience.

BIBLIOGRAPHY

The following are the works chiefly consulted in making this Lexicon:

"An Seabhach," ed., *Toraíocht Dhiarmada agus Ghráinne*, Áth Cliath agus Corcaigh (n.d.).

Dinneen, Rev. Patrick S., *Foclóir Gaedhilge agus Béarla: an Irish-English Dictionary*, Dublin and Cork (1927).

Fournier d'Albe, Edmund E., *An English-Irish Dictionary and Phrase Book*, Dublin (n.d.[1905]).

Glasheen, Adaline, *A Second Census of Finnegans Wake*, Evanston (1963).

Hart, Clive, *A Concordance to Finnegans Wake*, Minneapolis (1963).

Hayman, David, ed., *A First-Draft Version of Finnegans Wake*, Austin (1963).

Joyce, Patrick Weston, *Irish Names of Places*, Vol. I, 7th ed., Dublin and London (1901); Vol. II, Dublin and London (1902); Vol. III, Dublin and London (1920).

Woulfe, Rev. Patrick, *Sloinnte Gaedheal is Gall: Irish Names and Surnames*, Dublin (1923).

MAPS

"An Seabhach," *Léarscáil na hÉireann*, Áth Cliath (n.d.).

Léarscáilíocht Éireann, Survey of Ireland (Ordnance Survey), *Map of Dublin*, Dublin (n.d.).

Contents

Key to the Glossaries

The Glossaries are arranged in three principal columns. On the left, preceded by the page and line numbers of *Finnegans Wake* and Joyce's other works, according to the convention established by Clive Hart's *Concordance*, occurs *verbatim et literatim* the word or phrase to be glossed. The central column prints in Irish the original of the word or phrase Joyce has used, together with a phonetic transcription (see Pronunciation). The third or right-hand column translates the word or phrase into English, or provides an explanatory comment, or on occasion does both.

PRONUNCIATION

The second or central column in the Glossaries consists of Irish words or phrases spelled in Irish, followed in parentheses by a phonetic transcript of the Irish pronunciation. Only an approximation of the more difficult Irish sounds is attempted, but on the whole the phonetic spelling should give a reasonable idea of the phonetic basis upon which Joyce is building. The phonetic spelling attempts something of a compromise between conventional English and conventional Irish spelling, and the letters used are intended to represent the following sounds:

VOWEL SOUNDS

á	all, law	(ál, lá)
a	act, bat	(akt, bat)
é	brave, weigh	(brév, wé)
e	ebb, set	(eb, set)
í	bee, machine	(bí, mashín)
i	if, big	(if, big)
ó	over, no	(óver, nó)
o	lot, top	(lot, top)
ú	ooze, rule	(úz, rúl) [*not* unite (yúneit)]
u	bun	(bun)
ei	ice, fight	(eis, feit)
ou	loud, out	(loud, out)

CONSONANTS

d a voiced plosive made with tongue spread behind upper teeth; like d in French *droit;* somewhat like th in "*th*en," "fa*th*er."

d' d + y as in "di*d y*ou"—approaching j as in "di*dj*a."

g as in "give," "beg," *not* "George."

h lighter than in English.

kh heavier than English h, lighter than German ch in "a*ch*."

ġ voiced velar spirant corresponding to kh; like a roughened y deep in the throat.

ñ as in "o*ni*on," "si*ng*er."

s as in "*s*ing," "hi*ss*" (siñ, his), *not* "his," "is," "pleasure."

sh as in "*sh*oe," "pu*sh*" (shú, push).

t unvoiced plosive made with tongue spread behind upper teeth; like t in French *trés;* somewhat like th in "*th*is," "tru*th*."

t' t + y as in "go*t y*ou"—approaching ch as in "got*ch*a."

w consonant only, as in "*w*ater," "*w*in" (wáter, win), *not* "new," "lawyer" (ñú, láyer).

y consonant only, as in "*y*ak," "*y*et" (yak, yet), *not* "early," "try" (erlí, trei).

All others approximately as in English.

ABBREVIATIONS AND SYMBOLS

abp.	archbishop
adj.	adjective
anc.	ancient
anglic.	anglicised, anglicé
Asp.	aspiration, aspirated form
c.	century; circa
Co./co.	County/county
Cos./cos.	Counties/counties
dat.	dative (case or form)
des./dess.	descendant/descendants
dim.	diminutive
E.	East, Eastern
fem.	feminine
g.	genitive (case or form)
I.	Ireland, Irish

interj.	interjection
lit.	literally, literal
masc.	masculine
N.	North, Northern
n.	name; noun; nominative (case or form)
pers. n.	personal name
pfx.	prefix
pl.	plural
prep.	preposition
pron.	pronounced
S.	South, Southern
sing.	singular
sp.	spelling, spelled
st./sts.	saint/saints
suffx.	suffix
trans.	translates, is a translation of; translation
v.	verb
W.	West, Western
*	see indicated Supplementary Note

Other abbreviations follow standard conventions. Ordinal numbers are abbreviated 1st, 2nd, 3rd, 4th, etc.

Glossary for Finnegans Wake

003.07	Oconee	ochón (okhón)	alas	
.08	doublin	Dubh-linn (*d*uvliñ)	Black Pool; *Dublin	
.09	mishe mishe	mise (mishi)	I, me (emphatic)	
.10	thuartpeatrick	tú (*tú*)	you	
		trans. Cruach Phádraig	Patrick's [Peat-] Rick (i.e., "heap"); Croagh Patrick, mnt., Co. Mayo	
.13	rory	Ruaidhrí (rúrí)	pers. n.; anglic. Roderick; *Ruaidhrí, Ó Conchobhair* (1116–1198) last high king	
.15	–gharaghtak–	gaireachtach (garokh*t*okh)	boisterous	
.16	–skawn–	scán (skán)	crack	
.16–17	–thurnuk	tórnach (*t*órnokh)	thunder	
.19	Finnegan	Ó Fionnagáin (ó finegáñ)	des. of *Fionnagán* (dim. of *Fionn*, "fair")	
.22	knock	cnoc (knuk)	hill	
.23	devlinsfirst	Dubh-linn (*d*uvliñ)	Black Pool; *Dublin	
.24	livvy	Life (lifi)	*Liffey River	
004.04	Malachus	Maelsheach-lainn (mélokhlin) mullach (mulokh)	Servant of *Seachlann* (St. Secundinus, baptized by St. Patrick); anglic. *Malachy head	
.04	Micgranes	Mag Ráighne (mográñe)	son of *Raighne* (pet form of *Raghnall* [Reginald])	

004.07–08	Killykillkilly	cill; coill (kil; kíl)	church; wood; both anglic. *Kil-, Kill- in place-names
		Cill Choin-nigh (kil khiní)	Church of *Coinneach* (pers. n., anglic. Canice); Kilkenny, S.E. co. & town
.08	cashels	caiseal (kashel)	stone fort; Cashel, Co. Tipperary, ecclesiastical acropolis frequently sacked and burned; *Brian Boru
.24	gueneses	Mag Aonghusa (mogénǧese)	son of *Aonghus* ("single-choice" [god of love]); anglic. Guinness
.28	Annie	eanaigh (aní)	fenny, marshy; *Anna
.32	Childeric	éiric (érik)	fine, ransom
005.03	o'toolers	Ó Tuathail (ó túhil)	des. of *Tuathal* ("people-mighty")
.05–06	Booslaeugh	buadh (búe) laoch (léokh)	victory warrior
.10	Finn	Fionn (fin)	fair, white
.23	bedoueen	-ín (ín), *dim. suff.*	little; darling
.31	carhacks	carraig (korig)	rock, stone
.31	fargobawlers	fág a' bealach (fágo byalokh)	clear the way; name for a useless person
.36	bore the more	bóthar mór (bóher mór)	highway, main road
006.01	twelvepins	binne (bini)	peaks, mountains; The Twelve Pins, group of mountains, Joyces' Country, Co. Galway
.02	derryjellybies	doire, daire (diri)	oakwood; pfx. of 1,300 place-names; anglic. Derry-
.05	thurum and thurum	tórramh (tórov)[?]	wake, funeral
		tabhairim (túrim)[?]	I give
		tabhar dhom (túrum)[?]	give me

		tuairim (*túrim*)[?]	opinion
.13	shee	síodh; sídhe (shí)	tomb, tumulus; fairy
.13	Macool	Mac Cumhail (mok kúil)	son of *Cumhal*; patro- nymic of *Fionn*, 3rd c. hero of saga cycle
.13	orra	ara (ore)	deprecatory or expos- tulatory interj.
.15	hoolivans	Uí Shúileabh- áin (í húl- iváñ) *Asp.	dess. of *Súil-dubhán* ("black-eyed"); anglic. Sullivan
.21	kinkin	cinn (kin) caoin (kín)	head, principal; heads wail, lament
.21	kinkin corass	Ceann Coradh (kyoun kuru)	Weir Head; Co. Clare home of *Brian Boru; anglic. Kincora
.21	kankan	can (kon)	sing
.21	keening	caoineadh (kínú)	wailing, lamenting
.26	Priam Olim	Príomh Ollamh (prív uluv)	Chief Poet; highest rank in anc. I. bardic system
.26	brawdawn	bradán (bra*d*án) breágh (brá)	salmon fine, handsome
.27	finisky	[Páirc an] Fionn-uisce (párk un finishki)	Clear-water [Field]; anglic. Phocnix [Park]
.27	guenesis	see 004.24	
.30	tautaulogically	tá (*tá*)	there is; yes
.33	Shopalist	Séipéal Iosaid (shépél isid′)	*Iosada*'s [Iseult's] Chapel; W. Dublin suburb, anglic. Chapelizod
.33	Bailywick	Baile (bolye)	Homestead; home- stead of *Criomhthan*, 1st c. king; anglic. Bailey; lighthouse, Howth Head
.33	baronoath	barr an . . . (bár un)	the top of . . .

.35–36	a horn!	ochón (ukhón)	alas
007.04	issavan essavan	a bhean (a van)	his wife, his woman
		is ea *Vanessa* a bhean (isha vanesa avan)	Vanessa is his wife
		eas (es, as)	waterfall
.04	patterjackmartins	Peadar (pa*d*er)	Peter
		paidir (pa*d*ir)	prayer, Pater Noster
.07	pool the begg	Poll Beig (poul beg)	Little Hole; anglic. Poolbeg (lighthouse), *Dublin
.08	kish	cis (kish)	wickerwork, basket; Kish (lighthouse), *Dublin
.08	crawsake	crádh (krá)	misery
		grádh (grá)	love
.09	boord	bórd (bór*d*)	table
.11	Kennedy	Ó Cinnéide (ó kinédi)	des. of *Cinnéidigh* ("helmeted-head"); *Brian Boru
.12	U'Dunnell	Ua Domh-naill (ú *d*ónil)	des. of *Domhnall* ("world-mighty"); an *Uí Néill family
.14	bodey	bod, boidín (bu*d*, bwid´ín)	penis
.25	Arrah	ara (ore)	expostulatory, deprecatory interj.; *Arrah-na-Pogue
.25–26	Anny . . . Anna	eanaigh (ání)	fenny, marshy; *Anna
.27	nannygoes	An Eanaigh (un aní)	The Fenny; river, Co. Meath, where *Malachy I drowned prince of Bregia (604.04); anglic. Nanny
.28	Benn Heather	Binn Éadair (bin édir)	*Éadar*'s (pers. n.) Peak; I. n. for Howth Head
.28	Seeple Isout	see 006.33	
.30	clay	clé (klé)	left (side)
.35	lyffing	Life (lifi)	*Liffey River
008.17	Sraughter	*L/R Inter-change	Slaughter

		srathughadh (srahú)	directing a battle, disposing troops
.21	boyne	Bóinn (bóñ)	river N. of Dublin, named for a goddess; anglic. *Boyne; battle, 1690
.23	inimyskilling	Inis-Cethlenn (inish keleñ)	*Cethlenn*'s Island; *C.*, wife of Balor, Fomorian king, killed the king of *Tuatha Dé Danann* (*colonists); anglic. Enniskillen
.24, 26	bog . . . beg . . . bag . . . bug	bog (bug) beag (byug)	soft small
.25	Gallawghurs	galgar (golugur) Ó Gallchobhair (ó goulhúwer)	noisy argument des. of *Gallchobhar* ("foreign help"); a Donegal family, marshals of the O Donnels; anglic. Gallagher
.25	argaumunt	argal (árgol)	contention, noise, confusion
.26	Touchole	tuachail (túkhil) Tuathal (túhel)	astute, prudent People-mighty; pers. n. anglic. Toole
.26–27	Tuomush	Tomáis, *g.* (tumásh)	[of] Thomas
.27	Mac Dyke	Mac an Deagánaigh (mokun d'agání)	son of the deacon; anglic. MacDigney, etc.
.27	Hairy O'Hurry	Ó hÍr (ó hír); Ó hAichir (ó hakhir) Ó hEarchaidh (ó hyorkhí) Ó hEaghra (ó hyoure)	des. of *ír* ("anger"); des. of *Aichear* ("bitter"); both anglic. O Hare des. of *Earchadh* ("noble-warrior"); anglic. O Hurroe, etc. des. of *Eaghra* ("death"?); anglic. O Hara

.36	hrosspower	ros-, *pfx.* (ros)	horse-
009.05	Leaper Orthor	léimtear orthu (lémter urhu)	they are leapt upon
.07	Shee, shee	síodh, *n.*; sídhe, *adj.* (shí)	tomb, tumulus; fairy
.10	bode	bod (bu*d*)	penis
.18	guinness	see 004.24	
.22	bawn	bán (bán)	white
.25	solphereens	sulfairín (sulfirín)	sulphur + dim. suffx.
.27	Finnlambs	fionn (fin)	fair
.32	cool	cúl (kúl)	bottommost part
.33	marathon	tón (*t*ón)	bottom, arse
.34	branlish	bran (bron)	raven, chief; name of *Fionn Mac Cumhail*'s dog
		lis, *g.* (lish)	[of a] fort
.36	porca	porca (purke)	pig, hog
		*P/K Split: corca (kurke)	offspring, race
.36	fimmieras	fimín (fimín) fimide (fimid'i)	tail, tuft pig's tail
		Éire (ére)	Ireland
010.04	hinnessy	Ó Fhionn-ghusa (ó hin-ġesi), *on analogy of*	des. of *Fionnghus* ("fair-choice")
		Ó hAonghusa (ó hénġesi)	des. of *Aonghus* ("single-choice"), anglic. Hennessy
.05	dooley	Ó Dubh-laoich (ó *d*úlíkh)	des. of *Dubhlaoch* ("black-warrior")
.06	the hinndoo Shimar Shin	an fhionn-dubh siomar sin (un hin*d*ú shimer shin)	that fair-dark trefoil (or, shamrock)

.06	boy	buidhe (bwí)	yellow (often derogatory)
.16	madrashattaras	madra (mo*d*re)	dog
.18	the . . . Shimar Shin	an siomar sin (un shimer shin)	that trefoil (shamrock)
.26	annaone	eanach (anokh)	fen, marsh
		áth na (áne) abhann (ouwen)	the ford of river; *Anna
.35	glav	claidheamh (klíev)	sword
011.01	three of crows	Badhbh, Macha, Neamhan (bauv, mokhe, naven)	the war-goddesses; each name is that of a kind of crow
.03–05	Thon	tón (*t*ón) tonn (*t*on)	bottom, arse wave; *Four Waves
.04	toom-	tuaim (*t*úim)	funeral mound; resounding blow
.05	gaels	Gaedheal (gél)	Irishman, Scotsman
.05	liv	Life (lifi)	*Liffey River
.11	beggybaggy	beag (byug)	small
.18	who goes cute goes siocur and shoos aroun	Siúl, siúl, siúl a rún, Siúl go socair Agus siúl go ciúin (shúl shúl shúl /arún/ shúl gu sukir/ogus shúl gu kyún)	Go, go, go my dear, Go securely And go calmly (a song)
.27	cearc	cearc (kark) ceart (kart)	hen correct
.28	Slain	slán (slán) sláinte (sláñt'i)	safety; Farewell! health; Health!

012.03	min	meann (myon)	stuttering
.16	tay	té (té)	tea
.21	heegills	giolla (gile)	fellow; servant
.21	collines	cailín (kolín)	girl
.22	aroont	a rún (arún)	my dear (lit., "O secret")
.24	mickos	a mhic-ó (avikó)	my boyo
		"idir mic agus ó" (id'ir mik ogus ó)	everyone, *tout le monde* (lit., "between sons and grandsons"; "between Mac's and O's")
.31	Olaf's	Amhlaoibh (oulév)	Norse n. in I. since 9th c.; anglic. *Humphrey; *Brian Boru
.31	Ivor's	Íomhar (íver)	Norse *Ivarr*; borrowed by I.
		Éibhear (éver)	see 014.35; *Brian Boru
013.11	Ptollmen	poll (poul)	hole (superimposed on Cornish *tol*, "hole" in *tolmen* ["dolmen"])
.13	Farrelly	Ó Fearghaile (ó farǧili)	des. of *Fearghal* ("super-strength")
.19	ollaves	ollamh (uluv)	poet, sage, professor
.22	Dyfflinarsky	Dubh-linn (duvliñ)	Black Pool; *Dublin
.23	Eire's	Éire (ére)	Ireland
.24	bulbenboss	Beann Gulbain (byoun gulbin)	*Gulban*'s [*gulba*, "beak"] Peak; anglic. Bengulbin, Ben Bulben, Co. Sligo; *Uí Néill
		bolb (bulub)	caterpillar
.25–26	puir old wobban	*trans.* Sean Bhean Bhocht (shan van vukht)	Poor Old Woman: Ireland (poetic)
.26	wobban	bean (ban)	woman
.26	o'brine	Ó Briain (ó bríin)	des. of *Brian Boru

		Ó Braoin (ó brín)	des. of *Braon* ("sorrow")
.26	a'bride	Mac a' Bhríghde (mokavríd'i)	son of *Giolla Bhríghde* ("servant of Brigid"); anglic. A'Bride
.27	desarted	díseart (díshart)	retreat, hermitage; cf. *Cill a' Díseart*, "Church of the Retreat," anglic. Killadysart, Co. Clare (across Shannon from Adare *q.v.*)
.27	Adear, adear!	Áth-Daire (ádare)	Oakwood-Ford, anglic. Adare, Co. Limerick (O Brien country; see preceding entry)
.27	desarted. Adear	Díseart Uí Deaghaidh (díshart í d'ayí)	Hermitage of the des. of *Deaghadh* ("beetle"), Co. Clare; anglic. Dysart O Dea; see *Magrath*
.36	Baalfire's	*half-trans.* Bealtaine (byoultini) [= Beal + teine]	May Festival, May Day, May (lit. *Beal's* [a god] fire)
014.01	Kish	cis (kish)	wickerwork, basket; Kish (lighthouse), *Dublin
.01	turves	tórramh (tóruv)	wake, funeral
.02	blay of her Kish	Baile Átha[a]Cis (bláakish)	Town of the Ford of [her] Wickerwork, Town of the Wickerwork Causeway; *Dublin
.02	sothisfeige	feighil (feil)	tend cattle, herd
.03	sawl	sabhall (sál)	barn, granary
.04	brogues	bróg (bróg)	shoe
.05	Hurdlesford	*trans.* Áth Cliath	*Dublin
.08	*sobralasolas*	solas (sulus) sólás (sólás)	light comfort, solace

.09–10	Ballyaugha-cleeaghbally	Baile Átha Clíath Baile (bolye áhe klíe bolye)	Town of the Hurdle Ford Town; *Dublin
.13	santryman	Sean-truibh (shan*tr*ív)	Old Tribe, village N. of Dublin, anglic. Santry
.28	farfatch'd	fear-feasa (farfase)	wizard; pers. n.—*Fear-feasa Ó Maol Chonaire* (Farfassa O Mulconry), one of the *"Four Masters"
.28	peragrine	Cúchoigcríche (kúkhigkríkhi)	Hound of the border; pers. n., latinized Peregrinus; *C. Ó Cléirigh* (Peregrine O Clery), one of the *"Four Masters"
.28	dingnant	Ó Duibhgean-náin (ó *d*ivgyenáñ)	des. of *Dubhgeannán* (dim. of *Dubh-ceann,* "dark head") family of hereditary chroniclers; one of the *"Four Masters" (see 349.24); anglic. O Duignan
.28	clere	Ó Cléirigh (ó klérí)	des. of *Cléireach* ("cleric"), family name of three of the *"Four Masters"; anglic. O Clery
.34	rock . . . shams	seamróg (shamróg)	shamrock
.35	-grey	*trans.* gorm (gurum)	blue; also grey or green
.35	Hebear	Éibhear (éver)	first Milesian ruler of S.I.; killed by his brother *Eireamhón;* *colonists
.36	Hairyman	Eireamhón (erawón)	first Milesian ruler of N.I.; killed his brother *Éibhear;* *colonists
.36	Ballymun	Baile Munne (bolye mune)	*Munne*'s (9th c. st.) Town; Dublin suburb

015.02	Rush	Ros-eó (rushó)	Yew-tree peninsula; town on N. Dublin coast
.03	mayvallies	Magh Bhealaigh (má vyalí)	Plain of a Road, Co. Kildare, W. of Dublin on Liffey; anglic. Moyvally
.04	Knockmaroon	Cnoc na Marbhan (knuk numarún)	Hill of the Dead-persons; at W. of Phoenix Park
.04	Formoreans	Fomhor (fówer)	legendary pirates harassing pre-Milesian *colonists; anglic. Fomorians
.05–06	tooath	túath (túe)	region, territory; folk
.05–06	tooath of the Danes	Túatha Dé Danann (túe dé donun)	Folk of the Goddess Dana (apparently really the dead); fourth legendary *colonists of I.; now the fairies
.06–07	Firebugs	Fir Bolga (fir bulgu)	Bags Men; third legendary *colonists, related to Tuatha Dé Danann, subjugated by Milesians; anglic. Firbolgs
.07	jerrybuilding	Diairmín (d'írmín)	little *Diarmaid, anglic. Jerry (*Shem)
.07–08	Kevanses	Ó Caomháin (ó kéván)	des. of Caomhán (dim. of caomh, "comely") (*Shaun)
.11	Killallwho	Cill Dhá Lúa (kilġálú)	Church of [St.] Dalua, Co. Clare, site of *Brian Boru's palace; anglic. Killaloe
.12	thangas	teanga (t'oña)	tongue, language
.13	thigging thugs	[an] tuigeann tú? ([un] tigin tú)	do you understand?
.15	thawed	tá (tá)	there is; yes

.16	thou may	tú mé (tú mé)	you me
.16	Kerry	Ciarraidhe (kírí)	[territory of the progeny of] Ciar ("black"), S.W. co.
.25	truath	truagh (trúe)	pity, mercy
.25	tallin	Táilgheann (tálǧen)	"Adze-head," n. given to St. Patrick, from tonsure or miter
.29	Anem	ainm (onim)	name
.29	thongs	teanga (t'oña)	tongue, language
.30	parth a lone	Parthalón (parhalón)	leader of second legendary *colonists
016.01	mahan	Ó Mathghamhna (ó mahúne)	des. of Mathghamhain ("bear"); anglic. Mahan, etc.; *Brian Boru
		maon (moun)	dumb
		meann (myan)	stuttering
.06	tolkatiff	tolca (tulke)	flood, surge; Tolka, N.E. Dublin river, site of battle of Clontarf, 1014
.11	Mukk's	muc (muk)	pig
.22	Inns	inn (iñ), ppn. inn, n.	we, us point of a spear; skull; death
.22	Dungtarf	tarbh (torev)	bull
.25	Boohooru!	buadh (búe) hurú (hurú) bóramha (bórúe)	victory hurrah tribute; agnomen of Brian Bóirmhe (Brian of the Tribute, *Brian Boru)
.27	rath in mine mines	Ráth Maoinis (rá mwínish)	Manus's Fort; S. Dublin district, anglic. Rathmines
,27	mine mines	minne (mini), compar. adj.	more stuttering (comparative of meann: see 016.01)

.30	qualm	*P/K Split	palm
.31	coyne	coinnmheadh (kiñva)	coynye: billeting of military upon private persons
		Ó Cadhain (ó koyn)	des. of *Cadhan* ("wild goose"); anglic. Coyne and also Barnacle
.31	Ghinees	Mag Aonghusa (mogénġesi)	son of *Aonghus* ("single-choice" [god of love]), anglic. Guinness
.34	Cead mealy faulty rices	Céad míle fáilte romhat/ roimhe (kéd míli fált'i rót/rivi)	A hundred thousand welcomes to you/to him
.35	dabblin	daba (*d*obe)	small heap of soft matter
		linn (liñ)	pool; *Dublin
017.09	clompturf	Cluain Tarbh (klún *t*orev)	Bull Meadow, N.E. Dublin, anglic. Clontarf; defeat of Danes by *Brian Boru, 1014
.12	d'of Linn	Dubh-linn (*d*uvliñ)	Black Pool; *Dublin
		O Fhlainn (ó lin)	des. of *Flann* ("ruddy"), anglic. O Lynn, O Flynn
.13	Boildoyle	Baile Dubhghaill (bolye *d*úġel)	Town of a Black Foreigner (i.e., Dane), N.E. Dublin suburb, anglic. Baldoyle
.13	rawhoney	Ráth Éanna (rá éne)	Enda's Fort, N.E. Dublin suburb, anglic. Raheny
.13	beuraly	Beurla, Béarla (bérle)	English language
.14	sturk	storc (s*t*urk)	bullock; corpse of one who dies upright
.17	dun	dún (*d*ún)	fort
		donn (*d*oun)	brown; staunch

.24	brack	breac (brak)	speckled; trout
.24	Morthering rue	maidrín ruadh (moderín rú)	fox (lit., red little dog)
.29	isges	uisce (ishki)	water
.34	alp	alp (olp)	lump; job of work; *Alp Uí Laoghaire*, Dublin in mason's jargon
.36	luv	lubh (luv)	herb; *Liffey
018.07	crumling	Cruimghlinn (krumliñ)	Curved Valley, S. Dublin district, anglic. Crumlin
.08–09	Be in your whist!	Bí i bhur thost! (bí i vúr hus*t*)	Be quiet!
.16	thonthorstrok	tón (*t*ón) stróc (s*t*rók) strac (s*t*rok)	bottom, arse pang, pain tear, rip
.17	claybook	clé (klé)	left (side)
.31	pourquose	*P/K Split	pourpose
.33	billycoose	bile (bili)	sacred tree
019.05	Wisha, wisha	mhuise (wishi), *interj*.	indeed, well
.07–08	mnice . . . mness . . . mnakes	*imitation* *Eclipsis	pron.: mice . . . mess . . . makes
.09	cormacks	Cormac (kurmok)	Charioteer-son; masc. pers. n.
.17	trilithon	tón (*t*ón)	bottom, arse
.25	con an	Conán (konán)	dim. of n. beginning *Con*- ("High-"); a companion of *Fionn*
020.17	mahomahouma	Mathghamhain (mahúñ)	Bear; masc. pers. n.; *Brian Boru
.23	torytale	toraidhe (*t*orí)	robber
		Toraigh (*t*orí)	Towery; island off N.W.I. coast, Fomorian stronghold (*colonists); anglic. Tory
		Toraidheacht	The Pursuit of Diarmaid

		Dhiarmada agus Ghráinne (*toríukht yírmede ogus ġráñi)*	*and Gráinne*, a *Fionn-*cycle tale
021.02	ee	í (í)	she
.06	delvin	Deilbhín (d'elvín)	Little Warp; river, N. Co. Dublin
.06	madameen	-ín (ín), *dim. suffx.*	little, darling
.08	everybuddy	bod, boidín (bud, bid'ín)	penis
.09	everybilly	bile (bili)	sacred tree
.14	dermot	Diarmaid (d'írmid')	Freeman; hero of *Toraidheacht Dhiarmada agus Ghráinne*; typical Irishman in adages; *Shem
.20–21	grace o'malice	Gráinne Ní Mháille (gráñíwályi)	*Gráinne* fem. des. of *Máille* ("Chief"); 16th c. pirate chieftainess, anglic. Grace O Malley
.21–22	shandy	seanda (shande)	old, antique
.23	dovesgall	Dubh-ghall (duvġoul)	"Black-foreigner," i.e., Dane
.24	earin	Éirinn (ériñ), *dat.*	[to, for] Ireland
.25	brannewail	bran (bron)	raven, chief; n. of *Fionn*'s dog
		Gráinne Ní Mháille (gráñíwályi)	see 021.20–21
.26	Erio	Ériu (éryú)	Ireland
.27	Tourlemonde	Tuath-Mumhan (túemún)	North Munster; anglic. Thomond
.30	luderman	ludramán (luderemán)	lazy idler
.31	redtom (*anagram of* dermot)	Diarmaid (d'írmid')	see 021.14

022.10	finegale	Fine Gaedhil (fini gél)	Tribe of the Irish (*Fine Gael* is a modern political party)
		Fine-Gall (finigoul)	Foreign Tribe; N. Co. Dublin district, anglic. Fingal
		Fionn-gall (fingoul)	"Fair-foreigner," i.e., Norwegian
.10	earring	Éirinn (ériñ), *dat.*	[to, for] Ireland
.12	grannewwail	Gráinne Ní Mháille (gráñíwályi)	see 021.20–21
.14	crom cruwell	Crom Crúach (krum krúkh)	Bloody Croucher; anc. I. idol; *Humphrey
.18	dom ter (*anagram of* dermot)	Diarmaid (d'írmid')	see 021.14
.25	poghuing	póg (póg)	kiss
.26	knavepaltry	Naomh Pádraig (név pádrig)	St. Patrick
.26	naive bride	Naomh Brighid (név bríd')	St. Bridget
.35	bullbraggin	Baile Brecain (bolye brekin)	*Brecan*'s Town (St. *B.* was baptized by St. Patrick); town, N. Co. Dublin
023.06	–gruauyagok–	grúagach (grúagokh)	hairy, ugly; wizard
.10	kirssy	*P/K Split Mac Fhiarais (mokírish)	pirssy var. of *Mac Phiarais*, "son of Piers"; family des. from a Piers Healy; n. sometimes anglic. Healy
.19	Irenean	Éireann (érun), *g.*	[of] Ireland
.20–21	Noanswa	ní h-annsa (níhounse)	not hard; formula for answering riddles
.22	dinn	dionn (din)	fortified hill

.27	wave of roary	*trans.* Tonn Rudhraighe (*ton rúrí*)	poetic n. for Dundrum Bay, Co. Down; *Four Waves
.29	–horselug–	*pseudotrans.* Loch nEachach (lukh nakhokh)	*Eachach*'s ("Horseman") Lake; largest I. lake, anglic. Lough Neagh
.29–30	Landloughed . . . neaghboormistress	Loch nEachach	Lough Neagh, see 023.29
.31	louthly	Lughbhadh (lúva)	pertaining to *Lugh*, sun-god; co. N. of Dublin, anglic. Louth
024.07	Unfru	Unfradh (unfru)	I. version of *Hunfrid*; *Humphrey
.14	Usqueadbaugham	uisce beatha (ishkebahe)	"water of life": whiskey
.15	Anam muck an dhoul!	Anam muic an diabhail (onum mwik un d'oul)	Soul of the devil's pig
.16	Finnimore	Fionn Mór (fin mór)	Great *Fionn* ("Fair")
		Fine Mór (fine mór)	Great Tribe
.18	Healiopolis	Ó hÉilidhe (ó hélí)	des. of *Ealadhach* ("ingenious"); anglic. Healy
.19	Kapelavaster	capall a mháistir [?] (kopul a váshtir)	his master's horse
.21	Bower Moore	bóthar mór (bóher mór)	highway, main road
.22	Cotterick's	Cothraighe (koríye)	Old I. version of *Patricius* (Patrick); folk-etymologized as "belonging to four"; *P/K Split
.25	Devlin	Ó Dobhail-ein (ó dovelin)	des. of *Dobhailen* (meaning unknown); anglic. Devlin
		Duibhlinn (divlin)	Black-pool; *Dublin

		Dealbhna (d'alvne)	[territory of the progeny of *Lughaidhe*] *Dealbhaeth* (3rd c. king); barony, Co. Westmeath, anglic. Delvin, see next entry
.26	Nugent	de Núinnseann (de núnshen)	"de Nogent"; Norman-I. family, barons of Delvin
.31	Tory's	toraidhe (*torí*)	robber
		Toraigh (*torí*)	Towery; island off N.W.I. coast, Fomorian stronghold (*colonists); anglic. Tory
.31	clay	clé (klé)	left (side)
.34	Broin	brón (brón)	grief
.34	Broin Baroke	Brian Bóirmhe (bríen bórwe)	*Brian* of the Tribute; *Brian Boru
.34	pole ole lonan	Pól Ó Lonáin [?] (pól ó lonáñ)	Paul des. of *Lonán* (dim. of *lon*, "blackbird")
.34	lonan	lonán (lonán)	little blackbird
.35	Guinnghis	Mag Aonghusa (mogénġesi)	son of *Aonghus* ("single-choice" [god of love]), anglic. Guinness
025.01	fenians	Fíanna (fíene)	3rd c. standing army led by *Fionn Mac Cumhail*
.04	Mieliodories	míle deóra (míli d'óre)	a thousand tears
		míle d'óir (míli *dór*)	a thousand in gold
.04	Faherty	Ó Fathartaigh (ó fahertí)	des. of *Fathartach* ("tempered" [?])
.09	Fintan	Fionntán (fintán)	dim. of *Fionn*, "fair"; *Fionntán Mac Bochra*, legendary *colonist, survived the Flood in

			form of a salmon; St. *Fionntán* owned a book illicitly copied by **Colmcille* (see 050.09 etc.)
.10	Lalors	Ó Leathlobh-air (ó lalór)	des. of *Leathlobhar* ("half-leper")
.12	talking	Táilcenn (*t*álken)	"Adze-head," n. given to St. Patrick, from tonsure or miter
.15	supershillelagh	Síol Élaigh (shíléli)	"Seed of *Éalach* (masc. n.)"; tribal territory Co. Wicklow, noted for blackthorn sticks
.17	Eirenesians	Éire (ére) Éireannaigh (érení)	Ireland Irish people
.25	buddhoch	bodach (bu*d*okh) bod (bu*d*)	churl, lout penis
.26	Tuskar	Torscar (*t*ursker)	Sea-wrack; rock and lighthouse, Co. Wexford
.27	Moylean	Sruth na Maoile (sru nu mwéle)	Sea-stream of the Bald Headland; North Channel betw. Ireland and Scotland, anglic. (poetically) Moyle
.27	Erinnes	Éirinn (ériñ), *dat.* inis (inish)	[to, for] Ireland island
.29	ardking	árd (ár*d*)	high
.31	Liam	Líam (lím) lía (líe)	William monumental stone
.31	Liam failed	Lía Fáil (líe fál)	monolith at Tara that shrieked at coronation of rightful high kings
.31–32	Maccullaghmore	Mac Collach Mór (mok kulokh mór)	Great son of *Colla* ("hero" [?])
.32	faunayman	fáinne (fáñi)	ring, halo; dawn-light
.36	Mick Mac	mac mic (mok mik)	son's son

.36	Mac Magnus	Mac Maghnuis (mok mánish)	son of *Manus* (Norman pers. n. from *Carolus Magnus*, Charlemagne) anglic. MacManus
.36	MacCawley	Mac Amhlaoibh (mok oulév)	son of *Amhlaoibh* (Norse *Ólafr*; *Humphrey)
026.03	kis	cis (kish)	wickerwork, basket; *Dublin
.03	tilly	tuile (*t*ili)	extra, supplement (as, 13th to a dozen)
.07	tayboil	té (té)	tea
.27	scrant	screain (skran)	bad luck!
.29	Man	Inis Manann (inish manon)	Island of *Manannan*, son of *Lear* the sea-god; Isle of Man
027.02	pathoricks	*P/K Split, *L/R Interchange	catholicks
.05	Kevin's	Caoimhghein (kívġin)	Comely-birth; 7th c. st.; anglic. Kevin; *Shaun
.05	oghres	ogham (oġom)	early I. writing by notches
.09	Jerry	Diairmín (d'írmín)	little *Diarmaid*, anglic. Jerry; *Shem
.09	tarandtan	tarrantach (*t*aron*t*okh)	attractive
		tarrainte (*t*arint'i)	drawn, stretched
.14	Shanahan	Ó Seanacháin (ó shanakháñ)	des. of *Seanachán* (dim. of *seanach*, "old, wise")
.19	Lanner's	leannóir (lanór)	brewer
.25	Clancartys	Clann Cárthaigh (klon kárhí)	dess. of *Cárthach* ("loving"); the Carthy's, MacCarthy's
.28	Wramawitch	ráiméis (rámésh)	nonsense, rubbish
.29	misches	mise (mishi)	I, me (emphatic)

.31	Behan	Ó Beacháin (ó byakháñ)	des. of *Beachán* (dim. of *beach*, "bee")
028.01	queenoveire	Éire (ére)	Ireland
.01	Arrah	ara (ore)	interj. (expostulatory, deprecatory)
.05	salig	salach (slokh)	dirty, impure
.12–13	Findrinny	Fionn-draighne (fin *d*ríni) fionndruine (fin*d*rini)	Fair sloe trees silver-bronze
.19	kanekannan	cál ceann-fhionn (kál kyounin)	"white-head cabbage": potatoes and cabbage mixed with butter; anglic. colcannon
.34	Finn	Fionn (fin)	Fair
029.01	haunt of the hungred bordles	Baile Átha Cliath (bláklíe)	Town of the Ford of Hurdles; *Dublin
.02	buaboabaybohm	buadh (búe)	victory
.03	bennbranch	benn (ben)	peak
.03	yardalong	Árd-Oileán (ár*d*ilán)	High Island, Co. Galway; anglic. Ardilaun: Arthur Guinness, Baron Ardilaun
.04	ivoeh	Uíbh-Eachach (ívakhokh)	[territory of the] dess. of *Eachach* ("horseman"), Co. Down; anglic. Iveagh: Edward Cecil Guinness, Baron Iveagh
.12	frailyshees	sidhe (shí)	fairy
.17	Toragh	Toraigh (*t*orí) toraidhe (*t*orí)	Towery; island off N.W.I. coast, Fomorian stronghold; anglic. Tory robber
.22	Dybbling	Dubh-linn (*d*uvliñ)	Black Pool; *Dublin

.34	is ee	is í (is í)	she is; it is she
		is é (is é)	he is; it is he
030.01–02	O'Rangans	Ó Rean-nacháin (ó ranakháñ)	des. of *Reannachán* (dim. of *reannach,* "spearlike")
.10	Eric	éiric (érik)	fine, ransom
.11	Hofed-ben-Edar	Beann Éadair (byoun édir)	*Éadar*'s Peak; I. n. for Howth Head
.23	solascarf	solas (sulus) sólás (sólás)	light comfort, solace
031.10	thon	tón (tón)	bottom, arse
.12	gorban	gorb (gurub)	glutton
.17	gallowglasses	gall-óglach (goulóglokh)	"foreign-youth"; heavy-armed I. soldier
.18	Leix	Laoighis (lísh)	[territory of the dess. of] *Laoiseach* [*Ceannmhór*], 1st c. ruler; central co.
.18	Offaly	Uí Fáilghe (ífályi)	[territory of] the dess. of [*Ros*] *Fáilghe*, 2nd c. ruler; central co.
.18	Drogheda	Droichead Átha (drihedá)	Ford Bridge, town at mouth of *Boyne
.21	Canavan	Ó Ceanndubh-áin (ó kyanduváñ)	des. of *Ceanndubhán* (dim of *Ceanndubh,* "dark-head"); often mistrans. "White-head"
		ceannabhán (kyanaván)	"white-heads," bog cotton; anglic. canawawn
		canamhain (kanawin)	interpretation, grammatical irregularity
.21–22	Canmakenoise	Clúain maca Nóis (klún moko nósh)	Meadow of the sons of *Nós*; monastic settlement; anglic. *Clonmacnoise
.24	hamlock	amladh (omlu)	curling, injury (to crops)
		amalach (omelokh)	curled (of the hair)

		thaimhleacht (havlokh*t*)	[of a] plague-grave; anglic. -hamlet in place-names; *Humphrey
.24	preties	préataí (prétí)	potatoes
.24–25	dilsydulsily	dílse (dílshi) duileasc (*d*ilisk)	fidelity edible seaweed
.35	. . . murphyc	Ó Murchadha (ó murukhu)	des. of *Murchadh* ("sea-warrior"); anglic. Murphy; *Shem
032.01	Mulachy	Maolsheachlainn (mélokhlin)	"Servant of *Seachlann* (St. Secundinus, baptized by St. Patrick)"; anglic. *Malachy
		mullach (mulokh)	chief, head, summit
.06	finikin	fine (fini) finne-cinn (finikin)	kindred "fair-heads"
.16	spalpeens	spailpín (spolpín)	laborer, workman
.16	Lucalizod	Leamhcán (loukán)	producing marshmallows; town on Liffey W. of Dublin; anglic. Lucan
		Iosaid (isid′)	*Iosada*'s [Iseult's, Isolda's]; suffx. of Chapelizod
.29	Semperkelly's	Ó Ceallaigh (ó kyalí)	des. of *Ceallach* ("contention")
033.02	Maccabe	Mac Cába (mok kábe)	son of *Cába* ("hood"); Hebridian-I. military family
.02	Cullen	Culann (kulen)	master served by *Cú-Chulainn*, hero of *Red Branch sagas
		Ó Cuileáin/ Cuilinn (ó kiláñ/kilin)	des. of *Cuileán* ("whelp")/*Cuileann* ("holly"); both anglic. Cullen, etc.
		cúilfhionn (kúlin)	fair-head; pretty girl

034.01	tarrk	tearc (t'ark)	scant
.06	sulhan	sulth (sulh)	sensual pleasure
.10	ar	ar (er) ár (ár)	on our
.11	boyles	Ó Baoighill (ó bwél)	des. of *Baoigheall* ("vain-pledge")
.16	shomers	seamar (shamer)	trefoil; honeysuckle
035.10	inverness	Inbhear Nis (invernish)	Rivermouth of a Forti- fication
.11	cad	cad? (ko*d*)	what?
.11	cad with a pipe	*allusion to* dúd (*dúd*)[?]	cad; pipe; penis (*slang*: lit., stump)
.15	Guinness	Mag Aonghusa	see 024.35
.15–16	Guinness thaw tool in jew me dinner ouzel fin?	Conas tá tú indiu mo dhuine uasal fionn? (kunus *tá tú* iñú mu ġini úsil fin)	How are you today my fair gentleman?
.16–17	Poolblack	*trans.* Linn- dubh (liñ *d*uv) lionn dubh (lin *d*uv)	Black Pool; *Dublin dark ale, stout; melan- choly
.24	fenian	Fíanna (fíene)	3rd c. standing army led by *Fionn Mac Cum- hail*
.32	speckled church	*mistrans.* Coill Bhreac (kílvrak) *as if* Cill Bhreac (kilvrak)	Speckled Wood, Co. Galway, anglic. Kyle- brack; *Kill
.32	Couhounin's	Cú-Chulainn (kúkhulin) *quasi* Cú-Cheann- fhionn (kúhyounin)	"Hound of *Culann*," hero of *Red Branch sagas; see 033.02 Hound of the Fair Head

036.14	drumdrum	drom (*d*rum)	back, ridge
		Dúndroma (*dúnd*rume)	Fort of a Ridge, S. Dublin suburb; anglic. Dundrum
.20	co-comeraid	comrádaidhe (kumrá*dí*)	comrade
		comharaidheach (kóworíokh)	one who lends a day's work
.21	five ones	*trans.* cúige (kúige)	one-fifth; province (anciently there were five provinces, now only four)
.26	sinnfinners	sinn féin (shin fén)	ourselves
		fionn (fin)	fair[-haired]
.35	Gill	Mac an Ghoill (mokuṅgil)	Son of the Foreigner
		Giolla Íosa (gilíse)	Servant of Jesus; both anglic. Gill
		gíall (gíl)	jaw
037.02–03	murrough	Murchadh (murukhu)	"Sea-warrior" masc. n.; also, bad fright, beating (from *M. Ó Briain na dTóiteán* ["of the Burnings"], 17th c. Earl of Inchiquin) *Brian Boru; *Shem
.03	dublnotch	Duibhlinneach (*d*ivlinokh)	Dubliner
.08	gildthegap	gíall (gíl)	jaw
.22	poghyogh	póg (póg)	kiss
		óg (óg)	young
		óigh (óí)	virgin
.22	Arvanda	ár bhean (ár van)	our wife/woman
.25	*mawshe dho hole*	má 'sé do thoil é (má shé *d*u hul é)	if you please

.30	thockits	dáfhichid [?] (dokhid)	forty
.32	Lukanpukan	Leamhcán (loukán)	producing marshmallows, W. Dublin suburb; anglic. Lucan
		púca (púke)	hobgoblin
		lúchorpán (lúkherpán)	leprechaun (*lit.*, "little body")
.33	pibered	piobar (piber)	pepper
.34	minnshogue	minnseóg (minshóg)	she-goat after first kidding
038.14	pispigliando	pis (pish)	vulva
.22	Esnekerry	Áth-na-Scairbhe (áneskarve)	Ford of the Rough Crossing; town Co. Wicklow, anglic. Enniskerry
.29	ruah	ruadh (rúe)	red
.30	Havvah-ban-Annah	bean (ban)	woman; *Anna
039.02	Baldoyle	Baile Dubhghaill (bolye dúġil)	Town of a Dark Foreigner (i.e., Dane); N.E. Dublin suburb
.06	ek	each (akh)	horse, steed
.06	nek	neach (nakh)	anyone
.07	Boy	buidhe (bwí)	yellow (derogatory)
.09	roe	ruadh (rúe)	red
.09	roe hinny	Ráth Éanna (rá éne)	Enda's Fort, N.E. Dublin suburb; anglic. Raheny
.09	Dalough	Dá Lúa (dá lú)	st.'s n.; see 015.11; St. Doolagh's, village N.E. of Dublin
		[Gleann] dálocha ([gloun] dálukhe)	[Valley] of Two Lakes; monastic settlement fndd. by St. Kevin, Co. Wicklow, S. of Dublin; anglic. Glendalough; *Shaun
.17	Kehoe	Mac Eochadha (mokyókhu)	son of *Eochaidh* ("horseman")

.17	Donnelly	Ó Donn-ghaile (ó donyeli)	des. of *Donnghal* ("staunch-valor")
.23	colleenbawl	cailín bán (kolín bán)	"white" girl; pretty girl; *The Colleen Bawn*
.30	capalleens	capaillín (kopilín)	little horse
.35	Duck and Doggies	deoch an dorais (d'ukh un durish)	drink at the door, parting drink
.36	Brigid	Brighid (bríd')	"strength"; fem. n.; goddess of poetry; st., patroness of I.
040.02	leababobed	leaba (lyaba)	bed
.10	martas	Márta (márte)	March
.16	Cloran	Mac Labhráin (moklouráñ)	son of *Labhrán* ("spokesman")
.16	O'Mara	Ó Meadhra (ó myare)	des. of *Meadhair* ("mirth")
.30	Downlairy	Dún Laoghaire (dún líri)	*Laoghaire*'s ("calf-keeper") Fort; harbor just S. of Dublin, anglic. Dun Laoghaire; *L.* was High King at Patrick's coming; *Uí Néill
.36	Kevin's	Caoimhghein (kívġen)	Comely-birth; 7th c. st., fndr. of Glendalough (see 039.09); anglic. Kevin; *Shaun
041.02	Sant Iago	Séam (shém)	*Shem
.03	jerrywangle	Diairmín (d'írmín)	little *Diarmaid*; *Shem
.04	O'Deavis	ó (ó) Dia fios [?] (díefis)	descendant [of] God knows
.04	Mongan	Ó Mongáin (ó moñgáñ)	des. of *Mongán* (dim. of *Mongach*, "hairy")
.18	Ebblinn's	linn (liñ)	pool; *Dublin

.18	hamlet	thaimhleacht (havlokh*t*)	[of a] plague-grave; anglic. -hamlet in place-names; *Humphrey
.22	crewth	cruit (kri*t*)	harp
.22	cronauning	crónán (krónán)	hum, drone
.22	levey	Life (lifi)	*Liffey River
.24	Finnerty the Festive	Fionnachta Fleadhach (finokh*t*e flahokh)	"Fair-snow" (or, "Made known") the Festive; 7th c. high king
.26	foyneboyne	fuine (fwini)	finish; sunset; west; Ireland; n. of Shannon isl. anglic. Foynes
		Bóinn (bóñ)	n. of a goddess; *Boyne River
.33	Ceolmore	ceól mór (kyól mór)	great music
042.11	bouckaleens	buachaillín (búkholín)	little boy; unmarried man
.11	roscan	rosc (rosk) can (kon) rosc-catha (roskohe)	inflammatory speech sing; *also*, a can battle hymn
.11–12	seinn	seinn (shen)	play music
.11–12	fion . . . fion's	fíon (fín)	wine
.12	araun	arán (arán) amhrán (ourán)	bread song
.11–12	seinn . . . araun	sinn féin, sinn féin amháin (shin fén shin fén awáñ)	ourselves, ourselves alone
.14	cumannity	cumann (kumun)	club, society
.17	lubeen	lúibín (lúibín)	looplet, curl; pretty girl
.18	Liviau	Life (lifi)	*Liffey River
.21	Lenster	Laighin (lein)	"Lance"; E. province, anglic. Leinster

.34	palesmen	*trans.* Feara Páil [?] (fare pál)	Men of Ireland
.35	dundrearies	dún (*d*ún)	fort; freq. pfx. in place-names
.35	Daly's	Ó Dálaigh (ó *d*álí)	des. of *Dálach* ("assemblist")
043.02	hamalags	amalach (omalokh)	curled; *Humphrey
		amalóg (omalóg)	simpleton
.07	gaels	Gaedheal (gél)	Irishman, Scotsman
.20	Caoch	caoch (kékh)	one-eyed man
.21	O'Leary	Ó Laoghaire (ó lírí)	des. of *Laoghaire* ("calf-keeper")
.29	five pussyfours	cúige (kúige)	one-fifth, province (anciently there were five provinces, now only four)
.33	Delaney	Ó Dubh-shláine (ó *d*úláñi)	des. of *Dubhshláine* ("Black of the Slaney [River]")
.36	Gaul	Gall (goul)	foreigner
044.07	rann	rann (ron)	verse; stanza, quatrain
.08	Boyles	buachaill (búkhel)	boy
		Ó Baoighill (ó bwéyil)	des. of *Baoigheall* ("vain-pledge")
.08	Cahills	caile (kalyi)	girl, wench
		Ó Cathail (ó kohil)	des. of *Cathal* ("battle-powerful")
.11	dub . . . Llyn	Dubh-linn (*d*uvliñ)	Black Pool; *Dublin
.11	Llyn	Ó Fhlainn (ó lin)	des. of *Flann* ("ruddy"); anglic. Lynn
.11	Phin	Fionn (fin)	fair
.11	Lug	Lugh (lú)	god of sun and genius
.12	Bug	bog (bug)	soft
		beag (byug)	little
.12	Dan Lop	Mac Duinn-shléibhe	son of *Donnshléibhe* ("Brown of the Moun-

		(mok dunlévi)	tain"); anglic. Dunlop, etc.
.12	Arth	Árt (árt)	stone; bear
.13	Coll	coll (kol)	hazel tree; letter C
.14	O'Reilly	Ó Raghallaigh (ó raġelí)	des. of *Raghallach* ("strong-armed" [?])
.15	Arrah	ara (ore)	interj. (expostulatory, deprecatory)
.16–17	rann	see 044.07	
.21	–graddagh–	greadadh (gradu)	clapping; driving rapidly
.22	*Ardite*	árduigh é (árdigé)	lift it, raise it (masc.)
.22	*arditi*	árduigh í (árdigí)	lift it, raise it (fem.) [the n. *rann* may be either masc. or fem.]
045.03	Olofa	Amhlaoibh (oulév)	I. form of N. *Ólafr*; anglic. *Humphrey
.03	Crumple	Cromail (krumil)	I. form of Cromwell; n. established in I. before Oliver's time
.19	Arrah	ara (ore)	interj. (expostulatory, deprecatory)
.21	Cassidy's	Ó Caiside (ó kashide)	des. of *Caiside* ("curled" [?])
.26	rann	see 044.07	
046.01	E'erawan	Eireamhón (erawón)	First (Milesian) ruler of all I. (*colonists)
.07	Clancy	Mac Fhlannchadha (moklonkhu)	son of *Flannchadh* ("ruddy-warrior")
.14	Gall's	Gall (goul)	Foreigner
.18	Poolbeg	Poll-beag (poulbyug)	Little Hole; Poolbeg lighthouse, *Dublin
.20	Fingal	Fionn-ghal (finġal)	"Fair-fight," *Macpherson's version of *Fionn Mac Cumhail*
		Fine-gall (finigoul)	"Foreign-kindred," N. Co. Dublin district, anglic. Fingal
.20	Mac	mac (mok)	son [of]

.20	Oscar	Oscar (usker)	"Combatant"; son of *Oisín* son of *Fionn Mac Cumhail*
.25	rann	see 044.07	
047.20	Gaels'	Gaedheal (gél)	Irishman, Scotsman
.28	Connacht	Connachta (kunukh*t*e)	[portions of the] dess. of *Conn*; W. province
048.03	Shanvocht	Sean [Bhean] Bhocht (shan [van] vukh*t*)	Poor Old [Woman]; Ireland (poetic)
.10	mick	Mic (mik)[?]	Mr. (in *Mac* names)
.11	nick	Nic (nik)[?]	Miss (in *Mac* names)
.11	maggies	Mac Uí (mokí)[?]	Mr. (in *O* names)
.12	Coleman	Colmán (kulumán)	Young Dove; n. of sixty I. sts.; a *Colmán* conducted the unsuccessful Celtic case at the Synod of Whitby
.12	Lucan	Leamhcán (loukán)	producing marshmallows; W. Dublin suburb
.13	O'Daley	Ó Dálaigh (ó *d*álí)	des. of *Dálach* ("assemblist"); hereditary family of poets
.13	O'Doyles	Ó Dubhghaill (ó *d*úǧel)	des. of *Dubhghall* ("dark-foreigner," i.e., Dane)
.14	Fenn Mac Call	Fionn Mac Cumhail (fin mok kúl)	Fair, son of *Cumhal*, 3rd c. hero of saga cycle; *Anna
.14	Mac Call	Mac Cathmhaoil (mok kowél)	son of *Cathmhaol* ("battle-chief" *Uí Néill
.14	Loch Neach	Loch nEachach (lokh nakhokh)	*Eachach*'s ("horseman") Lake; anglic. Lough Neagh
.16–17	Eyrawiggla	Eire (ére)	Ireland
049.03	A'Hara	Ó hEaghra (ó hyare)	des. of *Eaghra* ("mastiff"[?]); anglic. O Hara

		a chara (akhore), *voc.*	friend, my friend
.04	Zassnoch	Sasanach (sosanokh)	Englishman (Saxon); English
.04	ardree	árd-rí (árdrí)	high king
.06	Shuley Luney	Siúl, a rún (shúl arún)	Go, my dear (see 011.18)
.07	Tyrone's	Tír Eoghain (tírówiñ)	*Eoghan*'s (*Shaun) Land, N. co.; patrimony of the O Neills; *Uí Néill. After 1607 Earls of Tyrone led I. volunteers in Spanish military service
.08	Bucklovitch	Ó Buachalla (ó búkheli)	des. of *Buachaill* ("boy"); anglic. Buckley
.09	cawer	cathair (koher)	city, citadel
		cath (ko)	battle
		Badhbh, Macha, Neamhan [?]	crow-goddesses of war; see 011.01
.15	louth	Lughbhadh (lúve)	pertaining to *Lugh* (sun-god); co. N. of Dublin, anglic. Louth
.15	*Booil*	buail (búil)	beat, defeat
.15	Horan	Ó hOdhráin (ó hóráñ)	des. of *Odhrán* (dim. of *odhar*, "pale")
.26	coulinclouted	cúl (kúl) cúilfhionn (kúlin)	back-, rear-, retro- "fair-head"; pretty girl
.33	O'Loughlins	O Lochlainn (ó lokhlin)	des. of *Lochlainn* ("Scandinavian")
050.05	Nolan's	Ó Nualláin (ó núláñ)	des. of *Nuallán* (dim. of *nuall*, "noble")
.09	Calomnequiller's	*Colm-cille (kulumkili)	Dove of the Church, 6th c. monastic missionary, latinized *Columba*. Illicitly copied a book owned by St. *Fionntán*

.12	mother of the book	"gurab leis gach máthair a mac"	"that to each mother belongs her son": legal principle upon which *Colmcille's illicit copy of St. *Finghin*'s book was awarded to *Finghin*
		mac [leabhair]	copy (lit. "son") [of a book]
.14	Levey	Mac Dhuinn-shléibhe (mok hinlévi)	son of *Donnshléibhe* ("Brown of the mountain")
.17–18	*Bhi she*	Bhí sé (ví shé)	he was
		Bhí sí (ví shí)	she was
.20	Iar-Spain	Iar-Spáinn (írspáñ)	Farther-Spain
.23	Nawlanmore	Ó Nualláin Mór (ó núláñ mór)	Great des. of *Nuallán* (dim. of *nuall*, "noble")
.23	Brawne	Ó Bioráin (ó biráñ)	des. of *Biorán* ("stripling"; dim. of *bior*, "spear")
.29	cark	cearc (kyark)	hen
.30	dunhill	Dún-aill (*d*únil)	Fortress of the Cliff; town, Co. Waterford, anglic. Dunhill
051.08	Slypatrick	slighe (shlí)	way; method
.12	Conn	Conn (kon)	"Intelligence"; masc. pers. n. *Shem
.16	da	dá (*d*á)	two of anything, pair
.17	gathery	ceathar (kaher)	four
.17	shesses	sé (shé) seisear (shesher)	six six persons
.19	wholebroader	*trans.* dearbh-bhráthair (*d*rihár)	brother (lit. "true-brother," as distinct from *bráthair*, brother-in-religion)

.21	lucal	Leamhcán (loukán)	producing marshmallows; W. Dublin suburb, anglic. Lucan
.25	brogue	barróg (beróg) bróg (bróg)	defect in speech
			shoe
.25	Meathman	Midhe (mí)	middle; E. co.; formerly high king's royal province
.27	clownturkish	Cluain-tuirc (klúntirk)	Boar Meadow, Dublin suburb, anglic. Clonturk
.28	craogs	cramhóg (kráóg)	refuse, residuum
		creag (krag)	rock cliff
		crannóg (kronóg)	lake-dwelling
.29	bryns	bruidhean (brín)	hostel; fairy palace
.31	pigs' older inselt	*trans.* muic-inis (mwik inish)	pig-island; anc. n. for I.
052.04	ruad	ruadh (rúe)	red
.09	Tolkaheim	Tolca (tulke)	Flood, surge; N. Dublin river, anglic. Tolka, scene of battle of Clontarf; *Brian Boru
.11–12	dearbraithers . . . dearbrathairs	dearbh-bhráthair (drihár)	brother (lit. "true-brother," as distinct from *bráthair*, brother-in-religion)
.16	Farfar	fear (far)	man
		Fear-feasa (farfase)	Wizard; pers. n., as of *Fear-feasa Ó Maol Chonaire*, one of the "Four Masters"
.17	Arthor	Artúr (ortúr)	"Stone" or "Bear"
.17	doyne	Ó Duinn (ó diñ)	des. of *Donn* ("brown")
.19	balefire's	*half-trans.* Bealtaine (byoultini)	May Festival, May Day, May (see 013.36)

.21	buckshee	boc (buk)	he-goat
		sidhe (shí)	fairy
.22	soorkabatcha	suairce	joyous, gay
		(súrke)	
		Sorcha	"Clear," fem. pers. n.
		(surkhe)	
.27	finndrinn	fionndruine	silver-bronze
		(find̃rini)	
.33	duskish	duscaidh	rashness
		(d̃uskí)	
053.01	fin	fionn (fin)	fair
.04	Ere	Éire (ére)	Ireland
.05	liss	lios (lis)	ring-fort; fairy-fort
.10	tussocks	tosach	beginning
		(t̃usokh)	
		Túsach	st., baptized by Patrick, priest at Patrick's deathbed; anglic. Tussach
		(t̃úsokh)	
.10	copoll	capall	horse
		(kopul)	
.12	tyrs	tír (tír)	land, country
.13	in eren	i nÉirinn	in Ireland
		(inériñ)	
.24	pluk	pluc (pluk)	cheek
.24	lekan	leicean	cheek
		(leken)	
		Leacán	Hillside; town, Co. Sligo, where "Yellow Book of Lecan" compiled; anglic. Lackan
		(lakán)	
.24	lukan	luachán	withered grass
		(lúkhán)	
		Leamhcán	producing marshmallows; W. Dublin suburb, anglic. Lucan
		(loukán)	
.25	pluggy	ag plucghail tobac (eg plugil t̃ubok)	smoking heartily
		pluctha	crammed, stuffed
		(pluke)	

.26	gothsprogue	barróg (beróg)	defect in speech
.29	Lorenzo Tooley	Lorcán Ó Tuathail (lurkán ó túhil)	*Lorcán* (dim. of *lorc*, "fierce") des. of *Tuathal* ("people-mighty") abp., patron st. of Dublin; anglic. Laurence O Toole
.29–30	the bannocks of Gort and Morya and Bri Head and Puddyrick	beannacht Dé agus Muire agus Brighid agus Phádraic (banokh*t* d'é ogus mwiri ogus bríd' ogus fá*d*rik)	the blessing of God and Mary and Bridget and Patrick
.29–30	bannocks	bannóg (banóg)	loaf, cake
.30	Gort	gort (gur*t*) gorta (gur*t*e)	field, oatfield; letter G hunger, famine
.30	Morya	mar bh'eadh (morya)	as if it were (derisive interj.)
.30	Bri Head	Brí (brí)	Hill; anglic. Bray, as in Bray Head, promontory S. of Dublin
.30	Puddyrick	*half-trans.* Cruach Phádraig	Patrick's [Peat-]Rick (i.e., heap); Croagh Patrick, mtn., Co. Mayo
.35	turrified	tórramh (*t*órev)	wake, funeral
.36	crow cru cramwells	Crom Cruach (krum krúkh)	Bloody Croucher; anc. I. idol
.36		crú (krú)	gore, clotted blood
054.01	Downaboo!	An Dún (un*d*ún) abú (abú)	The Fort; N.E. co., anglic. Down to victory!
.04	Poolaulwoman	*trans.* Sean Bhean Bhocht	Poor Old Woman: Ireland (poetic)
.04	Charachthercuss	Cárthach (kárhokh)	"Loving"; masc. pers. n.; O. Celtic *Caratacos*

.04–05	his Ann van Vogt	Sean Bhean Bhocht (shan van vukh*t*)	Poor Old Woman: Ireland (poetic)
.08	Halley's	Ó hAilche (ó halkhi)	des. of *Ailche* (Danish pers. n. "English")
.08	ulemamen	Uladh (ule)	N. province, anglic. Ulster
.09	dumagirls	Dún na nGall (*d*úneñoul)	Fort of the Foreigners; N.W. co., anglic. Donegal
.10	Huru	hurrú (hurú)	hurrah, huzza
.10	more	mór (mór) Mór (mór)	great, big "Sun," fem. pers. n.; typical peasant woman in adages
.10	Nee	ní (ní)	daughter [of]
.14	O thaw bron orm, A'Cothraige, thinkinthou gaily?	Ó tá brón orm, a Chothraighe, [an] tuigeann tú Gaedhealg? (ó *t*á brón urum a hohríye, [un] *t*igin *t*ú géliñ)	Oh I am sorry, Patrick [*P/K Split], do you understand Irish?
.19	Gomagh	go maith (gumoh)	well (adv.)
.22	bag belly	*trans.* bolg (bulug)	bag, belly
.24	moyliffey	Magh Life (málifi)	*Liffey Plain
.25	mamooth	Magh Nuadhat (mánú*t*)	*Nuadhat*'s (2nd c. king of Leinster) Plain; town, Co. Kildare, anglic. Maynooth. See also *Shaun: *Mogh Nuadhat*
.30	firbalk	Fir-bolga (firbulgu)	Bags Men; third legendary *colonists
055.03–04	Maeromor	méar mór (mér mór)	big finger

.04	Mournomates	Mughdhorna (múyórne)	dess. of *Mughdhorn* ("Ankle"); tribal n. of MacMahons; anglic. Mourne
.05	Fennyana	Fianna (fíene)	anc. **I.** standing army led by *Fionn Mac Cumhail*
		eanach (anokh)	fen; *Anna
.05	Life	Life (lifi)	*Liffey River
.10	manorwombanborn	bean (ban)	woman
.25–26	the clad . . . the cladagain	Do chuir Éire trí monga agus trí maola dhí	"Ireland has been thrice clad and thrice bare"; "Ireland has passed through three afforestations and three deforestations"— celebrated (and untranslatable) opening sentence of Keating's *Forus Feasa ar Éirinn* model of **I.** prose
.32	Castlebar	Caisleán an Bharraigh (kashlán unvarí)	Castle of the Barry (either Norman *de Barra* or Irish *Ó Báire* [des. of *Báire*, short for *Barrfhionn*, "Fairhead"])
.34	Dyas	Dia (d'íe) deas (d'as)	God nice; south; right (side)
056.07	Thounawahallya	Tonn a' mhaith-sháile (*t*oun a wa hálye)	Wave of the good salt-sea
.16	dropeen	ín (ín), *dim. suffx.*	little; darling
.23	zooteac	teach (t'okh)	house
.24	brogue	bróg (bróg)	shoe
.26	poteen	poitín (put'ín)	"little pot"; illicit whiskey
.26	praties	préataí (pré*t*í)	potatoes

.30–31	tothink	toth (*tu*) tothball (*tu*bol)	female "female-place": vulva
.32	O'Breen's	Ó Briain (ó bríin)	des. of *Brian [Boru]
		O Braoin (ó brín)	des. of *Braon* ("sorrow"); *Clonmacnoise
057.08	torroar	tórramh (*tó*rev)	wake, funeral
.08	Armagh	Árd Macha (árd*m*okhe)	*Macha*'s (war-goddess) Height; N. co. & town [in Ulster]
.09	Clonakilty	Cluain na Coillte (klún nakílti)	Meadow of the Woods; fishing port, Co. Cork [in Munster]
.10	Barna	Beárna (bárne)	Gap; village, Co. Galway [in Connacht]
.11	alplapping	alp (olp)	snarl; lump, heap; mouthful
.13	Allen	Almhain (alún)	"Whitened"; hill, Co. Kildare, HQ of the *Fianna*
.13	Barrow	Bearbha (barú)	"Seething"; river, connected to Liffey by canal
.14	an	an (un)	the
.31	Ceadurbar-atta-Cleath	céad (ké*d*)	first, chief
		cathair (koher)	city
		Áth Cliath (áklíe)	Hurdle Ford; *Dublin
.32	Dablena	daba (*d*obe)	small heap of anything soft
058.04	Dunlop	Mac Duinn-shléibhe (mok *d*inlévi)	son of *Donnshléibhe* ("Brown of the mountain")
.10	sullivans	Ó Súileabháin (ó súleváñ)	des. of *Súileabhán*, i.e., *Súil-dubhán*, "black-eyed"
.11	Graunya	Gráinne (gránye)	"Spearpoint[?]"; fem. pers. n.; *O Malley;

Toraidheacht Dhiarmada agus Ghráinne

.16	Begge	Ó Beig (ó beg)	des. of *Beag* ("little")
.17	bog . . . Bugge	bog (bug)	soft, vulnerable
.28	Finner	Fionn (fin)	Fair
		Fianna (fíene)	3rd c. standing army led by *Fionn Mac Cumhail*
		fine (fini)	kindred, tribe, family
.30	Coninghams	Ó Connagáin (ó konegáñ)	des. of *Connagán* (dim. of *Conn*, "intelligence")
059.01	derry	daire (*d*ari)	oakwood
.18	Glintalook	Gleann-dá-loch (gloun*d*álokh)	Two Lake Valley, Co. Wicklow; anglic. Glendalough; monastic settlement fndd. by St. Kevin; *Shaun
.21	thankeaven	Caoimhghein (kívġen)	"Comely-birth," 7th c. st., fndr. of Glendalough; anglic. Kevin. *Shaun
.23	O'Dea's	Ó Deaghaidh (ó d'ayí)	des. of *Deaghadh* ("beetle"[?])
.28	brehemons	breitheamhain (brehúñ)	judges, lawgivers (in old I. legal system)
.35	Braddon	Ó Bradáin (ó bra*d*áñ)	des. of *Bradán* ("salmon")
060.01	Dole Line	Dubh-linn (*d*úliñ)	Black Pool; *Dublin
.08	Drumcollakill	Drom Coll-choille (*d*rum kolkhíli)	Hazelwood Ridge, I. n. of Thomas St., Dublin; also town, Co. Limerick, anglic. Drumcolliher
		Drom Cholmchille (*d*rum khulumkili)	Colmcille's Ridge; anglic. Drumcolumb
.09	Tyrrel	Tirial (t'iryel)	N. *Thorvaldr*; family n. of Barons of Castleknock, Dublin, until 1385

		tíoramhail (tírúl)	native
.11	Brian Lynsky	Brian Ó Loinscigh (bríen ó linshkí)	*Brian*, des. of *Loingseach* ("pertaining to a fleet")
.12	Bawlonabraggat	Baile na Bragoide (bolye nubragid)	Town of the Pot-ale, Co. Down; anglic. Ballynabragget
.21	torrifried	tórramh (*tó*rev)	wake, funeral
.26	Magrath	Mag Raith (mogra)	son of *Mac Raith* ("son of grace")
061.01	una	úna (úne)	famine
		Úna (úne)	"Famine," fem. pers. n.; typical mother of a family in adages
.01	mona	móna (móne), *g.*	[of a] peat bog; peat, turf
.02	Doveland	Dubh-linn (*d*uvliñ)	Black Pool; *Dublin
.11	Jarley	Iarfhlaith (írla)	Feudal Lord; masc. pers. n., anglic. Jarlath
.13	Meagher	Ó Meachair (ó myakher)	des. of *Meachar* ("hospitable")
.14	cromlech	crom-leac (krumlak)	stooping flagstone; I. popular n. for dolmen; *Toraidheacht Dhiarmada agus Ghráinne*
.19	gobbit	gob (gob)	beak, snout
.24	piscman	pis (pish)	vulva
.25	Puellywally	*half-trans.* toth-bhall (*t*uwol)	"female-place"; fem. genitals
.26	blarneys	blárna (blárne)	Little Field, Co. Cork, anglic. Blarney
.27	Keysars	Ceasair (kasir)	queen of first *colonization
062.05	Rahoulas	Ráth hUbhla (ráhúle)	Apple-fort; *Macpherson

		Ráth Uladh (rá ule)	Ulster Fort; *Macpherson
.09	papishee	sidhe (shí)	fairy
.25	Errorland	Éire (ére)	Ireland
.30	Boore	bóthar (bóher)	road
.35	Lucalizod	Leamhcán (loukán) Iosaid (isid'), *g.*	Marshmallow-produc- ing; W. Dublin sub- urb, anglic. Lucan [of] *Iosada*, fem. pers. n.
.35–36	Glendalough	Gleann-dá- Loch (gloun*d*á- lokh)	Two Lake Valley; St. Kevin's monastic set- tlement, S. of Dublin; *Shaun
063.01	crawsopper	crádh (krá) sopaire (sopere)	torment, misery unkempt lazy fellow
.06	gaeilish	gaedhalach (gélokh)	Irish
.06	gall	gall (goul)	foreigner
.07	Kane's	Mac Aodháin (mokéáñ) Ó Catháin (ó kaháñ)	son of *Aodhán* (dim. of *Aodh*, "firc") des. of *Cathán* (pet form of n. beginning *Cath-*, "battle-")
.13	ann	ean (an)	water-; *Anna
.14	liv	Life (lifi)	*Liffey River
.22	hoshoe fine	[a] thoise fíon ([a] hushe fín)	[his] capacity of wine
.27	Murray	Ó Muireadh- aigh (ó mwiraí)	des. of *Muireadhach* ("mariner")
.35	Maurice	Muirgheas (mwiryas)	"Sea-choice"; anglic. Maurice by conflation with Anglo-Norman
.35	Behan	Ó Beacháin (ó byakháñ)	des. of *Beachán* (dim. of *beach*, "bee")
.36	barra	barra (bore)	top, tip, point
.36	tinnteack	*pseudo-Irish?* teinteach (tint'ukh)	tin-tack lightning

		tinnteach (tínt'okh)	scabbard
		tinnteog (tínt'óg)	stove
064.03	Dulyn	Dubh-linn (*dú*liñ)	Black Pool; *Dublin
.08	oonagh! oonagh!	úna (úne)	famine
		Úna	"Famine," fem. pers. n.
		abhnach (ounokh)	watery place; in place-names anglic. Ounagh, Onagh; *Anna
.09	Mullingcan	An Muileann Cearr (un mwilen kyar) Ó Maolagáin (ó mwélegáñ)	The Left-handed Mill, Co. Westmeath, anglic. Mullingar des. of *Maolagán* (dim. of *maol*, "bald"); anglic. Mulligan
.17	liffopotamus	Life (lifi)	*Liffey River
.23	astrolajerries	Diairmín (d'írmín)	dim. of *Diarmaid*, anglic. Jerry; *Shem
.24	Keavens	Ó Caomháin (ó kíváñ)	des. of *Caomhán* (dim. of *caomh*, "comely") [n. of 15 sts.]; anglic. Kevans; *Shaun
065.04	Colley	coll (kol) coillidhe (kulí)	hazel; see 064.34 destroyer; castrater
.04	Macaires	mac (mok) machaire (mokheri)	son [of] battlefield
.12	missymackenzies	Mise [?] Mac Coinnigh (mishi [?] mok kiní)	Myself [?], son of *Coinneach* ("fair-one"): formal signature of head of a family
.31	missymissy	mise (mishi)	I, me (emphatic)
.33	Finny	Ó Fianna (ó fíni)	des. of *Fiannaidhe* ("soldier")
066.24	Owen K.	Abhainn Caoch (ouwinkékh) Eoghan/Eoin Caoch (ówen/ ówin kékh)	Blind River, Co. Cork; anglic. Owenkeagh; *Anna; *Shaun One-eyed *Eoghan* ("Wellborn")/John (biblical); *Shaun

.25	litterish	litir (lit'ir) litreach (lit'rokh)	letter literary, lettered, literal
.36	oscar	Oscar (usker)	"Champion," son of *Oisín* son of *Fionn*
.36– 067.01	lily boleros	*various frag- mented, fake, & distorted I. words*	*Lillibullero,* Williamite song (c. 1690) ridicul- ing Irish & Jacobites; many unconvincing at- tempts (incl. one by Brendan Behan) have been made to recon- struct the originals
.11	Lally	Ó Maolalaidh (ó mwélalí)	des. of *Maolaladh* ("speckled chief"); Lally of Tullaghnadaly became Lally de Tol- lendal in Fr. nobility
.14	tailliur	táilliúr (*t*ályúr)	tailor
.18	Limericked	Luimneach (limnokh)	Barren spot, town & co. on Shannon River, famous for hams; an- glic. Limerick; scene of treaty betw. I. Jacob- ites and William III
.19	dun and dorass	dún an doras (*d*ún un *d*urus)	shut the door
.25	Mack Partland	Mac Par- thaláin (mok paraláñ)	son of Bartholomew; *colonists
.26	nick	nic (nik)	daughter, Miss in Mac names
.31–32	magretta	mo grádh (mugrá)	my love
.32	posque	póg (póg) pósadh (póse)	kiss marriage
068.06	greenawn	grianán (grínán)	solar (of medieval castle); sun-room, solarium
.10	Graunya	Gráinne (gráñe)	fem. pers. n.; daughter of King *Cormac Mac Airt*; *Toraidheacht*

			Dhiarmada agus Ghráinne; *Ó Malley
.11	Oscar	Oscar (usker)	"Champion," son of *Oisín* & grandson of *Fionn Mac Cumhail*
.11	son of a Coole	Mac Cumhail (mok kúil)	son of *Cumhal*; patronymic of *Fionn*
.11	Coole	Mac Dhubh-ghaill (mokġúil)	son of *Dubhghall* ("Black Foreigner," i.e., Dane), anglic. Coole
.12	arrah of the . . . poghue	ara na bpóg (ore nu bóg)	one given to kissing; *Arrah-na-Pogue*
.13	leinster	Laighin (lein)	"Lance"; E. province, anglic. Leinster
.14	dearmud	Diarmaid (dírmid′)	"Freeman", masc. pers. n.; *Toraidheacht Dhiarmada agus Ghráinne*; *Brian Boru; *Shem
.14	pitch	pit (pit′)	vulva
.19	farfar	fear (far) fear-feasa (farfase)	man wizard, wiseman
.21	shee	sidhe (shí)	fairy
.21	shebeen	síbín (shíbín)	illicit tavern
.30	pobalclock	pobal (pubel) cloch (klukh) clog (klug)	people, the public stone bell, clock
.31	Tomar's Wood	Coill Tómhair (kíl *tó*wir)	Thor's Wood, Clontarf, Dublin
069.03	the times the fairies were in it	*lit. trans.* an t-am a bhí na sidhe ann	the time when the fairies existed
.06	Peannlueamoore	peann-luaidhe mór (pyounlúí mór)	big pencil
.08	Dair's	dair (*d*er)	oak tree; letter D
.11	doun	dún (*d*ún) donn (*d*oun)	fort brown
.13	shoodov	dubh (*d*uv) ubh (uv)	black egg

.30	praties	préataí (préti)	potatoes
070.01	Gaul	gall (goul)	foreigner
.04	broguen	barróg (beróg)	defect in speech
.04	eeriesh	Éire (ére)	Ireland
.07	Lynn	Ó Fhloinn (ó lin)	des. of *Flann* ("ruddy")
.07	O'Brien	Ó Briain (ó bríin)	des. of *Brian [Boru]
.14	clan	clann (kloun)	family, progeny
.15	Bullfoost	Béal-feirste (bélferishti)	Sandbank River-mouth; city, Co. Antrim, anglic. Belfast
.29	o'connell	Ó Conaill (ó kunil)	des. of *Conall* ("high-mighty"); *Uí Néill
.30	irskusky	uisce (ishki)	water
071.04	guineese	Mag Aonghusa (mogénġesi)	son of *Aonghus* ("single-choice" [god of love]); anglic. Guinness
.07	foinne	foinne (fwiñi) fionn (fin)	knead, bake; dress; make tidy fair
.10	clean turv	Cluain Tarbh (klún toriv)	Bull Meadow; N.E. Dublin district, site of *Brian Boru's defeat of Danes, 1014; anglic. Clontarf
.10	turv	tórramh (tórev)	wake, funeral
.17	*Blau Clay*	Baile Átha Cliath (bláklíe)	Hurdle Ford Town; *Dublin
.23	*Arthur*	Artúr (ortúr)	"Bear"; "Stone"
.24	*Donald*	Domhnall (dónel)	"World-mighty"
.25	*O'Reilly's*	Ó Raghailligh (ó raġelí)	des. of *Raghallach* ("having [strong] fore-arms")
.29	*Connies*	Connachta (kunukhte)	[territory of the] progeny of *Conn* ("intelligence"); W. province, anglic. Connacht, Connaught

.33	*Turf*	tórramh (*tó*rev)	wake, funeral
.33	*Clandorf*	Clann (kloun) Cluain Tarbh (klún *t*orev)	family, progeny Bull Meadow, N.E. Dublin district, site of *Brian Boru's defeat of Danes, 1014; anglic. Clontarf
.36	*Kennealey*	Ó Cinnfhao- laidh (ó kinélí)	des. of *Ceannfhaoladh* ("wolf-head")
072.01	*Mac Noon*	Mac Nuadhan (mok nún)	son of *Nuadha* (n. of sea-divinity)
.01	*Annie's*	eanaighe (aní)	fens, marshes; *Anna
.04	*O'Phelim's*	Ó Feidhlim (ó felim)	des. of *Feidhlim* (short for *Feidhlimidhe*, "ever- good")
.05	*Castlecostello*	Caisleán Mhic Oisdealbhaigh (kashlán vikoshd'alví)	Castle of *Oisdealbh*'s ("shaped like [the god] *Os*") son. *Mac* *Oisdealbhaigh* was earliest I. n. adopted by Normans
.07	*Fingal*	Fine Gall (fini goul) Fionn-ghal (fingal)	Foreign Tribe, N. Co. Dublin district "Fair-Fight," *Mac- pherson's version of *Fionn Mac Cumhail*
.16	*Boawwl's*	buail (búil) bual (búl)	strike, hit water, stream
.24	so slaunga vollayed	So slán abhaile (su slán avolye)	Safe home here! Here's a "safe home"! (a farewell)
.34	diablen	Dia linn (d'íe liñ) diabhal (d'oul)	God with us! Goodness! devil
.34	lionndub	lionndubh (lyon*d*uv) lionn dubh (lyon *d*uv)	black bile, melancholy porter, stout

		linn dubh (liñ duv)	black pool; *Dublin
.35	flegm	*trans.* lionn fionn	phlegm
.35	purse	*P/K Split [?]	curse [?]
073.02	Hyland	Í (í)	Isle; in place-names anglic. Hy
		Uí (í)	descendants [of]; clan designation as *Uí Néill; anglic. Hy
.05	Mockerloo	machaire (mokheri)	battlefield
.06	Crumlin	Croim-ghlinn (krumliñ)	Curved Valley; S. Dublin district
.07	brianslog	Brian (bríen) brianna (bríene) slog (slug) sluagh (slúe)	*Brian Boru pieces, bits mouthful, gulp army, host
.10	Cacao	cac (kok)	excrement
.10	Campbell	Caimbéal (kambél)	"Wry-mouthed"
.12–13	a brisha a milla a stroka a boola	ag briseadh ag milleadh ag stracadh ag buaileadh (eg brishe a mile a *s*troke a búle)	breaking destroying tearing beating
.18–19	Hubbleforth	Áth Cliath (áklíe)	Hurdle Ford; *Dublin
.19	*Heli*	Ó hÉilidhe (ó hélí)	des. of *Ealadhach* ("ingenious"); anglic. Healy, etc.
.20	duff	dubh (duv)	black
.23	Bully Acre	*trans.* Cluain Tarbh (klún *t*orev)	"Bull Meadow," N.E. Dublin district, anglic. Clontarf
.26	Dog-an-Doras	deoch an dorais (d'ukh un durish)	drink at the door, parting drink
.29	Cloudletlitter	litir (lit'ir)	letter

.30	coombe	cúm (kúm)	hollow
.31	Coolock	Cúlóg (kúlóg)	Back-part; Little pocket; N.E. Dublin suburb
.31	Enniskerry	Áth-na-Scairbhe (áneskervi)	Ford of the Rocky Shallow; town, Co. Wicklow, S. of Dublin
.36	Arthur-	Artúr (ortúr)	"Bear," "Stone"
074.01	some Finn, some Finn avant	sinn féin, sinn féin amhain (shin fén shin fén awáñ)	ourselves, ourselves alone
		Fionn (fin)	Fair
.03	dun	dún (dún)	fort
		donn (doun)	brown
.09	Truiga	trúig (trúig)	occasion, fact; cause, cause of death
		truagh (trúe)	pity, mercy
		trú (trú)	condemned man
.13	Liverpoor	*Metathesis; *L/R Interchange	Riverpool; *Dublin
.13	coolt	cúl (kúl)	back of the head
.15	Fengless	Fionn-glais (finglash)	Clear Stream; N. Dublin district & stream, anglic. Finglas; *Anna
.16	Baldowl	Baile Dubhghaill (bolye dúğil)	Town of a Dark Foreigner (i.e., Dane), N.E. Dublin suburb, anglic. Baldoyle
.16	is in his	trans. idiom: tá . . . ina . . .	is a
.17	Rethfernhim	Ráth Farannain (rá farenin)	Farannan's (masc. pers. n.) Fort; S. Dublin suburb, anglic. Rathfarnham
075.02	Boghas	bogha (bóa)	bow (in archery); bow (of a boat)
.11	shamed	Séamus (shémus)	James; *Shem
.11	shone	Seón (shón)	John; *Shaun
.14	shamanah	seamanna (shamena)	quotations, sophistries, rigmarole

.16	Finglas	Fionn-glais (finglash)	Clear Stream; see 074.15
.21	rab	rab (rob)	hog
076.01	connemaras	Conmhaicne Mara (kun-vikni more)	Sea Tribe, district W. Co. Galway, anglic. Connemara. "Black-faced Connemara": a breed of sheep
.04	Meadow of Honey	Cluain Meala (klún male)	town, Co. Tipperary; also N. Dublin suburb; anglic. Clonmel
.13	porpus	*P/K Split	corpus; corcus
.21	Moyelta	Magh-gheilte (máyelti)	Grazing plain; pastureland
.21–22	Lough Neagh	Loch nEachach (lokh nakhokh)	*Eachach*'s ("horse-man") Lake, largest lake in I.
.23	Isle of Man	Inis Manann (inish manun)	Island of *Manannan*, son of *Lear*, the sea-god
.24	Fianna's	Fianna (fíene)	3rd c. standing army led by *Fionn Mac Cumhail*
.25–26	deeplinns	linn (liñ)	pool; *Dublin
.27	osiery	*trans*. cis, cliath	*Dublin
.32	Donawhu	Donnchadh (*d*unukhu)	"Strong-warrior," masc. pers. n. anglic. Donough, Denis, etc.
077.02	O. Tuohalls	Ó Tuathail (ó *t*úhil)	des. of *Tuathal* ("People-mighty"); anglic. O Toole
.04	Sowan	Samhain (souwen)	November; Allhallow-tide; Feast of the Dead; close of harvest, beginning of winter half-year
.05	Belting	Bealtaine (byoultini)	May; May Day; Spring Festival; close of winter, beginning of summer half-year

.14	the Ryan vogt	an ríoghan bhocht (un ríen vukh*t*)	the poor queen: Ireland
.14	Ryan	Ó Riain, Ó Riaghain (ó ríin)	des. of *Rian* ("track"), *Riaghan* ("queen")
.25	Mac	Mac (mok)	Son [of]
.25	Pelah	peile (pele) píoladh (píle)	football simpleton; anything big
.29	blasses	blas (blos)	flavor; accent in speech
.30	poteentubbs	poitín (put'ín)	"little pot," illicit whiskey
078.17	Breedabrooda	Brighde (bríd'e), *g.* bruaide (brúd'e)	[of] Bridget morsels
.18	Cian	Cian (kín)	"Ancient," n. of father of *Lugh* the sun-god
.18	Finntown	Fionntán (fin*t*án)	dim. of *Fionn*, "Fair"; masc. pers. n. anglic. Fintan
		Fionn-Tamhnach (fin*t*ounokh)	Fair Arable-Field, town, Co. Tyrone, anglic. Fintona
.25	Celtiberian	ceilt (kelt') Iberiu (iberíú)	concealing earlier form of *Eriu*, oldest form of *Éire*, "Ireland," whence Latin *Iberio*, *Hibernia*, etc.
.27	Uladh	Uladh (ule)	N. province, anglic. Ulster
.29	cons	con (kun)	pure
.29	mor	mór (mór)	big, great
079.08	atta	áit tigh (át'tí)	house site; anglic. -atta- in place-names
.15	Danadune	Dana-dún (*d*oned*ú*n)	Fort of *Dana* (*Ana*) [goddess of dead]; *Anna

		Danair-Dún	Danes' Fort
		(*d*anir*d*ún)	
		Dána-dún	Bold fort
		(*d*áne*d*ún)	
.19	inyon	inghean	daughter, young
		(inyen)	woman
.21	lugod!	Lugh (lú)	god of sun and genius
.21	lugodoo!	dubh (*d*ú)	black
.29	elvanstone	Ailfinn	"Rock of the Clear
		(elfin)	[Spring]," or perhaps
			"Fionn's Rock," town,
			Co. Roscommon,
			anglic. Elphin
.30	pusshies	puisín	lip
		(pushín)	
.30	moggies'	magaidhe	mocker
		(mogí)	
		madaí	dogs, curs
		(mo*d*í) [?]	
.33	smithereen	smiodairín	small fragment
		(smi*d*erín)	
.35	Hamlaugh's	Amhlaoibh	Norse *Ólafr* ("ancestral
		(oulév)	relic"), anglic.
			*Humphrey
080.01	macadamized	Mac Ádaim	son of Adam
		(moká*d*im)	
.02	footbatter	bóthar	road, path; anglic.
		(bóher)	-batter in place-names
.07	Finewell's Keeps-acre	*trans.* Páirc	Field of the Clear
		an Fionn-	Water; anglic.
		uisce (párk un	Phoenix Park
		finishki)	
		Fionnghuala	"Fair-shoulders," prin-
		(finúle)	cess transformed into a
			swan by evil magic un-
			til released by St.
			Patrick's coming
.07	tautaubapptossed	tá (*t*á)	is, there is, yes
.08–09	oh flaherty	Ó Flaith-	des. of *Flaithbheartach*
		bheartaigh	("bright ruler")
		(ó flaver*t*í)	
.10	stunned's turk	sturc (s*t*urk)	corpse of one who dies
			upright

.10	turk	torc (*t*urk)	wild boar, hog
.14	leabhar	leabhar (lyour)	book
.22	morphyl	Ó Murchadha (ó murukhu)	des. of *Murchadh* ("Sea-warrior"), anglic. Morphy, Murphy, etc.
.29	O'Fluctuary	Ó (ó)	descendant [of]; see 080.08–09
.32	Mac Shane's	Mac Seagháin (mok shaáñ)	son of *Jehan* (Norm.-Fr., "John")
.36	lucans	Leamhcán (loukán)	"producing marshmallows," W. Dublin suburb, anglic. Lucan
081.06	cheadmilias faultering	céad míle fáilte (ké*d* míli fált'i)	a hundred thousand welcomes
.09	So more boher O'Connell	Seo mór-bhóthar Uí Chonaill (shu mórvóher í khunil)	This is O Connell highway
.11	Fiacre	Fiachra (fíkhre)	"Raven"; n. of I. fndr. of Breuil monastery, France
.14–15	saddle of the Brennan's . . . pass	Cnoc Bréanainn (knuk brénen)	Brendan's Hill, Co. Kerry, has anc. stone causeway leading to summit
.14	Brennan's	Ó Braonáin (ó brénáñ)	des. of *Braonán* (dim. of *braon*, "sorrow")
		Ó Branáin (ó branáñ)	des. of *Branán* (dim. of *bran*, "raven")
.16–17	Beneathere! Benathere!	Beinn Éadair (ben é*d*ir)	*Éadar*'s (masc. pers. n.) Peak; I. n. for Howth Head
.17	livland	Life (lifi)	*Liffey River
.18	cropatkin	Cruach Phádraig (krúkh fá*d*rig)	Patrick's Rick [conical heap], mtn., Co. Mayo, anglic. Croagh Patrick
.28	patrecknocksters	Cnoc Phádraig (knuk fá*d*rig)	Patrick's Hill, anglic. Knockpatrick

.28	hellmuirries	Muire (mwiri)	Mary (n. of mother of Jesus *only*)
082.03	tipperuhry	Ṭiobraid Árann (tibrid áren)	"Well of *Ára* [n. of district]," S. co., anglic. Tipperary
.09	Pautheen	Páidín (pád'ín) poitín (put'ín)	Paddy (dim. of *Pádraig*) "little pot": illicit whiskey
.29	Billi	bile (bili)	sacred tree
.33	loo	lua (lú)	vigor
083.13	kish	cis	basket, wickerwork; *Dublin
.13	sprogues	bróg (bróg) barróg (beróg)	shoe defect in speech
.15	languidoily	dáil (dál)	assembly; *Dáil Éireann*, I. national legislative assembly
		Ó Dubhghaill (ó dúġil)	des. of *Dubhghall* ("Black-foreigner," i.e., Dane), anglic. Doyle
.17	Dun	donn (doun)	brown
.19	Ruadh	ruadh (rúe)	red
.19	Tallaght	Támhlacht (toulokht)	Plague-grave; village S.W. of Dublin
.20	Ringsend	Rinn (riñ)	Point, Headland; S.E. Dublin district betw. Liffey mouth and Bay
.20	Conway's	Ó Connmhaigh (ó konvé)	des. of *Connmhach* ("son of intelligence")
.21	atte	attha (ate)	swollen
.22	fain real	fé'n riaghail (fén ríel)	under the government; under religious rules
.23	Tailte	Tailte (tolt'e)	Firbolg queen after whom is named *Tailtean* (anglic. Teltown, Co. Meath), site of annual Games
.24	Declaney	Déaglán (déglán)	"Capacity [?]," 5th c. st., anglic. Declan

			Ó Dubh-shláine (ó dúláñi)	des. of Dubhshláine ("Black of [the] Slaney [River]"); anglic. Delaney
.33	poghue		póg (póg)	kiss (from Latin pax)
.34	killelulia		cill (kil)	church; *Kill
.34	allenalaw		Almhain (alún)	"Whitened," HQ of Fianna, anglic. Hill of Allen, Co. Kildare
			bullen-a-law	corrupt I. words of Lillibullero; see 066.36–067.01
.35	torgantruce		tuargain (túrgen)	battering, bombardment
			'tuigeann tú? (tigin tú)	do you understand?
084.02	hurooshoos		hurrú (hurú)	hurrah
.08	delaney		Ó Dubh-shláine (ó dúláñi)	des. of Dubhshláine ("Black of [the] Slaney [River]")
.14	O'Daffy		Ó Deabh-thaigh (ó d'afí)	des. of Deabhthach ("quarrelsome")
.32–33	Hamlaugh		Amhlaoibh (oulév)	Norse Ólafr ("ancestral relic"); anglic. *Humphrey
.36	Dunelli		Ó Donnghaile (ó douñeli)	des. of Donnghal ("brown-valor")
085.02	burral		burral (burel)	bit, jot
.15	blackpool		trans. dubh-linn (duvliñ)	*Dublin
.23	Maam		Mám (mám)	Breach, Mountain pass; village, Co. Galway
.23	Festy		Feichín (fekhín)	dim. of Fiach, "raven"
.25	Mayo of the Saxons		Magh-Eó-na-Sacsan (máyónu-soksun)	"Yew-Plain of the Saxons"; 7th c. monastery fndd. by Colmán at Magh-Eó, anglic. Mayo, Co. Mayo; resorted to by English monks, whence the tag

.26	potheen	poitín (put′ín)	"little pot," illicit whiskey
.33	Kersse's	Mac Fhiarais (mokírish), *var. of* Mac Phiarais (mok fírish)	son of *Piers*
.36	cymtrymanx	Coimbrice (kimbriki)	Welsh (Welsh *cymry*)
086.02	padderjagmartin	Peadar (pader) paidir (pad′ir)	Peter prayer
.05	himcell	cill (kil)	church; *Kill
.05	feacht	feacht (fyokht) fuacht (fúukht)	turn, time, occasion cold, coldness
.06	coold raine	Cúil-Rathain (kúlrahin)	Fern-Angle, Co. Derry, anglic. Coleraine. When St. Patrick was offered the land for a church, boys set the fern on fire
.08	Crowbar	Crobh-dhearg (kró-yareg)	Red-fist; *Cathal Crobh-dhearg Ó Conchobhair* in 1189 deposed his kinsman, *Ruaidhrí Ó Conchobhair*, last high king
.08	Meleky	Maelsheach-lainn (mélokhlin)	Servant of *Seachlann* (St. Secundinus), anglic. *Malachy
.09	plucks	pluc (pluk)	cheek
.10	pussas	pusa (puse)	lips, mouth
.10	clanetourf	Cluain-Tarbh (klún torev)	Bull Meadow, N.E. Dublin, anglic. Clontarf; *Brian Boru's defeat of Danes, 1014
.11	Mudford		*Dublin, *Anna
.12	feishts	feis (fesh) feiste (feshti)	festival, convention accommodation, entertainment

.13	Rabworc	rab (rob) Crobh-dhearg (kró-yareg)	hog see 086.08
.15	Ir	Éire (ére)	Ireland; *Children of Lir
		íar (ír)	west, western
.21	muck	muc (muk)	pig
.24	scattery	Inis-Cathaighe (inishkohí)	Cathach's ["Battler"] Island; monastic settlement by St. Senan (6th c.), who expelled Cathach, a demon
.24–25	ballybricken	Baile Breacáin (bolye brekáñ)	Breacán's [st. baptized by Patrick] Town, N. Co. Dublin, anglic. Balbriggan
087.02	Molroe	Ó Maol-ruaidh (ó mulrúí)	des. of Maolruadh ("red-chief")
.03	gobbless	gob (gob)	beak, snout
.08	Temorah	Teamhair (t'our)	Prospective Hill, Co. Meath, anc. seat of high king; anglic. Tara; distorted to Temora by *Macpherson
.12	O'Donnell	Ó Domhnaill (ó dónel)	des. of Domhnall ("world-mighty"); *Uí Néill
.14	Gaeltact	Gaedheal-tacht (géltokht)	Irishness; Irish-speaking districts
.15	bullycassidy	Baile Uí Chaiside (bolyí khoshidi)	Town of the Descendants of Caiside ("curled"), Co. Fermanagh; anglic. Ballycassidy
.17	Gush Mac Gale	'ghus Mac Cathail (ġus mok kohil)	"-choice, son of Battle-mighty"
.17	Roaring	Ruaidhrí (rúrí)	masc. pers. n., anglic. Roderick

.18	O'Crian	*quasi* Ó Chríoin (ó khríin) Ó Briain (ó bríin)	des. of *Críon* ("worn-out") des. of *Brian [Boru]
.18	unlucalized	Leamhcán (loukán)	producing **marsh-**mallows; W. Dublin suburb anglic. Lucan
.21	boer's . . . bull	Cluain Tuirc (klún *t*irk) Cluain Tarbh (klún *t*orev)	Boar's Meadow, N. Dublin, anglic. Clonturk Bull Meadow, N.E. Dublin, anglic. Clontarf
.24	meace . . . meathe	Midhe (mí)	"Middle," former fifth (royal) province, now Co. Meath, N.W. of Dublin
.25	congsmen	Conga (kuñge)	"Strait," religious settlement, Co. Mayo, anglic. Cong, where *Ruaidhrí Ó Conchobhair*, last high king, retired in old age
.25	donalds	Domhnall (*d*ónel)	"World-mighty"; *Uí Néill
.25	arans	Oileáin Árann (iláñ áren)	"Kidney"[?] Islands, anglic. Aran; islands off Co. Galway; also Aran Island, Co. Donegal; Arran, Scotland
.25–26	dalkeys	Deilginis (delginish)	Thorn-island, S. Dublin coast; anglic. Dalkey
.26	tory	Toraigh; Tor-inis (*t*orí; *t*orinish)	"Towery"; "Tower-isle," off Donegal coast; anglic. Tory; Fomorian stronghold
.26	Killorglin	Cill Orglain (kilorglin)	*Orglan*'s Church, Co. Kerry; annual fair at which a goat is crowned

.30	macdublins	Maca Dhuibh-linn (moke ġivliñ)	Sons of Black-pool; *Dublin
.31	bohernabreen	Bóthar na Bruidhne (bóher nu bríne)	Road of the Hostel; townland, Co. Dublin, anglic. Bohernabreena
.31	Banagher	Beannchar (byanekher)	"Pinnacled," Co. Offaly
.31	Mick	Mic (mik), voc.	Son; Mr. in Mac names
.32	O'Donner	Ó Donna-bhair (ó donawir)	des. of Donnabhar ("brown eyebrow")
.32	Bu!	Abú! (abú)	To Victory!
.32–33	tongue mor	tungc mór (tunk mór)	big push
088.13	cad	cad? (kod)	what?
.21	Crumwall	Cromall (krumel)	Cromwell; English n. known in I. long previous to Oliver
.23	Dysart	díseart (díshart)	hermitage; common in place-names; see 013.27
.26	de Vologue	de bholóig (de vológ)	of/from an ox
.34	laving . . . leaftime	Life (lifi)	*Liffey River
.34–35	Blackpool	Dubh-linn (duvliñ)	Black Pool; *Dublin
089.06–07	Macchevuole	Mac (mok)	Son
.07	Rooskayman	rúscaidh (rúskí)	moor, fen; oozing; common in place-names: Rooskey, Rooscagh, Roosca
		Roscomáin (roskumáñ)	Comán's Wood; W. co., anglic. Roscommon
.07	Gallwegian	Gaillimh (goliv)	"Foreign," W. co., anglic. Galway
.10	Crosscan	rosc-catha (ruskohe)	battle hymn
		rosc-ghairm (ruskarim)	battle cry

.10	Crosscan Lorne	crúiscín lán (krúshkín lán)	full jug (n. of drinking song)
.10	Lorne	[Cineal] Loarna (kinel lórne)	[territory of the dess. of] *Loarn*, 6th c. colonist of Scotland; W. Scotland
.10	cossa	cosa (kuse)	legs, feet
.13	O'Dowd	Ó Dubhda (ó *dúde*)	des. of *Dubhda* ("black")
.17	dtheir gcourts	*Eclipsis	*pron.* deir gourts
.18	Dthat nday in ndays	*Eclipsis	*pron.* dat nay in nays
.18	Lindendelly	Ó Liondáin (ó lin*dáñ*), *var. of* Ó Leannáin	des. of *Leannán* (dim. of *leann*, "cloak"); anglic. Linden
		Mac Giolla Fhionntáin (mok gilin*táñ*)	son of *Giolla Fhionntán* ("servant of *Fionntán* [dim. of *Fionn*, fair]"); anglic. Linden
		Doire (*d*iri)	Oakwood; N. city & co., anglic. [London]-derry, Derry
.18	coke	Corcaigh (kurkí)	Swamp; S. city & co., anglic. Cork
.19	skilllies	sceillig (shkelig)	Reef; rocky islands off Co. Kerry, anglic. Skelligs; also, the Scillies
.19	gart	gart (gor*t*)	planted field; letter G; hospitality
.28	Siar	siar (shír)	westward, backward
.30	macoghamade	mac (mok) cogadh (kuge)	son war
.35	atac	athach (ahokh)	peasant; stammerer; giant
090.02	Solasistras	solas (sulus) sólás (sólás)	light comfort
.10	bettygallaghers	Ó Gall-chobhair (ó galekhúr) gealach (gyalokh)	des. of *Gallchobhar* ("foreign help"); anglic. Gallagher moonlight, moon

.10	Mickmichael's	Mac Giolla Mhichil (mok gilevikhil)	son of *Giolla Mhichil* ("servant of Michael"); anglic. McMichael
.10	soords	Sórd (sórd)	Sward, town N. Co. Dublin, anglic. Swords
.12	tunnybladders	Ó Tonnaigh (ó tuní)	des. of *Tonnach* ("glittering"); anglic. Tunny
.24	Multifarnham	Muilte Farannain (mwilti farenin)	*Farannan*'s Mills, town Co. Westmeath, anglic. Multyfarnham
.26	Thomar's	Tómhar (tór)	Thor
.28	Rhian	Ó Riaghain/ Riain (ó ríin)	des. of *Ríoghan* ("queen")/*Rian* ("distinguished"); anglic. Ryan
.28–29	Rhian O'kehley	trí n-a chéile (t'ríne-khéli)	mixed-up, confused
.28–29	O'kehley	Ó Ceallaigh (ó kyalí)	des. of *Ceallach* ("contention"); anglic. O Kelly
.29	turly	Mac Toirdhealbhaigh (mok tiryalví)	son of *Toirdealbhach* ("shaped like Thor"); *Brian Boru
.31	Bladyugh–	bladaireacht (bladerokht)	flattery
.32	–whurawhora–	Mhuire, Mhuire (wiriwiri)	Mary, Mary (mother of Jesus)
.32	–scorta–	scártadh (skárte)	shouting
.32	–corta–	córta (kórte)	right, proper
.32	–cortas–	córtas (kórtes)	courtesy
.32	–trumpa–	trúmpa (trúmpe)	trumpet, bugle
.32	–nanenny–	na n-éan (nanén)	of the birds
.33	–puck–	poc (puk)	he-goat; sudden blow
.33	–anach	eanach (anokh) anach (anokh)	marsh, fen; *Anna path, pass

		-annach (anokh), *suffx.*	one-who-is
.34	Meirdreach	méirdreach (mérdrokh)	whore
.34	an	an (un)	the
.34	Oincush	óinseach (ónshukh)	harlot, giddy woman
		Aonghus (éngus)	Single-choice; god of love
091.01	Festy	Fiachán (fíkhán)	dim. of *fiach*, "raven"
		feiste (feshti)	accommodation, entertainment
.04–05	mhuith peisth mhuise as fearra bheura muirre hriosmas	*English spelled as Irish* (wi*t* pesh*t* wishi as fare vére mwiri hrismos)	with best wishes for a very merry Christmas
.04	peisth	peist (pesht)	beast, serpent
.04	mhuise	mhuise (wishi)	indeed, well (interj.)
.04	as fearra	as fearra (as fare)	best
.06	bouchal	buachaill (búkhel)	boy; herdboy
.06	Cliopatrick	clíth (klí)	sexual heat in swine (N.B. St. Patrick was a swineherd as a boy slave in I.)
.08, 09	Tierney	Ó Tighearnaigh (ó tíerní)	des. of *Tighearnach* ("lordly")
		tighearna (tíerne)	lord; *Clonmacnoise
.08–09	Dundalgan	Dún Dealgan (dúndalgen)	*Dealga*'s (n. of Firbolg chief) Fort; Co. Louth, N. of Dublin; Cúchulain's home; anglic. Dundalk
.09	thurkells	Mac Turcaill (mok turkil)	son of Thorkell (Norse n.)
		turcail (turkil)	cart
		turcalach (turkelokh)	well-fed person

.09	folloged	faológ (fwélóg)	seagull
.13	Markarthy	Mac Carth- aigh (mok kárhí)	son of *Cárthach* ("loving")
		[Cormac] Mac Airt (mokart)	C. son of Bear/Stone; high king in *Fionn Mac Cumhail*'s time (3rd c.)
.14	Baalastartey	*pseudoplace- name beginning* Bealach-a, Béal-Átha, *or* Baile (byalokha, bélá, bolye)	Way-of-the, Ford- Mouth, Town; anglic. Balla-, Bella-, Bally-
.22	Inishman	inis (inish) Inis Meádhoin (inishmain)	island Middle Island, central island of Aran group, anglic. Inishmaan
.25–26	Tyre-nan-Og	Tír na nÓg (tírnenóg)	Land of the Young; legendary elysium in Atlantic
.28	iskybaush	uisce-beatha (ishki bahe)	"water of life," whiskey
.34	castleknocker's	Caisleán Cnucha (kashlán knukhe)	Hill Castle, prehistoric burial mound on W. of Phoenix Park, anglic. Castleknock
.34	kithoguishly	ciotógach (kitógokh)	left-handedly, awk- wardly
.35–36	Godhelic	*P/K Split	Irish, Scots, Manx
092.07	*isce*	uisce (ishki)	water
.11	duasdestinies	duas (*dús*) duais (*dúsh*)	labor reward, prize, pay
.15	Swiney	Mac Suibhne (mok swíni)	son of *Suibhne* ("well- going")
.17	feen	fíon (fín)	wine
.17	deur	deur, déar (dér)	tear; also, precise
.18	Oirisher	oiris (irish) Leabhar Oiris	knowledge, science; chronicle; landmark Chronicles (bible)
.18	cleur	cléir (klér)	clergy

.20	mechree	mo chroidhe (mukhrí)	my heart, my darling
.20–21	me postheen	mo pháistín (mufáshtín)	my little child
		mo phuistín (mufushtín)	my little post
.26	Makegiddyculling's Reeks	Cruacha Mhic Giolla Chuda (krúkhe vikgilikhude)	Ricks [heaps] of the son of the servant of [St.] *Mochuda*, mtn. range, Co. Kerry, anglic, Macgillycuddy's Reeks
.28	shaym	Séam (shém)	Sant Iago; *Shem
.31	wishwish	mhuise (wishi)	indeed, well (interj.)
.31	sheeshea	Ó Séaghdha (ó shé)	des. of *Séaghdha* ("stately"); anglic. O Shea
		sí sé (shí shé)	she he
		sí 'sé (shí shé)	she it is; he is she
.32	shayshaun	'sé Seán (shé shán)	it is John
.35	Muncius	mún (mún)	urine
093.01	Nolans	Ó Nualláin (ó núláñ)	des. of *Nuallán* (dim. of *nuall*, "noble")
.03	scotfree	scot- (skut), *pfx.*	Irish-
.04	pitch	pit (pit')	vulva
.05	britgits	Brighid (bríd')	fem. pers. n., from *brigh*, "strength"; anglic. Bridget
.05	rael	réal (rél)	sixpenny
.08	rawdownhams	Ráth-dúin (rádúñ)	Circumvallation of a Fort, Co. Wicklow, anglic. Rathdown
		Ráth Domhnach, *correctly* Ráth Tamhnaigh (rádounokh, rátouní)	Church- [or, Sunday-] Fort; correctly Greenfield Fort, Co. Laoighis, anglic. Rathdowney
.09	tumass	Tomás (tumás)	Thomas
.13	Shun	Seán (shán)	John; *Shaun

.15	gratiasagam	gratiasagam (grot′esogum)	nickname for St. Patrick, from his reiteration of Latin *gratias agamus*
		agam (ogum)	"at-me," I have
.19	dun	dún (*dú*n)	shut
		donn (*d*oun)	brown
.21	Nau!	náire (náre)	shame
.24	litter	litir (lit′ir)	letter
.28	Coogan	Mac Eochagáin (mokyokhegáñ)	son of *Eochagán* (dim. of *eochaidh*, "horseman")
		Ó Cuagáin (ó kúgáñ)	des. of *Cuagán* (dim. of *cuach*, "cuckoo")
.28	Barry	Ó Báire (ó bári)	des. of *Báire* (short for *Barrfhionn*, "Fairtop")
.28	Coogan Barry	Gúgán Barra (gúgán bore)	*Barra*'s [short for *Barrfhionn* or *Fionnbharr*, "Fairtop," st., anglic. Finbar] Rock-cleft, Co. Cork, source of River Lee; anglic. Gougane Barra
.29	Sean Kelly's	Seán Ó Ceallaigh (shán ó kyalí)	John, des. of *Ceallach* ("contention")
.30	I am the Sullivan	Mise Ó Súileabháin (mishi ó súleváñ)	Myself (or, I am) the Descendant of *Súileabhán*, i.e., *Súil-dhubhán* ("black-eyed"); formal signature of head of a family
.30	Dufferin	Ó Dábhoireann (ó *d*áverin)	des. of *Dubhdábhoireann* ("Black of the two Burrens [stony districts]"), a brehon family from Co. Clare
.31	Kathleen May Vernon	Caitlín mo mhúirnín (kat′lín muvúrñín)	My darling Catherine; song, "Kathleen Mavourneen"
.32	Curran	Ó Corráin (ó kuráñ)	des. of *Corrán* (dim. of *Corradh*, "spear")

.32–33	machreether	mo chroidhe (mukhrí)	my heart, my beloved
		mo chréatúir (mukhrétúr)	my [poor] creature
.33	leery	Laoghaire (líri)	Calf-keeper; high king (428–458) at Patrick's arrival
.35	Finn	Fionn (fin)	Fair
.35	Finn again's	Ó Fionnagáin (ó finegáñ)	des. of *Fionnagán* (dim. of *Fionn*, "fair"); anglic. Finnegan
.36	sowheel	samhail (souwil)	ghost, apparition
094.01	Mullen	Ó Maoláin (ó mwéláñ)	des. of *Maolán* (dim. of *maol*, "bald")
.02	Mallon	Ó Mealláin (ó maláñ)	des. of *Meallán* (dim. of *meall*, "pleasant")
.02	Meldon	Ó Maoldúin (ó mwéldúñ)	des. of *Maoldún* ("chief of a fort")
.03	Muldoons	Ó Maoldúin (ó mwéldúñ)	des. of *Maoldún* ("chief of a fort")
.12	shaun	Seán (shán)	John; *Shaun
.12	Una	Úna (úne)	"Famine," fem. pers. n.; typical mother of a family
.12	Ita	Íde (íde)	"Thirst," fem. pers. n.
.14	Danaides	danaid (donid)	pitiful
		Dana (done)	goddess of the dead; eponymous deity of *Tuatha Dé Danann*; *Anna
.16	ana	ana (one)	plenty, prosperity
		Ana (one)	see 094.14 Dana; *Anna
.16	mala	mála (mále)	bag, sack
.19	finfin	fionn (fin)	fair
.26	Lally	Ó Maolalaidh (ó mwélalí)	des. of *Maolaladh* ("speckled chief")
.27	Solans	Solán (sulán)	Sollane River, said to drown a man at regular intervals

		Solamh (solev)	Solomon
.30	beetyrossy	rásaidhe (rásí)	wandering woman; jilt
.30	beetyrossy betty-doaty	Biadhtach (bítokh)	Victualler; anglic. Beatty, Betty
.31	a'duna	a' Dúna (adúne)	"of the Fort," Kerry family n.
.31	o'darnel	Ó Domhnaill (ó dónil)	des. of *Domhnall* ("world-mighty"); anglic. O Donnell
.36	sheemen's	sidhe (shí)	fairy
095.02–03	Ballybock	Baile-bocht (bolyebukh*t*)	Poor-town; N. Dublin district anglic. Bally- bough
.03	O'Moyly	Sruth na Maoile (sru nu mwíle)	"Sea-stream of the Bald-headland," channel between I. & Scotland, anglic. (poetically) Moyle
.03–04	O'Moyly gracies	Gráinne Ní Mháille (gráñí wályi)	*Gráinne* fem. des. of *Máille* ("chief"); Grace *O Malley
.04	O'Briny	Ó Briain (ó bríin)	des. of *Brian [Boru]
.04	rossies	rásaidhe (rásí)	rambling woman; jilt
.09	Cunningham	Ó Cuinnea- gáin (ó kunegáñ)	des. of *Cuinneagán* (dim. of *Conn*, "intelligence")
.11	cork	Corcaigh (kurkí)	Swamp, S. city & co.
.17	Thawt I'm glad a gull	Tá t-am [glad] agat [?] (*tá* *t*oum [glad] agu*t*)	You have a [glad] time
.17	a gull	eagal (ogul) [?] a dhul (a ġul)	fear to go
.17–18	pawsdeen fiunn	páistín fionn (páshtín fin)	fair-haired child; *An Páistín Fionn*, "The Fair-haired Girl," a song
.18	Goborro	go barradh (gubore)	excellently

.18	Gobugga	go bog (gubug)	easily, softly
.19–20	when I was in my	*lit. trans. of* nuair a bhíos i-m'	when I was a
.20	farfather	fear-feasa (farfase)	wizard; masc. pers. n. of one of the *Four Masters
.22	kissabetts	*P/K Split	pissabetts
.22	kool	*P/K Split	pool
.22	kurkle	*P/K Split corcra (kurkere)	purple purple
.27–28	unguam	ungaim (uñgim)	I anoint
.28	lunguam	longaim (luñgim)	I lap up
.34	craigs	craig (krag)	crag, rock
.36	buds	bod (bud)	penis
096.04–05	Niall of the Nine Corsages	Niall Naoi-Ghiallach (níl néyílokh)	*Niall* ("Soldier") Nine-Hostager, anc. high king, ancestor of *Uí Néill
.05	arrah	ara (ore)	interj. (deprecatory)
.12	mushymushy	muise (mwishi)	indeed, well (interj.)
.13	*a drahereen o machree!*	a dearbhráth-airín óg mo chroidhe (a dráhirín óg mukhrí)	O young little brother of my heart!
.20	pasht	paist (pasht)	spirit
.23–24	And schenkusmore	An Seanchas Mór (un shanekhus mór)	The Great Register; corpus of early I. law
.24	Craig	de Carraig (de korig)	of *Carraig* ("Rock," place-name anglic. Carrick), Norm.-I. family n.
097.03	Mullinahob	Muilinn a' Hob (mwilina hob)	Hobbs' Mills

.10	Loughlinstown	Ó Lochlainn (ó lokhlin)	des. of *Lochlainn* ("Scandinavia"), anglic. Loughlin
.10	Boolies	buaile (búlyi)	milking place; anglic. booley
098.04–05	shunshema	Seán (shán) Séamus (shémus)	John; *Shaun James; *Shem
.09	Magrath's	Mag Raith (mog ra)	son of *Mac Raith* ("son of grace")
.16	saggarth	sagart (sogert)	priest
.28	gar	gearr (gyar)	cut, cut off
.28	Dub's	dubh (duv)	black; *Dublin
.30	Hogan	Ó hÓgáin (ó hógáñ)	des. of *Ógán* ("youth")
.31	Cassidy	Ó Caiside (ó kashidi)	des. of *Caiside* ("curled")
.33	immor	immór (imór)	very big
.35–36	Maply . . . your- selves	*Imitation I. tree letters*, e.g., ailm, beith, coll	elm, birch, hazel; A, B, C; therefore, M, W, H, Y
099.03	Guinnesses	Mag Aonghusa (mogénġesi)	son of *Aonghus* ("single- choice"; n. of god of love)
.11	fullybigs	filleadh beig (filibeg)	"little fold," kilt
.11	sporran	sparán (sporán)	pouch
.15	Hvidfinns	fionn (fin)	fair, white
.25	moliamordhar	míle- marbhadh (mílyemorú)	"a thousand murders," great commotion & destruction
.26	Breffnian	Breifneach (brefnokh)	of *Breifne* ("porous," N. central district, an- lic. Breffny)
.26–27	Tullymongan	Tullach Mongáin (tulokh moñgáñ)	*Mongán*'s (dim. of *mongach*, "hairy") Hillock, Cavan town; recently called Gallows Hill
.27	rayheallach	Uí Raghal- laigh (írayelí)	of the descendants of *Raghallach* ("of a fore-

			arm"); distinguishing n. of E. Breffny (incl. Tullymongan), anglic. Breffny O Reilly
		ré (ré) geallach (gyalokh)	moon; month, phase moon; moonlight
.27	royghal	ríoghamhail (ríúl)	royal, kingly
		geal (gyal) -ghal (ġal), *suffx.*	bright -fight, -valor
.28	MacMahon	Mac Math- ghamhna (mok mahúne)	son of *Mathghamhain* ("bear")
.32	clontarfminded	Cluain Tarbh (klún *t*orev)	Bull Meadow, N.E. Dublin district, site of *Brian Boru's defeat of Danes, 1014
.32	Bawle	báille (bálye)	bailiff
.33	O'Roarke	Ó Ruairc (ó rúirk)	des. of *Ruadhrac* (Norse *Hrothrekr*)
		Uí Ruairc (í rúirk)	of the descendants of *Ruadhrac*; distinguish- ing n. of W. Breffny; anglic. Breffny O Rourke
100.03	Macfarlane	Mac Phartha- láin (mok faraláñ)	son of Bartholomew
.04	Bartholoman's	Parthalán (paralán)	2nd *colonizer; buried at Tallaght, Co. Dub- lin
.06	Tri Paisdinernes	Trí Páistíní Éireannaigh (trí páshtíní erení)	Three little Irish Chil- dren
.06	Lochlanner	Lochlannach (lokhlenokh)	Scandinavian, Norwegian
.07	Fathach I Fiounn- isgehaven	Fathach i [bPáirc an] Fionn-uisce (fohokh i [bárk un] finishki)	Giant in Clear-water [Field] (anglic. Phoe- nix [Park])

.06–07	Tri . . . Fiounnisgehaven	Eachtra Trí Páistíní Éireannaigh le Fathach Lochlannach i bPáirc an Fionn-uisce	Adventures of Three little Irish Children with a Norwegian Giant in Phoenix Park
.07	Bannalanna	bean na leanna (ban ne lane)	ale-woman
.07	Ballyhooly	Baile Atha hUbhla (blá húle)	Appletree Ford Town, Co. Cork, proverbial for faction fights
.08	Buddaree	bodaire (budere) bod (bud) rí (rí)	churl; rich vulgar farmer penis king
.08	Bullavogue	bullabhóg (bulevóg)	bullock; bully
.13	Parteen	Pairtín (part'ín)	Little Landing Place, Co. Clare
.14	fir	fir (fir)	men
.23	fineglass	Fionn-ghlais (finglash)	Clear Stream; village & stream N. of Dublin, anglic. Finglas
101.06	ards	árd (árd)	high; height
.06	downs	dún (dún)	fort; anglic. -down- in place-names
.06	liss	lios (lis)	circular fort; anglic. -lis- in place-names
.08	Moore	Ó Mórdha (ó mórġe)	des. of *Mórdha* ("majestic")
.09	Toemaas	Tómás (tómás) tómas (tómes)	Thomas sake
.11–12	Lucalizod	Leamhcán (loukán) Iosaid (isid')	producing marshmallows; W. Dublin suburb, anglic. Lucan [of] *Iosada* (fem. pers. n., Iseult)
.15	Buckley	Ó Buachalla (ó búkhele)	des. of *Buachaill* ("boy")

.17	colleen bawl aroof	cailín bán a rún (kolíñ bán arún)	my darling white-haired girl
.29	owenglass	*multiple puns* abhainn (ouwin) Eoghan (ówen)	see 101.36: anngreen river; anglic. -owen- in place-names "wellborn," masc. pers. n. anglic. Owen; *Shaun
		glas, glais (glos, glash)	cold, raw, green
		glais, glas (glash, glos)	rivulet
.33	mackavicks	maca mhic (moke vik)	sons of a son
.36	anngreen		see 101.29: owenglass
		half-mistrans. eanglais (anglash)	milk-and-water; any diluted unsatisfactory drink
		ean- (an), *pfx.*	water-; *Anna
		glas, glais (glos, glash)	cold, raw, green
102.02	keen	caoin (kín)	wail, weep
.08	danworld	dán (*d*án) Dana (*d*one)	treasure, art; fate goddess of the dead; *Anna
.09	finickin	Ó Fionnagáin (ó finegáñ)	des. of *Fionnagán* (dim. of *Fionn*, "fair")
.10	brogues	bróg (bróg) barróg (beróg)	shoe defect in speech
.11	little bolero boa and all	*garbled Irish*	words of "Lillibullero," anti-I. Williamite song (c. 1690)
.15	pookas	púca (púke)	hobgoblin
.18	Morandmor	mórán mó (mórán mó) mór (mór)	much more big
.19	Ogrowdnyk's	Ó Gramhna (ó groune) *corrupt for* Mac Carrghamhna	son of *Carrghamhain* ("spear-calf"); anglic. O Growny
.20	tay	té (té)	tea
.28–29	tomauranna	Tómhar (*t*ówer)	Thor

		eanach (anokh)	marsh, fen; *Anna
103.03	*Fin*	Fionn (fin)	Fair
104.01, 08	Annah, *Anna*	eanach (anokh)	marsh, fen; *Anna
.06	*Rockabill*	Craig Dhá Bille (krag gá bili)	Rock of Two Stones; double rock, light-house, off N. Co. Dublin
.09	*Arishe*	arís (arísh)	again
.10	*Siseule*	Sisile (shishili)	fem. pers. n., Cecelia; n. for a hen
.21	*Coombing*	Cúm (kúm)	Hollow; S. Dublin slum anglic. Coombe
.21	*Cammmels*	Caimbéal (kambél)	"Wry-mouth," anglic. Campbell
105.02	*Oremunds*	Urmhumha (urúe)	East Munster; anglic. Ormond
.03	*Granny*	Gráinne (gráñye)	"Grain"/"Spear-point"; fem. pers. n.; *Toraidheacht Dhiarmada agus Ghráinne*
.03	*Fain Me Cuddle*	Fionn Mac Cumhail (fin mok kúl)	Fair son of *Cumhal*, 3rd c. hero of saga cycle; *Toraidheacht Dhiarmada agus Ghráinne*
.09	*Log*	log (lug)	pool from which a river rises
.09	*Anny*	eanaigh (aní)	marshy, fenny; *Anna
.11	*Orel Orel*	Óirghialla (óryíle)	Golden Hostages; anc. principality in S.E. Ulster; anglic. Oriel
.12	*Juckey*	deoch (d'ukh)	drink
.12	*Dhoult*	a dhalta (a youl*t*e)	"foster-child," endear-ment to one much younger
.14	*Nuancee . . . Noahnsy*	ní h-annsa (níhounse)	not hard; formula for answering riddles
.16	*Bonnbtail*	banbh (bonev)	young pig
.18	*Culpreints*	cúl (kúl)	back of the head
.19	*Whisht*	thost (hus*t*)	silence

.22	*Rush*	Ros-eo (rusyó)	Yew-tree peninsula; town, N. Co. Dublin
.26	*Tory Island*	Tor-inis (*t*urinish)	Tower-island; Fomorian stronghold off Co. Donegal
.26	*Milchcow*	Milchó (milkhó)	masc. pers. n., owner of St. Patrick as boy slave in I.
.27	*Crowalley*	Cruadh-bhaile (krúvolye)	Hard-town, Co. Waterford, anglic. Crowbally
.32	*Columbkisses*	Colm Cille (kulum kili)	Dove of the Church, 6th c. st., latinized Columba
106.01–02	*Glen, O'Donogh, White Donogh*	Ó Donnchadha (ó *d*unukhu)	des. of *Donnchadh* ("brown-warrior"), n. of about 7 families, variously anglic.; the head of the surviving branch of the original stock is *Ó Donnchadha an Ghleanna, "Ó D.* of the Glen"; *Brian Boru
.05	*Torsker*	Carraig an Turscair (korig un *t*urskir)	Sea-wrack Rock; shoal, lighthouse off Co. Wexford, anglic. Tuskar Rock
.06	*Tonnoburkes*	tonn (*t*oun)	wave, billow
.07	*O'Loughlin*	Ó Lochlainn (ó lokhlin)	des. of *Lochlainn* ("Scandinavia")
.07	*Pit*	pit (pit′)	vulva
.08	*Moohr*	Ó Mórdha (ó mórġe)	des. of *Mórdha* ("majestic")
.11	*Mackeys*	Mac Aoidh (mokéí)	son of *Aodh* ("fire")
.15	*Thonderbalt*	tón (*t*ón)	bottom, arse
.17	*Fingallians*	Fine-Gall (finigoul)	Foreign Tribe; N. Co. Dublin district, anglic. Fingal
.26	*Delvin*	Deilbhín (d'elvín)	Little Warp; river, N. Co. Dublin
.26	*Vuggy's*	*Asp.	Muggy's
.34	*O'Mollies*	Ó Máille (ó mályi)	des. of *Máille* ("chief"); anglic. *O Malley

107.05	*Lucalizod*	Leamhcán (loukán)	producing marshmallows, W. Dublin suburb, anglic. Lucan
		Iosaid (isid′)	of *Iosada* (fem. pers. n.: Iseult)
108.12–13	Carprimustimus	Cairbre (karbri)	Charioteer; n. of several kings, incl. opponents of *Fionn Mac Cumhail* and St. Patrick; anglic. Carberry, Cairpre
.17	Kinihoun	Ó Cuinneacháin (ó kiniháñ)	des. of *Coinneachán* (dim. of *Conn*, "intelligence")
.17	Kahanan	Ó Catháin (ó kaháñ)	des. of *Cathán* (pet form of some n. beginning *Cath-*, "Battle-")
.18	mear	méar (mér)	finger, toe
.18	measenmanonger	meas (myas)	act of measuring
.18	darnall	dárnael (*d*árnél)	covering of straw
.19	Carrageehouse	Cairrgín (karigín)	Little Rocks, Co. Waterford, anglic. Carragheen; also (from the place), an edible seaweed
.21	Fionn	Fionn (fin)	Fair
.25	gall	gall (goul)	foreigner
110.02	Brien	Ó Briain (ó bríin)	des. of *Brian [Boru]
.03	dindin	dionn (din)	fortress
.08	Isitachapel	Iosada (isi*d*e)	fem. pers. n., Iseult, Isolda
.08	Asitalukin	Leamhcán (loukán)	Producing marshmallows, W. Dublin suburb, anglic. Lucan
.09	madh vaal	Magh Bhealaigh (mávalí)	Plain of a Way, Co. Kildare, on Liffey; anglic. Moyvalley
.11	tay	té (té)	tea
.23	kischabrigies	*half-trans.* droichead cise (*d*rihe*d* kishi)	wicker bridge, hurdle bridge; *Dublin

.32	Kevin	Caoimhghin (kívġin)	Comely-birth; 7th c. st.; *Shaun
.35	Ardagh	Árd-achadh (árdokhe)	High-field, Co. Limerick; chalice found here, silver, gold, bronze, enamel, crystal (9th c.) in Nat'l. Museum
.35	heily	Ó hÉilidhe (ó hélí)	des. of *Éaladhach* ("ingenious"), anglic. Healy
.36– 111.01	Tipperaw raw	Tiobraid Árann (tibrid' áren)	Well of *Ára* (district n.), S. central co., town, anglic. Tipperary
.01	raw	ráth (rá) rádh (rá)	fort speech
.01	reeraw	rí-rá (rírá)	fuss, confusion, revelry
.05	Dorans	Ó Deóráin (ó d'óráñ)	des. of *Deóradhán* (dim. of *deóradh*, "exile")
.12	*the van*	an bhean (un van)	the woman
.14	Chriesty	Mac Críosta (mok kríste)	son of *Críosta* (pet form of Christopher); anglic. Christy
		Críostaidhe (krístí)	Christian
112.07	shoolerim	siubhlóir (shúlór)	wanderer, vagrant
.27	Doran	Ó Deóráin (ó d'óráñ)	des. of *Deóradhán* (dim. of *deóradh*, "exile")
.33	Arin	Éireann (érun), *g.*	[of] Ireland
		árann (áren), *g.*	[of a] kidney; *fig.*, heart
113.01	graith	graithe (grahi)	business, occupation, duty
.02	grigs	griog (grig)	excite desire, tantalize
.07	anakars	anacair (anekir)	affliction, distress
.10	–kinkin–	cinn (kin)	[of a] head; heads; principal
		caoin (kín)	wail, lament
,10	–kankan–	ceann (kyoun) can (kon)	head sing

114.12	shillelagh	Síol Éalaigh (shíléli)	Seed of *Éalach* (masc. pers. n.); tribal territory, Co. Wicklow, renowned for blackthorn
.17	litters	litir (lit'ir)	letter
.24	karrig	carraig (korig)	rock
.24	darka	dorcha (*d*urukhe)	dark
.24	disheen	duisín (*d*ishín)	dozen
.25	Dalbania	Alba (olbe)	Scotland
.36	Boyne	Bóinn	*Boyne River
115.20	grace a mauling	Gráinne Ní Mháille (gráñí wályi)	G. dghtr. of a des. of *Máille* ("chief") anglic. Grace *O Malley
116.13	Dumbil's	bile (bili)	sacred tree
.15	swords	Sórd (sór*d*)	Sward; N. Co. Dublin village
.16	O'Dwyer	Ó Dubhuidhir (ó *d*uvír)	des. of *Dubhodhar* ("black *Odhar* ['dun']")
117.04	Feueragusaria	agus (ogus)	and
.11	michemiche	mise (mishi)	I, me (emphatic)
.14	sheltafocal	seilte (shelte)	"Bog Latin," jargon, argot, cant (featuring arbitrary distortion of basic language)
		focal (fukcl)	word
.18	talkatalka	Tolca (*t*ulke)	Flood, Torrent; river, N.E. Dublin, site of battle of Clontarf
.29	combled	Cúm (kúm)	Hollow; S. Dublin slum, anglic. Coombe
.30	cup on tay	cupán té (kupán té)	cup of tea
118.05	olmund	Urmhumha (urúe)	East Munster; anglic. Ormund (domain of the Butler family)
.13	Coccolanius	Cúchulainn (kúkhulin)	Hound of *Culann* (pers. n.); 2nd c. hero of *Red Branch saga cycle
.13	Gallotaurus	gall (goul)	foreigner
.36	coignings	coinnmheadh (kínva)	quarters, billets (military); anglic. cognye

119.20	alp	alp (olp)	lump, bite, snarl, job; *Alp Uí Laoghaire* ("O Leary's job") : Dublin, in mason's jargon
120.01	pews	*P/K Split	kews
.02	pristopher polombos	*P/K Split	cristopher colombos
.02	Kat Kresbyterians	*P/K Split	Pat Presbyterians
.22–23	kakography	cac (kok)	excrement
121.12, 14	*Aranman*; Aran	Oileáin Árann (iláñ áren)	Kidney Islands, off Co. Galway, anglic. Aran
.14	keen	caoin (kín)	wail, lament
.16	disdotted aiches	*Aspiration	indicated by super-script dot *or* post-fixed h
122.09	*O'Remus*	*as if* Ó Remus	des. of Remus
.16	rossy	rásaidhe (rásí)	wandering woman; jilt
.16, 19	O'Mara	Ó Meadhra (ó myare)	des. of *Meadhair* ("mirth")
.23	Kells	Ceanannas (kyanenus); *altered to* Ceannlios (kyanlis)	chief residence; chief fort; anglic. Kenlis, then Kells, royal resi-dence, Meath, con-verted by St. Colmcille to monastic center where famous Gospel MS made
.29	Columkiller	Colmcille (kulumkili)	Dove of the Church; 6th c. fndr. of Kells monastic settlement; latinized Columba
123.02	dhee	dia (d'íe) I. sound of consonant d (*d*)[?]	god
.08	ogham	ogham (oyum)	early I. writing by notches
.11	Duff	Dubh (*d*uv)	Black; descriptive epi-thet replacing real sur-name
.25	*MacPerson*'s	Mac an Phearsúin (mokun farsúñ)	son of the parson; *Macpherson

.25	*Oshean*	Oisín (ushín)	Little Deer; Fawn; son of *Fionn Mac Cumhail* *Macphersonized into Ossian
.32	Hanno O'Nonhanno's	Ó hAinchín (ó hankhín)	des. of *Ainchín* (perhaps *Ainghein*, "unborn")
		Ó hAnnach-áin, hAnnagáin (ó hanekháñ, hanegáñ)	des. of *Annagán* (dim. of *annadh*, "delay")
		Ó hAnnaidh (ó haní)	des. of *Annadh* ("delay")
		Ó hAnnáin (ó hanáñ)	des. of *Annán* (dim. of *annadh*, "delay") all anglic. Hannan, Hannon, etc.
124.09	àth	áth (á)	ford; *Dublin
.09	é's	é (é)	he
.09	Brèak	breac (brak)	"speckled"; trout
.25	Pratiland	prátaí (prátí)	potatoes
.29	Fjorgn Camhelsson	Fionn Mac Cumhail (fin mok kúl)	Fair son of *Cumhal*, 3rd c. hero of saga cycle
125.04	Tulko	tulc (tulk)	strong blow
		Tolca (tulke)	Flood, Torrent; N.E. Dublin river
.04	MacHooley	Mac Uallaigh (mokúlí)	son of *Uallach* ("proud")
.06	the day was in it	*lit. trans.* an lá bhí ann	that day, on that day
.06	morrow Diremood	Diarmaid Mac Murchadha (d'írmid' mok murukhu)	Freeman son of *Murch-adh* ("sea-warrior"); anglic. Dermot Mac Morrough, Leinster king who invited Anglo-Norman inva-sion; *Shem
.06–07	is the name is on the writing chap of the psalter	*lit. trans.* an ainm atá ar fear scríobhtha na saltrach	is the name of the man who wrote the psalter
.08	dearmate	Diarmaid (d'írmid')	Freeman; masc. pers. n., *Shem

.09	Torba's	Ó Torpa (ó turpe)	des. of *Tarpach* ("sturdy")
.22	kak	cac (kok)	excrement
.22	poteen	poitín (put'ín)	little pot; illicit whiskey
126.04	Shaun Mac	Seán Mac (shán mok)	John son of
.07	Mic	Mic (mik)	Son (vocative; genitive)
.12	buaboababbaun	buadh (búe) bábán (bábán) bán (bán)	victory baby white
.15	esker	eiscir (eshkir)	sandy ridge
.19	serebanmaids	bean (ban)	woman
.22	boyne	Bóinn (bóñ)	*Boyne River
127.07	cad a'clog	cad a chlog (kod a khlug)	what o'clock
.11–12	shoolbred	siubhal (shúl)	walking, traveling; commotion
.19	sosannsos	sos (sus)	peace; *Anna
.26	Iren	Éirinn (érin), *dat.*	[to, for] Ireland
128.01	Benn	Beinn (ben)	mountain, headland
.04	faunonfleetfoot	fán (fán) ar fán (er fán)	straying in exile (lit., "on straying")
.06	buglooking	bog (bug)	soft
.14	Anna Livia	eanach Life (anokh lifi)	*Liffey-fen; *Anna
.25	O'Bruin's	Ó Brúin (ó brúñ)	des. of *Braon*, ("sorrow")
.26	Noolahn	Ó Nualláin (ó núláñ)	des. of *Nuallán* (dim. of *nuall*, "noble")
.33	flawhoolagh	flaitheamh-lach (flahúlokh)	princely; generous, hospitable
129.01	cowcarlows	Ceatharlach (kahirlokh)	Quadruple Lake; S.E. town & co., anglic. Carlow

.04	Cattermole Hill	Cathair Maoth-Aill (kahir mwéhil)	Soft-cliff Citadel, Co. Limerick, anglic. Cahermohill
.09	Cellbridge	Cill-Droichid (kil*d*rihid')	Bridge-Church; on the Liffey; anglic. Celbridge (half-trans.)
.10	biguinnengs	Mag Aonghusa (mogénġesi)	son of *Aonghus* ("single-choice" [god of love]); anglic. Guinness
.12	Danes	Dana (*d*one)	goddess of the dead; *Anna
.20	dub	dubh (*d*uv)	black
.21	limn	linn (liñ)	pool; *Dublin
.24	Ratheny	Ráth Éanna (rá éne)	Enda's Fort; N.E. Dublin suburb, anglic. Raheny
.26	Domhnall, Domhnall	Domhnall (*d*ónel)	World-mighty; masc. pers. n., anglic. Donnell, Donal, Donald, Daniel
.33–34	thick-in-thews	'tuigeann tú? (*t*igin tú)	do you understand?
.34	thews	tiugh (t'ú)	thick
.34	in Aryania	i nÉirinn (inérin)	in Ireland
.35	Collesons	*trans.* Mac Cuill (mok kil)	Son of *Coll* ("hazel-tree"); one of last *Tuatha Dé Danann* kings; *colonists
130.04	Lug	lug (lug)	mountain-hollow; n. of several mtns.
.04	Luk	luch (lukh)	mouse
.13	bawn	bán (bán)	white
.13–14	Roh re	Ruaidhrí (rúrí)	Norse *Rothrekr* ("fame-ruler"); n. of last high king
.21	annesleyg	Áth na Slighe (áneshlí)	Ford of the Way; Co. Donegal, anglic. Annasley; also bridge in Dublin

.21	binn	binn (bín)	melodious
.21	atolk	Tolca (*t*ulke)	Flood, Torrent; N. Dublin river, site of battle of Clontarf; anglic. Tolka
.25	dulse	duileasc (*d*ilesk)	edible seaweed
.30	young rose	[?] bod (bu*d*)	penis
.33	Glintylook	Gleann-dá-loch (gloun *d*álokh)	Two-lake Valley, Co. Wicklow; St. Kevin's monastic settlement; anglic. Glendalough
.34	Elin's	Éireann (érun), *g.*; *L/R Interchange	[of] Ireland
131.01	Mount of Mish	Sliabh Mis (slív mish)	*Mis*'s (fem. pers. n.) Mountain; mtn., Co. Antrim, where Patrick tended swine as boy slave, anglic. Slemish; mtn., Co. Kerry, anglic. Slieve Mish
.01	Mell of Moy	Magh Meall (má myal)	Honey Plain; anc. I. elysium
.05	topperairy	Tiobraid Árann (tibrid' áren)	Well of *Ara* (district n.); S.-central co. & town, anglic. Tipperary
.09	fenians . . . *fainéants*	Fíanna (fíene)	3rd c. standing army led by *Fionn Mac Cumhail*
.09	Tiara	Teamhair (t'our)	Prospective-hill; anc. royal capital, anglic. Tara
.10	Liam	Líam (lím)	William
.10	Liam Fail	Lia Fáil (lí fál)	fetish stone at Tara, shrieked at accession of rightful high king
.10–11	Westmunster	Mumha[n] (mú[n])	S. province; anglic. Munster
,13	Buddapest	bod (bu*d*) péist (pésht)	penis serpent

.25	curach	curach (kurokh)	coracle, canvas canoe
		cuirreach (kwirokh)	racecourse
		Cath-reacht (korokh*t*)[?]	Battle-vigor; *Macpherson explains n. Curach as "Cu-raoch . . . the madness of battle"
.28	fidhil	*English spelled as I.:* (fíl)	feel; *Macpherson
.28	morvenlight	Mór-Bheanna (mórvane)[?]	Great Peaks; *Macpherson's Fingal was king of Morven, "which signifies a ridge of very high hills"
.35	Taishantyland	tigh (tí)	house; anglic. Ty- in place-names
		sean (shan)	old
		sean-tigh (shant'í)	old house
132.02	cavin	cabhán	hollow, slope
.04	Badderstown	*half-trans.* Baile an Bóthair (bol-yunbóher)	Town of the Road, Co. Meath; anglic. Batterstown
.05	modareds	madradh (mo*d*re)	dog
		madradh-ruadh (mo*d*erúe)	"red-dog": fox
.06	Camlenstrete	Cam-líne (komlíni)	Crooked-line; n. of several rivers, anglic. Camlin
.13	costellous	Mac Oisdealbh (mokushd'alv)	son of *Oisdealbh* ("shaped like *Os* ['deer'—n. of a god]"); anglic. Costello
.15	Monstrucceleen	strucáil (s*t*rukál)	huckstering
		trucailín (*t*rukelín)	little cart
.17	tav	támh (*t*áv)	sleep, death

.19	tradertory	tóraidhe (*tórí*)	robber, persecuted person
.22	Cromlechheight	Crom-leac (krumlak)	stooped flagstone; popular n. for dolmen
.22	Crommalhill	Cromail (krumil)	English n. Cromwell; *Humphrey
.24	Lubar	Lúbar (lúber)	Convolutions; according to *Macpherson, a n. for the Six-Mile River, Co. Antrim
.26	Banba	Banba (bonbe)	Ireland (poetic); n. of a *Tuatha Dé Danann* queen
.27	Beurla	Beurla, Béarla (bérle)	English language
.33	Irskaholm	Éire (ére) uisce (ishki)	Ireland water
133.01–02	Costello	Mac Oisdealbh (mokushd'alv)	see 132.13
.02	Kinsella	Cinnsealach (kinshelokh)	des. of *Éanna Cinnsealach*, son of *Diarmaid Mac Murchadha*, Leinster king who invited Anglo-Normans. *Cinnsealach* ("ostentatious") is an agnomen replacing the real surname
.02	Mahony	Ó Mathghamhna (ó mahoune)	des. of *Mathghamhain* ("bear"), leader in *Brian Boru's army killed at Clontarf
.02	Moran	Ó Móráin (ó móráñ) Ó Mughróin (ó múróñ)	des. of *Mórán* (dim. of *mór*, "great") des. of *Mughrón* ("slave-sealion")
.07	Roseoogreedy	Ó Gráda (ó grá*de*)	des. of *Gráda* ("illustrious"); anglic. O Grady
.08–09	mack . . . micks	mac (mok)	son
.24	brehons	breitheamhain (brehúñ)	judges, lawgivers
.26	Mac Milligan's	Mac Maoil-eacháin (mok mwélekháñ)	son of *Maolagán* (dim. of *maol*, "bald")

.28	boro	bóramha (bórúe)	"cow-counting"; tribute; *Brian Boru
.36	ardree	árd-rí (árdrí)	high king
134.01	Baulacleeva	Baile Átha Cliath (bláklíe)	Hurdle Ford Town; *Dublin
.03	laveries	Ó Labhradha (ó laverú)	des. of *Labhraidh* ("spokesman")
.22	gale	Gaedheal (gél)	Irishman, Scotsman
.22	gall	Gall (goul)	Foreigner
135.01	murry	Ó Muireadh-aigh (ó mwiraí)	des. of *Muireadhach* ("mariner")
.06	annacrwater	eanach (anokh)	marsh, fen; *Anna
.13–14	brow of a hazelwood	*trans.* Drom Coll-Choille	Hazelwood Ridge, now Thomas Street, Dublin
.14	pool . . . dark	Dubh-linn (*d*uvliñ)	Black Pool; *Dublin
.14	blowicks	Ó Bláthmhaic (ó bláwik)	des. of *Bláthmhac* ("blossom-son")
.15	well of Artesia . . . bird of Arabia	[Páirc an] Fionn-uisce ([párk un] finishki)	Clear-water [Field], anglic. Phoenix [Park]
.18	pleasant little field	*as if* Glaisín Aoibhinn (glashínívin) *for* Glas Naoidhean (glosníen)	*as if* Pleasant Little Green *for* [St.] *Naoidhe*'s Stream, anglic. Glasnevin; N. Dublin district with cemetery
.31	Dundrums	Dún Droma (*d*ún*d*rume)	Ridge Fort, Dublin suburb, anglic. Dundrum
.36	saggarts	sagart (sogur*t*)	priest
136.03–04	cushlin his crease	cúislín a chroidhe (kúshlín a khrí)	little pulse of his heart (endearment)
.08	borèd	bóthar (bóher)	road

.09	Moyle	Sruth na Maoile (sru nu mwéli)	Sea-stream of the Bald-headland; sea between I. & Scotland; anglic. Moyle (poetic)
.13	geulant	Gaedhealach (gélokh)	Irish
.13	duiv	dubh (duv)	black
.14	Boaro	bodhradh (bóre)	deafness
		bóramha (bórúe)	"cow-counting"; tribute; *Brian Boru
.22–23	king's brugh	Brugh Ríogh (brúrí)	King's Palace, Limerick, anglic. Bruree
.23	brugh	brugh (brú)	palace
.28	bannucks	bannach (banokh)	loaf
		beannacht (banokht)	blessing
.30	duv	dubh (duv)	black
.33	bally clay	Baile Átha Cliath (blá klíe)	Hurdle Ford Town; *Dublin
.33	clay	clé (klé)	left (side)
.36	moontaen	mún (mún)	urine
137.01	succar	Succat (sukot)	St. Patrick's supposed baptismal n.
.01	boinyn	Bóinn (bóñ)	(n. of goddess) River Boyne
		boinín (buñín)	calf
.02	Miss MacCormack	Níc Cormaic (ník kurmik)	Daughter of a Son of Cormac ("chariot-son") [construed as Daughter of Cormac?]
.02	Ni Lacarthy	Ní Cárthaigh (ní kárhí)	Daughter of a Grandson of Cárthach ("loving") [construed as Granddaughter of Cárthach?]
.02	Miss MacCormack Ni Lacarthy	[Gráinne] inghean Cormaic Mhic Airt [not Cárthaigh]	["Grain"] daughter of Chariot-son Son of Bear: Gráinne, dgtr. of King Cormac Mac Airt [not Mac Cárthaigh],

			heroine of *Toraidh- eacht Dhiarmada agus Ghráinne
.03	Dermod	Diarmaid (d'írmid')	Freeman; hero of *Toraidheacht Dhiar- mada agus Ghráinne; *Shem
.03, 04	diamond, dammat	Diarmaid	see 137.03
.04	garnet, groany	Gráinne	see 137.02
.05	Florence	Finghin (finyin)	"Fair-birth," masc. pers. n. common among MacCarthys, who anglic. it Florence. Fionn ("Fair") Mac Cumhail was Gráinne's jilted & vengeful fiancé
.05	Wynn's	de Bhuinn (devwin)	I. version of Welsh Gwyn, "white," cog- nate with I. Fionn
.08	Cockran	Ó Cogaráin (ó kugeráñ)	des. of Cogarán ("confidant")
.08	tays	té (té)	tea
.11	prities	préataí (prétí)	potatoes
.22	kersse	Mac Fhiarais (mokírish) var. of Mac Phiarais (mok fírish)	son of Piers [Healy]
138.10	ath . . . cleah	Áth Cliath (áklíe)	Hurdle Ford; *Dublin
.11	fingallian	Fine Gall (fini goul)	Foreign Tribe, N. Co. Dublin district, anglic. Fingal
.11	hoolies	[Baile Átha] hUbhla ([blá] húle)	Appletree [Ford Town], Co. Cork, famous for faction fights: wild, uninhib- ited party
.12	brabanson	breágh (brá) bean (ban)	fine, handsome woman
.14	buckeley	Ó Buachalla (ó búkhele)	des. of Buachaill ("boy")

.19	Mullingar	An Muileann Cearr (un mwilin kyar)	The Left-handed Mill, Co. Westmeath
.20	nuasilver	nua (núe) Nuadha Airgead- lámh (núa arigidláv)	new *Nuadha* Silver-hand, king of *Tuatha Dé Danann*
.21	Iron	Éireann (érun), g.	[of] Ireland
.23	Ebblannah	eanach (anokh) leanbh (lanev)	marsh, fen; *Anna child
.25	Olives	ollamh (ulev)	scholar
.26	Otooles	Ó Tuathail (ó túhil)	des. of *Tuathal* ("people-mighty"); anglic. O Toole
.27	durc's	dorcha (durukhu)	dark
139.06	farfar	fear-feasa (farfase)	wizard
.10	pearly	*trans.* fionn (fin)	white speck or "pearl" on eye
.13	wan	*trans.* fionn (fin)	pale
.13	wubblin wall	*trans.* falla fionntrach (fole fintrokh)	wall liable to collapse
.14	Finn Mac Cool	Fionn Mac Cumhail (fin mok kúl)	Fair Son of *Cumhal*; 3rd c. hero of saga cycle; *Macpherson's Fingal
.19	Ann alive	Eanach Life (anokh lifi)	*Liffey-fen; *Anna
.19	grig	griog (grig)	excite desire, tantalize
.22	Ossean	Oisín (ushín)	Little Deer, Fawn; poet, son of *Fionn Mac Cumhail*; *Macpherson's Ossian
.22	Dann	Danann (donon), g. Danar (daner)	[of] *Dana* (goddess of dead); *Anna Dane
.22	Ann's	ean- (an) *pfx.*	water-; *Anna

.24	dabblin	daba (*d*obe)	small soft heap; *Dublin
.29	Tick	tig (tig)	house (S.)
.30	Teac	teach (t′okh)	house (W.)
.36	Ebblawn	lán (lán)	full
140.02	Corry's	Ó Corra (ó kure)	des. of *Corra* ("spear"); by mistaking *corra* for *cora*, anglic. Weir
.02	Weir's	*mistrans.* Ó Corra *as if* Ó Cora (ó kore)	des. of *Corra* ("spear") des. of Cora ("weir"); anglic. Weir
.03	Uval	úbhall (úl) Umhall (úl)	apple suggested correct n. of *Fionn Mac Cumhail*'s/ *Umhaill*'s father
.08	a dea o dea!	a dhia (a ġíe)	o god!
.09	nuinous	nuin (nwin)	ash tree; letter N
.15	Delfas	Béal Feirste (bél ferishti)	Sandbank River-mouth; anglic. Belfast
.21	Dorhqk	dorcha (*d*urukhu) Corcaigh (kurkí)	dark Swamp; anglic. Cork
.27	Isha	ise (ishi) 'uise (ishi)	she (emphatic) well, indeed
.28	avourneen	a mhúirnín (a vúrñín)	sweetheart, my dear
.36	Dalway	dál (*d*ál) Gaillimh (goliv)	territory of a tribe Foreign; anglic. Galway "of the Tribes"
141.01	Mayo	Magh-eó (máyó)	Yew-plain; W. town & co. (N. of Galway)
.02	Tuam	Tuaim (túim)	Funeral-mound, Co. Galway; "Mayo & Tuam": the arch-diocese of Tuam
.02	Sligo's	Sligeach (shligokh)	Shell-mound; W. city & co.
.02	Galway's	Gaillimh	see 140.36
.06	Shand . . . gon	Sean-Dún (shan*d*ún)	Old Fort, Cork, anglic. Shandon

.06	gon	gan (gon)	without
.06	ness	neas (nas)	fortified place; anglic. -ness in place-names
.06–07	*Shandeepen*	sean (shan)	old
.07	moy	magh (má)	plain; anglic. moy- in place-names
.08	loughlad	loch (lokh)	lake; anglic. lough in place-names
		Lochlainn (lokhlin)	Lake-country; Scandinavia, Norway
.20	skreve	scríobh (shkrív)	write
.25	aleconnerman	Ó Conchobhair (ó konehur)	des. of *Conchobhar* ("high-will"), anglic. O Connor
.28	slogan	sluagh-ghairm (slúgorim)	"host-summons": call for mobilization
.30	Galory	go leor (gulyór)	enough, plenty
.35	blackcullen	Ó Cuileáin (ó kuláñ)	des. of *Cuileán* ("whelp"); anglic. Cullen
		cúilfhionn (kúlin)	"fair-head": pretty girl
.35	Tomorrha's	Teamhair (t'our)	Prospective-hill; anc. royal capital, anglic. Tara, *Macpherson's Temora
142.04	kilkenny	Cill Ceannaigh/ Choinnigh (kil kyaní/ khiní)	Church of *Ceannach/ Coinneach*, "Fair One"; S.E. co. & town
.12	Donnybrook	Domhnach/ Tamhnach Broc (*d*ounokh/ *t*ounokh brok)	Badger Church/Field (1st commonly accepted; 2nd correct); S. Dublin suburb
.13	Crumglen's	Crom-ghlinn (krumglin)	Bent Valley, S.W. Dublin district; anglic. Crumlin

.13	Kimmage's	Cam-ínse (koumínshi)	Curved water-meadows, S.W. Dublin suburb
.14	Cabra	Cabrach (kabrokh)	"Badland," N.W. Dublin district
.14	Finglas	Fionn-glais (finglash)	Fair Stream; river & village N. of Dublin
.15	Santry	Sean-treabh (shantrav)	Old Tribe; village N. of Dublin
.15	Raheny	Ráth Éanna (rá éne)	Enda's Fort; N.E. Dublin suburb
.15–16	Baldoygle	Baile Dubhghaill (bolye dúġil)	Town of a Dark For-eigner (i.e., Dane), an-glic. Baldoyle; village N.E. of Dublin
.22	condam	conda (kunde)	doglike, canine
.26	doyles	dáil (dál)	assembly; Dáil Éireann, I. Legislative Assembly
		Ó Dubhghaill (ó dúġil)	des. of Dubhghall ("black-foreigner" [Dane]); anglic. Doyle
.26	sullivans	Ó Súileabháin (ó súleváñ)	des. of Súileabhán, i.e., Súil-dubhán ("black-eyed")
.28	Mor	Mór (mór)	great; the Great
.28	Mac Carty	Mac Cárthaigh (mok kárhí)	son of Cárthach ("loving")
.29	Morphios	Ó Murchadha (ó murukhu)	des. of Murchadh ("sea-warrior"); anglic. Murphy, Morphy
143.07	camelot	cam (koum)	crooked
.12	tory	tóraidhe (tórí)	robber, persecuted person
.17	gallicry	gall (goul)	foreigner
.17	lucan	Leamhcán (loukán)	producing marsh-mallows; W. Dublin suburb, anglic. Lucan
.19	tother	toth (to)	female; fem. genera-tive organs
.30	shee	sidhe (shí)	fairy
.30	dothe	toit (tit')	smoke

.35	pigaleen	-ín (ín), *dim. suffx.*	little, darling
		pigín (pigín)	small wooden pitcher
144.05	Clancarbry	Clann/Cineal Cairbre (klon/kinel korbri)	Race of *Cairbre* (son of *Niall* Nine-Hostager); a clan settled in Co. Sligo; *Uí Néill
.09	Ornery's	Orbhraighe (orvrí)	Posterity of *Orb* (masc. pers. n.); barony, N. Co. Cork, anglic. Orrery
.10	Balldole	Baile Dubhghaill (bolye *d*úġil)	Town of a Black Foreigner (i.e., Dane), village N.E. of Dublin, anglic. Baldoyle
.10	Eilish	Eilís (elísh) Éire (ére); *L/R Interchange	Elizabeth Ireland
.19	Iran	Éirinn (érin), *dat.*	[to] Ireland
145.05	Tay	té (té)	tea
.07	toughturf	tórramh (*t*órev)	wake, funeral
.07–08	mishymissy	mise (mishi)	I, me (emphatic)
.22	Magrath	Mag Raith (mogra)	son of *Mac Raith* ("son of grace")
.35–36	bannan	Ó Banáin (ó banáñ) bean (ban)	des. of *Banán* (dim. of *bán*, "white") woman
146.08	Daveran	Ó Dábhoireann (ó *d*áviron)	des. of *Dubhdábhoireann* ("Black of the Two Burrens [stony wasteland]")
.16	gleison	Ó Glasáin (ó glosáñ)	des. of *Glasán* (dim. of *glas*, "grey, green")
.27	dear mot's	Diarmaid (d'írmid')	Freeman; hero of *Toraidheacht Dhiarmada agus Ghráinne*; *Shem
.29	granny	Gráinne (gráñi)	Grain; heroine of *Toraidheacht Dhiarmada agus Ghráinne*

.31	more on more	mórán mó (mórán mó)	much more
147.11	Ena	Aodhnait (énat')	fem. dim. of *Aodh* ("fire"), anglic. Ena
.12	Ita	Íde (ídi)	"Thirst," fem. pers. n.
.14	Una	Úna (úne)	"Famine," fem. pers. n.
.30	Holohan	Ó hUalla- cháin (ó húleháñ)	des. of *Uallachán* (dim. of *uallach*, "proud")
148.02	*Misi, misi!*	mise (mishi)	I, me (emphatic)
.07	duvetyne	dubh (*d*uv)	black
.19	Brinbrou's	Brian Bóroimhe (bríen bórivi)	*Brian* of the Tribute, high king killed at Clontarf, 1014, while defeating Danes; *Brian Boru
.22	alpin	ailpín (alpín)	knob; *Macpherson substitutes "son of Alpin" for St. Patrick
.23	cantalang	canntal (kon*t*el)	sorrow
.26	Liss, liss!	lios (lis)	ring-fort; anglic. Lis- in place-names
.31	amorandmore	mórán mó (mórán mó)	much more
.33	Ailing	Éirinn (érin), *dat.*, *L/R Interchange áilne (álñi)	[from] Ireland beauty
.34	shimmy	Siomaidh (shimí)	Jimmy
.34	on shin	annsin (unshin)	then, thereupon
.36	Lyon	Ó Laighin (ó lein)	des. of *Laighean* ("lance")
.36	O'Lynn	Ó Fhloinn (ó lin)	des. of *Flann* ("ruddy")
149.06	diffle	Ó Duibh- ghiolla (ó divġile)	des. of *Dubhghiolla* ("black-lad"); anglic. Diffley
.07	fain	féin (fén)	self
.07	shinner	sinn-ne (shini)	we, us (emphatic)

.07	fain shinner	Sinn Féin (shin fén)	Ourselves
150.02	hree	rí (rí)	king
.21	Cavantry	Cabhán (kaván) Ó Caomháin (ó kéváñ)	Hollow; N.-central co. & town; anglic. Cavan des. of *Caomhán* (dim. of *caomh*, "comely"); anglic. Cavan
151.20	taradition	Teamhair (t'our)	Prospective-hill; anc. royal capital, anglic. Tara
.24	Mullocky	Ó Maol- aithche (ó mélakhi) Maelsheach- lainn (mélokhlin)	des. of *Maolaithghein* ("votary of regenera- tion") Servant of [St.] Secundinus [disciple of Patrick]; anglic. *Malachy
152.05	lattlebrattons	*trans.* Breatain Beag (bra*t*in byug)	"Little Britain": Brittany; Wales
.06	Cadwan	céad (ké*d*)	first
.11	Nowlan	Ó Nualláin (ó núláñ)	des. of *Nuallán* (dim. of *nuall*, "noble")
.36	Shinshone	sinn (shin) Seón (shón)	we, us John; *Shaun
153.04	colliens	cailín (kolín) Ó Coileáin (ó koláñ)	girl des. of *Coileán* ("whelp"); anglic. Collins
.07	*down*	donn (*d*oun)	brown
.10	olum	Oilioll Olum (ilil olum)	3rd c. king of Munster, father of *Eoghan Mór*; *Shaun
.18	Dubville	dubh (*d*uv) bile (bili); *Asp.	black sacred tree
154.02	lowry	Labhraidh (lourí)	Spokesman; masc. pers. n. of several kings
155.11	inchies	ínse (ínshi)	water-meadows; anglic. inchi- in place- names

.34	Malachy	Maelsheach-lainn (mélokhlin)	Servant of [St.] Secundinus (disciple of St. Patrick); anglic. *Malachy
156.22	MacHammud's	Mac (mok)	son [of]
.34	mear's	méar (mér)	finger
157.03	Unuchorn	chorn (khorn) ochón (ukhón)	horn, chalice alas
.05	Uvuloid	ubh (uv)	egg
.06	Uskybeak	uisce-beatha (ishkibahe)	"water of life"; whiskey
.15	Moonan	Ó Maonáin (ó mónáñ)	des. of *Maonán* (dim. of *maon*, "dumb")
.33	*Petite Bretagne*	*trans.* Breatain Beag	"Little Britain": Brittany; Wales
158.04	dubliboused	dubh (*d*uv)	black
.11	an	an (un)	the
.16	morrokse	Murchadh (murukhu)	Sea-warrior; masc. pers. n.; severe fright— from *Murchadh Ó Briain na dTóiteán* (M. O Brien of the Burnings), Earl of Inchiquin, 17th c. pro-English terrorist; *Brian Boru
159.08	bannistars	bean (ban)	woman
.12–13	Missisliffi	Life (lifi)	*Liffey River; *Anna
.30	baileycliaver	Baile Atha Cliath (bláklíe)	Hurdle Ford Town; *Dublin
160.06	Curraghchasa	Cuirreach Life (kwirokh lifi)	Moor/Racecourse of the *Liffey [Plain], anglic. the Curragh of Kildare
.08	deodarty	dair (*d*ar)	oak tree; letter D
.12	Conna Hill	Conachail (konakhil)	Firewood-cliff, Co. Cork
.15	awn	áin (áñ)	pleasure, desire
.15	alum	ailm (elim)	elm; letter A
.27	billfaust	Béal Feirste (bél ferishte)	Sandbank River-mouth; anglic. Belfast

.27	curks	Corcaigh (kurkí)	Swamp; anglic. Cork
.27	coolskittle	cúl (kúl)	back of the head
161.29	Murphybuds	Ó Murchadha (ó murukhu)	des. of *Murchadh* ("Sea-warrior")
162.12	Fonnumagula	fonn (foun)	longing desire
		Fionn Mac Cumhail (fin mok kúl)	Fair son of *Cumhal*, 3rd c. hero of saga cycle
		Fionnghuala (finúle)	Fair-shoulders; heroine of *Children of Lir
163.09	tyron	Tír Eoghain (tír ówiñ)	*Eoghan*'s ("wellborn"; *Shaun) Land; anglic. Tyrone; *Uí Néill
.30	tyrondynamon	see 163.09	
164.12	kish	cis (kish)	wickerwork; *Dublin
.22	drisheens	drisín (drishín)	stuffed sheep's intestine cooked as pudding
167.16	cong	Conga (kuñge)	Strait between lakes; Cong, Co. Mayo, monastic retirement of *Ruaidhrí Ó Conchobhair*, last high king
168.05	Mac	mac (mok)	son
.14	*Semus*	Séamus (shémus)	James; *Shem
169.01	Shemus	Séamus (shémus)	James; *Shem
.01	joky	Seóigh (shóí)[?]	son of *Joie* (Norman pers. n.); anglic. Joyce
.11	adze of a skull	Táilcenn (tálken)	Adze-head; n. for St. Patrick, from tonsure or miter
.20	Shemmy	Siomaidh (shimí)	Jimmy; *Shem
170.01	annas . . . annas	eanach (anokh)	marsh, fen; *Anna
.04	sweestureens	siuirín (shúrín)	little sister; sweetheart
.15	sem	Sem (shem)	*Shem (biblical)
.24	rocks, —Sham	seamróg, seamar (shamróg, shamer)	shamrock, trefoil

.33	Balaclava	Baile Átha Cliath (blá klíe)	Hurdle Ford Town; *Dublin
171.04	farsoonerite	pharsún (forsún) *Aspiration	parson
.06	split little pea	*reference to*	*P/K Split
.31	Tulloch	tulach (*t*ulokh)	hill
172.02	*Sar shin*	saor sinn (sér shin)[?]	free us
.23	Nearapoblican	pobal (pubel) poblacht (publokh*t*)	people, the public republic
.31	Munda	mún (mún)	urine
173.15	tamileasy	tamall (*t*omel)	a while, a time
.22	Poppamore	Pápa (pápe) mór (mór)	Pope big, great
.25–26	cruaching	crúach (krúokh) cruach (krúkh)	gory conical heap, rick
.26	Peppybeg	beig (beg)	little
174.15	is their girlic-on-you?	*trans.* an bhfhuil Gaedhealg agat?	do you know Irish?
.22	hailcannon	cál ceannfhionn (kál kyonin)	"fair-head cabbage": dish of cabbage, butter, potatoes; anglic. colcannon
.25	soggert	sagart (sogur*t*)	priest
.26	Leafy	Life (lifi)	*Liffey River
.29	rahilly	Ó Raithile (ó rahili)	des. of *Raithile* (meaning unknown); family distinguished by greatest mod. I. poet & by hero killed in 1916 Rising
175.14	*Witchywithcy*	mhuise (wishi)	indeed, well (interj.)
.25	*Tory Island*	Tor-Inis (*t*orinish)	Towery Island; Fomorian stronghold off Donegal
.25–26	*Eirewhiggs*	Éire (ére)	Ireland

176.01	*Thonderman*	tón (*tón*)	bottom, arse
.03	*Sheila*	Síle (shíle)	fem. pers. n., from Latin Cecilia
.07	*Henressy*	Ó hAonghusa (ó hénġesi)	des. of *Aonghus* ("single-choice" [god of love]); anglic. Hennessy
.08	*Bearstone*	*trans.* Árt (árt)	masc. pers. n.: Bear/ Stone
.10	*Dreamcolohour*	Drom Coll-choile (*d*rum kolkíle)	Hazelwood Ridge, Co. Limerick, anglic. Dromcolliher; also, Thomas Street, Dublin
.12	*Heali*	Ó hÉilidhe (ó hélí)	des. of *Ealadhach* ("ingenious")
.13	*Theagues*	Tadhg (*t*eig)	Poet.; masc. pers. n. of typical country laborer
.14	*Cooney*	Ó Cuana (ó kúne)	des. of *Cuana* ("handsome")
.17	*Farrel*	Ó Fearghail (ó faryil)	des. of *Fearghal* ("super-valor")
.18	*Mac Garvey*	Mac Gairbh-aith (mok garve)	son of *Gairbhith* ("rough-peace")
.20	germogall	gall (goul)	foreigner
.27	Talviland	talamh (*t*olev)	land
.27	ahone	ochón (okhón)	alas
177.04	pawdry's	Pádraig (pádrig)	Patrick
.30	Sheames	Séamus (shémus)	James; *Shem
178.01	Lumdrum	Lom-drom (loum*d*rum)	Bare-ridge
.02	ruvidubb	dubh (*d*uv)	black
.04	scrufferumurraimost	Ó Muirea-dhaigh (ó mwirayí)	des. of *Muireadhach* ("mariner"); anglic. Murray
.09	Lucalizod	Leamhcán (loukán)	producing marshmallows; W. Dublin suburb, anglic. Lucan
		Iosaid (isid'), g.	[of] *Iosada* (Iseult, Isolda)

.16	Gillooly	Mac Giolla Ghuala (mok gileġúle)	son of *Giolla Ghuala* ("servant of gluttony" —i.e., glutton)
.22–23	MacJobber	Mac (mok)	son of
.26	dia	dia (d'íe)	god; day
.26	Finnados	Fionn (fin)	Fair
.33	kules	cúl (kúl)	goal (ball games)
.33	oving	ubh (uv)	egg
.35	Duvvelsache	dubh (*duv*)	black
179.02	*lennones*	Ó Leannáin (ó lanáñ)	des. of *Leannán* (dim. of *leann*, "cloak"); anglic. Lennon
.13	Calumnious Column	*Colmcille (kulumkili)	Dove of the Church; st., latinized Columba
.14	Annamite	eanach (anokh)	fen, marsh; *Anna
.30	mor	mór (mór)	big, great
.31	aisling	aisling (ashliñ)	vision, dream
180.06	*Shemlockup Yellin*	Seamróg Éireann (shamróg érun)	Shamrock (trefoil) of Ireland
.08	McGluckin	Mag Eochaidhín (mog yokhín)	son of *Eochaidhín* (dim. of *Eochaidh*, "horseman"); anglic. McGuckin
.10	macfarlane	Mac Pharthaláin (mok faraláñ)	son of Bartholemew
.11	kerssest	Mac Fhiarais (mokírish) *for* Mac Phiarais (mok fírish)	son of Piers [Healy]
.13–14	Lindundarri	*as if* Linn Dún Daire (lin *d*ún *d*ari)	Oakwood Fort Pool
		Daire (*d*ari)	Oakwood, N. city & co., anglic. [London]-derry, Derry
,14	Carchingarri	Corcaigh (kurkí)	Swamp, S. city & co., anglic. Cork
		Ciarraidhe (kírí)	Race of *Ciar* ("black"), S.W. co., anglic. Kerry

.14	Loriotuli	Lorcán Ó Tuathail (lurkán ó *t*úhil)	*Lorcán* (dim. of *lorc*, "fierce") des. of *Tuathal* ("people-mighty"); 12th c. abp., patron st. of Dublin, anglic. Law- rence O Toole
.16	hurdles	*trans.* cliath	*Dublin
.24	bullugs	bolg (bulug)	belly
.25	suil	súil (súl)	eye
181.18	Sluttery's	Ó Slatarra (ó slo*t*ere)	des. of *Slatra* ("bold"); anglic. Slattery
.35	Drumcondriac	Drom Conaire (*d*rum kuneri)	*Conaire*'s ("high-care") Ridge; N. Dublin dis- trict, anglic. Drumcon- dra
.36	Hamis	Shéamuis (hémish), *g.*	[of] James; *Shem
182.13	scriobbled	scríobh (shkrív) scríob (shkríb)	write scratch
.18	Uldfadar	*half-trans.* oll-athair (ul ahir) Ul-fhada (ulo*d*e)	mighty father, father of all; surname of *Dághdha*, anc. god Long-bearded; *Ulfada*, warrior in *Macpher- son's *Fingal*, is glossed as "long beard"
.22	goyls	Gaedheal (gél) gall (goul)	Irishman, Scotsman foreigner
.27	anna	eanach (anokh)	fen, marsh; *Anna
.30	O'Shea	Ó Séaghdha (ó shéa)	des. of *Séaghdha* ("stately")
.30	O'Shame	*as if* Ó Séam/ Séim (ó shém)	des. of *Séam* (St. Iago)/ *Sem* (Shem)
.34	phwinshogue	fuinneóg (fwinyóg) fuinnseóg (fwinshóg)	window ash tree
183.05	ballyfermont	Baile Thor- maid (bolye hormid')	*Tormad*'s (Norse masc. n. *Thormodr*) Town; Dublin suburb, anglic. Ballyfermot

.17	brogues	bróg (bróg)	shoe
.22	quotatoes	*P/K Split	potatoes
184.02	thaws	tá (*tá*)	there is; yes
.13	lithargogalenu	litir (lit'ir)	letter
		go (gu)	to
.21	Carrageen	Cairrgín (karigín)	Little Rocks, Co. Waterford; also (from the place), an edible seaweed
.29	uves	ubh (uv)	egg
185.10	porporates	*P/K Split	corporates
.11	dunsky	Dún na Sciath (*d*únneshkí)	Shield-Fort, Co. Westmeath; stronghold of Meath kings; *Brian Boru; *Malachy
.11	tunga	teanga (t'oñe)	tongue, language
.25	O'Ryan's	Ó Riaghain (ó ríen)	des. of *Riaghan* ("vigor")
.33	gallic	gall (goul)	foreigner
.33	iron	Éireann (érun), *g*.	[of] Ireland
186.24	eveling	aoibhinn (íviñ)	pleasant
.25	Knockmaree	Cnoc na Riaghadh (knuk nu ría)	Execution Hill, Co. Sligo; anglic. Knocknarea
.25	Mea	Midhe (mí)	Middle; co., anc. royal province; anglic. Meath
187.08	Lieutuvisky	uisce (ishki)	water
.11	arrahbejibbers	ara (ore)	deprecatory interj.
.18	Putterick O'Purcell	Pádraig Ó [P.] (pá*d*rig ó)	Patrick des. of [P.]
.27	Baus	bás (bás)	death
.35	Macadamson	Mac Ádaim (moká*d*im)	son of Adam
188.05	Sheem	Sím (shím)	[St.] Swithin (*Suítín*), by conflation with *Séam* (St. Iago), since Swithin's Day is also the day of another St. James (of Nisibis); *Shem

.05	avick	a mhic (avik)	son; my boy
189.01	pish	pis (pish) piseóg (pishóg)	vulva; pea superstition
.11	cantreds	ceanntar (kyan*t*er)	district
.11	catchaleens	Caitlín (kat'lín)	fem. pers. n., from Gk. Katherine
.19	Anguish	Aonghus (énġus)	Single-choice; masc. pers. n. (of god of love)
.25	Morna	Múirne (múrñe)	Tenderness; fem. pers. n. (of *Fionn*'s mother); Morna in *Macpherson's *Fingal* is glossed as "woman beloved of all"
		as if múir-neach	lovable person
190.29	Galway	Gaillimh (goliv)	Foreign; W. co. & town
.30	cuthone	*as if* Caoi-tuinne (kí *t*ini)	Lamenting-of-the-wave; place-name Cu-thon in *Macpherson's *Fingal* and fem. pers. n. Cuthona in *Conlath and Cuthona* are both glossed as "mournful sound of waves"; derivation is improbable
		Cú-tuinne (kú*t*ini)	Hound of the Wave; masc. pers. n. which may be *Macpherson's original
		cú (kú)	hound
		tón (*t*ón)	bottom, arse
.32	mooner	mún (mún)	urine
191.07	gob	gob (gob)	snout
.11–12	on his keeping	*trans.* ar a choimhead	in flight from authorities
.36	wishywashy	mhuise (wishi)	well, indeed (interj.)
192.04	Morrisons	Ó Muir-gheasáin (ó mwiryasáñ)	des. of *Muirgheasán* (dim. of *Muirgheas*, "sea-tabu")

.08	schamer	seamar (shamer)	trefoil, shamrock
.26	Airish	Éire (ére)	Ireland
.26–27	nawboggaleesh	ná bac leis (ná bok lesh)	pay no attention to him/it
.30	moonshee	sidhe (shí)	fairy
193.02	crawsick	crádh (krá)	misery
.12	Whisht!	thoist (hisht)	silence
.14	barishnyas	bárr-thuisleadh (bárishlya)[?]	accident, stumble
.18	Mullah	mullach (mulokh)	top, summit, head, heap
.18	Mull	mull (mul)	heap, eminence; n. of several mtns.
.24	Kelly	Ó Ceallaigh (ó kyalí)	des. of *Ceallach* ("contention")
.24	Kenny	Ó Cionaodha (ó kiné)	des. of *Cionaodh* ("fire-sprung")
.24	Keogh	Mac Eochadha (mok yókhe)	son of *Eochaidh* ("horseman")
194.02	Cathmon	Cathmhór (kowór)	Battle-great; masc. pers. n. Cathmor in *Macpherson's Temora* is glossed as "great in battle"
		Cathmhín (kowín)	Battle-mild [an unlikely n.]; masc. pers. n. Cathmin in *Macpherson's Temora* & *Lathmon* is glossed as "calm in battle"
.02	Carbery	Cairbre (korbri)	Charioteer; n. of several I. kings; in *Macpherson's Temora* Cairbar is the brother of Cathmor
.05	athands	atha (aha)	creek; in *Macpherson's Temora* Cairbar is lord of Atha, a n. glossed as "shallow river"
.12	la	lá (lá)	day

.14	Ulerin's	Ol-Éirinn (ulérin)[?]	Over-Ireland; Of/About-Ireland
		Oll Éireann (ulérun)[?]	Splendor of Ireland
		Ul Éireann (ulérun)[?]	Edge of Ireland; Ulerin, a star in *Macpherson's *Temora*, is explained as "the guide to Ireland"
.29	Cooney	Ó Cuana (ó kúne)	des. of *Cuana* ("handsome")
.35	Tallaght	Taimhleacht (*t*alokh*t*)	Plague-grave; hill & village S.W. of Dublin; supposed burial place of early *colonists
.36	pools of the phooka	Poll a' Phúca (poul a fúke)	Goblin's Hole; chasm of Liffey S.W. of Dublin, anglic. Poulaphuca
195.04	Anna	eanach (anokh)	fen, marsh; *Anna
.04	Livia	Life (lifi)	*Liffey River
196.03 ff.	Anna Livia	Eanach Life (anokh lifi)	*Liffey Fen; *Anna
.08	dubbling	Dubh-linn (*d*uvliñ)	Black Pool; *Dublin
.12	water black	Abhainn Mór (ouwin mór)	Great River, anglic. Blackwater; but see *Dublin, *Shaun
.20	loch and neagh	Loch nEachach (lokh nakhokh)	*Eachach*'s ("horseman") Lake, largest lake in I.; anglic. Lough Neagh
197.01	Drughad	droichead (*d*rihe*d*)	bridge
.04	derry's	Daire (*d*ari)	Oakwood, N. city & co., anglic. Derry
.05	corksown	Corcaigh (kurkí)	Swamp; S. city & co., anglic. Cork
.05	blather	bladar (bl*ad*er)	flattery, coaxing
.05	doubling	Dubh-linn (*d*uvliñ)	Black Pool; *Dublin (E. city & co.)
.06	gullaway	Gaillimh (goliv)	Foreign, W. city & co., anglic. Galway

.07	Garda	Gárda (gárde)	Policeman (since independence)
.20	delvan	Deilbhín (d'elvín)	Little Warp; stream, N. Co. Dublin
.20	duvlin	Dubh-linn (duvliñ)	Black Pool; *Dublin
.21	asthore	a stór (astór)	dear, darling
.31	kelp	ceilp (kelp)	seaweed reduced to ashes
.35	Pilcomayo	Magh-eó (máyó)	Yew-plain, W. co., anglic. Mayo
198.05	buah . . . bueh	buadh (búe)	victory
.05	Boyana	Bóinn (bóñ)	*Boyne River
.10	badher	bóthar (bóher)	road; anglic. Batter-, Badder- in place-names
.10	Anna Livia		see 196.03
.20	skol	scoil (skul)	school
.25	reedy derg	Loch Dearg-dhearc (lokh d'argyark)	Lake Red-Eye, on Shannon River; anglic. Lough Derg
.26	bogans	bogha (bóye) bogán (bugán)	bow egg laid without shell
.28	moher	mothar (moher)	pile of stones; cloud
.33	Funglus	Fionn-glais (finglash)	Clear streamlet; stream & village N. of Dublin, anglic. Finglas
199.08	buddy	bod (bud)	penis
.11	Anna Livia		see 196.03
.14	neuphraties	phréataí (frétí)	potatoes
.17	weeshywashy	mhuise/mhaise (wishi/washi)	well, indeed (interj.)
.27	esk	easc (ask)	channel cut by water; anglic. -esk- in place-names
.28	*Mallow*	Magh-Ealla (máyale)	Plain of *Ealla* ("Swan" —a river), Co. Cork
200.03	Cullen	Ó Cuilinn (ó kulin)	des. of *Cuileann* ("holly")
.03–04	MacCabe	Mac Cába (mok kábe)	son of *Cába* ("hood")

.14	Bothar	bóthar (bóher)	road
.14	Bheri-Bheri	*English spelled as I.*	Very-Very
.16	Anna Liv		see 196.03
.18	dudheen	dúidín (*d*úd'ín)	short tobacco pipe
.20	Milucre	Miluchradh (milukhru)	fem. pers. n., sense unknown; perhaps "honey-breasted"
.20	Awny	Áine (áñi)	Delight; fem. pers. n., anglic. Anna
.20	Graw	grádh (grá)	love
.34	Denis	Donnchadh (*d*unukhu)	Brown-warrior; anglic. Denis
.34	Florence	Finghin (finyin)	Fair-offspring; anglic. Florence (common MacCarthy n.)
.35	MacCarthy's	Mac Cárthaigh (mok kárhí)	son of *Cárthach* ("loving"); *Shaun
.36	Anna Livia		see 196.03
201.18	*slobs*	slab (slob)	reclaimed or alluvial land
.18	*Tolka*	Tolca (*t*ulke)	Flood, Torrent; N.E. Dublin river, site of battle of Clontarf
.19	*Clontarf*	Cluain Tarbh (klún *t*orev)	Bull Meadow, N.E. Dublin district, defeat of Danes by *Brian Boru, 1014
.24	mahun	Mathghamhain (mahúñ)	Bear; n. of brother of *Brian Boru killed at Clontarf
.26	Clondalkin	Cluain Dealgan (klún d'algen)	Thorn Meadow; Dublin district
.35	Pluhurabelle	bile (bili)	sacred tree; *Anna
202.03	Messamisery	mise (mishi) maise (moshe)	I, me (emphatic) well, indeed (interj.)
.06	owen	abhann (ouwen)	river; anglic. -owen-; *Anna, *Shaun
.07	cam	cam (koum)	crooked

.07	camlin	Cam-líne (koumlíni)	Crooked Line; n. of several rivers
.15	esk	easc (ask)	channel cut by water; anglic. -esk- in place-names
.20–21	Albern, O Anser . . . Nuancee	ní h-annsa (níhounse)	not hard; formula for answering riddles
.24	Leinster	Laighin (lein)	"Lance"; E. province
.24	a wolf of the sea	Murchadh (murukhu)	Sea-warrior; patronymic of *Diarmaid Mac Murchadha*, Leinster king who invited Anglo-Norman invasion; *Shem
		as if Muirchú (mwirkhú)	Sea-hound (but *faolchú* ["wildhound"] = "wolf," also "warrior")
.29	Curraghman	Cuirreach Life (kwirokh lifi)	Moor/Racecourse of the *Liffey, Co. Kildare; anglic. the Curragh of Kildare
.31	Kildare	Cill-dara (kildore)	Church of the Oak; co. on Liffey W. of Dublin
203.01	Erin	Éireann, *g.*, Éirinn, *dat.* (érun, érin)	[of] Ireland, [to, for] Ireland
.02	Kilbride	Cill-Bhrighde (kilvríd'i)	Bridget's Church; n. of 35 places
.06	lifey	Life (lifi)	*Liffey River
.07	fordofhurdlestown	Baile Átha Cliath (blá klíe)	Hurdle Ford Town; *Dublin
.08	dove	dubh (duv)	black
.08	dunas	dún (dún) donas (dunes)	fort misfortune, bad luck; substitute for *diabhal* ("devil") in colloq. expressions
.10	Mourne	Mughdhorna (múyorne)	progeny of *Mughdhorn* ("ankle"); N.E. district incl. mtn. range, anglic. Mourne

		Múirne (múrñe)	Tenderness; n. of *Fionn Mac Cumhail*'s mother
.10	the Nore	An Fheoir (unyór)	The Shore; S.E. river
.10	takes lieve of Bloem	Sliabh Bladhma (slív bláme)	*Bladhm*'s ("blaze," masc. pers. n.) Mountain; mtn., anglic. Slieve Bloom
.11	Braye	Brí (brí)	Hillside; n. of several places, anglic. Bray: S. Dublin coast resort; lake at Liffey source
.11	Moy	Muidhe (múí)	Milk churn; river in N. Mayo, draining Lough Cullin
.12	Cullin	Loch Cuilinn (lokh kulin)	Holly Lake, N. Mayo, just S. of Lough Conn
.12	Conn	Loch Con (lokh kon)	Pure Lake, N. Mayo, just N. of Lough Cullin
.14	narev	ná raibh (ná rev) ní raibh (ní rev)	that was not was not
.14	Ow	Abha (ouwe)	River; n. of river, Co. Wicklow
.15	Ovoca	Abha; Abhann Mór (ouwe; ouwen mór)	River; Great River; river, Co. Wicklow, recently called Ovoca, from Ptolemy's *Oboka* (n. of a river in I., doubtless from *Abha*)
.15	Lucan	Leamhcán (loukán)	producing marshmallows; W. Dublin suburb on Liffey
.17	Luggelaw	Log an Lagha (lugunlá)	Hollow of the Hill; valley, Co. Wicklow
.20	venersderg	Lough Dearg/ Dhearg-dhearc (lokh d'arg/ d'argyark)	Red/Red-Eye Lake; lakes in Co. Donegal & on Shannon River, both anglic. Lough Derg
.24	cushlas	cúisle (kúshle)	pulse, vein
.29	Wish a wish!	mhuise (wishi)	well, indeed (interj.)

.35	kisokushk	coisceadh (kushke)	stop, enough
.36	Anna-na-Poghue	[A] na póige ([A] nupógye) ara na bpóg (ore nubóg)	[A] of the kiss one given to kissing
204.05	navn	neamh (nyav) An Uaimh (unúiv)	heaven The Cave, Co. Meath; anglic. Navan
.05	Lugnaquillia	Log na Coille (lug nukíle)	Hollow of the Wood; highest mtn. in Co. Wicklow, S. of Dublin
.13	Kippure	Cip Iubhair (kipyúwir)	Yew Trunk; mtn. in Co. Wicklow, headspring of Liffey River
.15	Sally	Sailighe [Neaganna] (salí[nagene])	Willow [Notches]; anglic. Sallynoggin, S. Dublin suburb
.18	black pools	Dubh-linn[te] (duvliñ[ti])	*Dublin
.19	innocefree	Inis Fraoigh (inishfrí)	Heather Island, island in Lough Gill, Co. Sligo, anglic. Inishfree
.31	Arran	ara (ore) Ára (áre)	deprecatory interj. Kidney; islands off Galway, anglic. Aran; island in Hebrides
.34	Magrath's	Mag Raith (mogra)	son of *Mac Raith* ("son of grace")
.35	aird	árd (árd)	height
205.09–10	Keown's	Mac Eoghain (mokyóñ)	son of *Eoghan* ("wellborn"); *Shaun
.11	Kinsella	Cinnsealach (kinshalokh)	des. of *Éanna Cinnsealach* ("ostentatious"), son of *Diarmaid Mac Murchadha* (who invited Anglo-Norman invasion); agnomen replaced surname
.22	Thaw, thaw	tá (tá)	there is; yes
.26	Nannywater	Na hEanaigh (nuhaní)	The Marshes, Co. Offaly, anglic. Nahana; *Anna

		An Eanaigh (unaní)	The Fenny; river, Co. Meath, where *Malachy I drowned prince of Bregia (604.04); anglic. Nanny
.26	Vartryville	Fir Tíre (firtíri)	Men of the Land, river, Co. Wicklow, anglic. Vartry
.28	cammocking	Camóg (kamóg)	dim. of *cam*, "crooked"; tributary of Liffey at Crumlin, S. Dublin, anglic. Cammock
206.02	crowders	cruit (kri*t*)	harp
.04	Lilt . . . a law	*corrupt & mutilated I.*	words of *Lillibullero*, anti-I. Williamite song (c. 1690)
.10	shammy	Siam (sham); seamar (shamer)	St. Iago; trefoil, shamrock; *Shem
.11	Shaun	Seán (shán)	John; *Shaun
.12	Casey's	Ó Cathasaigh (ó kahasí)	des. of *Cathasach* ("watchful")
.18	dargle	Deargail (d'argil)	Red; stream, valley, near Bray, S. of Dublin
.24	slaney	Sláine (sláñi)	Full; river, Co. Wexford
.27–28	Ower more	Abhann Mór (ouwen mór)	Great River; n. of several rivers, anglic. Owenmore, Avonmore, Ovoca
207.08	Annushka	ean-uisce (anishki)	marsh water; *Anna
.15	Brie-on-Arrosa	Brían a' Rosa (brían a ruse)	Little Hillside of the Wood
.19	Anna Livia		see 196.03
208.02	werra	Mhuire (wiri)	[Virgin] Mary (interj.)
.25	gawan	gabhann (goun), *g.*	[of a] smith
.25	siouler's	siubhlóir (shúlór)	wanderer, vagrant
.31	Fenny	*trans.* Eanaigh (aní)	*Anna

.35	murrayed	Ó Muirea-dhaigh (ó mwiraí)	des. of *Muireadhach* ("mariner"); anglic. Murray
209.06	Avondale's	abhann (oven)	river; (in. I.) anglic. -avon-; (in England -avon- is Welsh *afen*, "river")
.09	*Alp*	alp (olp)	heap, lump, job; *Alp Uí Laoghaire* (O Leary's Job) is Dublin in mason's jargon
.20	diliskydrear	duileasc (*d*ilesk)	edible seaweed
.30	glashaboys	Glaise-buidhe (glashebwí)	Yellow streamlet; n. of several streams in Co. Cork, anglic. Glasha-boy
210.01	culdee	Céile Dé (kyéledé)	Servant/Spouse of God; masc. pers. n. also title, in early Christian I.
.04	dribblederry	Daire (*d*ari)	Oakwood; N. city & co., anglic. Derry
.07	bann	Banna (bone)	Active [?], river, Co. Derry, draining Lough Neagh
.10	MacFarlane	Mac Phar-thaláin (mok fareláñ)	son of Bartholomew
.13	Beg	beig (beg)	little
.13	papar	*L/R Inter-change	papal
.14	Kevineen	Caoimhghinín (kívyinín)	Little *Caoimhghin* ("comely-birth"); *Shaun
.14	O'Dea	Ó Deaghaidh (ó d'ayí)	des. of *Deaghadh* ("beetle"[?])
.14	Pudge Craig	Páid de Carraig (pád' de korig)	Pat[rick] of the Rock
.16	Hayes	Ó hAodha (ó hé)	des. of *Aodh* ("fire")

.16	Hartigan	Ó hArtagáin (ó hartegáñ)	des. of *Artagán* (dim. of *Art*, "bear")
.18	Clonliffe	Cluain Luibh (klún liv)	Herb Meadow, N.E. Dublin district on Tolka River; *Liffey
.19	Skibereen	Scibirín (shkibirín)	Skiff-harbor; port, Co. Cork
.19	Doolin	Ó Dubhlainn (ó *d*úlin) Dubh linn (*d*ú lin)	des. of *Dubhfhlann* ("black ruddy") Black Pool; *Dublin; Doolin, Co. Clare
.19	Ballyclee	Baile Atha Cliath (blá klíe)	Hurdle Ford Town; *Dublin
.19	jackeen	*half-trans.* Seóinín (shóñín)	"Johnny," "Jacky"; flunky, aper of English ways; countryman's derogation of Dubliner; *Shaun
.20	Teague	Tadhg (*t*eig)	Poet; typical rural laborer
.20	O'Flanagan	Ó Flannagáin (ó flanegáñ)	des. of *Flannagán* (dim. of *Flann*, "ruddy")
.21	Jerry	Diairmín (*d*'írmín)	dim. of *Diarmaid*, "freeman"; *Shem
.21	Coyle	Mac Dhubhghaill (mokúyil)	son of *Dubhghall* ("black-foreigner," i.e., Dane)
.21–22	Mackenzie	Mac Coinnigh (mok kiní)	son of *Coinneach* ("fair one")
.25	Wildairs' breechettes	Brighid Cill-Daire (bríd' kil*d*ere)	*Brighid* of Oak Church, St. Bridget of Kildare
.31	Eileen Aruna	Eibhlín a rún (eilín arún)	"Eileen [Helen] my dear"; a song
.32	Helen Arhone	Eibhlín a rún	"Eileen my dear"
.33	Coleraine	Cúil-rathain (kúlrahin)	Fern-recess; town, Co. Derry
.35	Puckaun	pocán (pukán) púcán (púkán) púcán (púkán)	dim. of *poc*, "he-goat" dim. of *púca*, "goblin" toadstool
.35	Dunne	Ó Duinn (ó *d*in)	des. of *Donn* ("brown")

211.04	Seumas	Seumas (shémus)	James; *Shem
.05	Congoswood	Conga (kuñge)	Strait; anglic. Congo, Co. Tyrone, Cong, Co. Mayo
		Cluain Gabha (klúngou)	Smith's Meadow, Co. Kildare; anglic. Clongowes
.09	Shannon	Ó Seanáin (ó shanáñ)	des. of *Seanán* (dim. of *sean*, "old")
		Sionann (shinon)	Chain [?], Quivering [?]; longest river in I.
.10	Tuami	Tuaim (túim)	Tumulus; town (episcopal see), Co. Galway; anglic. Tuam
.11	Blarney	Blárna (blárne)	Little Field; town, castle, Co. Cork
.11	Meagher	Ó Meachair (ó myakhir)	des. of *Meachar* ("hospitable")
.12	Elsie Oram	Éilís Óram (élísh órem)	folklore character, notorious liar
.23	Felim	Feidhlimidh (félimí)	Ever-good; masc. pers. n.
.25	naves	naomh (név)	saint
.27–28	Brennan	Ó Braonáin (ó brénáñ)	des. of *Braonán* (dim. of *braon*, "sorrow")
.31	Shemus O'Shaun	Séamus Ó Seáin (shémus ó sháñ)	James des. of John; *Shem, *Shaun
.32	Donn	Donn (*d*oun)	Brown
.34	Billy	bile (bili)	sacred tree
.34	Dunboyne	Dún-buinne (*d*únbwini)	Fort of the Flood; town, Co. Meath
.35	Ida Ida	Íde (íde)	Thirst; fem. pers. n.
212.01	Yuinness	Mag Aonghusa (mogénġesi)	son of *Aonghus* ("single-choice" [god of love]); anglic. Guinness
.01	Yennessy	Ó hAonghusa (ó hénġesi)	des. of *Aonghus* ("single-choice" [god of love]); anglic. Hennessy
.03	Behan	Ó Beacháin (ó byakháñ)	des. of *Beachán* (dim. of *beach*, "bee")

.03	Sully	O Súiligh (ó súlí)	des. of *Súileach* ("quick-eyed")
.03	Magrath	Mag Raith (mogra)	son of *Mac Raith* ("son of grace")
.03	Cloran	Mac Labhráin (moklouráñ)	son of *Labhrán* (dim. of *Labhraidh*, "spokesman")
.04	O'Delawarr Rossa	Ó Donnabháin/Donnamháin Rosa (ó dounaváñ rose)	des. of *Donndubhán* (dim. of *donn-dubh*, "brown-black")/ *Donndamhán* (dim. of *donn-damh*, "brown-poet") of the Grove; O Donovan Rossa, 19th c. patriot
.04	MacPacem	Mac Péice (mok péki)	son of *Péic* ("pike")
.07	Quilty	Ó Caoilte (ó kílt'i)	des. of *Caoilte* ("hardness")
.07	Brosna	Brosna (brusne)	Faggot (bundle of firewood); river & town, Co. Kerry
.08	Kieran	Ó Ciaráin (ó kíráñ)	des. of *Ciarán* (dim. of *ciar*, "black")
.08	Camac	Camac (komok)	dim. of *cam*, "crooked"; S. Dublin tributary of Liffey; also sp. Cammock
.09	Bradogue	Brághadóg (brádóg)	dim. of *brághad*, "throat"; N. Dublin tributary of Liffey
.10	Greaney	Greanach (granokh)	Gravelly; river, Co. Limerick
.11	Rohan	Ó Robhacháin (ó roukháñ)	des. of *Robhachán* (dim. of *robhach*, "crafty")
.13	O'Farrell	Ó Fearghail (ó faryel)	des. of *Fearghal* ("super-valor")
.13	Foyle	Feabhail (fyouil)	Wealthy [?]; river between Cos. Derry & Donegal
.15	Macleay	Mac an Leagha (mok un léa)	son of the physician

.18	shone	Seón (shón)	John; *Shaun
.20	bakereen	-ín (ín), *suffx.*	little, darling
		bachairín (bokherín)	dim. of *bachaire,* "drunkard"
.21	tillies	tuille (*t*ili)	increase; small addition, as 13th to "baker's dozen"
213.04	isker	uisce (ishki)	water
.16	clogh	clog (klug)	clock, bell
.34	Shannons	Ó Seanáin (ó shanáñ)	des. of *Seanán* (dim. of *sean,* "old")
		Sionann (shinon)	Chain [?], Quivering [?], longest river in I., anglic. Shannon
.35	Dunnes	Ó Duinn (ó *d*in)	des. of *Donn* ("brown")
.35	Brendan's	Breanndán (broun*d*án)	Putrescence [?]; n. of several sts., including supposed discoverer of America
214.04	Meaghers	Ó Meachair (ó myakhir)	des. of *Meachar* ("hospitable")
.07	Ussa	usa (use) 'uise (ushi)	easier well, indeed (interj.)
.07	Ulla	olla (ule)	splendid
.07	Mezha	maise (mashi)	well, indeed (interj.)
.11	Finnleader	Fionn (fin) Ó Fionn-ghalaigh (ó finyalí)	Fair des. of *Fionnghalach* ("fair-valorous") anglic. Finlay (*Fionnghalach Mac Donnchuan* was a leader of *Brian Boru's army at Clontarf)
.13	On	an (un)	the
.13	Fallareen	falairín (falerín)	dim. of *falaire*: ambler, pacing horse
.20	Conway's	Ó Connmhaigh (ó konvei)	des. of *Connmhac* ("intelligence-son")
.21	Carrigacurra	Carraig a' Chuirrigh (korigakhurí)	Rock of the Moor/Racecourse

.23–24	Corrigan's	Ó Corragáin (ó koregáñ)	des. of *Corragán* (dim. of *corradh*, "spear")
.30	Carlow	Ceatharlach (kaherlokh)	Quadruple-lake; S.E. co. & town
.33	dwyergray	Ó Dubhuidhir (ó *d*úwír)	des. of *Dubhodhar* ("black-palegreen")
.34	Tarpey	Ó Tarpaigh (ó *t*orpí)	des. of *Tarpach* ("stout")
.34	Lyons	Ó Laighin (ó lein)	des. of *Laighean* ("lance") [cf. *Laighin* "Leinster"]
.36	MacDougal	Mac Dubhghaill (mok *d*úǵel)	son of *Dubhghall* ("black-foreigner," i.e., Dane)
215.01	Poolbeg	Poll Beig (poul beg)	Little Hole; light-house, *Dublin Bay
.02	Kishtna	Cis (kish)	Wickerwork; light station, *Dublin Bay
.10–11	moyvalley	Magh Bhealaigh (mávalí)	Plain of a Way; on Liffey, Co. Kildare, W. of Dublin; anglic. Moyvally
.11	rathmine	Ráth Maoinis (rámwénish)	Magnus's Fort; S. Dublin district, anglic. Rathmines
.12	skeowsha	sceoidhte (shkyóít′e)	worn-out
		scamhaite (skout′e)	person with attenuated face
.12	Anna Livia		see 196.03
.14	fingalls	Fine-Gall (finigoul)	Foreign Kindred; N. Co. Dublin district; anglic. Fingal
		Fionn-ghal (finǵal)	"Fair-Fight"; appar-ent basis of Fingal, *Macpherson's version of *Fionn Mac Cumhail*
.14	dotthergills	Mac an Ghoill (mokunǵil)	son of the foreigner; anglic. Gill
		gile (gili)	bright
.24	Anna . . . Livia		see 196.03

.24	Plurabelle	bile (bili)	sacred tree; anglic. -belle in place-names
.27	eryan	Éireann (érun), g.	[of] Ireland
.33	Malone	Ó Maoileóin (ó mwélóñ)	des. of *Maol-Eóin* ("servant of [St.] John"; *Shaun)
.35	Shaun	Seán (shán)	John; *Shaun
.35	Livia's	Life (lifi)	*Liffey River
216.01, 02	Shaun	Seán (shán)	John; *Shaun
219.11	Findrias	Fionn-tráigh (fintráí)	White-strand, Co. Kerry; anglic. Ventry
.11	Murias	múr (múr) muir (mwir)	wall, rampart sea
.11	Gorias	Guaireach/ Gabhraigh (gúrokh/ gourí)	Bristles/Goat-ful [rival explanations], town, Co. Wexford, anglic. Gorey
.11	Falias	Fáil (fál) falla (fole)	n. of fetish stone at Tara; by extension, Ireland wall
.11	Coarbs	comharba (kóorbe)	coheir; vicar; successor to ecclesiastical bene- fice
.11–12	Clive Sollis	Claidheamh Solais (klív sulish)	Sword of Light
.19	Ballymooney	Baile Uí Maonaigh (bolyí mwéní)	Town of the descend- ant of *Maonach* ("wealthy"); n. of 3 towns near Dublin
.20	Blackdillain	Ó Duibh- leacháin (ó dilakháñ)	des. of *Dubhlachán* ("black reed"), anglic. Dillon
.22	GLUGG	glogar (gluger)	empty rattle; addled egg; *Shem
.22	Seumas McQuillad	Seumas Mac Cuill (shémus mok kwil)	James son of *Coll* ("hazel tree"): James McQuill; *Shem
220.03	Bride's	Bríghid (bríd')	Strong; fem. pers. n.; goddess of poetry, also st., patroness of I.

.10, 14	Glugg		see 219.22
.11	CHUFF	tiomhailteach (t'uvilt'okh)	full after eating; *Shaun
.11	Sean	Seán (shán)	John; *Shaun
.11	O'Mailey	Ó Máille (ó málye)	des. of *Máille* ("chief"); anglic. *O Malley, O Mailey, etc.
		Ó Mála (ó mále)	des. of *Mála* ("sack")
.19	Grischun	gríosán (grísán)	blusher
.19	scuola	scoile (skule), g.	[of a] school
.20	Poder	Peadar (pader)	Peter
.35	Caherlehome	Ceatharlach (kaherlokh)	Quadruple-lake; S.E. co. & town, anglic. Carlow
		cathair (kohir)	city, mansion; anglic. Cahir-, Caher- in place-names
.35	Eskur	eiscir (eshkir)	sand-ridge; anglic. Esker in place-names
		uisce (ishki)	water
221.08	Glen of the Downs	Gleann-Doimhin (gloun dowin)	Deep Valley; anglic. Glendowan, Co. Donegal, etc.
.23	Coachmaher	Ó Meachair (ó myakher)	des. of *Meachar* ("hospitable"); anglic. Maher, Meagher, etc.
.23–24	Rocknarrag	Roc na Raig (ruknurag)	Gully of the Chasm
.27	Finnegan	Ó Fionnagáin (ó finegáñ)	des. of *Fionnagán* (dim. of *fionn*, "fair")
.27	R.I.C.	*P/K Split	R.I.P. (Royal Irish Constabulary/ Requiescat in Pace)
.29	pibe	píob (píb)	pipe
.29	Kappa	*P/K Split	Pappa
.33	silktrick twomesh	Tomás Síodach (tumás shídokh)	Silken [soft-spoken] Thomas Fitzgerald, 16th c. Earl of Kildare

.34	Sowry	Ó Samhraidhe (ó sourí)	des. of *Samhradh* ("summer")
.35	Cork	Corcaigh (kurkí)	Swamp; S. city & co.
.36	Buckley	Ó Buachalla (ó búkheli)	des. of *Buachaill* ("boy")
222.07	MockComic	Mac Cormaic (mok kurmik)	son of *Cormac* ("chariot-son"); anglic. McCormack
.08	Souslevin	Ó Súileabháin (ó súleváñ)	des. of *Súil-dubhán* ("black-eyed"), anglic. Sullivan
.22	Chuffy	tiomhailteach (t'uvilt'okh)	full after eating; *Shaun
.25	duvlin	Dubh-linn (*d*uvlin)	Black Pool; *Dublin
.25	Glugger	glogar (gluger)	empty rattle, addled egg; *Shem
.28	liubbocks	lúbach (lúbokh)	deceitful, meandering
.29	clayblade	claidheamh (klív) clé (klé)	sword; anglic. clay- [e.g., claymore] left (side)
.31	Djowl	diabhal (d'oul)	devil
223.03	airish	Éire (ére)	Ireland
.04	an Father	*part trans.* an tAthair (un *t*ahir)	the Father: Father (clerical title)
.04	Hogam	Ó hÓgáin (ó hógáñ)	des. of *Ógán* ("youth"); anglic. Hogan
		ogham (oyum)	anc. I. system of writing by notches
.05	Glugg	glug (glug)	rattle, gurgle; see 219.22
.10	drim . . . drumming	druim/drom (*d*rim/*d*rum)	back, ridge
.13	owen	abhann (ouwen) Eoghan (ówen)	river; anglic. -owen- in place-names Wellborn; masc. pers. n., anglic. Owen; *Shaun; *Uí Néill

.13	hugh	Aodh (é)	Fire; *Uí Néill
.17	Glenasmole	Gleann na Smól (gloun ne smól)	Valley of the Thrushes; valley in S. Dublin mtns.
.18	O'Sheen	Ó Síodhacháin (ó shíkháñ)	des. of *Síodhachán* (dim. of *síodhach*, "peaceful")
		Oisín (ushín)	Fawn; son of *Fionn Mac Cumhail*; *Macpherson's Ossian
.18	ascowl	as Cumhail (os kúl)	out of *Cumhal* (father of *Fionn*; grandfather of *Oisín*)
224.06	fourd . . . hurtled	Áth Cliath (áklíe)	Hurdle Ford; *Dublin
.09, 16	Glugg		see 219.22, 223.05
.11	colline born	cailín bán (kolín bán)	white (i.e., pretty) girl; *The Colleen Bawn*
.19	mearly	méar (mér) mear (myar)	finger swift
.20	skoll	scol (skul)	lamentation
.23	bud	bod (bu*d*)	penis
.29	Lifay	Life (lifi)	*Liffey River
.33	thother	toth (*to*)	female; female organs
.35	thong	teanga (t'oñe)	tongue, language
225.06	Ni	ní (ní)	not, is not
.08	Toboo!	abú! (abú)	To victory!
.13–14	worrawarrawurms	Mhuire (wiri)	[Virgin] Mary (interj.)
.20	Mitzymitzy	mise (mishi)	I, me (emphatic)
.29	Glugg		see 219.22, 223.05
.30	Chuff . . . Chuffchuff's		see 220.11, 222.22
.34	Jerry	Diairmín (d'írmín)	dim. of *Diarmaid* ("Freeman"); *Shem
226.07	gone of a cool	Mac Cumhail (mok kúl)	son of *Cumhal* [*Fionn*]
.10	Clare	Clár (klár)	Level surface; S.W. co.
.19	Chuffy		see 222.22

.20	Glugg's		see 219.22, 223.05
.31	greeneriN	grían Éireann (gríenérun)	sun of Ireland
		grian Éireann (grínérun)	soil of Ireland
.35	Anems	ainm (onim)	name
227.01	Eirae	Éire (ére)	Ireland
.06	Megrievy	Mag Riabhaigh (mogríví)	son of *Riabhach* ("brindled"); anglic. McGreavy, etc.
.14	Ida	Íde (íde)	Thirst; fem. pers. n.
.22	divlun	Duibhlinn (*d*ivlin)	Black Pool; *Dublin
.29	Murrey	Ó Muirea-dhaigh (ó mwirayí)	des. of *Muireadhach* ("mariner")
.29	Ryall	Ó Raghaill (ó reil)	des. of *Raghallach* ("having a [strong-] fore-arm")
.29	puck	poc (puk)	sudden blow
.30	Gillie Beg	giolla beig (gili beg)	little lad/servant
.32	MacFearsome	Mac an Pharsúin (mokun farsúñ)	son of the parson; *Macpherson
.33	MacIsaac	Mac Íosaic (mokísik)	son of Isaac
.33	McAdoo	Mac Condubh (mok kon*d*ú)	son of *Cú-dubh* ("black-hound")
228.01	Machonochie	Mac Dhonnchaidh (mokonekhí)	son of *Donnchadh* ("brown-warrior")
.02	MacSiccaries	Mac Siocaire (mok shikeri)	son of *Siocaire* ("dwarf")
.03	moush	muise (mushi)	well, indeed (interj.)
.03	missuies	mise (mishi)	I, me (emphatic)

.04	Everallin	Iubhar-áluinn (yúver-áliñ) or Eibhear-(ever)	Beautiful yew tree; n. of wife of *Macpherson's Ossian [Beautiful] Highspirits
.04	Macnoon	Mac Nuadhan (mok nún)	son of *Nuadha* (n. of anc. god)
.07	Mocknitza	Mac Neasa (mok nase)[?]	son of *Neas* ("fortified hill" [?]); patronymic of *Conchobhar Mac Neasa*, 2nd c. king of Ulster; *Red Branch
.08	dagrene	Deo-gréine (d'ogréne)	Spark of the sun; *Macpherson explains fem. pers. n. Degrena in *Fingal*: "Deogréna signifies a sunbeam"
		ga-gréine (gogréne)	sun-beam
		dagh/dé-grían (da/dé gríen)	excellent-sun; Joyce's correction & more probable etymology of Degrena
		grían (gríen)	sun; day
.12	cumman	cumann (kumon)	society, club
.12	Brassolis	Brágha-solais (brásulish)	Throat of Light; *Macpherson explains fem. pers. n. Brassolis in *Fingal* as signifying "a woman with a white breast"
.13	conansdream	Conán (konán)	dim. of n. beginning *Con-* ("high-"); *Conán Maol* ("the Bald"), a companion of *Fionn Mac Cumhail*
.13	lodascircles	ó Ladhan [Laighin] (ó lein)	"from Leinster," ballad phrase conjectured by W. Shaw (1781) to be misconstrued basis of *Macpherson's Loda, Scandinavian evil spirit

.14	Gelchasser	Geal-chosach (gyalkhusokh)	Bright-footed; *Macpherson explains n. Gelchossa in *Fingal* as "white-legged"
.15	Shimach	siomach (shimokh)	kind of trout; tall slender man; *Shem
.15	eon	Eóin (óin)	[St.] John; *Shaun
.15	Era	Éire (ére)	Ireland
.16	ban's	bean (ban)	woman, wife
.16	Dora	Doire (*d*ire)	thicket on a steep incline; *Macpherson glosses Dora, n. of a hill in *Temora*, as "the woody side of a mountain"
.18	carberry	Cairbre (korbri)	Charioteer; extremely common anc. masc. pers. n.
.21	laracor	Láthrach-cora (lárokh kure)	Site-of-a-weir, Co. Meath, anglic. Laracor (ecclesiastical living held by Jonathan Swift)
.25	O'Tuli	Ó Tuathail (ó *t*úhil)	des. of *Tuathal* ("people-mighty")
.26	cashel	Caiseal (kashel)	Stone-fort; anc. royal capital of Munster; monastic settlement & fortified bishop's seat, Co. Tipperary; anglic. Cashel; *Brian Boru
.32	knockonacow	Cnocán an Gabha (knukán nugou)	The Smith's Hillock; anglic. Knocknagow
.34	Toumaria	Teamhar (t'our)	Prospective-hill; anc. royal capital, anglic. Tara
.35	Anteach	an teach (un t'okh)	the house
229.03	Fenlanns	*half-trans.* Eanach-lann (anokhlon)	Fen-place; *Anna

.04	logh	loch (lokh)	lake; anglic. lough
.11	Gilligan	Ó Giollagáin (ó gilegáñ)	des. of *Giollagán* (dim. of *giolla*, "lad, servant")
.12	Crowhore	Conchobhar (kruhúr)	High-will; masc. pers. n.
.17	Maleesh!	mailís (malísh)	malice, wickedness
.24	down low	Dún Loich (*d*ún lokh)	*Loch*'s (masc. pers. n.) Fort; anglic. [Gap of] Dunloe, mtn. pass, Co. Kerry
230.24	coronaichon	corónach (kerónokh)	funeral dirge
.25	liffe	Life (lifí)	*Liffey River
231.12	Fonar	Fonn-fhear (founar)	Song-man; *Macpherson explains masc. pers. n. Fonar in *Temora* as "the man of song"
		Fonnmhar (founewor)	Diligent/Melodious; more probable etymology for Fonar
.28	Malthos	Mall-thost (moulhus*t*)/ Mall-tas (moul*t*os) [?]	Slow-silence/Slow-dwelling; *Macpherson explains masc. pers. n. Malthos in *Temora* as "slow to speak"
		[mall-labharthach/ -rádhach]	[slow-spoken]
.28	Moramor	Móra (móre)	Sun (pers. n. of; also fem. pers. n.)
		mór (mór)	big, great
.29	Ferchios	Fir-cheas/ Fir-chíos (fir khyas/khís)	Men-affliction/trib ute; *Macpherson ex-plains masc. pers. n. Ferchios in *Fingal* as "the conqueror of men"
		Fearghus (farġus)	Superchoice; masc. pers. n., true original of Ferchios; anglic. Fergus

.29	Allad	Aill-liath (al líe)[?]	Rock-greyhaired person; *Macpherson identifies Allad in *Fingal* as "the greyhaired son of the rock"; the n. is most unconvincing
232.06	Dinny	Ó Duibhne (ó díñi)	des. of *Duibhne* ("ill-going")
.06	Finneen	Finghin (finyin)	Fair-birth; masc. pers. n.
.06	Dinny Finneen	Ó Duinnín (ó dinín)	des. of *Duinnín* (dim. of *donn*, "brown"); anglic. Dinneen, n. of Prof. of I. during Joyce's time at University, compiler of standard I. dictionary
.06	canty	Ó an Cháinte (ó un khánt'i) cáinteach (kánt'okh)	des. of the satirist; anglic. Canty satirist
.16	errind	Éirinn (érin), *dat.*	[to, for] Ireland
.19–20	dearmate ashore	Diarmaid a stór (d'írmid' astór)	Freeman (masc. pers. n.) my dear; *Toraidheacht Dhiarmada agus Ghráinne* *Shem
.24	mavrone	mo bhrón (muvrón)	my grief, sorrow
.28	sifadda	Sithe fada (shihi fode)	Long lunge; *Macpherson explains Sifadda, n. of a horse in *Fingal*, as "Sithfadda—i.e., a long stride"
		sith-fada (shifode)	very-long
		síoth fada (shífode)	long peace; see next entry
.28	sosson	sos (sus) Sasana/ Sasanach (sosone/ sosonokh)	peace, respite England/Englishman

.28	bran . . . speedhount	Bran (bron)	Raven; n. of *Fionn Mac Cumhail*'s dog
.29	sos	sos (sus)	peace, respite
233.13	can	con- (kon), *pfx.*	dog, canine
.21	jauneofergs	fearg (farig)	anger
.27	Asky, asky, asky!	aisce (aski)	gift
		asca (oske)	rival
		uisce (ishki)	water
.36	Gelagala	geal (gyal)	bright
		Gaedheal (gél)	Irishman, Scotsman
		gall (goul)	foreigner
234.10	kevinly	Caoimhghin (kívġin)	Comely-birth; anglic. Kevin; *Shaun
.14	buddhy	bod (bu*d*)	penis
.20	kerilour	*P/K Split	perilour
.20	kevinour	Caoimhghin	see 234.10
.31–32	arrahbeejee	ara (ore)	deprecatory interj.
235.03	evings	aoibhinn (íviñ)	delightful, pleasant
.04	blossful	blas (blos)	taste, flavor
.16	Oncaill's	on-caill (onkeil)	great damage
.16	Luccombe	Leamhcán (loukán)	Producing marshmallows; W. Dublin suburb on Liffey; anglic. Lucan
		cúm (kúm)	Hollow; S. Dublin slum, anglic. the Coombe
.19	U'Thule	Ua Tuathail (ú *t*úhil)	des. of *Tuathal* ("people-mighty"); anglic. O Toole
.19	Manelagh	Raghnallach (ráñelokh)	belonging-to-*Raghnall* (Norse *Rognvaldr*, Norman *Ragenald*); S. Dublin district, anglic. Ranelagh
		mana (mone)	omen
.27–28	Chuffs . . . chuffeur	tiomhailteach (t'uvilt'okh)	full after eating; *Shaun

.36	Bootiestown	*half-trans.*	Town of a Road, S.
		Baile Bóthair	Dublin suburb, anglic.
		(bolye bóhir)	Booterstown
236.07	Cork	Corcaigh	Swamp; S. city & co.
		(kurkí)	
.09	Fomor's	Fomhór	legendary pirates,
		(fowór)	anglic. Fomorians;
			*colonists
.09	Fin	Fionn (fin)	Fair
.09, 10	paaralone	Parthalón	leader of legendary
		(paralón)	*colonization
.14	billy	bile (bili)	sacred tree
.17–18	Anneliuia	Eanach-Life	*Liffey-Fen; *Anna
		(anokh lifi)	
.21	Ballybough	Baile Bocht	Poor Town; N. Dublin
		(bolyebukh*t*)	district
.31	teapucs	*P/K Split	teacups
237.12	aboutobloss	blas (blos)	taste, flavor
.15	barnaboy	Beárna	Yellow Gap; anglic.
		Buidhe	Barnaboy
		(bárnebwí)	
		beárna	gap of danger; favorite
		baoghail	phrase in patriotic
		(bárne-bwél)	literature
.16	gab	gob (gob)	snout
.16	borab	bó (bó)	cow
		rab (rob)	rooting animal; hog
.18	Daneygaul	Dún na nGall	Fort of the Foreigners;
		(*d*un nu ñoul)	N.W. town & co., an-
			glic. Donegal
.20	celtech	ceilteach	denying, concealing
		(kyelt'okh)	
		Ceilteach	Celt, Celtic
		(kyelt'okh)	
.33	Labbeycliath	Baile Átha	Hurdle Ford Town;
		Cliath (bláklíe)	*Dublin
238.04	ishibilly	ise (ishi)	she (emphatic)
		bile (bili)	sacred tree
.24	finnishfurst	fionn (fin)	fair
.29	smithereens	smiodairíní	(dim. pl. of *smiodar*,
		(smi*d*eríní)	"fragment"): tiny frag-
			ments

239.21	catholeens	Caitilín (kat'ilín)	fem. pers. n., from Gk. Katherine
.29	chiuff		see 235.27
.30	mearing	méar (mér)	finger
240.03	Glugger	glogar (gluger)	empty rattle; addled egg; *Shem
.12	dooly	Ó Dubhlaoich (ó dúlékh)	des. of *Dubhlaoch* ("black-warrior")
.13	allbigenesis	Mag Aonghusa (mogéngesi)	son of *Aonghus* ("single-choice" [god of love]); anglic. Guinness
.13	henesies	Ó hAonghusa (ó héngesi)	des. of *Aonghus* ("single-choice" [god of love]); anglic. Hennessy
.13	golls	goll (gol)	blind person; *Goll Mac Mórna*, companion & rival of *Fionn Mac Cumhail*
.21	Calembaurnus	Colmán (kulumán)	dim. of *Colm* ("dove"); n. of many sts. latinized Columbanus
.23	Flinn	Ó Floinn (ó flin)	des. of *Flann* ("ruddy")
.25	mussymussy	muise (mwishi)	well, indeed (interj.)
241.01	crumm	crom (krum) Crom (krum)	crooked, stooping n. of anc. idol
.16–17	mish . . . mountain	Slíabh Mis (slív mish)	*Mis*'s (fem. pers. n.) Mountain, Co. Antrim, where St. Patrick was a boy slave; anglic. Slemish
.16	myrries	Muire (mwiri)	[Virgin] Mary
.22	Milchku	Milchó (milkhó)	Greyhound [?]; n. of master for whom St. Patrick worked as slave
.24	lochkneeghed	Loch nEachach (lokh nakhokh)	*Eachach*'s ("horseman") Lake; largest lake in I.; anglic. Lough Neagh
.32	osghirs	Oscar (osker)	Combatant; n. of *Fionn*'s grandson, son of *Oisín*

242.01	sorestate hearing	Saorstát Éireann (sérstát érun)	Irish Free State
.09	gobstick	gob (gob)	snout
.20	samhar	samhradh (soure)	summer
		Samhaoir (souír)	fem. n.; dgtr. of *Fionn Mac Cumhail*; also Morning Star River, Limerick
.20	tionnor	teine (tini)	fire
		teintreach (tintrokh)	lightning
		tionnúr (tinúr)	sleep, doze
.23	stoney badder	*half-trans.* Bóthar na gCloch (bóher-nuglukh)	Road of the Stones; Dublin street, anglic. Stonybatter
.28	Avenlith	abhainn (avin)	river; anglic. -aven- in place-names
.29	fenny	*trans.* eanaigh (aní)	*Anna
.34	iern	Éireann (érun), *g.*	[of] Ireland
.36	Cooley-Couley	Mac Giolla Chúille (mok gilekhúli)	son of *Giolla Mhochúille* ("servant of St. Mochuille"); anglic. Cooley
		Mac Amhlaoibh (mok oulév)	son of *Amhlaoibh* (Norse Ólafr); *Humphrey; anglic. Cowley
243.02	annams	anam (onem)	soul
.03	magrathmagreeth	mo ghrádh mo chroidhe (mu ġrá mu khrí)	my love of my heart
		Mag Raith (mogra)	son of *Mac Raith* ("son of grace"); anglic. Magrath
.12	damman	Damhán (dawán)[?]	Ox; Damman is masc. pers. n. in *Macpherson's *Fingal*
.14	MacCumhal	Mac Cumhail (mok kúl)	son of *Cumhal*: *Fionn*

.22	devlins	Duibh-linn (*di*vlin)	Black Pool; *Dublin
.22	streelwarkers	straoille (st*rí*lye)	untidy wench
.23	honeycoombe	Cúm (kúm)	Hollow; S. Dublin slum, anglic. the Coombe
.25	savuneer dealinsh	's a mhúirnín dílis (sa vúrñín dílish)	and my dearest darling: phrase from a song
.29	Alpoleary	Alp Uí Laoghaire (olp í lírí)	"the lump of the des. of Calf-keeper"— O Leary's Job: Dublin, in mason's jargon
.34	Orelli	Ó Raghaillaigh (ó rayelí)	des. of *Raghallach* ("[strong-]forearmed"); anglic. O Reilly
244.04	lolave	ollamh (olev)	sage, poet, professor
.06	Tubbournigglers	tobar (*t*uber)	well, spring
.06	Inisfail	Inis Fáil (inishfál)	Island of *Fál* (fetish stone at Tara): Ireland
.06	Timple	timcheall (tímpel)	around
.16	There is a wish on them	*lit. trans.* Tá fonn orthu	They wish
.23	Gill	Mac an Ghoill (mokunġil) gil (gil)	son of the foreigner bright
.23	benn	beinn (ben)	peak, headland
.30	Luathan	Luath (lúe)	Swift; n. of one of *Fionn*'s dogs
.31	Nuathan	Nuadha (núe)	n. of anc. god, king of *Tuatha Dé Danann* (Nuath, masc. pers. n. in *Macpherson's Lathmon*)
.31	avond	abhainn (avin)	river
.34	leabarrow	leaba (lyabe)	bed
245.01	tusker	toscar (*t*usker)	retinue; trekking party; dinner party

.06	Yul	Iúl (yúl)	July
.09	lissaned	lios (lis)	ring-fort; anglic. Lis- in place-names
.13	Lubbernabohore	liobar na bóthair (lyuber nubóhir)	ne'er-do-well of the road: tramp
.16	Finnyland	Fionn (fin)	Fair
.23–24	Livmouth	Life (lifi)	*Liffey River
.28	Marely	Maor (mér)	Steward, Stuart
246.04	Gorey	Guaireach/ Gabhraighe (gúrokh/gourí)	Bristles/Goat-ful [rival etymologies] town, Co. Wexford, scene of battle in 1798 Rebellion
.05	Hushkah, a horn!	Uisce, ochón! (ishki ukhón)	Water, alas!
.06	God es El?	Cad é [El]? (kod é [El])	What is [El]?
.19	Finn	Fionn (fin)	Fair
.21	Ninan ninan	naoidheanán (nínán)	infant, young child
247.09	go poltri	go pailt (gupolt') pailtire (polt'iri)	abundantly generous person
.10	mor	mór (mór)	big, great
.14	mavrone	mo bhrón (mu vrón)	my grief, sorrow
.16	Kod	cad (kod)	what?
.18	momourning	Mughdhorna (múyorne)	[belonging to the descendants] of *Mughdhorn* ("ankle"); N.E. district, incl. mtn. range, anglic. Mourne
.20	ross	ros (ros)	wood, grove, peninsula
.27	moramor	mórán mó (mórán mó)	much more
.28	Tarara	Teamhar (t'our)	Prospective-hill; anc. royal capital, anglic. Tara
248.02	Shee	sídhe (shí)	fairy

.04	Angus Dagdasson	Aonghus Mac Dághdha (énǧus mok dáye)	Single-choice son of *Dághdha* [father-god], the god of love
.07	Doubtlynn	Dubh-linn	Black Pool; *Dublin
.08	Land-under-Wave	Tír Fó Thuinn	legendary country in Atlantic; also, the Netherlands
.11	Achill's	Acaill (akil)	Narrows; island off Co. Mayo, largest island off I.
.16	Cucullus	Cúchulainn (kúkhulin)	Hound of *Culann* (masc. pers. n.); 2nd c. hero of Red Branch saga cycle
.22	Dalton	dallán (*do*lán)	blind person
.23	thicketloch	loch (lokh)	lake
.27	threaspanning	treasna (*t*rasne)	across
.30	Glendalough	Gleann-dá-loch (gloun *d*á lokh)	Two-lake Valley; St. Kevin's monastic settlement, Wicklow Mtns., S. of Dublin
.33	Awabeg	Abha Beig (ouwebeg)	Little River; n. of several streams
.35	Rab	rab (rob)	rooting animal; pet
249.07	elfinbone	Ailfinn (elfin)	Rock of the Clear [spring], Co. Roscommon, anglic. Elphin
.29	Misha Misha	mise (mishi)	I, me (emphatic)
.31	Ogh! Ogh!	Ógh (óǧ)	virginal; virgin
250.03	rossy	rásaidhe (rásí)	wandering woman; jilt
.11	be hushy	bí id' thost (bí i*d* hus*t*)	"be in your silence": be silent
.17–18	Lack breath	Mac Beatha (mok bahe)	son of life; anglic. (in Scotland) MacBeth
.27	Aghatharept	Achadh a' . . . (akha . . .) *cp.* Achadh a' tSathairn	Field of . . . Field of the Saturday, Co. Mayo, anglic. Aghataharn

		Achadh a' tSearradh (akha t'are)	Field of the Mowing; would be anglic. Aghathara
.34	cac	cac (kok)	ordure, excrement
.34	duff	dubh (*d*uv)	black
.36	minymony	minne (mini) maon (món)	stuttering dumb
251.01	far	fear (far)	man
.01	Nic	Níc (ník)	daughter, Miss (in Mac names)
.04	mun	mún (mún) maon (moun)	urine dumb
.31	exaspirated, letters		*Aspiration
.34	Rohan	Ó Robhacháin (ó roukháñ) Ó Ruadhacháin (ó rúkháñ)	des. of *Robhachán* ("crafty") des. of *Ruadhachán* (dim. of *ruadh*, "red")
252.01	shoolthers	siubhal (shúl) siubhaltach (shúl*t*okh)	walking, traveling disposed to roam
.04	Dvoinabrathran	bráthair (bráhir)	kinsman; brother (in religion); friar
.07	Mowy	Mo-'bhí (muví)	My-[some n. contracted]; 7th c. st., fndr. of monastery at Glasnevin
.07	Pleasant Grin	*as if* Glaisín Aoibhinn (glashíníviñ) *for correct* Glas Naoidhean (glosníen)	Pleasant Little Green *Naoidhe*'s (masc. pers. n.) Stream; N. Dublin stream & district, anglic. Glasnevin
.07–08	everglass	glas (glos)	green
.07–08	everglass and even	Glas Naoidhean	Glasnevin, as above
.21	bawn	bán (bán)	white, pretty
.24	gar	gar (gor) gearr (gyar)	short, soon cut

253.01–02	I have done it equals I so shall do	Tá sé déanta agam	I have done it/I have it done [promise]
.23–24	gossan	gasán (gosán)	stalk; boy
.24	duad	dúd (*dúd*)	stem, pipe; penis (slang)
		duadh (*dúe*)	hardship
.32	Lucanhof	Leamhcán (loukán)	Producing marshmallows; W. Dublin suburb on Liffey; anglic. Lucan
.35	mauromormo	mór (mór) mó (mó)	big, great more; bigger, greater
.35	milesian	míleadh (míla)	warrior; des. or follower of *Miledh*, leader of Celtic *colonization
254.02	Rurie	Tonn Rudhraighe (*t*oun rúrí)	Wave of *Rudhraighe* (masc. pers. n., symbolizes Ulster, N. province): Dundrum Bay, Co. Down, E. of *"Four Waves of I."
.02	Thoath	Tonn Tuaithe (*t*oun *t*úyi)	Wave of the North: mouth of the Bann River, Co. Derry, N. of *"Four Waves"
.02	Cleaver	Tonn Chlíodhna (*t*oun khlíne)	Wave of *Clíodhna* ("wasted from sickness," fem. pers. n. of fairy): Glandore Bay, Co. Cork, S. of *"Four Waves"
		Tonn Scéine (*t*oun shkéñi)[?]	Wave of a Knife: Kenmare Bay, Co. Kerry, W. of *"Four Waves"
.03–04	MacMuhun	Mac Mathghamhna (mok mahúne)	son of *Mathghamhain* ("bear"); anglic. MacMahon
.13	minnelisp	minne (mini)	stuttering
.16	abu	abú (obú)	to victory
.16	abiad	biadh (bíe) abiadh [?]	food to food [?]
.17	dub	dubh (*d*uv)	black
.20	Finnfinn	Fionn (fin)	Fair

.20	Faineant	Fiannaidhe (fíení)	Warrior; member of *Fianna*, 3rd c. standing army commanded by *Fionn Mac Cumhail*
.25	Costollo	Mac Oisdeal- bhaigh (mok oshd'alví)	son of *Oisdealbhach* ("resembling *Os* ['deer,' n. of a god]")
.26	Mahun	Ó Math- ghamhna (ó mahúne)	des. of *Mathghamhain* ("bear"); anglic. Mahon; *Brian Boru
.28	Merodach	Mac Muir- cheartaigh (mok mwirkhyartí) méirdreach (mérdrokh)	son of *Muircheartach* ("navigator"); anglic. Murdoch whore
.30	ee	í (í)	she
.31–32	selm ashaker	Seall-maith (shalmo)[?]	Good-view; Selma is *Macpherson's Fingal's castle
.33	berrathon	Barra-tonn (boretoun)/ Bior a' tuinn (biretin)	Wave-top/Point of the wave; *Macpherson explains Berrathon, island in *Berrathon*, as "a promontory in the midst of waves"
		barr (bor) tón (tón)	top bottom, arse
.36	gillyflowrets	gile (gili)	brightness
.36	Artho	Árt (árt)	Bear/Stone; masc. pers. n.
.36– 255.01	the name is on	*lit. trans.* an t-ainm atá ar	the name of
.04	clay, Tamor	claidheamh mór (klív mór) Teamhar (t'our)	great sword; anglic. claymore Prospective Hill; anc. royal capital, anglic. Tara
.13	Moykill	Magh Cille (má kili)	Plain of a Church
.15–16	Danamaraca	Dana (done)	goddess of the dead; eponymous goddess of *Tuatha Dé Danann*; *Anna

		Danmhairg (*d*aneworrig)	Denmark
.20	Micmacrobius	mac, mic, *g*. (mok, mik)	son, of a son
.21	Lukan	Leamhcán (loukán)	Producing marshmal-lows; W. Dublin sub-urb on Liffey; anglic. Lucan
.22	Kongdam	Conga (kuñge)	Strait; monastic re-treat of *Ruaidhrí Ó Conchobhair*, last high king, Co. Mayo, an-glic. Cong
.22	Coombe	Cúm (kúm)	Hollow; S. Dublin slum
.23	duckindonche	deoch (d'ukh) deoch an dorais (d'ukh un *d*urish)	drink "drink of the door": parting drink
256.02	Gallus	gall (goul)	foreigner
.23	Eire	Éire (ére)	Ireland
.25	mongafesh	monga (moñge) feis (fesh)	growth of hair, grass, trees, etc.; afforestation convention, assembly
.28	doil	dáil (*d*ál)	assembly; *Dáil Éireann*, I. Legislative Assembly
.33	isky	i (i) uisce (ishki)	in water
.36	gueroligue	Gaedhealg (gélg)	I. language
.36	Gaylegs	Gaedhealg (gélg)	I. language
.36	Gallocks	Gaedhealg (golik) Gall (goul) Gallda (goul*d*e) geallach (gyalokh)	[Scottish pronuncia-tion] I./Scots language Foreigner Foreign moon
257.17	Burleigh	Béarla (bérle)	English language
.24	Farley	Ó Faircheal-laigh (ó farkhalí)	des. of *Faircheallach* ("superwar")

.27	-dunandurras-	dún an doras (dún un durus)	shut the door
.27	-fermoy-	Feara-Muighe (faremwí)	Men of the Plain, Co. Cork, anglic. Fermoy
.33	Uplouderamain	ludramán (luderamán)	lazy idler
.36	Fionia	Finne (fini)	Fairness; fem. pers. n., anglic. Fiona
		Tír na bhFionn (tír nevin)	Land of the Fair: Ireland (also Finland)
258.09	dud	dúd (dúd)	stem, pipe; penis (slang)
.09–10	Yarrah!	a Dhia ara (yare)	O God well! (interj.)
.10	Nek	Níc (ník)	daughter
.10	Mak	Mac (mok)	son
.17	mekanek	each (akh)	horse
.17	Mak	Mac (mok)	son
.19	Uplouderamain-again	ludramán (luderamán)	lazy idler
.28	shin	sinn (shin)	we, us
.30	Garda	Gárda (gárde)	(I. national) Policeman
.31	Domas	domasach (domesokh)	light dry soil
.35	krubeems	crúibín (krúbín)	dim. of crúb, "hoof": pig's or sheep's trotter
260.09, 13	Livius	Life (lifi)	*Liffey River
.15	fahr . . . fear	fear (far)	man
.F1	Rawmeash	ráiméis (rámésh)	"romance": nonsense
.F1	girlic	Gaedhealg (gélg)	I. language
.F1	teangue	teanga (t'oñe)	tongue, language
261.L1	*Swiney*	Mac Suibhne (mok swíni)	son of *Suibhne* ("well-going")
.15–16	Hymanian	Uí Máine (í máñi)	descendants of *Máine Mór*: tribal territory, Co. Galway; anglic. Hymainy
.16	donnery	donn (doun)	brown

.L3	*Ardrey*	árd-rí (árdrí)	high king
.19	Tumulty	Ó Tomaltaigh (ó *t*umel*t*í)	des. of *Tomaltach* ("bulky")
.23	Ainsoph	aon (én) ain- (an), *pfx.*	one in-, un-, not-; very-
.F2	Kellywick	Ó Ceallaigh (ó kyalí)	des. of *Ceallach* ("contention"); anglic. Kelly
.F2	Co. Mahogany	Muineachán (mwinekhán)	Bramble-thicket; N. central co., anglic. Monaghan
262.05–06	castle. Knock.	Caisleán Cnuca (kashlán knuke)	Hill Castle; W. of Phoenix Park, anglic. Castleknock
.15	Erdnacrusha	Árd na Croise (ár*d*ne krushe)	Height of the Cross; on Shannon, Co. Limerick; anglic. Ardnacrusha
.25	Baws	bás (bás)	death
.25–26	ballyhouraised	Baile Shamhraidh (bolye hourí)	Summer Town
.25	pubblicam	cam (koum)	crooked
.F2	salg	salach (slokh)	dirty
.F5	dinn	duinn (*d*in)	palace
.F7	Begge	beig (beg)	little, small
.F7	buggey	bog (bug)	soft
264.06	Life	Life (lifí)	*Liffey River
.15	Eblinn	linn (lin)	pool; *Dublin
.16	carr	cathair (kaher)	city
.16	fen	*trans.* eanach (anokh)	*Anna
.19	philim	Feidhlim (félim)	Ever-good; masc. pers. n., anglic. Phelim
.L2	*Mackinerny*	Mac an Airchinnigh (mok unerkhiní)	son of the *Airchinneach* (steward of church lands)
.L2	*Muckinurney*	muc an airchinnigh (muk unerkhiní)	the *airchinneach*'s pig

.27	glen of marrons	Gleann na Marbhain (gloun numorún)	Valley of the Dead; W. of Phoenix Park; anglic. Glenmaroon
.28	Gleannaulinn	Gleann Áluinn (gloun álin)	Lovely Valley; W. of Phoenix Park; home before his death of Tim Healy; anglic. Glenaulin
.28	Ardeevin	Árd Aoibhinn (árd iviñ)	Pleasant Height; W. of Phoenix Park
.28–29	purty glint	*trans.* Gleann Áluinn	pretty glen
.29	plaising height	*trans.* Árd Aoibhinn	pleasant height
.31	Ereland	Éire (ére)	Ireland
.F2	pool beg	Poll Beig (poul beg)	Little Hole; lighthouse, *Dublin Bay
265.06	Agus	agus (ogus)	and
.14	an	an (un)	the
.18	tho . . . tho	toth (*t*o)	female; female organs
.20	Angoisse	Aonghus (éngus)	Single-choice; god of love
.28	Finntown's	Fionn (fin)	Fair
.F2	jerryhatted	Diairmín (d'írmín)	dim. of *Diarmaid* ("Freeman"); anglic. Jerry; *Shem
266.03	Lynne	linn (lin)	pool; *Dublin
.F2	Halpin	Ó hAilpín (ó halpín)	des. of *Ailpín* (dim. of *alp*, "lump")
.F2	Glens	gleanna (glone)	valleys
.F2	Antrim	Aontruim (éntrim)	One-elder [tree]; N.E. co.
.F2	Brophy	Ó Bróithe (ó bróhyi)	des. of *Brothach* ("fierce")
.F3	dove deelish	dubh dílis (*d*uv dílish)	dark dearest
267.03	maymeaminning	meann, minne (myan, mini)	stuttering

.03	maimoomeining	maon (mwén, món)	dumb
.07	gael	Gaedheal (gél)	Irishman, Scotsman
.07	gillie	giolla (gile)	lad, servant
.07	gall	gall (goul)	foreigner
.L1	Cis	cis (kish)	wickerwork; *Dublin
.13	grene	grían (gríen)	sun
.13	ray	ré (ré)	moon
.13	earong	Éireann (érun), *g.*	[of] Ireland
.18	Adamman	Adhamhnán (ounán)	dim. of *Adhamh* ("Adam"); anglic. Adamnan, 7th c. st., author of Life of *Colmcille*
		Damhán (dawán)	Ox; Damman, masc. pers. n. in *Macpherson's *Fingal*
.19	Emhe	Émhe, *properly* Éabha (éve)	Eva, Eve
.19	Issossianusheen	is (is) Oisín (ushín)	and Fawn; son of *Fionn Mac Cumhail*; *Macpherson's Ossian
		Is Ossian Oisín (is O. ushín)	*Oisín* is Ossian
.20	ogs	óg (óg) agus (ogus)	young and
.25	Una	Úna (úne)	Famine; fem. pers. n.
.F1	Inishmacsaint	Inis Muighe Samh (inish mwísou)	Island of the Sorrel Plain; island in Lough Erne, Co. Fermanagh, unaccountably anglic. Inishmacsaint
.F4	Anama	anama (onema)	souls
		ainm, anma (onim, onma)	name, names
,F4	anamaba	anama ba (onema ba)	souls of cows

.F6	Tarararat	Teamhar (t'our)	Prospective-hill; anc. royal capital; anglic. Tara
268.L1	annaryllies	eanach (anokh)	fen, marsh; *Anna
.15	bodikin	bod (bu*d*)	penis
.26	Bott's	bod (bu*d*)	penis
.F6	Locklaun	Lochlainn (lokhlin)	Scandinavia, Norway
269.19	O'Meghisthest	Ó [M.]	des. of [M.]
.29	Murrey's	Ó Muirea- dhaigh (ó mwirayí)	des. of *Muireadhach* ("mariner")
270.04	alanna	a leanbh (alanev)	child, my child
.L2	*O'Mara*	O Meadhra (ó myoure)	des. of *Meadhair* ("mirth")
.L2	*Farrell*	Ó Fearghail (ó faryel)	des. of *Fearghal* ("super-valor")
.26	burly	Béarla (bérle)	English language
.31	The O'Brien	Ó Briain (ó bríin)	Descendant of *Brian [Boru]; surname used alone denotes chief of those bearing n.; an- glic. The . . . ; *O Briain* has nominal claim to defunct I. kingship & provincial kingship of Munster
271.01	The O'Connor	Ó Concho- bhair (ó konehur)	Descendant of *Concho- bhar* ("high-will"); *Ó Conchobhair Donn*, des. of last high king, has nominal claim to king- ship and claim to pro- vincial kingship of Connacht
.01	The Mac Loughlin	Mac Loch- lainn (mok lokhlin)	Son of *Lochlainn* (Scan- dinavia); *Mac Lochlainn* is head of N. *Uí Néill* and most anc. claimant of kingship, as well as provincial kingship of Ulster

.01–02	The Mac Namara	Mac Conmara (mok kon- mare)	Son of *Cú-Mara* ("hound of the sea"); *Mac Conmara* inaugu- rated Ó Briain kings but has no separate claim to kingship
.18	gossans	gasan (gosan)	stalk; boy
.19	Heber	Éibhear (éver)	coleader of Celtic *col- onization; ruled S.I. until killed by brother
.20	Heremon	Eireamhón (erawón)	coleader of Celtic *col- onization; ruled N.I., killed brother, became first high king of all I.
272.23	Lough	loch (lokh)	lake
.24	Murph	Ó Murchadha (ó murukhu)	des. of *Murchadh* ("sea- warrior"), anglic. Murphy
.25	Brock	broc (brok)	badger; filth
.27	Ghinis	Mag Aonghusa (mogénġesi)	son of *Aonghus* ("single- choice" [god of love]); anglic. Guinness
.F4	shessock	seasachas (shasokhes)	truce, cessation
273.L1	*Curragh*	Cuirreach Life (kwirokh lifi)	Moor/Racecourse of the Liffey [Plain]; an- glic. the Curragh of Kildare
.L1	*machree*	mo chroidhe (mukhrí)	of my heart
.L1	*bosthoon*	bastún (bostún)	poltroon, blockhead
.L1	*Curragh machree, me bosthoon fiend*	A chara mo chroidhe, mo bhastún féin/ fionn (a khore mukhrí mu vostún fén/fin)	Friend of my heart, my own/fair-haired block- head
.20	gar	gar (gor) gearr (gyar) gáir (gár)	short, soon cut laugh
.22	laubhing	*English spelled as I.* (láviñ)	laughing [?], loving [?]

.25	muckwits	muc (muk)	pig
.F8	tathair	an t-athair (un *t*ahir)	the father
274.05	Dathy	Dáithí (*d*áhí)	Nimbleness; n. of last pagan king
.09	mac	mac (mok)	son [of]
.12	Barmabrac's	bairghean breac (baryen brak)	speckled loaf: currant cake for Halloween; anglic. barmbrack
.24	fieldgosongingon	gasán (gosán) inghean (inyen)	stalk; boy daughter
275.01	Bryan Awlining	Brian Ó Fhloinn (bríen ó lin)	*Brian des. of Flann* ("ruddy"); anglic. Brian O Lynn
.01	Awlining	áluinn (áliñ)	lovely
.01	Erin's	Éirinn (érin), *dat.*	[to, for] Ireland
.05	Eire	Éire (ére)	Ireland
.09	macotther	Mac Artúir (mok or*t*úr)	son of Arthur
.14	Airyanna	Éire (ére) Éireannach (éranokh) eanach (anokh)	Ireland Irishman/woman fen, marsh; *Anna
.F1	pengeneepy	pingin (piñin)	penny
276.05	gale	Gaedheal (gél)	Irishman, Scotsman
.05	blost	blas (blos)	taste, flavor; correct accent in speaking I.
.05	dove	dubh (*d*uv)	black
.05	gall	gall (goul)	foreigner
.05	dove . . . gall	Dubhghall (*d*úġoul)	Black-foreigner, i.e., Dane
.07	lettereens	litirín (lit'irín) Leitirín (let'irín)	little letter dim. of *leitir* ("wet hill-side"), anglic. Lettreen, Co. Roscommon
.12	gabhard	gabhar (gour)	goat
.21	Brannan's	Ó Branáin (ó branáñ)	des. of *Branán* (dim. of *bran*, "raven")
.22	Fanagan's	Ó Fionnagáin (ó finegáñ)	des. of *Fionnagán* (dim. of *fionn*, "fair")

.F7	liss	lios (lis)	ring-fort
277.01	Ochone!	ochón (ukhón)	alas!
.02	Ochonal!	ochón (ukhón)	alas!
		Ó Conaill (ó kunil)	des. of *Conall* ("high-powerful"); anglic. O Connell
.03	Mogoul	Mac Cumhail (mok kúl)	son of *Cumhal*; patronymic of *Fionn*
.05–06	fiannians	Fianna (fíene)	3rd c. standing army led by *Fionn Mac Cumhail*
.07	duggedy	deoch (d'ukh)	drink
.11	Mishy	mise (mishi)	I, me (emphatic)
.11	Mushy	muise (mushi)	well, indeed (interj.)
.12	gobleege	go bliaist (gu blísht')	to a large feast
		gob (gob)	snout
.15	Drommheim	drom (*d*rum)	back, ridge
.L5	*budders*	bod (bu*d*)	penis
.16	little black rose	*trans.* Róisín Dubh	Ireland (poetic); Mangan's "Dark Rosaleen"
.20	herbest country	*trans.* Magh Life	*Liffey Plain
.21	Blath	bláth (blá)	flower
		Baile Átha Cliath (bláklíe)	Hurdle Ford Town; *Dublin
.23	Eric	éiric (érik)	fine, ransom
.23	aboy!	abú! (obú)	to victory!
.F1	Millickmaam's	míolach (mílokh)	lousy
		maodhm (mám)	mountain pass; anglic. Maam in place-names
.F4	Roe	ruadh (rúe)	red (of hair)
.F4	Bewey	buidhe (bwí)	yellow
.F4	Gorham	gorm (gurum)	blue
.F4	McEndicoth	Mac an tSagairt (mok un togirt)	son of the priest
.F6	Thickathigh . . . Thinathews	'tuigeann tú? (*t*igen tú)	do you understand?
		tiugh (t'ú)	thick

278.11	Coalmansbell	Colmán (kulumán)	dim. of *colm* ("dove"); n. of several sts.; latinized Columbanus
.20	dun	dún (*dún*)	fort
.20	fen	*trans.* eanach (anokh)	*Anna
279.03	Erigureen	Éire (ére) -ín (ín), *dim. suffix.*	Ireland little, darling
.07–08	athclete . . . bally	Baile Átha Cliath (bláklíe)	Hurdle Ford Town; *Dublin
.08–09	Towntoquest, fortorest . . . hurley	Baile Átha Cliath	Hurdle Ford Town; *Dublin
.F1/22	Carr	Ó Carra (ó kore)	des. of *Carr* ("spear")
.F1/24	bean	bean (ban)	woman, wife
.F1/24	Mullans	Ó Maoláin (ó mwéláñ)	des. of *Maolán* (dim. of *maol*, "bald")
.F1/25	kill	cill (kil)	church, monastic cell
.F1/27	coolesdas	cúil-deas (kúld'as)	pretty-head (girl)
280.01	dreamoneire	dream (*d*roum) Éire (ére)	partisans; crowd Ireland
281.F2	Teague . . . Thady	Tadhg (*t*eig)	Poet; masc. pers. n. of typical peasant laborer; anglic. Teague, Thady, etc.
.F3	donnelly	Ó Donnghaile (ó *d*ounyeli)	des. of *Donnghal* ("staunch-valor")
282.23	O'Kay	Ó Caoich (ó kékh)	des. of *Caoch* ("one-eyed")
.32	Niall Dhu	Niall Dubh (níl *d*ú)	Black *Niall* ("champion"); *Niall Glúndubh* ("black-knee"), high king killed fighting Danes, 919; ancestor of O Neills; *Uí Néill
283.02	cap, pac	*P/K Split	
.L1	*cashellum*	caiseal (kashel)	bulwark, stone fort; *Brian Boru

.17	gallants	gall (goul)	foreigner
.17	gells	Gaedheal (gél)	Irishman, Scotsman
.28	jerrybly	Diairmín (d'írmín)	dim. of *Diarmaid* ("free-man"); anglic. Jerry; *Shem
284.05	Tullagrove	tullach (*t*ulokh)	hill; anglic. Tulla- in place-names
.06	Fearmanagh	Fir Monach (firmonukh)	Men of *Monach* (masc. pers. n.); N.W. tribal territory now Co. Fermanagh
		fear (far)	man
		manach (monokh)	monk
.08	Monachan	Muineachán (mwinekhán)	bramble-thicket; co. W. of Fermanagh, anglic. Monaghan
		monachán (munukhán)	dim. of *manach* ("monk")
		Monachán (munukhán)	one of the *Fir Monach* (see 284.06)
.F4	Braham Baruch	Brian Bó-roimhe (bríen bórivi)	Brian of the Tribute; high king killed defeating Danes at Clontarf, 1014; anglic. *Brian Boru
.F4	Massach	másach (másokh)	person with large buttocks
		measach (masokh)	fruitful, fecund
.F4	McKraw	Mag Raith (mogra)	son of *Mac Raith* ("son of grace"); anglic. McGraw, etc.
		crádh (krá)	misery
.F4	Braham the Bear	Mathghamh-ain (mahúñ)	Bear; brother of *Brian Boru, also killed at Clontarf
285.L1	*Finnfinnotus*	Fionn (fin)	Fair
.25–26	bully clavers	Baile Átha Cliath (blá klíe)	Hurdle Ford Town; *Dublin
.F3	rossies	rásaidhe (rásí)	wandering woman; jilt

286.02	aosch	aois (ésh)	age, era
.09	Casey's	Ó Cathasaigh (ó kahasí)	des. of *Cathasach* ("watchful")
.10	Hickey's	Ó hÍceadha (ó híkya)	des. of *Íceadh* ("healer")
.14	radmachrees	rad mo chroidhe (ro*d* mu khrí)	kick of my heart
.14–15	rossecullinans	ros chuilinn (ros khulin)	hollywood
		Ó Cuileannáin (ó kulináñ)	des. of *Cuileannán* (dim. of *cuileann*, "holly"); anglic. Cullinan
.19	ann	ean- (an), *pfx.*	water-; *Anna
.22	trilitter	trí litir (t′rílitir)	three letter[s]
.22	the tizzer	an t-athair (un *t*ahir)	the father
.L3	*Mullingar*	An Muileann Cearr (un mwilin kyar)	The Left-handed Mill; town, Co. Westmeath
.27	Kev	Caomh (kív) Caoimhghin (kívġin)	Comely Comely-birth; anglic. Kevin; *Shaun
.F5	sugans	súgán (súgán)	hay rope
287.05	Puddlin	linn (lin)	pool; *Dublin
.06	big . . . bog	beig, beag (beg, byug) bog (bug)	little soft
.07	Anny	eanaigh (aní)	fenny, marshy; *Anna
.07	liffle	Life (lifi)	*Liffey River
.08	doob	dubh (*d*ú) dába(*d*ábe)	black soft heap
.09	alp	alp (olp)	lump, heap; job; Dublin
.15	Mun	mún (mún)	urine
.F4	Finnican	Ó Fionnmhacáin (ó finakáñ)	des. of *Fionnmhacán* (dim. of *Fionnmhac*, "fair-son"); anglic. Finnucan
.F4	Teangtaggle	teanga (toñe)	tongue, language

288.09	shee	sidhe (shí)	fairy
.14	leinster	Laighin (lein)	Lance; E. province, anglic. Leinster
.14	*Eva*	Aoife (ífe)	fem. pers. n.; dgtr. of *Diarmaid Mac Murchadha*, Leinster king who invited Anglo-Norman invasion, married Strongbow, leader of invasion
.16	nataves	naomh (név)	saint
.17	maderaheads	madradh (mo*d*ere)	dog
.17	unguished	Aonghus (énġus)	Single-choice, god of love
.24	galloroman	gall (goul)	foreigner
.26	braim	braim (bram)	fart
.28– 289.01	Wickerworks . . . ford	Áth Cise/ Áth Cliath (á kishi/ áklíe)	Wickerwork/Hurdle Ford; *Dublin
288.F5	jerried	Diairmín (d'írmín)	dim. of *Diarmaid* ("freeman"), anglic. Jerry; *Shem
.F6	erring	Éirinn (érin), *dat.*	[to, for] Ireland
.F6	Ryan	Ó Riain (ó ríñ)	des. of *Rian* ("distinguished")
.F7	fearfurther	fear (far) fear-feasa (farfase)	man wise man, seer, wizard
289.04	o'ralereality	Ó Raghailligh (ó raġelí)	des. of *Raghallach* ("[strong-]forcarmed"); anglic. O Reilly, etc.
.11	cummal	Cumhal(kúl)	masc. pers. n., father of *Fionn*
.13	Byrne's	Ó Broin (ó brin)	des. of *Bran* ("raven")
.14	Hayses's	Ó hAodha (ó hé)	des. of *Aodh* ("fire")

.20	murty	Muircheart-ach(mwir-khar*t*okh)	Navigator; *Muircheart-ach na gCóchall Croicionn* ("of the leather cloaks") became high king 941
.24	Conn	Conn(kon)	Intelligence; masc. pers. n.
.24	Shaughraun	seachrán (shokhrán)	wandering, straying; *Arrah-na-Pogue*
.28	Liv's	Life (lifi) Lir (lir), *g.*	*Liffey River [of] *Lear* ("Ocean"); god of the sea; *Children of Lir ("Lir's lonely daughter"—T. Moore)
290.01	Shee	sidhe (shí)	fairy
.03	tompull	teampall (toumpul)	temple, church (esp. Protestant)
.05	O Shee	sidhe (shí) Ó Séaghdha (ó shéye)	fairy des. of *Séaghdha* ("stately")
.06	Mac Auliffe	Mac Amh-laoibh (mok oulév)	son of *Amhlaoibh* (Norse *Ólafr*); *Humphrey
.06–07	MacBeth	Mac Beatha (mok bahe)	son of *Mac Beatha* ("son of life")
.07	MacGhimley	Mag Fhionn-ghaile (mogin-ġeli)	son of *Fionnghal* ("fair-valor") [*Macpher-son's Fingal?]; anglic. McGinley
.09	MacAdoo	Mac Con-duibh (mok kon*d*ú)	son of *Cú-dubh* ("black-hound")
.09	MacDollett	Mac Dubh-ghaill (mok *d*úġel)	son of *Dubhghall* ("black-foreigner," i.e., Dane)
.10	Devine	Ó Daimhín (ó *d*avín)	des. of Daimhín (dim. of *dámh*, "bard" or *damh*, "ox")
.19	vartryproof	Fir-Tíre (firtíri)	Men of the Country; district & river, Co. Wicklow, anglic. Vartry

.24	mavourneens	mo mhúirnín (muvúrñín)	my darling
.24–25	Louth super Luck	Lughbhadh (lúva)	pertaining to *Lugh* (god of light & poetry), co. N. of Dublin
.F1	Muckross	Muc-ros (mukros)	Pig Peninsula; site of abbey at Killarney
.F7	bookley	buachaill (búkhil)	boy
		Ó Buachalla (ó búkheli)	des. of *Buachalla* ("boy")
291.02	mavrue	mo bhrú (muvrú)	my belly
.02	mavone	mo bhun (muvun)	my bottom
		mo bhrón (muvrón)	my grief
.10	O'Kneels	Ó Néill (ó nél)	des. of *Niall* ("champion") *Glúndubh* ("black-knee") [10th c. king]; anglic. O Neill
.10	O'Prayins	Ó Briain (ó bríin)	des. of *Brian [Boru]
.10	O'Hyens	Ó hEidhin (ó hein)	des. of *Eidhean* ("ivy"); *Maolruanaidhe Ó hEidhin* fell at Clontarf
.10	Lochlaunstown	Lochlainn (lokhlin)	Scandinavia, Norway
.11	O'Hollerins	Ó hAllmhuráin (ó halwuráñ)	des. of *Allmhurán* ("overseas-stranger"), anglic. O Halloran
.11	Staneybatter	*half-trans.* Bóthar na gCloch (bóher nuglukh)	Road of the Stones; Dublin street, anglic. Stoneybatter
.24	Dammad	Diarmaid (d'írmid')	Freeman; hero of *Toraidheacht Dhiarmada agus Ghráinne*; *Shem
.24	Groany	Gráinne (gráñi)	Grain/Spearpoint; heroine of *Toraidh-

			eacht Dhiarmada agus Ghráinne
.28	diarmuee	Diarmaid	see 291.24
292.01	granyou	Gráinne	see 291.24
.05	Lubbock's	lúbóg (lúbóg)	noose
		lúbaire (lúbere)	rogue
.10	Huggin	Ó hAodhagáin (ó hégáñ)	des. of Aodhagán (dim. of aodh, "fire")
.17	laggin	Lagán (logán)	dim. of Log ("hollow"); river, anglic. Lagan
		lag (log)	weak
.23	launer's	leannóir (lanór)	brewer
		lánamha (lánú)	married couple; complete set
.26	mearbound	méar (mér)	finger
.30	whisth	thost (hust)	silence
.F1	Buickly	Ó Buachalla (ó búkheli)	des. of Buachaill ("boy")
293.01	Coss?	Cad? (kod) cos (kus)	What? foot, leg
.09–10	murphy	Ó Murchadha (ó murukhu)	des. of Murchadh ("sea-warrior")
.10–11	maryamyriameliamurphyes	míle marbhadh (míli morú)	a thousand murders: great commotion
		míle Murchadha (míli murukhu)	a thousand bad frights [from Murchadh na dTóiteán, 17th c. pro-English Earl of Inchiquin]
.14	Mearingstone	méar (mér)	finger
.15	linch	O Loingsigh (ó liñshí)	des. of Loingseach ("having to do with a fleet"); anglic. Lynch, etc.
.19	liv	Life (lifi)	*Liffey River
.21	Lo, lo	ló (ló)	water; day (poetic)

.21	La, la	lá (lá)	day
.F1	Draumcondra's Dream-country	Drom Conaire (*d*rum kunere)	*Conaire*'s (masc. pers. n.) Ridge; N. Dublin district, anglic. Drumcondra
		dream (*d*roum)	followers, partisans
294.13	Makefearsome's	Mac an Phearsain (mokun farsen)	son of the parson; anglic. *Macpherson
.13	Ocean	Oisín (ushín)	Fawn; son of *Fionn Mac Cumhail*; *Macpherson's Ossian
.16	galehus	Gaedheal (gél)	Irishman, Scotsman
.17	Bigdud	dúd (*dúd*)	stump, pipe; penis (slang)
.19	turvku	tarbh (*t*orev) tórramh (*t*órev)	bull wake, funeral
.21	Owens	Ó hEoghain (ó hówiñ)	des. of *Eoghan* ("well-born"); *Shaun
.23	Dockrell	Dealg-inis (d'alginish)	Thorn Island; S. Dublin suburb; Norsified Dalkey
.F4	Bagnabun	bac na buinn (baknabwin)	hollow of the sole
.F4	Banbasday	Banba (bonbe)	Ireland (poetic)
295.13	Dairy	Éire (ére)	Ireland
.19	Loosh	luis (lush)	quicken tree; letter L
.20	Luccan	Leamhcán (loukán)	Producing marshmallows; W. Dublin suburb on Liffey; anglic. Lucan
.F1	Killykook	cill (kil)	church; anglic. Kill- in place-names; *Kill
.F1	Kelleiney	Cill na nInghean (kilne niñen)	Church of the Daughters; on S. Dublin coast; anglic. Killiney
296.12	kink	*P/K Split	pink; pinp

.13	kurkle	*P/K Split corcra (kurkure)	purple purple
.13	keek	*P/K Split cíoc (kík)	peep peep
.20	arrahquinonthiance	ara (ore)	deprecatory interj.
.21	Eggsmather	smeadar (smader)	mess
.F3	Thargam then goeligum?	Tuigeann tú Gaedhealg? (tigen tú gélg)	Do you understand Irish?
297.04	Arrah	are (ore)	deprecatory interj.
.04	Fin	Fionn (fin)	Fair
.11	Ocone! Ocone!	ochón (ukhón)	alas!
.12	fearfully	fear (far)	man
.15	mear	méar (mér)	finger
.20	Hurdlebury	trans. Baile [átha] Cliath	Hurdle [Ford] Town; *Dublin
.20	Fenn	trans. Eanach (anokh) Fionn (fin)	*Anna Fair
.27	usquiluteral	uisce (ishki)	water
.F2	Ugol egal ogle	eagal (ogel)	fear
299.08	superpbosition	*Eclipsis	superposition
.10–11	grannyamother	Gráinne (gráñi)	Grain/Spearpoint; heroine of *Toraidheacht Dhiarmada agus Ghráin- ne; *O Malley
.19	bolgylines	bolg (bulug)	belly
.23	O'Haggens	Ó hAgáin (ó hagáñ)	des. of Ogán ("youth")
.27	Kelly	Ó Ceallaigh (ó kyalí)	des. of Ceallach ("con- tention")
.30	Guinness's	Mag Aonghusa (mogénġesi)	son of Aonghus ("single- choice" [god of love])
.F1	bens	beinn (ben)	peak, headland
300.04	gossoon	garsún (gorsún)	boy, lad

.09	Wherapool	Mhuire (wiri) *trans.* linn	[Virgin] Mary (interj.) whirlpool; *Dublin
.12	me ah	mí-ádh (mí á)	misfortune, bad luck
.15	P. Kevin	*P/K Split Caoimhghin (kívġin)	Comely-birth; 7th c. st., fndr. of monastic settlement at Glenda-lough; *Shaun
.18	ravenostonnori-ously	tonn (*t*oun) tón (*t*ón)	wave, billow bottom, arse
.30	thur	tabhair (*t*úr)	give
301.04	feacemaker	*Aspiration	peacemaker
.05	bosthoon	bastún (bos*t*ún)	blockhead, poltroon
.07	foyne	Fuin, Fuineadh (fwin, fwinú)	Finish; West; Setting sun; place on Shannon River, anglic. Foynes
.15	waggy	mhagaidhe (wogí); *Asp.	mocker
.17	jerry	Diairmín (d′írmín)	dim. of *Diarmaid* ("Freeman"); anglic. Jerry; *Shem
.19	purate	*P/K Split	curate
.22	Law	lá (lá) lámh (láv, lá)	day hand, arm
.27	rawside	ráth (rá)	fort, castle
.30	croakpartridge	Cruach Pádraig (krúkh pá*d*rig)	Patrick's Rick [conical heap]; mtn., Co. Mayo, anglic. Croagh Patrick
302.13	Butt	bod (bu*d*)	penis
.13–14	Skibbering's	Sciobairín (shkibirín)	Skiff-harbor; town, Co. Cork, anglic. Skibbereen
.28	bennyache	beinn (ben)	peak, headland
.F1	Macbeths	Mac Beatha (mok bahe)	son of *Mac Beatha* ("son of life")
.F1	Plumpduffs	dubh (*d*uv)	black
303.04	illpogue	póg (póg)	kiss
.07	Doubbllinn-	Dubh-linn (*d*uvlin)	Black Pool; *Dublin

.09, 12	Connolly	Ó Conghal-aigh (ó konyalí)	des. of *Conghalach* ("valorous")
.13	L'arty	Árt (ár*t*)	Bear; Stone
.13–14	Magory	Mac Gothraidh (mok gorí)	son of *Gothfhraidh* (Godfrey)
.14	Eregobragh	Éire go bráth (ére go brá)	Ireland until Judgment Day
.15	Kev	Caomh (kív)	Comely
.17	Kevvy	Caoimhghin (kívġin)	Comely-birth; anglic. Kevin
.R2	FIG . . . PIG	pig/phig (pig/fig)	*Aspiration
.R2	THISTLE . . . WHISTLE	tuiseal/ thuiseal (*t*ishel/ hwishel)	*Aspiration; stumble, fall
.27	bladdy	bladar (bla*d*er)	flattery, coaxing
.F3	Castlehacknolan	Ó Nualláin (ó núláñ)	des. of *Nuallán* (dim. of *nuall*, "noble")
304.R3	PUCKING	poc (puk)	sudden blow
.17	maily	mála (mále)	sack
305.08	celebridging	*half-trans.* Cilldroichid (kil*d*rikhid)	Church of the Bridge, Co. Kildare, on Liffey W. of Dublin; anglic. Celbridge
.14	toobally	tothbal (*t*obol)	female genitals
.R2	LUG IN A LAW	Log an Lagha (lugelá)	Hollow of the Hillside; valley, Co. Wicklow, S. of Dublin, anglic. Luggelaw
.18–19	Keane	Ó Céin (ó kén)	des. of *Cian* ("ancient"); this was the n. of Edmund Keane the actor; sometimes anglic. Cain
.20	Quin	Ó Cuinn (ó kwin)	des. of *Conn* ("intelligence")

.23–23	shanty	sean-tigh (shant'í)	old house; asserted as origin of English "shanty"
.23	slanty	sláinte (slánt'i)	health
.24–25	Bide in your hush! Bide in your hush, do!	Bí i do thost! Bí i do thost, tú! (bí i du hust . . . tú)	Be silent! Be silent, you!
.33	whaboggeryin	bog (bug) ná bac (ná bok) Éirinn (érin), dat.	soft; soft-spot pay no attention; never mind [to, for] Ireland
.F2	Kilty	Ó Caoilte (ó kílt'i)	des. of Caoilte ("hardness")
.F2	MacGusty	Mag Oiste (mogusht'i)	son of Hodge (pet form of Roger); family descended from Hodge Merrick, killed 1272
306.03	Heavysciusgard-addy	gárda (gárde)	policeman (I. national)
.07	cong	Conga (kuñge)	Strait; monastic retreat of Ruaidhrí Ó Conchobhair, last high king, anglic. Cong, Co. Mayo
.17	Banshee	bean-sidhe (banshí)	fairy-woman
.28	Diarmuid and Grania	Diarmaid agus Gráinne (d'írmid'/ gráñi)	hero & heroine of *Toraidheacht Dhiarmada agus Ghráinne; *Shem
307.01	Guinness'	Mag Aonghusa (mogéñgesi)	son of Aonghus ("single-choice" [god of love])
.05	Clontarf	Cluain Tarbh (klún torev)	Bull Meadow; N.E. Dublin district, site of *Brian Boru's defeat of Danes, 1014

.09	Kettle	Mac Coitil (mok kitil)	son of *Ketill* (Norse masc. pers. n.) *Ketill Hviti*, alleged original of *Fionn Mac Cumhail*
.09	Griffith	Ó Gríobhtha (ó grífe)	des. of *Gríobhtha* ("griffin-like")
.09	Moynihan	Ó Muimh-neacháin (ó mwín-ekháñ)	des. of *Muimhneachán* ("Munsterman")
.20	Sharkey	Ó Searcaigh (ó sharkí)	des. of *Searcach* ("loving")
.F2	spookeerie	Éire (ére)	Ireland
308.01–02	Gobble Ann	Dubh-linn (*d*uvlin) leann (lan) ean- (an), *pfx.*	Black Pool; *Dublin ale water-; *Anna
.05	Aun	aon (én)	one
.06	Do	dó (*dó*)	two
.07	Tri	trí (t'rí)	three
.08	Car	ceathar (kaher)	four
.09	Cush	cúig (kúig)	five
.10	Shay	sé (shé)	six
.11	Shockt	seacht (shokh*t*)	seven
.12	Ockt	ocht (ukh*t*)	eight
.13	Ni	naoi (ní)	nine
.14	Geg	deich (d'e)	ten
.24	livvey	Life (lifi)	*Liffey River
.F1	Kish	cis (kish)	wickerwork basket; *Dublin
309.01	Guinnesses	Mag Aonghusa (mogénġesi)	son of *Aonghus* ("single-choice" [god of love])
.09–10	Finnfannfawners	Fionn (fin) fann (fon) fonn (foun) fánaidhe (fání)	Fair faint, languid desire wanderer, exile

		trans. Oisín (ushín)	Fawn; son of *Fionn Mac Cumhail*
		Sinn Féin (shin fén)	Ourselves
		fáinne (fáñi)	ring; association of Irish speakers
.11	Miletians	Míleadha (mílyaú)	Warriors; traditional n. for Celtic *coloniz- ers of I.
.11	Noremen	An Fheoir (unyór)	The Shore; S.E. river, anglic. Nore
.14	Himana	Uí Máine (í máñi)	descendants of *Máine*; W. tribal district, an- glic. Hy-mainy
.14	daildialler	dáil (*dál*)	assembly; *Dáil Éire- ann*, I. national Legis- lative Assembly
.16	ruad	ruadh (rúe)	red
.20	skybuddies	bod (bu*d*)	penis
310.05	liffing	Life (lifi)	*Liffey River
.08	serostaatarean	Saorstát Éireann (sérs*tát* érun)	Irish Free State
.10	Piaras UaRhuam- haighaudhlug	Piaras Ua Raghallaigh (píres ú rayelí) ruamghail (rúmyel)	Piers des. of *Raghallach* ("[strong-]fore- armed"); Piers O Reilly rumbling
.12	Bauliaughacleeagh	Baile Átha Cliath (blá- klíe)	Hurdle Ford Town; *Dublin
.13	Naul	An Áill (un ál)	The Cliff; village N. of Dublin; anglic. The Naul
.13	Santry	Sean-treabh (shan*t*rav)	Old Tribe; village N. of Dublin
.13	Corthy	[Inis] Coirthe ([inish] korhi)	[Island of the] Memo- rial Stone; village Co. Wexford, S. of Dublin, anglic. Enniscorthy
.16	O'Keef	Ó Caoimh (ó kív)	des. of *Caomh*, ("comely"); *Shaun

.16	Rosses	Rosach (rusokh) rásaidhe (rásí)	[of the] Grove/Peninsula jilt; wandering woman
.17	Rhosso	Rosach; rásaidhe	as above
.17	Keevers	Mac Íomhair (mokíver)	son of *Ivaar* (Norse masc. pers. n.)
.20	Iren	Éireann (érun), *g.*	[of] Ireland
.27	orel orioled	Óir-ghialla (óryeli)	Golden-hostages; anc. principality, N. & W. of Dublin; anglic. Oriel
		na hOirthir (nu hirhir)	the Eastern parts; eastern Oriel, anglic. Orior
.28	o'connell's	Ó Conaill (ó kunil)	des. of *Conall* ("highpowerful")
.32	Culsen	Mac Cumhail (mok kúl)	son of *Cumhal*; patronymic of *Fionn*
.32	Patagoreyan	patghlórach (po*t*glórokh)	boring
.32	chokanchuckers	deoch (d'ukh)	drink
.34	Lougk Neagk	Loch nEachach (lokh nakhokh)	*Eachach*'s ("horseman") Lake; largest lake in I., anglic. Lough Neagh
311.01	slaunty	sláinte (slánt'i)	health
.07	Kersse	Mac Fhiarais (mokírish) *for* Mac Phiarais (mokfírish)	son of Piers [Healy]
.17	Our svalves are svalves aroon!	Sinn féin, sinn féin amháin! (shin fén shin fén awáñ)	Ourselves, ourselves alone!
.17	are	ár (ár)	our
.17	aroon	a rún (arún)	my darling
.17	Baass	bás (bás)	death

.18	Connibell	Ó Conaill (ó kunil)	des. of *Conall* ("high-powerful"); anglic. O Connell
		Conn (kon)	Intelligence; masc. pers. n.
		béal (bél)	mouth
.25	Ahorror	a chara (a khore)	friend, my friend
		Ó hEadhra (ó hyare)	des. of *Eadhra* (masc. pers. n.); anglic. O Hara
.27	an	an (un)	the
.33	buthock	bodach (budokh)	lout, churl; rich stupid farmer
312.01	Moy Eireann	Magh Éireann (má érun)	The Plain of Ireland: Ireland (poetic)
.15	Kersse	Mac Fhiarais (mokírish) *for* Mac Phiarais (mokfírish)	son of Piers [Healy]
.29	Gill	Mac an Ghoill (mokunġil)	son of the foreigner
		giall (gyel)	jaw
.29	gob	gob (gob)	snout
.30	ceilidhe	céilidhe (kélí)	evening visit; musical entertainment & dance
.30	gailydhe	*English spelled as I.* Gaedhealach (gélokh)	gaily Irish, Irish-speaking
.30	shaunty	seanda (shande)	ancient
		sean-tigh (shantí)	old house
313.07	acordial	a cháirde (akhárd'i)	friends, my friends
.07	Kersse	Mac Fhiarais	see 312.15
.16	pengeypigses	pingin (piñin)	penny (pig is on I. half-penny)
.17	coyne	coinnmheadh (konve)	billeting of soldiers; anglic. coynye

.18	dearagadye	dearg-daol (daregdíl)	"red-beetle": earwig
.19	duff	dubh (duv)	black
.19	dorkland	dorcha (durukhu)	dark
.22	pigses		halfpennies
.22	hare		threepenny
.22	chicking		penny
.23–24	lewdbrogue	barróg (beróg)	defect in speech
		bróg (bróg)	shoe
.24	coppels	capall (kopel) *L/R Interchange	horse: halfcrown coppers
.26	Twomeys	Ó Tuama (ó túme)	des. of Tuaim ("tumulus")
.27–28	fain make glories	Fionn Mac Cumhail (fin mok kúl)	Fair son of Cumhal; 3rd c. hero of saga cycle
.29	bullyon		shilling
.30	pengapung	pingin (piñin)	penny
.30	finnence	Fionn (fin)	Fair
.31	little bratton	trans. Breatain Beag (braten byug)	"Little Britain": Wales; Brittany
.34	Meade	Midheach (míukh)	Meathman
.34	Lynn-Duff	Ó Fhloinn (ó lin)	des. of Flann ("ruddy"); anglic. Lynn
		Dubh (duv) Linn Dubh lionn dubh (lin duv)	Black; anglic. Duff black pool; *Dublin porter, stout; black bile, melancholy
.35	pookal	púca (púke) buachaill (búkhel)	hobgoblin boy
314.03	meade	Midheach	see 313.34
.05	dyfflun's	Duibh-linn (divlin)	Black Pool; *Dublin

.09	-looderamaun-	ludramán (lu*d*eremán)	lazy idler
.15	go lore	go leór (gu lyór)	plenty, enough
.21–22	Ballaclay	Baile Átha Cliath (bláklíe)	Hurdle Ford Town; *Dublin
.22	Barthalamou	Parthalón (paralón)	early *colonist
.22	thonder	tón (*t*ón)	bottom, arse
.30	murtagh	Muircheart-ach (mwir-khar*t*okh)	Navigator; masc. pers. n.
.32	bouchal	buachaill (búkhel)	boy
315.12	Moyle	Sruth na Maoile (srunu mwíle)	Sea-stream of the Bald Headland; sea be-tween I. & Scotland
.14	skibber	scibeoir (shkibór)	steersman, skipper
.22	bierhiven	Béarra (bére)	fem. pers. n.; harbor, Co. Cork, anglic. Bearhaven
.24	Publin	linn (lin) lionn (lin)	pool; *Dublin ale
.24	lug in the lee	Log an Lagha (lugalá)	Hollow of the Hillside; valley, Co. Wicklow, S. of Dublin, anglic. Luggelaw
.25	slaunter	sláinte (slánt'i)	health
.29	endnew	indiu (iñú)	today
.31	talka	Tolca (*t*ulke)	Flood; N. Dublin river, site of battle of Clontarf, anglic. Tolka
.31–32	clown toff	Cluain Tarbh (klún *t*orev)	Bull Meadow, N.E. Dublin district, site of defeat of Danes by *Brian Boru, 1014; anglic. Clontarf
.34	Skibbereen	Sciobairín (shkiberín)	Skiff-harbor; town, Co. Cork

.35	lauwering	labhair (louwer, lour)	speak
.35	gallic	gall (goul) Gaedhealg (gélg)	foreigner Irish/Scots language (pron. golik in Scotland)
316.01	Pukkelsen	púca (púke) buachaill (búkhel) Ó Buachalla (ó búkheli)	hobgoblin boy des. of *Buachaill* ("boy"); anglic. Buckley
.04	aerian	Éireann (érun), *g.*	[of] Ireland
.06	Kish	Cis (kish)	Wickerwork; Light station, *Dublin Bay
.07	mear	méar (mér) mear (myar)	finger swift
.08	eric	éiric (érik)	fine, ransom
.09	Brewinbaroon	Brian Bóroimhe (bríen bórivi)	Brian of the Tribute; anglic. *Brian Boru; high king killed defeating Danes at Clontarf, 1014
.12	skerries	Sceire (shkeri)	Sea-rocks; resort, N. Dublin coast
.13	Kinkincaraborg	Ceann Cora (kyoun kure)	Weir Head; on Shannon River, residence of *Brian Boru; anglic. Kincora
.18	Erinly	Éirinn (érin), *dat.*	[to, for] Ireland
.21	Morya	mar bh'eadh (mor ya)	as if it were so (ironic interj.)
.21	ballshee	bean-sidhe (banshí) ball-sidhe (bolshí)	fairy-woman fairy-spot
.28	Blasil the Brast	*L/R Interchange Í Breasal (í brasel)	Brasil the Blest Joyful [?] Isle; anc. I. elysium in Atlantic

.28–29	furt . . . turn . . . hurdies	Baile Átha Cliath (bláklíe)	Hurdle Ford Town; *Dublin
.35	ogos	agus (ogus)	and
317.01	t.d.	*initials of* Teachta Dáil	Deputy to *Dáil Éireann*, I. Legislative Assembly
.01–02	kennedy's	Ó Cinnéididh (ó kinédí)	des. of *Cinnéididh* ("helmeted-head"); *Brian Boru
.05	dallkey	Dealg-inis (d'alginish)	Thorn-island, S. Dublin suburb, Norsified Dalkey
		dall (*d*oul)	blind
.07	tolk	Tolca (*t*ulke)	see 315.31
.08	cater	ceathar (kaher)	four
.08–09	cater million falls	céad míle fáilte (ké*d* míli fált'i)	a hundred thousand welcomes
.14	fin	fionn (fin)	fair
.18	Maldemaer	maor (mér)	steward
.22	kersse	Mac Fhiarais	see 312.15
.30	bailey	Baile (bolye)	Homestead, lighthouse, Howth Head, anglic. Bailey
.30	O'Colonel	Ó Conaill (ó kunil)	des. of *Conall* ("high-powerful"), anglic. O Connell
.31	O'Conner Dan	Ó Conchobhair Donn (ó konuher *d*oun)	Brown des. of *Conchobhar* ("high-will") anglic. The O Conor Don: head of senior branch of I. royal family
.32	obliffious	Life (lifi)	*Liffey River
.34	dun	dún (*d*ún)	fort
.36	gragh	grádh (grá)	love
318.05	duinnafear	duine (*d*ine) fear (far)	person man
.12	Ethna	Eithne (ene)	Kernel; fem. pers. n., anglic. Annie; *Anna
.15	amilikan	mil (mil)	honey

.16	bannock	bannóg (bonóg)	loaf, cake
.30	knocker	cnoc (knuk)	hill; anglic. Knock- in place-names
.32	Alpyssinia	alp (olp)	lump, heap; *Dublin
319.03	fine me cowheel	Fionn Mac Cumhail (fin mok kúl)	Fair son of *Cumhal*, 3rd. c. hero of saga cycle
.04	usquebauched	uisce beatha (ishkibahe)	"water of life": whiskey
.04	aleconner	Ó Conchobhair (ó konuher)	des. of *Conchobhar* ("high-will")
.04–05	Bembracken	Beinn Breacáin (benbrakáñ)	*Breacán*'s (dim. of *breac*, "speckled") Peak
		bairghean breac (boryen brak)	speckled loaf; currant cake used at Halloween; anglic. barmbrack
.06	stircus	stiorc (shtirk)	corpse of one who dies upright
.20	gobbos	gob (gob)	snout
.23	Pukkelsen		see 316.01
.25	Tarra	Teamhar (t'our)	Prospective-hill; anc. royal capital, anglic. Tara
.27	kersse	Mac Fhiarais	see 312.15
320.02	kersse	Mac Fhiarais	see 312.15
.05	budinholder	bod (bud)	penis
.05	cummanisht	cumann (kumon)	society, club
.12	kersse	Mac Fhiarais	see 312.15
.13	eeriesk	Éire (ére)	Ireland
.18	acarras	a chara (a khore)	friend, my friend
.21	dhruimadhreamdhrue	druim a' dhreama dhruadha (drime ġroume ġrúe)	ridge of the druidical adherents
.22	turs	túr (túr)	tower

.24	May Aileen	Magh Éireann (má érun) magh áluinn (má áliñ)	Plain of Ireland: Ireland (poetic) lovely plain
.24	Aileen	Eibhlín (eilín)	fem. pers. n., from Gk. *Elené* (Helen)
.33	Bullysacre	*half trans.* Cluain Tarbh (klún *t*orev)[?]	Bull Meadow; N.E. Dublin district, site of *Brian Boru's defeat of Danes, 1014; anglic. Clontarf
.34	billy	bile (bili)	sacred tree
321.08	Glasthule	Glas Tuathail (glos *t*úhil)	*Tuathal*'s ("people-mighty") Stream; stream & village near Dun Laoghaire, S. Co. Dublin
.08	Boehernapark	Bóthar na páirc (bóherne-párk)	Road of the Field; Park Road, street in Glasthule end of Dun Laoghaire
.08	Nolagh	An Ulaigh (un ulí)	The Altar-tomb; town, Co. Cavan
.11	galler	gall (goul)	foreigner
.12	gael	Gaedheal (gél)	Irishman, Scotsman
.17	Irinwakes	Éirinn (érin), *dat.*	[to, for] Ireland
.23	giel	giall (gíl)	jaw; hostage
.23	gail	Gaedheal (gél)	Irishman, Scotsman
.23	geil	Gaedheal (gél) giall (gíl)	Irishman, Scotsman jaw; hostage
.23	gaul	gall (goul)	foreigner
.26	hens		pennies
.26	hounds		sixpences
.26	horses		halfcrowns
.27	biddy		penny
.27	bunny		threepence
.29	sows		halfpennies

.29	topple	capall (kopel)	horse: halfcrown
.33	mulligar	An Muileann Cearr (un mwilin kyar)	The Left-handed Mill; town, Co. Westmeath, anglic. Mullingar
		Ó Maolagáin (ó mwélegáñ)	des. of *Maolagán* (dim· of *maol*, "bald"); an-glic. Mulligan
322.01	Kersse	Mac Fhiarais	see 312.15
.02	Boildawl	Baile Dubhghaill (bolye *dú*ġil)	Black-Foreigners' [i.e., Danes'] Town, N.E. Dublin suburb, anglic. Baldoyle
.02	rushirishis Irush-	Ros-eó (rushó)	Yew-tree peninsula; N. Co. Dublin town, anglic. Rush
.03	Conan	Conán (konán)	dim. of n. beginning *Con-* ("intelligence")
.05	Kersse	Mac Fhiarais	see 312.15
.09	bekersse	Mac Fhiarais	see 312.15
.16	doyle	Dáil (*d*ál)	Assembly; *Dáil Éire-ann*, I. Legislative As-sembly
		Ó Dubhghaill (ó *d*úgel)	des. of *Dubhghall* ("black-foreigner," i.e., Dane); anglic. Doyle
.17–18	kersey	Mac Fhiarais	see 312.15
.18	Kersse	Mac Fhiarais	see 312.15
.19	acurraghed	Cuirreach Life (kwirokh lifi) a chara (a khore)	Moor/Racecourse of the Liffey [Plain]; Co. Kildare, anglic. the Curragh of Kildare friend, my friend
.33	Kongbullies	Conga (kuñge)	Strait; monastic re-treat of *Ruaidhrí Ó Conchobhair*, last high king, Co. Mayo, an-glic. Cong
.34	Domnial	Domhnall (*d*ónel)	World-mighty; masc. pers. n.
.35	muncipated	mún (mún)	urine

323.04	Ship Alouset	Séipéal Iosaid (shépél isid')	*Iosada*'s (fem. pers. n.: Iseult, Isolda) Chapel; W. Dublin district, anglic. Chapelizod
.09	Donnerbruch	Domhnach [*properly* Tamhnach] Broc (*d*ounokh/ *t*ounokh brok)	Badger Church [properly, Green-field]; S. Dublin district, anglic. Donnybrook
.21	Drumadunderry	Drom an Dún Daire (*d*rum a*d*ún *d*eri)	Ridge of the Fort of the Oakwood
.21	Mecckrass	Muc-ros (mukros)	Pig-peninsula; site of abbey near Killarney, Co. Kerry; anglic. Muckross
.34	sham cram bokk	Sean Bhean Bhocht (shan van vukh*t*)	Poor Old Woman: Ireland (poetic)
324.06	ruad	ruadh (rúe)	red
.07	pairc	páirc (párk)	field
.08	murrainer	Ó Muireadh-aigh (ó mwirayí)	des. of *Muireadhach* ("mariner"); anglic. Murray, etc.
.10	Tullafilmagh	*pseudoplace-name*: Tulach (*t*ulokh) magh (má)	Hill; anglic. Tulla- in place-names plain
.18	Rowdiose wodhalooing	Ráidió Átha Luain (rád'ó áhelúñ)	Radio Athlone [Ford of *Luan* ("warrior")]; station identification of I. (prewar) broadcasting service
.20	Clontarf	Cluain Tarbh (klún *t*orev)	Bull Meadow; N.E. Dublin district, site of *Brian Boru's defeat of Danes, 1014
.22	Finucane	Ó Fionn-mhacáin (ó finwokáñ)	des. of *Fionnmhacán* (dim. of *Fionnmhac*, "fair-son")
.22	Lee	Ó Laoidhigh (ó lí)	des. of *Laoidheach* ("poetic")

.26	Colunnfiller	*Colmcille (kulumkili)	Dove of the Church; st., latinized Columba
.32	lucal	Leamhcán (loukán)	Producing marshmallows; W. Dublin suburb on Liffey; anglic. Lucan
325.04	Lynchya	Ó Loingsigh (ó liñshí)	des. of *Loingseach* ("having to do with a fleet")
.08–09	honnessy	Ó hAonghusa (ó héngesi)	des. of *Aonghus* ("single-choice" [god of love]); anglic. Hennessy
.13	ahorace	a chara (a khore)	friend, my friend
.14	a laun	a lán (a lán)	many, much
.23	Mac Namara	Mac Conmara (mok konmore)	son of *Cú-mara* ("hound of the sea")
.24	Banba	Banba (bonbe)	Ireland (poetic)
.25	Idyall	Iodáil (idál)	Italy
.32	luusk	Lusc (lusk)	Cave; village N. of Dublin; anglic. Lusk
.32	cong	Conga (kuñge)	Strait; see 322.33
.33	bray	Brí (brí)	Hillside; coast resort S. of Dublin; anglic. Bray
326.02	mardhyr	marbhadh (morú)	murder
.05	ouishguss	uisce (ishki) Aonghus (énġus)	water Single-choice, god of love
.06	cruisk	crúisce (krúshki)	jug, pitcher
.06	Ocean	Oisín (ushín)	Fawn; son of *Fionn Mac Cumhail* (baptized by St. Patrick)
.07	Oscarvaughther	Oscar (usker)	Combatant; son of *Oisín*
		uisce beatha (ishki bahe)	"water of life": whiskey

.07	Erievikkingr	Éire (ére)	Ireland
.08–09	gielgaulgalls	giall (gíl)	jaw; hostage
		Gaedheal (gél)	Irishman, Scotsman
		gall (goul)	foreigner
.09	clansakiltic	Cluain Uí Chaoilte (klúní khílt'i)	Meadow of the Descendants of *Caoilte* ("hardness"), Co. Cork; anglic. Clonakilty
		Clanna Ceilteach (klone kyeltokh)	Celtic race
.10	cuddycoalman's	Colmán (kulumán)	dim. of *Colm*, ("dove"); n. of many sts. incl. disciple of Patrick; latinized Columbanus
.11–12	pukkaleens	púca (púke)	hobgoblin
		poc (puk)	sharp blow
		buachaillín (búkhelín)	little boy
		cailín (kolín)	girl
.13	danned	Domhnall (dónel)	World-mighty; anglic. Daniel
.13–14	roomyo connellic	Ó Conaill (ó kunil)	des. of *Conall* ("high-powerful"); anglic. O Connell
.16	osker	Oscar (usker)	Combatant; son of *Oisín*
.18	osion	Oisín (ushín)	Fawn; son of *Fionn Mac Cumhail*
.18	Edar	Éadar (éder)	masc. pers. n.: in *Beann Éadair*, "*Éadar*'s Peak," I. n. for Howth Head
.19	Anomyn and awer	I n-ainm an Athair (in anim un ahir)	In the name of the Father
.22–23	bigbug	beag, beig (byug, beg)	little
		bog (bug)	soft

.25	Diaeblen	Dia (d'íe) diabhal (d'oul)	God devil
.25	Balkley	Baile Átha Cliath (bláklíe)	Hurdle Ford Town; *Dublin
.25	Domnkirk	Domhnach (dounokh)	Sunday; Church (founded by Patrick)
.26	aaherra	a chara (a khore)	friend, my friend
.26	peadar	Peadar (pader)	Peter
.29-30	we brought your summer with us	trans. thugamair féin an samhradh linn	we even brought the summer with us: from a song
.34	Dybblin	Duibh-linn (divlin)	Black Pool; *Dublin
327.02	praties	préataí (prétí)	potatoes
.02	a Cara	a chara (a khore) cara (kore)	friend, my friend friend
.03	Fynlogue	Fionn-laoghóg (finléóg)	Fair young-calf; masc. pers. n. (of St. Brendan's father)
.04	Talur	táilliúr (tályúr)	tailor
.05	astore	a stór (astór)	my treasure (endearment)
.12	invairn	inbhear (inver)	harbor, estuary
.12	Roners	rón (rón)	seal (the mammal)
.16	rossies	rásaidhe (rásí)	wandering woman; jilt
.17	Dinny	duine (dini)	person
.18	Dargul	Deargail (d'argel)	Red; valley & stream Co. Wicklow near Bray; anglic. Dargle
.24	Kilbarrack	Cill Bearach (kilbarokh)	Church of Bearach ("judgment"?), district near Clontarf

.32–33	Eriweddyng	Éire (ére)	Ireland
.36	munin	mún (mún)	urine
328.02	Bruin	Brian (bríen)	*Brian Boru
		Bran (bron)	Raven
.02	O'Luinn	Ó Fhloinn (ó lin)	des. of *Flann* ("ruddy")
.04	Kersse	Mac Fhiarais	see 312.15
.10	donochs	donacht (*d*unukh*t*)	evil, badness
.14	Nanny	An Eanaigh (unaní)	The Fenny; river, Co. Meath, where *Malachy I drowned prince of Bregia (604.04); anglic. Nanny
.14	Ni Sheeres	Ní Saoraidhe (ní sírí)	daughter of des. of *Siocfhraidh* (Norse *Sigefrith*, "victory-peace")
.17	Lif . . . lif	Life (lifi)	*Liffey River
.23	taylight	té (té)	tea
.25	ringsengd ringsengd	Rinn (riñ)	Point, Peninsula; point of land, S. Dublin, anglic. Ringsend
.25	Concorant	Conchobhar (konuher)	High-will; masc. pers. n., anglic. Conor, etc.
.26	Referinn	Éirinn (érin), *dat.*	[to, for] Ireland
.27	Thingavalley	[T.] an Bhealaigh ([T.] a valí)	[T.] of the Way; frequent place-name element
329.03	bud	bod (bu*d*)	penis
.03	divlin's	Duibh-linn (*d*ivlin)	Black Pool; *Dublin
.14	Dub	dubh (*d*uv)	black; *Dublin
.14	Fingal	Fine Gall (finigoul)	Foreign Kindred; N. Co. Dublin district
.14	Fingal of victories	Fionnghal na buaidh/ mbuadha	Fair-fight of the victory/victories; title attributed by *Macpherson to his Fingal: "*Fiön gal na buai*, Fingal of Victories" (*Temora*)

.14–15	Cannmatha	Ceann- mathghamhna (kyoun mahúne)	Bear's-Head; Can- mathon, star in *Mac- pherson's *Temora*
		Maithe (mohe)[?]	Goodness; Matha is a warrior in *Macpher- son's *Fingal*
.15	Cathlin	Ga-linn (go lin)[?]	Ray of the sea; Cath- lin, star in *Macpher- son's *Temora*, is ex- plained as "beam of the wave"
		Caitlín (kat′lín)	fem. pers. n., from Gk. Katherine; Cathlin is the n. of a girl in *Mac- pherson's *Cathlin of Clutha*
.16	Tuhal	Tuathal (*t*úhel)	People-mighty, Ty- rant; masc. pers. n.; *Macpherson glosses Tuathal in *Fingal* as "surly"
		tuathamhail (*t*úhúl)	rustic, boorish; per- haps source of *Mac- pherson's gloss
		tuathalach (*t*úhelokh)	awkward, tactless, sin- ister; perhaps source of *Macpherson's gloss
.17	Darthoola	Dart-shúile (*d*or*t* húle)	Heifer-eyes; *Mac- pherson explains Dar- Thula in *Dar-Thula* as "Dart-'huile, a woman with fine eyes"
.17	Roscranna's	Ros-chranna (ruskhrone)	Shrub-trees; Ros- crana, fem. pers. n. in *Temora* is glossed by *Macpherson (inexpli- cably): "the beam of the rising sun"
		Rosc-ghréine (ruskġréñi)	Eye of the sun; possi- ble basis for *Macpher- son's gloss
		crann (kroun)	tree, beam (of wood), beam of light (fig.)

.17	bolgaboyo	Fir-Bolga (firbulge)	Bags Men; legendary *colonists; *Macpherson calls S.I. Bolga in *Temora*, "from the . . . Belgae"
		ga bolga (go bulge)	"gapped spear," weapon of *Cúchulainn*, *Red Branch
.18	Cormac	Cormac (kurmok)	Chariot-son; in *Fionn's* time high king was *Cormac Mac Airt*, father of *Gráinne*; in *Macpherson's* *Temora* Roscrana was "the daughter of Cormac"
.21	bragues	bréag (brég)	lie, falsehood
.31	glaives	claidheamh (klív)	sword
.33	Fathach	fathach (fohokh)	giant
.33–34	louthmouthing	Lughbhadh (lúva)	pertaining to *Lugh* (god of light & genius), co. N. of Dublin anglic. Louth
.34	Healy	Ó hÉilidhe (ó hélí)	des. of *Ealadhach* ("ingenious")
.34	Mealy	Ó Máille (ó mályi)	des. of *Máille* ("chief"); anglic. Mealy, *O Malley
.35	Tarar	Teamhar (t'our)	Prospective-hill; anc. royal capital; anglic. Tara
330.01	gafr	gabhar (gour)	goat [*gafr* (gover) is Welsh]
.06	taytotally	té (té)	tea
.07	lanv	leanbh (lanev)	child
.09	Laxembraghs	brágha (brá) bráth (brá)	neck, throat doom, judgment (sometimes anglic. bragh)
.16	Mick na Murrough	Mac Murchadha (mok murukhu)	son of *Murchadh* ("seawarrior"); anglic. McMurrough; *Diarmaid Mac Murchadha*,

			Leinster king who invited Anglo-Norman invasion; *Shem; *Brian Boru
.16	na Murrough	na murchadha (nu murukhu)	of the sea-warrior
.17	Burke-Lees	Ó Buachalla (ó búkheli)	des. of *Buachaill* ("boy"); anglic. Buckley
		Ó Laoidhigh (ó lí)	des. of *Laoidheach* ("poetic")
.16	Coyle-Finns	Mac Dhubhghaill (mokúġil)	son of *Dubhghall* ("black-foreigner," i.e., Dane), anglic. Coyle, McCool, etc.
		Ó Finn (ó fin) Fionn Mac Cumhail (fin mok kúl)	des. of *Fionn* ("fair") Fair son of *Cumhal*, 3rd c. hero of saga cycle
		cúilfhionn (kúlin)	fair-head
.18	feines . . . sinns	sinn féin (shin fén)	ourselves
.18	Coolie	Mac Giolla Chúile (mok gili khúli)	son of *Giolla Mhochúille* ("servant of [St.] Mochuille")
.21	banbax	Banba (bonbe) bean (ban)	Ireland (poetic) woman
.24	Finn's	Ó Finn (ó fin)	des. of *Fionn* ("fair")
.35	kathareen	Caitrín (kat′rín)	fem. pers. n. from Gk. Katherine
.36	moder of moders	modar (moder)	dark, dingy
331.04	liamstone	Liam (lím) lia (líe)	William stone monument
.10	Peganeen	Peigeáinín (pegáñín)	Little Peggy
.12	Melooney	Ó Maoldhomhnaigh (ó mwélouní)	des. of *Maoldomhnaigh* ("devoted to Sunday"); anglic. Moloney, etc.

		Mac Cluanaigh (mok klúní)	son of *Cluanach* ("deceitful"), anglic. MacLoonie, etc.
.19	diublin's	Dubh-linn (*d*uvlin)	Black Pool; *Dublin
		diu (d'ú)	day
.23	eira	Éire (ére)	Ireland
.25	formor	Fomhór (fowór)	Fomorian, giant, pirate; *colonists
.26	Bil	bile (bili)	sacred tree
.26–27	Brine Borumoter	Brian Bóroimhe (bríen bórivi)	Brian of the Tribute, anglic. *Brian Boru, high king killed defeating Danes at Clontarf, 1014
332.04	hanigen	Ó hAnnagáin (ó hanegáñ)	des. of *Annagán* (dim. of *annadh*, "delay")
.04	finnd	Fionn (fin)	Fair
.05	hinnigen	Ó hÉineacháin (ó hénekháñ)	des. of *Eidhneachán* (*Aonachán* [?], "solitary")
.05–06	-parrassannuaragh-eallachnatullagh-mongan-	Piaras an Ua Raghailleach na Tulaighe Mongáin (píres un úrayelokh nu *t*ulí muñgáñ)	Piers *the* Descendant of *Raghallach* ("[strong-] fore-armed") of the Hill of *Mongán* (dim. of *mongach*, "hairy") [anglic. Tullymongan, Co. Cavan]; *Tulach Mongáin* is at the heart of *Breifne Uí Raghailligh*, anglic. Breffny O Reilly; see 099.26–27
.05	-parrassan-	pearsa (parse) pearsún (parsún)	person parson
.05	-rassa-	rás (rás) rásaidhe (rásí)	race wandering woman; jilt
.05	-as-	as (os)	out of
.05	-san-	'san (sun)	in the
.05	-ann-	ann (oun)	in it
.05	-nua-	nua (núe)	new

.05	-gheallach-	gealach (gyalokh)	moon, moonlight
.06	-macmacmac-	mac (mok)	son
.06	-dubb-	dubh (*d*uv)	black; *Dublin
.07	anruly	an (un) an- (on), *pfx.*	the un-, in-, not-, anti-; very-
.08	Fine again	Ó Fionnagáin (ó finegáñ)	des. of *Fionnagán* (dim. of *Fionn*, "fair")
.08	Cuoholson	Mac Cumhail (mok kúl)	son of *Cumhal*; patronymic of *Fionn*
.10	tolk of	Tolca (*t*ulke)	Flood; N. Dublin river, site of battle of Clontarf; anglic. Tolka
.10	Doolin	Dubh linn (*d*úlin) Ó Dubhlainn/ Dubhláin (ó *d*úlin/*d*úláñ)	Black Pool; *Dublin des. of *Dubhfhlann* ("black *Flann* ['ruddy']")/*Dubhshlán* ("black-defiance"); both anglic. Doolin
.14	roammerin	Éirinn (érin), *dat.*	[to, for] Ireland
.26	fiounaregal	fionn (fin) fionna (fine) fionnadh (finú) Fianna (fíene)	fair hair fur 3rd c. standing army led by *Fionn Mac Cumhail*
.27	fenians	Fianna (fíene) fiannaidhe (fíení)	3rd c. standing army led by *Fionn Mac Cumhail* warriors, soldiers; members of *Fianna*
.28	Inverleffy	inbhear (inver) Inbhear Life (inver lifi)	estuary, harbor "*Liffey Estuary": Dublin Bay
.32	Paudheen	Páidín (pád'ín)	dim. of *Pádraig*: Paddy

.33	Kenny's	Ó Cionaodha (ó kiné)	des. of *Cionaodh* ("fire-sprung")
.33	Kenny's thought ye, Dinny Oozle	Conas tá tú, a dhuine uasal (kunes *tá tú* a ģini úsil)	How are you, gentle person [= sir]
333.10	cavarnan	Ó Caomháin (ó kéváñ)	des. of *Caomhán* (dim. of *caomh*, "comely"); anglic. Cavan
		Caomhánach (kévánokh)	des. of *Caomhán*; anglic. Cavanaugh
		Cabhán (kaván)	Hollow; N. central town & co., anglic. Cavan
.17	juinnesses	Mag Aonghusa (mogénģesi)	son of *Aonghus* ("single-choice" [god of love]); anglic. Guinness
.27	fain a wan	féin amháin (fén awáñ)	self alone
.30	lillabilla	bile (bili)	sacred tree
.32	Murphy's	Ó Murchadha (ó murukhu)	des. of *Murchadh* ("sea-warrior")
.33	gnockmeggs	cnoc (knuk)	hill
.34	whishtful	thoist (hish*t*)	silence
.36	Naul	An Áill (unál)	The Cliff; village N. Co. Dublin
334.03	Kostello	Mac Oisdealbhaigh (mok oshd'alví)	son of *Oisdealbhach* ("shaped like *Os* ['deer']"; n. of a god)
.04	billybobbis	bile (bili)	sacred tree
.08	Delgany	Dergne (d'ergini)	dim. of *dearg*, "red"; Co. Wicklow, S. of Dublin, anglic. Delgany (*L/R Interchange)
.11	mahonagyan	Ó Mathghamhna (ó mahúne)	des. of *Mathghamhain* ("bear"); anglic. Mahoney, etc.; *Brian Boru
		Ó Manacháin (ó monekháñ)	des. of *Manachán* (dim. of *manach*, "monk"); anglic. Monaghan

.15	cummal	Cumhal (kúl)	father of *Fionn Mac Cumhail*
.24	pobbel	pobal (pubel)	people; public
.29–30	dunneth . . . the. Duras	dúnann an doras (*d*únen un *d*ures)	shuts the door
.32	thon	tón (*t*ón)	bottom, arse
.33	Finndlader's	Fionn (fin)	Fair
.33	Tallaght	Taimhleacht (*t*alokh*t*)	Plague-grave; village S.W. of Dublin
.35	Donnicoombe	Domhnach/ Tamhnach	Sunday; Church/ Green-field; anglic. Donny- in place-names
		Cúm (kúm)	Hollow; S. Dublin slum, anglic. The Coombe
.36	Carlowman's	Ceatharlach (kaherlokh)	Quadruple-lake; S.E. co. & town; anglic. Carlow
335.13	Bullyclubber	Baile Átha Cliath (blá klíe)	Hurdle Ford Town; *Dublin
.13	burgherly	Ó Buachalla (ó búkheli)	des. of *Buachaill* ("boy"), anglic. Buckley
.16–17	leish . . . laleish	leis (lesh)	with him
.18	maormaoring	maor (mér)	steward
.22	wukeleen	bhuachaillín (wúkhelín)	*Asp.; little boy
.24	Paud	Páid (pád')	dim. of *Pádraig*: Pat
.28	olives	ollamh (olev)	sage, poet, professor
.28	ocolombs	Ó Cuilm (ó kulim)	des. of *Colm* ("dove"); anglic. Colum
.31	grace so madlley	Gráinne Ní Mháille (gráñí wályi)	Grain/Spearpoint, daughter of a des. of *Máille* ("chief"); anglic. Grace *O Malley
336.06	louthly	Lughbhadh (lúva)	pertaining to *Lugh* (god of light & genius); co. N. of Dublin, anglic. Louth

.06	meathers	Midhe (mí)	Middle; anc. royal province; co. W. & N. of Dublin; anglic. Meath
.20	Slant.	sláinte (sláñt'i)	health
.20	Shinshin. Shinshin	sinn (shin)	we, us
.28	tauth	tát (*tát*)	opinion
.33	The Nolan	Ó Nualláin (ó núláñ)	The des. of *Nuallán* (dim. of *nuall*, "noble") [designation of head of n.]
337.11	maleybags	mála (mále)	bag
.15	brian	Brian	*Brian Boru
.16	billy	bile (bili)	sacred tree
.19	Omnibil	bile (bili)	sacred tree
.26	Budlim	bod (bu*d*)	penis
.28	Faunagon	Ó Fionnagáin (ó finegáñ) fánach (fánokh)	des. of *Fionnagán* (dim. of *Fionn*, "fair") idle, useless; vagrant
.30	Donn	donn (*d*oun)	brown; staunch
.30	Teague	Tadhg (*t*eig)	Poet; masc. pers. n. of typical rustic laborer
.30	Hurleg	Ó hUrthuile (ó hurili)	des. of *Urthuile* ("heath-abundance"); anglic. Hurley
.32–33	Bud . . . Bud Budderly . . . Bud Budderly boddily	bod (bu*d*) bodaire (bu*d*ere) bodairlín (bu*d*erlín)	penis lout, churl; rich vulgar farmer minnow
.33	Borrisalooner	buirghes (buryis)	burgage; anglic. Borris- in place-names
.36	Flavin	Ó Flaitheamháin (ó flaváñ)	des. of *Flaitheamhán* (dim. of *Flaitheamh*, "lord, ruler")
.36	Ulick	Uilleac (ulak)	dim. of *Uilliam*, William
.36	Dunne	Ó Duinn (ó *d*in)	des. of *Donn* ("brown")

338.02	Burghley	Ó Buachalla (ó búkheli)	des. of *Buachaill* ("boy"); anglic. Buckley
.03	Ehren	Éirinn (érin), *dat.*	[to, for] Ireland
.03	gobrawl	go bráth (gu brá)	until Judgment (i.e., forever)
.09	moriartsky	Ó Muircheartaigh (ó mwirkhyartí)	des. of *Muircheartach* ("navigator"); anglic. Moriarty
.14	mwilshsuni	milseánaí (milshání)	sweets, confections, candies
.19	Baltiskeeamore	Bailte Scíth Mór (bolt'i shkí mór)	Town of a Great Wickerwork-Partition
.21	saillils	sail (sal) saill (sal)	willow; letter S grease
.21	Shelltoss	seilte (shelte)	jargon, argot
.22	aghom	agam (agum)	at me; (with verb "to be") I have
		ogham (oġem)	anc. I. writing with notches
.26	d'airain	d'Éirinn (dérin)	from Ireland
		Árainn (árin), *g.*	[of a] Kidney; islands off Co. Galway, anglic. Aran
.28	Bruyant	Brian	*Brian Boru
.32	hear in	Éirinn (érin), *dat.*	[to, for] Ireland
.36	*Aerin*	Éireann (érun), *g.*	[of] Ireland
.36	*laugh neighs*	Loch nEachach (lokh nakhokh)	*Eachach*'s ("horseman") Lake; largest lake in I.; anglic. Lough Neagh
339.02	Ullahbluh!	Uladh abú! (ule abú)	Ulster (N. province) to victory!
.05	metchennacht	meath (mya) ceannacht (kyanokht)	weak, pliable person headship; purchasing, buying

.06	Bog	bog (bug)	soft
.06	carsse	Mac Fhiarais	see 312.15
.08	ros	ros (ros)	wood, grove; horse
.11	roscians	ros (ros)	wood, grove; horse
		rosc (rusk)	inflammatory speech, call to valor
		scian (shkín)	knife
.13	gaelstorms	Gaedheal (gél)	Irishman, Scotsman
.14	Obriania's	Ó Briain (ó bríin)	des. of *Brian Boru; anglic. O Brien
.15	shimars	siomar (shimer)	trefoil, shamrock
.31	*lusky*	Lusca (luske)	Cave; village N. of Dublin, anglic. Lusk
.34	*Krumlin*	Crom-ghleinn (krumġlin)	Crooked Valley; S. Dublin district, anglic. Crumlin
340.02	fitchid	fichid (fikhid')	twenty
.06	*Lissnaluhy*	Lios na Luigh (lisnelúí) [?]/ na Luaithe (nelúhi)	Fort of the Little [People]/of the Ashes
.06	*Djublian*	Dubh-linn (*d*uvlin)	Black Pool; *Dublin
.06	*Alps*	alp (olp)	heap; job; *Alp Uí Laoghaire*: Dublin in mason's jargon
.08	karhags	carraig (korig)	rock
.09	Oghrem	ogham (oġem)	anc. I. writing of notches
		Each-dhruim (akhġrim)	Horse-ridge, Co. Galway, scene of Jacobite–Williamite battle, 1691; anglic. Aughrim
.10	glunn	gleann (gloun)	valley
		glún (glún)	knee
.11	buddies	bod (bu*d*)	penis
.14	*keening*	caoineadh (kínu)	wailing, lamenting
.15	*blank sheets*	bean-sidhe (banshí)	fairy-woman

.16	rath . . . mines	Ráth Maoinis (rá mwémish)	Magnus's Fort; S. Dublin district, anglic. Rathmines
.17	Mac Mahahon	Mac Math-ghamhna (mok mahúne)	son of *Mathghamhain* ("bear"); anglic. Mac-Mahon
.17	Osro	Osraighe (osrí)	[belonging to the] posterity of *Os* ("deer"); S.E. tribal district, anglic. Ossory
		*L/R Interchange	Oslo
.20	*applehooly*	na h-ubhaillí (nahúlí) ubhaillí (úlí)	the apple trees/orchards apple trees/orchards
.20	Bruinoboroff	Brian Bóroimhe (bríen bórivi)	Brian of the Tribute, anglic. *Brian Boru, high king killed defeating Danes at Clontarf, 1014
.21	Meideveide	Midh (mí)	Middle; anc. royal province; co., W. & N. of Dublin, anglic. Meath
.24	Finnland	Fionn (fin)	Fair
.32	dargman	dearg (d'areg)	red
341.05	Buckily buckily	Ó Buachalla (ó búkheli)	des. of *Buachaill* ("boy"); anglic. Buckley
.06	boyne	Bóinn (bóñ)	n. of goddess; River *Boyne, scene of defeat of I. Jacobites by Williamites, 1690
.09	balacleivka	Baile Átha Cliath (blá klíe)	Hurdle Ford Town; *Dublin
.17	mlachy	Maoilsheach-lainn (mwélokhlin)	Servant of Secundinus (st.); masc. pers. n.; anglic. *Malachy
.24–25	*Twomass Nohoholan*	Tomás Ó Nulláin (*t*umás ó núláñ)	Thomas des. of *Nuallán* (dim. of *nuall*, "noble")

.27	*Saint Dhorough's*	Cill Dúilech (kil *d*úlekh)	Church of St. *Dúileach*, village N. of Dublin, anglic. Saint Doolaghs
342.06–07	*Baldawl . . . baledale*	Baile Dubhghaill (bolye *d*úġil)	Town of the Black Foreigner (i.e., Dane), N.E. Dublin suburb, anglic. Baldoyle
.17	*Riley*	Ó Raghailligh (ó rayelí)	des. of *Raghallach* ("[strong-]fore-armed")
.17–18	*turn of the fourth of the hurdles*	Baile Átha Cliath (blá klíe)	Town of the Ford of Hurdles; *Dublin
.23	*Bailey*	Baile (bolye)	Homestead; lighthouse, Howth Head, anglic. Bailey
.24	*Ratatuohy*	Ráth an Tuathaigh (rá a *t*úhí)	Fort of the Territorial-Lord
.25	*Leavybrink*	Life (lifi)	*Liffey River
.30	eeridreme	Éire (ére)	Ireland
.36	*tiomor*	tiomar (timer)	bequest
343.03	Boyle	Ó Baoighill (ó bwél)	des. of *Baoith-gheall* ("vain-pledge")
.03	Campbell	Caimbéal (kambél)	Wry-mouth
.09	ingain	inghean (inyen)	daughter
.10	Galwegian	Gaillimheach (golivokh)	foreign, strange; pertaining to Galway
.11	micramacrees	mac, mic (mok, mik)	son, of a son
		mo chroidhe (mukhrí)	of my heart
.11	na Bogaleen	na Bogairliúin (nu bugerlyúñ)	of the spongy turnip (Myles na gCopaleen [*na gCapaillín*, "of the little horses"]: pseudonym of a journalist); *The Colleen Bawn*
.25	Foinn	Fionn (fin)	Fair
.25	duhans	Ó Dubháin (ó *d*úáñ)	des. of *Dubhán* (dim. of *dubh*, "black")

.31	cromlecks	Crom-leac (krumlak)	Stooped stone; popular n. for dolmen; *Humphrey
.32	lewdbrogue	barróg (beróg) bróg (bróg)	defect in speech shoe
.33	santry	Sean-Treabh (shan*t*rav)	Old Tribe; village N. of Dublin
344.01	*unglucksarsoon*	garsún (gorsún)	boy, lad
.06	Gambanman	gaimbín (gombín) gamba (gombe) bean (ban)	usury, interest; "gombeen-man": usurer jamb, leg woman
.07	cawraidd's	raid (rad') *trans.* Táin-bó [?]	kick Cattle-raid; Cow-raid; famous *Red Branch saga
.18	cowruads	ruadh (rúe) bó-ramha (bórúe)	red "cow-counting": tribute; *Brian Boru
.18	airish	Éire (ére)	Ireland
.31	meac Coolp	Mac Cumhail (mok kúl)	son of *Cumhal*; patronymic of *Fionn*
.31–32	Eirzerum	Éire (ére)	Ireland
.32	Deer Dirouchy	Deirdre (d'írd'ri)[?]	heroine of *Red Branch saga cycle; fig., a sweetheart
.35–36	there was fear on me	*lit. trans.* bhí eagla orm	I was afraid
.36	Nuad	Nuadha (núa)	king of *Tuatha Dé Danann*; god surnamed *Airgead-lámh*, "silver-hand"
345.02	achaura moucreas	a chara mo chroidhe (a khore mukhrí)	friend of my heart
.09	Fonn	fonn (foun)	desire, longing; tune
.11	*waitawhishts*	thoist (hish*t*)	silence
.12	*kuldrum*	cúl (kúl) drom (*d*rum)	back of the head back; ridge
.19	*lagan*	Lagán (logán)	dim. of *Lag* ("hollow"); River Lagan

.25	orafferteed	Ó Raithbh-eartaigh (ó rafertí)	des. of *Robhartach* ("crafty"); anglic. O Rafferty
.33	fiennd	fionn (fin)	fair
.35	*Mullingaria*	An Muileann Cearr (un mwilin kyar)	The Left-handed Mill; town, Co. Westmeath; anglic. Mullingar
346.02	*muckinstushes*	Mac an Taoisigh (mok un *t*íshí) muc (muk)	son of the chieftain; anglic. Mackintosh pig
.14	*Peadhar*	Peadar (pa*d*er)	Peter
.15	*Colliguchuna*	Colg a' tiuine (koliga t'úni)	Fury of the tune (imaginary place-name)
.17	*agamb . . . agam*	agam (agum)	at me; (with verb "to be"): I have
.19	Buccleuch	Ó Buachalla (ó búkheli)	des. of *Buachaill* ("boy")
.21	gow	gabha (gou)	smith
.22	piddyawhick	Páid a mhic (pád' awik)	Pat, my son
.22	Ath	áth (á)	ford; *Dublin
.24	Ballygarry	Baile-garrdha (bolye gore)	Garden-town; Co. Mayo
.25	cooll . . . feign	Fionn Mac Cumhail (fin mok kúl)	Fair son of *Cumhal*; 3rd c. hero of saga cycle
.25	Harkabuddy	bod (bu*d*)	penis
.26	shimwhir	siomar (shimer)	trefoil, shamrock
.27	Shinfine . . . fainman	Sinn féin amháin (shin fén awáñ)	Ourselves alone
.28	slog	slog (slug)	swallow, gulp
.28	Tuan	tuan (*t*ún) Tuan [Mac Cairill]	advanced in years legendary *colonist, survivor of the Flood, baptized by *Colmcille*
.29	arrah	ara (ore)	deprecatory interj.
.30	budd	bod (bu*d*)	penis

.31	*cushlows*	cúisle (kúshle)	pulse, heartbeat
.32	*niallist of the ninth homestages*	Niall Naoi-ghiallach	*Niall* ("champion") Nine-hostager; high king, 379–406, ancestor of *Uí Néill
.35	*angush*	Aonghus (éngus)	Single-choice; god of love
.35	Horrasure	ara (ore)	deprecatory interj.
347.01	bulg	bolg (bulug)	belly
.08	Reilly	Ó Raghailligh (ó rayelí)	des. of *Raghallach* ("[strong-]fore-armed")
.11	Ayerland	Éire (ére)	Ireland
.15	banshee	bean-sidhe (banshí)	fairy-woman
.19	annam	anam (onem) ainm (onim)	soul name
.20	is in it	*lit. trans.* atá ann	exists, occurs
.20–21	Bok of Alam	Móin Almhain (món alúñ)	Bog of *Almha* ("whitened"), Co. Kildare, surrounding *Almhain*, HQ of Fianna; anglic. Bog of Allen
.21	columnkill	Colmcille (kulumkili)	Dove of the Church; st., latinized Columba
.21	Erin gone brugk	Éire go bráth (ére gubrá)	Ireland until Judgment Day
.36	*smolking*	smalcadh (smolku)	devouring, eating greedily
.36	*turfkish*	cis (kish)	wickerwork basket
348.17	currgans	Ó Corragáin (ó kuregáñ)	des. of *Corragán* (dim. of *corra*, "spear")
.18	Gormleyson	Mac Gormfhlaith (mok gurm la)	son of *Gormfhlaith* ("blue-lady"); mother of Sitric, 11th c. Danish king of Dublin was *Gormfhlaith*
		Ó Goirmshleaghaigh (ó gurmlayí)	des. of *Goirmshleaghach* ("blue-spearman"); anglic. Gormley

.19	Danno O'Dun-nochoo	Domhnall Ó Donnchadha (*dó*nel ó *d*unukhu)	World-mighty des. of *Donnchadh* ("brown-warrior"); *Brian Boru
.19	Conno	Conn (kon)	Intelligence
.19	O'Cannocher	Ó Concho-bhair (ó koneher) ceannacht (kanokh*t*)	des. of *Conchobhar* ("high-will"); sur-name of last high king headship; purchase
.21	Kong	Conga (kuñge)	Strait; monastic re-treat of *Ruaidhrí Ó Conchobhair*, last high king; Co. Mayo; an-glic. Cong
.21	Kong Gores	Cluain Gabha (klún gou)	Smith's Meadow, Co. Kildare; anglic. Clongowes
.21	thurkmen	torc (*t*urk)	boar, hog
349.03	keaoghs	Mac Eochadha (mokyokhu)	son of *Eochaidh* ("horseman"); anglic. Keough
.19	*O'Donoshough*	Ó Donn-chadha (ó *d*unukhu) donas (*d*unus)	des. of *Donnchadh* ("brown-warrior") bad luck, misfortune
.24	*Gorman*	Ó Gormáin (ó gurmáñ)	des. of *Gormán* (dim. of *gorm*, "blue"); *Mael-muire Ó Dúnáin Ó Gormáin*, latinized Mari-anus Gorman (d. 1181), Augustinian ab-bot composed his "Martyrology" (calen-dar of sts.) in 2,780 lines of verse during reign of *Ruaidhrí Ó Conchobhair*
.35	*comfoderacies*	rásaidhe (rásí)	wandering woman; jilt
350.07	*O'Dungaschiff*	Ó Donnagáin (ó *d*unegáñ)	des. of *Donnagán* (dim. of *donn*, "brown")
.09	*Dtin, dtin, dtin, dtin*	*Eclipsis	Din, din, din, din

.12	*Oldbally*	baile (bolye)	town, homestead
.17	kughs	Mac Eochadha	see 349.03
.20	cossakes	cos (kus)	foot
.21	eskermillas	eiscir (eshkir)	sand-ridge; anglic. -esker-
		míle (míli)	thousand
		milleadh (mile)	destruction
.21	billyfell	bile (bili)	sacred tree
.22	rawmeots	ráiméis (rámésh)	nonsense, "romance"
.24	sassenacher	Sasanach (sosenokh)	Englishman ("Saxon")
.27	Parishmoslattary	Moslatra (muslotre)	Saint (*lit.*, "My") *Slatra* ("strong")
.28	daun	dán (*d*án)	song; art
		dána (*d*áne)	bold; shameless
		donn (*d*oun)	brown; staunch
.29	Slobabogue	Slab Ó Buadhaigh (slob ó búíg)	*Slab* ("soft-fleshed person") des. of *Buadhach* ("victorious") [anglic. Bogue]
.31–32	sand us . . . saint us . . . sound us	sláinte (sláñt'i)	health
.32	agun	again (agin)	"at-us"; (with verb "to be"): we have
351.01	nowells	nuall (núl)	noble
.02	curry	Ó Corra (ó kure)	des. of *Corra* ("spear")
.02	fanagan's	Ó Fionnagáin (ó finegáñ)	des. of *Fionnagán* (dim. of *Fionn*, "fair")
.09	durck rosolun	*trans.* Róisín Dubh	Dark Little Rose: Ireland (poetic)
.13	poppyrossies	rásaidhe (rásí)	wandering woman; jilt
.14	Sczlanthas!	Sláinte! (sláñt'i)	Health!
.23	meelisha's deelishas	miliseach dílis (milishokh dílish)	dearest sweetheart

352.01	urssian	Oisín (ushín)	Fawn; son of *Fionn Mac Cumhail*; *Macpherson's Ossian
.12	meath	Midhe (mí)	Middle; anc. royal province; co. N. & W. of Dublin
.16	*bron*	brón (brón)	grief, sorrow
.16	*nuhlan*	Ó Nualláin (ó núláñ)	des. of *Nuallán* (dim. of *nuall*, "noble")
.23	bullyclaver of ye	Baile Átha Cliath (blá klíe)	Hurdle Ford Town; *Dublin
.27	*Dann Deafir*	déan deifir (d'én d'efir)	make haste, hurry
.29	*finngures*	fionn (fin)	fair
.31	gayl	Gaedheal (gél)	Irishman, Scotsman
.33	Russkakruscam	rosc (rusk)	call to valor
		cac (kok)	excrement
		crúisc (krúshk)	jug, pitcher
		cam (koum)	crooked
.34	Allaf	Amhlaoibh (oulév)	masc. pers. n. (Norse *Ólafr*); *Humphrey
.34	O'Khorwan	Ó Ciardubháin (ó kírduváñ)	des. of *Ciardubhán* (dim. of *ciardubh*, "jet-black"); anglic. Kerwan, etc.
.34	connundurumchuff	Conn (kon)	Intelligence; masc. pers. n.
		tiomhailt (t'uvilt')	full from eating
353.06	*maomant*	maon (món)	dumb
.11	Killtork	Coill-tuirc (kílturk)	Boar-wood, Co. Fermanagh, anglic. Kilturk
.13	bull in a meadows	*trans.* Cluain Tarbh	Bull Meadow; N.E. Dublin district, site of *Brian Boru's defeat of Danes, 1014, anglic. Clontarf
.17	claimhis	claimhe (klavi)	itch, mange

		claimhiscín (klavishkín)	gnashing of teeth
.17	puddywhuck	Páid a mhic (pád' awik)	Pat my boy
.18	culothone	cúl- (kúl), *pfx.* tón (*tón*)	back-, rear-, retro- bottom, fundament, arse
		Caoi-tuinne (kítini)	Lamenting of the wave; place-name Cu- thon in *Macpherson's *Fingal* glossed as "mournful sound of waves"
		[cúl- *for* barra-	rear- for top-; see 254.33: berrathon]
.23	*Hurtreford*	Áth Cliath (áklíe)	Hurdle Ford; *Dublin
.24	*Parsuralia*	Piaras Ua Raghailligh (píres ú rayelí)	Piers des. of *Raghal- lach* ("[strong-]fore- armed")
.24	*ivanmore-*	mór (mór)	big, great; the Great
.31	*dawnybreak*	Domhnach (*correctly* Tamhnach) Broc (*d*ounokh/ *t*ounokh brok)	Badger Church/ Green-field; S. Dublin district, anglic. Don- nybrook
.32	*Aira*	Éire (ére)	Ireland
.34	*cromlin*	Crom-ghleinn (krumġlin)	Curved valley; S. Dub- lin district, anglic. Crumlin
.35	*artheynes*	Árd Aidhin (ár*d* ein)	*Aidhean's* (n. of 9th c. st.) Height; N.E. Dub- lin suburb with indus- trial school for boys, anglic. Artane
.36	*fullfour fivefirearms*	cúige (kúge)	"one-fifth": province; there are only four provinces
354.01–02	Shattamovick	mo mhic (muvik)	my son
.03	*doog at doorak*	deoch an dorais (d'ukh un *d*urish)	"drink of the door": parting drink

.06	Faun	*trans.* Oisín (ushín)	Fawn; son of *Fionn Mac Cumhail*
.06	Faun MacGhoul	Fionn Mac Cumhail (fin mok kúl)	Fair son of *Cumhal*; 3rd c. hero of saga cycle
.10	*mulattomilitiaman*	*trans.* Fianna	"Militia": 3rd c. standing army led by *Fionn Mac Cumhail*
.13	*Goll's*	Goll (gol)	Blind, masc. pers. n.; *Goll Mac Mórna* companion & rival of *Fionn Mac Cumhail*
.13	*gillie*	giolla (gili)	lad, servant
.15	*fonngeena*	fonn (foun) fonn-diadha (found'íye) faingín (fongín)	tune; desire; bottom "divine-tune": hymn tall useless girl
.15	*barney*	beárnach (bárnokh)	gap-toothed; peevish
.15	*brawl*	breágh (brá)	fine, handsome
.17	*Lanigan*	Ó Lonagáin (ó lonegáñ)	des. of *Lonagán* (dim. of *lon*, "blackbird")
.18	*mormor*	go mór mór (gu mórmór)	especially
.18	*blathrehoot*	bláth (blá) bladar (blader)	flower, blossom flattery, coaxing
.19	*fiannaship*	Fiannas (fíenes)	*Fiann*-ship; membership in 3rd c. standing army led by *Fionn Mac Cumhail*
.31	*gulling*	gall (goul)	foreigner
.31	*gells*	Gaedheal (gél)	Irishman, Scotsman
.33	*duff*	dubh (duv)	black
.33	*duff as a bettle*	ciaróg (kíróg)	"black-thing": bcetle
.34–35	*butagain budly . . . bodley*	bod (bud)	penis
355.08	*bud*	bod (bud)	penis
.15	*Be of the housed!*	Bí i do thost! (bí i du hust)	"Be in your silence": Be silent!

.19	arooned	a rún (arún)	my precious
.32	An-Lyph	Ean-Life (anlifi)	*Liffey-water; *Anna
356.03	Gow	gabha (gou)	smith
.17	sowansopper	Samhain (soun)	Autumn feast of the dead; November; All-hallowtide
.18	sodhe gudhe rudhe brodhe wedhe swedhe medhe	*appearance of I. spelling; no consistent sense* (só gú rú bró wé swé mé) sódh (só) bródh (bró)	"sowed good red bread with sweet mead" [?] turning dirt
357.04	Bismillafoulties	míle fáilte (míli fált'i)	thousand welcomes
.17	dovely	dubh (*d*uv)	black
.18	oreillental	Ó Raghailligh (ó rayelí)	des. of *Raghallach* ("[strong-]fore-armed"); anglic. O Reilly
.35	Flannagan	Ó Flannagáin (ó flanegáñ)	des. of *Flannagán* (dim. of *flann,* "ruddy")
358.12	bottery	bod (bu*d*)	penis
.19	Meschiameschianah	mise (mishi) meiseamh-nacht (meshúnokh*t*)	I, me (emphatic); I am judgment
.20	Perseoroyal	Piaras Ó Raghailligh (píres ó rayelí)	Piers des. of *Raghal-lach* ("[strong-]fore-armed")
.20	padar	paidir (pad'ir) Peadar (pa*d*er)	prayer; paternoster Peter
.20	madar	máthair (máher)	mother
.21	Ere	Ére (ére)	Ireland
.21	Iran	Éireann (érun), *g.*	[of] Ireland
.21	Amick amack amock	a mhic (avik) mac (mok) amach (amokh)	my son, my boy son outside

.22	mucktub	muc (muk)	pig, swine
.23	Fenegans	Ó Fionnagáin (ó finegáñ)	des. of *Fionnagán* (dim. of *Fionn*, "fair")
.25	baillybeacons	Baile (bolye)	Homestead; lighthouse, Howth Head, anglic. Baily
.27	baskatchairch	cearc (kyark)	hen
.31	O cara	a chara (a khore)	friend, my friend
.32	Agrah	a ghrádh (a ġrá)	love, my love
.34	slammocks	slamach (slomokh)	loose handful
359.02	toork	torc (*t*urk)	boar, hog
.03	taratoryism	Teamhar (t'our)	Prospective-hill; anc. royal capital, anglic. Tara
		toraidhe (*t*orí)	fugitive, robber
.03	orenore	óir (ór)	gold
		An Fheoir (unór)	The Brim; S. river, anglic. Nore
.05	Fintan	Fionntán (fin*t*án)	dim. of *Fionn*, "fair"; legendary *colonist, survivor of the Flood
.26	pinginapoke	pingin i póca (piñin i póke)	penny in a pocket
.26	Tory	toraidhe (*t*orí)	fugitive, robber
.26	Eeric	éiric (érik)	fine, ransom
.27	*Fearson*'s	Pharsúin (farsúñ)	of the parson
.28	Lucan	Leamhcán (loukán)	Producing marshmallows; W. Dublin suburb on Liffey
360.07	Heeny	Ó hÉanna (ó héne)	des. of *Éanna* (masc. pers. n.)
.08–09	wheckfoolthenairyans	Éircannaigh (érení)	Irish people
.09	peanas	péanach (pénokh)	malicious
.16	thorush	toras (*t*ures)	weariness
.26–27	O gui, O gui!	guidhe (gwí)	prayer, beseeching

.27	Salam, salms, salaum	salm (solem)	psalm, hymn
361.02	fairs fears	fear (far)	man
.05	guineases	Mag Aonghusa (mogénġesi)	son of *Aonghus* ("single-choice" [god of love]); anglic. Guinness
.07	tongue irish	*half-trans.* teanga Gaedhealach	Irish language
.07	may goh too	mé go tú (mé gu *tú*)	I to you
.07	Quicken	*trans.* luis	letter L
.07	aspen	*trans.* eabhadh	letter E
.07	ash	*trans.* nuin	letter N
.07	yew	*trans.* íodha	letter I
.08	willow	*trans.* sail	letter S
.08	broom	*trans.* oir	letter O
.08	oak	*trans.* dair	letter D
.07–08	[LENISOD]	le'n (len) Iosada (isi*d*e)	with the fem. pers. n.: Isolda
.08	for	*trans.* teithne [?]	furze; letter T
.08	you	*trans.* íodha [?]	yew; letter I
.11	Ingean	inghean (inyen)	daughter, girl
.11	mingen	miongáin (mingáñ), *g.*	of a seashell
.13	ovful	ubh (uv)	egg
.15	Poddy	bod (bu*d*)	penis
.15	pitted	pit (pit′)	vulva
.16	Kelly	Ó Ceallaigh (ó kyalí)	des. of *Ceallach* ("contention")
.16	Killykelly	Cill/Coill Uí Ceallaigh (kil/kíl íkhalí)	Church/Wood of the des. of *Ceallach* ("contention")
.20	Shillelagh	Síol Éalaigh (shílélí)	Progeny of *Éalach* ("swanlike" [?]); district, Co. Wicklow, noted for blackthorns (see 361.19)

.25	budkley	bod (bud)	penis
		clé (klé)	left (side)
		Ó Buachalla (ó búkheli)	des. of *Buachaill* ("boy"); anglic. Buckley
.25	boyne	Bóinn (bóñ)	(n. of goddess; from *bó*, "cow"); River *Boyne, scene of defeat of I. Jacobites by William III, 1690
.33	unrawil	rámhaille (ráwili)	delirium
.36	sowriegueuxers	samhradh (soure)	summer
362.02	Clandibblon	Clann Duibh-linn (kloun divlin)	Progeny/Race of a Black Pool; *Dublin
.03	burleys	Béarla (bérle)	English language
.05	nollcromforemost	crom (krum)	stooped, crouching; n. of anc. idol; *Humphrey
.05	camnabel	Caim-béal (kombél) cam (koum) na béil (nubél)	Wry-mouth; anglic. Campbell crooked of the mouth
.12	finn	fionn (fin)	fair
.22–23	yearin . . . yearin	Éirinn (érin), dat.	[to, for] Ireland
363.05	rann . . . rann	rann (roun)	verse, stanza
.05	keen	caoin (kín)	bewail, lament
.12	bann	bean (ban)	woman, wife
.19	bonnick lass	beannacht leat (banokht lat)	"a blessing with you": farewell
.35	barely	Béarla (bérle)	English language
364.08	Shaum Baum's	Seán Bán (shán bán)	White John; *Shaun
.09	bode	bod (bud)	penis
.09	shool	siubhal (shúl)	move, travel, march
.13	budsome	bod (bud)	penis
.15	gall	gall (goul)	foreigner

.19	Kinahaun	Ó Coin-neacháin (ó kinekháñ)	des. of *Coinneachán* (dim. of *conn*, "intelligence")
.21	Elin	Éirinn (érin), *dat.*	*L/R Interchange; [to, for] Ireland
.25	duvlin	Dubh-linn (*d*uvlin)	Black Pool; *Dublin
365.17	tarafs	tarbh (*t*orev)	bull
.19	barran	barrán (barán)	bite
		bearrán (byarán)	small bundle; annoyance
.22	thonther	tón (*t*ón)	bottom, arse
.24–25	Mac Gurk	Mag Cuirc (mogkirk)	son of *Corc* ("heart")
.25	O'Duane	Ó Dubháin (ó *d*úáñ)	des. of *Dubhán* (dim. of *dubh*, "black")
.26	MacElligut	Mac Uileagóid (mok ilegód')	son of Wilecot (double dim. of William)
.27	pud	bod (bu*d*)	penis
.32	weedeen	-ín (ín), *dim. suffx.*	little, darling
.36	folced	folc (fulk)	flood, downpour
366.09	buntad	bun (bun)	bottom
.11	fain	féin (fén)	self
.12	biguidd	guidhe (gwí)	pray, beseech
.17	Milcho	Miolchó (milkhó)	masc. pers. n.; master Patrick served as boy slave
.19	turk	torc (*t*urk)	boar, hog
.20	Jambuwel's	buail (búl)	beat, strike, defeat
.21	Terry Shimmyrag's	Tír na Simearóig (tírne shimeróg)	Land of the Shamrock
.28	sowill	samhail (souwil)	likeness, ghost
.32	Magongty	Mag Fhion-nachtaigh (mog inokhtí)	son of *Fionnachta* [*Fionn-shneachta*] ("fair-snow"); anglic. McGinty, etc.

			Mac an tSaoi (mokun*t*í)	son of the scholar; an- glic. McGinty
	.34	Whisht	thuist (hish*t*)	silence
367.11		Kullykeg	Tulach Beag (*t*ulokh beg)	Little Hill; anglic. Tullybeg
	.12	Dan Leary	Dún Laoghaire (dún líre)	*Laoghaire*'s ("calf- keeper") Fort; town & harbor directly S.E. of Dublin
	.22	fionnling	fionn-linn (finlin)	clear pool; *Dublin
	.22	dubhlet	dubh (*d*uv)	black; *Dublin
	.23	dun	donn (*d*oun)	brown
	.28	breide	bréid (bréd') Brighid (bríd')	canvas; rug; kerchief (from *brigh*, "strength"); fem. pers. n. goddess of poetry; st., patroness of I.
	.30	attaim	atáim (a*t*ám)	I am
	.32	kingcorrier	Cean Coradh (kyoun kure)	Weir Head; home of *Brian Boru on Shan- non River; anglic. Kincora
	.33	eyriewinging	Éire (ére)	Ireland
	.35	envery	inbhear (inver)	river-mouth, harbor, estuary
368.04		greatgrandgoster- fosters	gastaire (gos*t*eri)	tricky person
			gastar (gos*t*er)	uppishness
	.12	Monabella	Móin a' bile (mónebili)	Peat bog of the sacred tree
	.33	Tarpinacci	Ó Tarpaigh (ó *t*orpí)	des. of *Tarpach* ("sturdy"); anglic. Tarpey
	.33–34	Duggelduggel	Ó Dubhghaill (ó *d*úyil)	des. of *Dubhghall* ("black-foreigner," i.e., Dane)
369.01		tuffbettle	dubh (*d*uv) ciaróg (kíróg)	black "black-one": beetle

.09	Carolan	Ó Cearrbh-alláin (ó karwoláñ)	des. of *Cearrbhallán* (dim. of *Cearbhall*, "stag-cliff" [?])
.12	Doon	dún (*dún*)	fort
.12	Botham	bothán (buhán)	hut
.18	rudrik	Ruaidhrí (rúrí)	Norse *Rothrekr* ("fame-ruler"); n. introduced to I. by Vikings; n. of last high king
.26	Paullabucca	Poll an Phúca (poulafúke)	Hobgoblin's Hole, chasm on Liffey S.W. of Dublin, anglic. Poulaphooka
.29	Poulebec	Poll Beig (poul beg)	Little Hole; light-house, *Dublin Bay
.30	Tighe	Ó Taidhg (ó *t*eig)	des. of *Tadhg* ("poet")
.31	daremood's a grownian	Diarmaid is Gráinne (d'ír mid' is gráñi)	Freeman & Spear-point; hero & heroine of *Toraidheacht Dhiarmada agus Ghráinne*
370.07	Cobra	Cabragh (kobra)	Bad-lands; N. Dublin district anglic. Cabra
.08	Jeremy	Diarmaid (d'írmid')	Freeman; anglic. Jeremy; *Shem
.08	Kepin	Caoimhghin (kívǧin)	Comely-birth; fndr. of Glendalough, anglic. Kevin
.08	O'Keepers	Ó Caoimh (ó kív)	des. of *Caomh* ("comely"); anglic. O Keefe
		Ó Ciabhaigh (ó kíví)	des. of *Ciabhach* ("long-locks"); anglic. O Keevey
.15	Onamassofmancy-naves	naomh (név)	saint
.17	Getobodoff	bod (bu*d*)	penis
.18	diliskious	duileasc (*d*ilisk)	edible seaweed
		dílis (dílish)	own, special

.19	milisk	milis (milish) míolasc (mílask)	sweet desire
.19	dunlearies	Dún Laoghaire (dún líre)	*Laoghaire*'s ("calf-keeper") Fort; town & harbor directly S.E. of Dublin
.20	Kelly	Ó Ceallaigh (ó kyalí)	des. of *Ceallach* ("contention")
.20	Grimes	Ó Gréacháin (ó grékháñ)	des. of *Créachán* (dim. of *créach*, "blind")
.21	Phelan	Ó Faoláin (ó féláñ)	des. of *Faolán* (dim. of *faol*, "wolf")
.21	Mollanny	Ó Maoilean-aigh (ó mwélaní)	des. of *Maol-Sheanaigh* ("servant of [St.] *Seanach* ['prosperous']")
.21	O'Brien	Ó Briain (ó bríin)	des. of *Brian [Boru]
.21	MacAlister	Mac Alastair (mok alas*t*ir)	son of *Alastar*, masc. pers. n. from Gk. *Alexandros*
.21	Coyle	Mac Dhubh-ghaill (mokúgil)	son of *Dubhghall* ("black-foreigner," i.e., Dane)
.21	Hynes	Ó hEidhin (ó héyin)	des. of *Eidhean* ("ivy"); *Maolrunaidh Ó hEidhin*, 1st of this n., fell at Clontarf, 1014
.22	Traynor	Mac Tréinfhir (mok trénir)	son of *Tréanfhear* ("strong-man")
.22	Gilligan	Ó Giollagáin (ó giligáñ)	des. of *Giollagán* (dim. of *giolla*, "servant, lad")
.22	Goll	Goll (gol)	Blind; *Goll Mac Mórna*, companion & rival of *Fionn Mac Cumhail*, killer of *Cumhal*, *Fionn*'s father
.22	Gilligan-Goll	giolla-goillín (giligulín)	"tormentor-lad": the devil

.28	Lochlunn	Lochlainn (lokhlin)	Scandinavia, Norway
.28	gonlannludder	lann (loun)	space, floor
.30	Sockerson boy	Sasanach buidhe (sosenokh bwí)	yellow (derogatory epithet) Englishman
.34	onem	anam (onem) ainm (onim)	soul name
.34	maynoother	Magh Nuadhat (má nút)	*Nuadhat's* (3rd c. king of Leinster) Plain; Co. Kildare, anglic. Maynooth
.34	endnow	indiu (iñú)	today
.35	clandoilskins	Clann Dálaigh/ Dubhghaill (kloun dálí/dúġil)	Race of *Dálach* ("assemblist"), 8th in desc. from *Conall Gulbain*, son of *Niall Naoighiallach*: clan name of O Donnell of Donegal; *Uí Néill/of *Dubhghall* ("black-foreigner," i.e., Dane)
371.16	blarneying	Blárna (blárne)	Little-field; Co. Cork, anglic. Blarney
.16	sockson	Sasanach (sosenokh)	Englishman ("Saxon")
.22	Fingool	Fionn-gall (fingoul) Fine-Gall (finigoul) Fionnghal (finġal) Fionn Mac Cumhail (fin mok kúl)	Fair-foreigner, i.e., Norwegian Foreign-Kindred, N. Co. Dublin district, anglic. Fingal Fair-fight: Fingal, *Macpherson's n. for *Fionn Mac Cumhail* Fair son of *Cumhal*; 3rd c. hero of saga cycle
.22	MacKishgmard	Mac Cise[ach] (mok kish e/okh)	son of a wickerwork [pontoon]; *Dublin

.26	almaynoother	Magh Nuadhat	see 370.34
.33	Awaindhoo's	Abhainn-dubh (ouwin*dú*)	Black River
.34	Mullinguard	An Muileann Cearr (un mwilen kyar)	The Left-handed Mill; town, Co. Westmeath; anglic. Mullingar
.36–372.01	errindwards	Éire (ére)	Ireland
.02	londmear	méar (mér)	finger
.07	beauyne	Bóinn (bóñ)	(n. of a goddess, from *bó*, "cow") : Boyne River, scene of defeat of I. Jacobites by William III, 1690
.11	seanad	seanad (shane*d*)	senate
.14–15	kaillykailly	caill (keil) caillseach (keilshokh)	loss, damage; lose earwig
		céilidhe (kélí)	musical entertainment & dance
.15	kellykekkle	Ó Ceallaigh (ó kyalí)	des. of *Ceallach* ("contention")
.15	Brownhazelwood		see 135.13–14, 469.18
.16	dinnasdoolins	duine (*d*ini) daoine Dubh-linne (*d*ini *d*úlini)	person the people of Black Pool (*Dublin)
		Donnchadh Ó Dubhlainn (*d*unukhu ó *d*úlin)	Brown-warrior des. of *Dubhfhlann* ("black-ruddy"); anglic. Denis Doolin
.28	corry awen	corraidh abhainn (korí ouwin)	river weirs
		Garrdha Eoghain (gorye ówin)	*Eoghan*'s ("wellborn" *Shaun) Garden, Co. Limerick, anglic. Garryowen
.29	glowry	gleadhradh (glouru)	noise, clatter

.29	Brownaboy	Brian abú! (bríen abú)	Brian to victory!
		buidhe (bwí)	yellow; as epithet anglic. boy
.29	Fuinnninuinn's	Fionn (fin)	Fair
		fuin (fwin)	end, limit, west
		fuinneamh (fwinyev)	energy, vigor
		Ó Fionnáin (ó fináñ)	des. of *Fionnán* (dim. of *Fionn*, "fair")
.30	lyncheon	Ó Loingsigh (ó liñshí)	des. of *Loingseach* ("having to do with a fleet"); anglic. Lynch
.30	burgherbooh	buadh (búe)	victory
.30–31	Shanavan Wacht	Sean-bhean Bhocht (shane-van vokht)	Poor Old Woman: Ireland (poetic)
.31	Dorans	Ó Deóráin (ó d'óráñ)	des. of *Deóradhán* (dim. of *deóradh*, "exile, stranger")
.32	O'Ryne	Ó Rinn (ó riñ)	des. of *Reann* ("spear")
		Ó Riain (ó rín)	des. of *Rian* ("track")
.32	O'Rann	Ó Rinn (ó riñ)	des. of *Reann* ("spear")
		reann (ran)	spear
		rann (roun)	verse, stanza
.33	keener	caoin (kín)	bewail, lament
.36	Bothersby	bóthar (bóher)	road
373.05	Moherboher	bóthar mór (bóher mór)	highway
		Mothar (moher)	thicket; ruined fort; village, cliffs, Co. Clare, anglic. Moher
.14	magreedy	Mag Bhrádaigh (mogvrádí)	son of *Brádach* ("spirited"); anglic. MacGrady, etc.
.20	pairk	páirc (párk)	field
.23	Arderleys	árd (árd)	high

.25	Broree aboo!	Brugh Ríogh abú! (brúrí abú)	King's Palace (anc. royal capital of Munster in Co. Limerick; anglic. Bruree) to victory!
.30	Rorke	Ó Ruairc (ó rúrk)	des. of *Ruarc* (Norse *Hrothrekr*); W. *Breifne* is *Breifne Uí Ruairc*, anglic. Breffny O Rourke
.30	relly	Ó Raghailligh (ó rayelí)	des. of *Raghallach* ("[strong-]forearmed"); E. *Breifne* is *Breifne Uí Raghailligh*, anglic. Breffny O Reilly; see 099.26 etc.
374.06	Torkenwhite	torc(*t*urk)	boar, hog
.12	aglove	eagla (ogle)	fear
.15	Doughertys'	Ó Dochartaigh (ó dokher*t*í)	des. of *Dochartach* ("disobliging")
.21	Finnish Make Goal	Fionn Mac Cumhail (fin mok kúl) cúl (kúl)	Fair son of *Cumhal*; 3rd c. hero of saga cycle goal (in ball games)
.22	Namar	namá (nemá)	alone
.36	sagasand	Sasanach (sosenokh)	Englishman
375.03	Greevy	Mag Riabhaigh (mog ríví)	son of *Riabhach* ("brindled")
.23	Dalymount	Ó Dálaigh (ó *d*álí)	des. of Dálach ("assemblist"); anglic. Daly; Dalymount Park: Dublin soccer stadium
.23	Buckley's	Ó Buachalla (ó búkheli)	des. of *Buachaill* ("boy")
.24	Tara	Teamhar (t'our)	Prospective-hill; anc. royal capital
.29	Fummuccumul	Fionn Mac Cumhail (fin mok kúl) muc (muk)	Fair son of *Cumhal*; 3rd c. hero of saga cycle pig, swine

.29	graneen	Gráinnín (gráñín)	dim. of *Gráinne* ("grain/spearpoint") *Fionn*'s faithless fiancée, heroine of **Toraidheacht Dhiarmada agus Ghráinne*
.29	aveiled	aithmhéala (avéle)	regret, contrition
.32	Benn	beinn (ben)	peak, headland
.32	Bree	brí (brí)	hillside, headland
.32	tear	tír (tír)	land, country
.36	moya!	mar bh'eadh (morya)	as if it were so! (ironic interj.)
376.01–02	Ineen . . . MacKundred	*parody of* Gráinne's *genealogy:* Inghean Cormaic Mhic Áirt Mhic Cuinn Céadcathach	Daughter of *Cormac* son of *Art* son of *Conn* Hundred-fighter
.01	Ineen	inghean (inyen)	daughter; Miss
.01	MacCormick	Mac Cormaic (mok kurmik)	son of *Cormac* ("chariot-son")
.01	MacCoort	Mac Áirt (mokárt')	son of *Árt* ("stone/bear")
		Mac Cuarta (mok kúrte)	son of *Cuairt* ("circuit, tour"); anglic. Mac-Coort
.01	MacConn	Mac Cuinn (mok kin)	son of *Conn* ("intelligence")
		Mac Míolchon (mok mílkhon)	son of *Míolchú* ("greyhound"), anglic. Mac-Conn
.01	O'Puckins	Ó Poicín (ó pukín) poc (puk)	des. of *Poicín* ("little he-goat") sharp blow
.02	MacKundred	Mac an Druaidh (mok un *drúí*)	son of the druid
.01–02	MacConn O'Puckins MacKundred	Conn Céadcathach	*Conn* ("intelligence") Hundred-Fighter 2nd–3rd c. high king,

grandfather of *Cormac Mac Áirt*, high king in *Fionn*'s time

.03	abog	bog (bug) go bog (gu bug)	soft softly
.08	Clontarf	Cluain Tarbh (klún *t*orev)	Bull Meadow; N.E. Dublin district, site of *Brian Boru's defeat of Danes, 1014
.08	O'Bryan	Ó Briain (ó bríin)	des. of *Brian [Boru]
.09	MacBruiser	Mac (mok)	son [of]
.08–09	O'Bryan MacBruiser	Brian Bóroimhe (bríen bórivi)	Brian of the Tribute, anglic. *Brian Boru, high king killed defeat- ing Danes at Clontarf, 1014
.10–11	doatereen	-ín (ín), *dim suffx.*	little, darling
.11	Delphin	Dealbhna (d'alvne)	[progeny of *Lughaidh*] *Dealbhaodh*; N. Dublin co. stream, anglic. Delvin
.16	demnye	Demni (d'emní)	Assurance [?]; infant n. of Fionn Mac Cum- hail
.17	Neffin	Néifin (néfin)	"sanctuary" [?]; mtn., Co. Mayo; anglic. Nephin
.18	Gormagareen	gorm (gurum)	blue
.19	arrah	ara (ore)	deprecatory interj.
.21	Poghue! Poghue! Poghue!	póg (póg)	kiss
.23	Huggins	Ó hAodhag- áin (ó hégáñ)	des. of *Aodhagán* (dim. of *aodh*, "fire")
.26	Skerry	sceire (shkeri)	reef
.27	Badbols	Bodhmall (bómoul)	Deaf-slow; one of *Fionn Mac Cumhail*'s nurses
.27	the Grey One	*trans.* Liathluachra	Grey of Frost [*or*, Hoar-Frost's]; one of

			Fionn Mac Cumhail's nurses
.30	Morialtay	Ó Muirche-artaigh (ó mwirkhartí)	des. of *Muircheartach* ("navigator") anglic. Moriarty, etc.
.32	brogue	bróg (bróg) barróg (beróg)	shoe defect in speech
.32	Clanruckard	Clann Rio-cáird (kloun rikárd')	Progeny of Rickard; clan n. assumed by Scottish family Sinclair
.33	Fenn . . . Fenn . . . Fenns	Fionn (fin) *trans.* eanach, eanaigh	Fair fen, fens; *Anna
.34	croonacreena	crú na chrí-onna (krúna khríne)	the old man's gore
.34	Fisht!	thoist (hisht)	silence
377.01	Angus! Angus! Angus!	Aonghus (énġus)	Single-choice; god of love
.04	Mawgraw	mo ghrádh (muġrá) Mag Raith (mogra)	my love son of *Mac Raith* ("son of grace"); anglic. Magrath, Magraw, etc.
.05	a gull	eagal (ogel)	fear
.06	Lannigan's	Ó Lonagáin (ó lonegáñ)	des. of *Lonagán* (dim. of *lon*, "blackbird")
.07	Shallburn	Síol-Brain (shílbrin)	Progeny of *Bran* ("raven"); tribal land Co. Wexford, anglic. Shelburne
.10	schlymartin	slighe (shlí)	way
.10	sloomutren	sluagh (slú)	host, army
.16	*Hall of Alum*	Almhain (alúñ)	Whitened (said to have been rubbed with a substance called *Alma*); hill, Co. Kildare, HQ of *Fianna* led by *Fionn Mac Cumhail*; anglic. Hill of Allen

.16	finnecies	fionn (fin) Ó Fionn- ghusa (ó finġesi)	fair des. of *Fionnghus* ("fair-choice"), anglic. Finnessy
.19	brideen	Brighdín (bríd'ín)	dim. of *Brighid*, fem. pers. n. (from *brigh*, "strength"); anglic. Bridget
.19–20	Alannah	a leanbh (a lanev)	child, my child
.21	gallus	geal (gal)	bright
.22	Dovlen	Dubh-linn (*d*uvlin)	Black Pool; *Dublin
.22	Rathfinn	Rath Finn (ráfin)	*Fionn*'s ("Fair") Fort
.25	gosson	gasán (gosán) garsún (gorsún)	"stalk": boy boy
.27	Shonny Bhoy	Seón Buidhe (shón bwí)	Yellow John: John Bull; *Shaun
.27	Poshtapengha	Post pingne (pus*t* piñine)	penny-post
.35	dathe	Dáithí (*d*áhí)	Swiftness, masc. pers. n.; last unbaptized high king
.36	Dinnin	dionn (din) Ó Duinnín (ó *d*inín)	fort des. of *Duinnín* (dim. of *donn*, "brown") anglic. Dinneen (n. of com- piler of I. dictionary)
378.01	dannies . . . dennises	Domhnall (*d*ónel) Donnchadh (*d*unukhu)	World-mighty; masc. pers. n. anglic. Daniel Brown-warrior; masc. pers. n. anglic. Denis
.06	Arrorsure	ara (ore)	deprecatory interj.
.06	Arrahland	ara (ore) ara (ore) Éire (ére)	deprecatory interj. one usually responsible for something Ireland
.10	-dalluck-	dall (*d*oul) dallbhach (*d*oulwokh)	blind mental blindness; puz- zledness

		dálach (dálach)	appropriate for holding assemblies
.10	-truckall-	trucail (trukil)	cart, sidecar
.13	Soideric O'Cunnuc	Sitreac (shitrok)	Sygtryg, 11th c. Danish king of Dublin
		Ó Conn- achtaigh (ó kunukhtí)	des. of *Connachtach* ("Connachtman")
		Ruaidhrí Ó Conchobhair (rúrí ó konukher)	*Ruaidhrí* des. of *Conchobhair* ("high-will"), anglic. Roderic O Connor, last high king
.19	agus	agus (ogus)	and
.25	Shea	Ó Séaghdha (ó shéya)	des. of *Séaghdha* ("stately")
.25–26	me gurk	Mag Cuirc (mog kwirk)	son of *Corc* ("heart"); anglic. McGurk
.26	like os	Oisdealbh (ushd'alv)	shaped like the god *Os* ("deer"); masc. pers. n.; ancestor of Costelloes
.28	drippindhrue gayleague	'tuigeann tú Gaedhealg? (tigen tú gélg)	do you understand Irish?
.31	brogue	barróg (beróg)	defect in speech
379.01	Knockcastle	Caisleán an Cnuca (kashlán aknuke)	Castle of the Hill, W. of Phoenix Park, anglic. Castleknock; site of battle at which *Goll Mac Mórna* killed *Cumhal*, *Fionn*'s father
.01	Muck!	muc (muk)	pig, swine
.03	Chiggenchugger's	'tuigeann tú (tigen tú)	do you understand; you understand
.10	Carlow	Ceatharlach (kaherlokh)	Quadruple-lake; S.E. co. & town
.11	Aerian's	Éireann (érun), *g.*	[of] Ireland
.15	Idas	Íde (íde)	Thirst; fem. pers. n.

.16	Nessies	Neasa (nase)	Nearest [?]; fem. pers. n.
.16	Phook!	phúca (fúke)	hobgoblin
.28	Gorteen	Goirtín (gert'ín)	Little tilled-field; n. of many villages
.31	Megantic	Mag Fhinn-eachtaigh (mog inokhtí)	son of *Fionnshneachta* ("fair-snow"), anglic. McGinty
		Mac an tSaoi (mok un tí)	son of the sage; anglic. McGinty
.36	Keyhoe	Mac Eochadha (mokyókhu)	son of *Eochaidh* ("horse-man"); anglic. Keogh
.36	Danelly	Ó Donnghaile (ó dounyeli)	des. of *Donnghal* ("brown-valor")
380.05	Malincurred	Malainn (malin)	Hill-brow; N.-most point in I., Co. Donegal, anglic. Malin
.09	Glenfinnisk	Gleann Finn-uisce (gloun finishki)	Clear-water Valley [*Fionn-uisce*, anglic. Phoenix]
.12	Roderick O'Conor	Ruaidhrí Ó Conchobhair	*Ruaidhrí* (Norse *Hrothrekr*, "fame-ruler") des. of *Conchobhar* ("high-will"), last high king (12th c.)
.21	Taharan	Teamhar (t'our)	Prospective-hill; anc. royal capital; anglic. Tara
.22	Arth Mockmorrow Koughenough	Árt Mac Murchadha Caomhánach (árt mok murukhu kévánokh)	Bear/Stone son of *Murchadh* ("sea-warrior") fosterling of *Caomhán* (dim. of *caomh*, "comely") [*Shaun]; anglic. Art MacMurrough Kavanagh, 14th c. king of Leinster; agnomen *Caomhánach* replaced original surname among dess. of *Domhnall Caomhánach*, son of *Diarmaid Mac Murchadha* [*Shem], 11th c.

			king of Leinster who invited Anglo-Norman invasion
.22–23	of the leathered leggions	na gCóchall Croicionn	of the leather cloaks; agnomen of *Muircheartach*, high king, 941
.31	Nolan's	Ó Nualláin (ó núláñ)	des. of *Nuallán* (dim. of *nuall*, "noble")
.33	Roderick O'Conor		see 380.12
381.02	McCarthy's mare	Mac Cárthaigh Mór (mok kárhí mór)	Great son of *Cárthach* ("loving"); *Mac Cárthaigh Mór* is head of senior branch of McCarthys, chief family of the *Eoghanacht* (dess. of *Eoghan Mór*; *Shaun)
.05	Parthalonians	Párthalónaigh (páralóní)	followers of *Parthalón*, 2nd legendary *colonist
.05	Firbolgs	Fir-Bolga (firbulge)	Bags Men; 3rd-last prehistoric *colonists
.06	Tuatha de Danaan	Tuatha Dé Danaan (túhe dé donon)	Folk of the Goddess *Dana*; 2nd-last prehistoric *colonists; a supernatural race, probably the dead
.06	Clane	Clochán (klokhán)	Stepping-stones; common place-name, anglic. Clahane, Clane, etc.
.12	Leary	Ó Laoghaire (ó líri) Laoghaire (líre)	des. of *Laoghaire* ("calf-keeper") Calf-keeper; son of *Niall Naoi-ghiallach*; high king at Patrick's arrival
.12	Brady's	Mac Brádaigh (mok brádí)	son of *Brádach* ("spirited")
.14	Macclefield's	Mac Giolla Faoil (mok gili fwíl)	son of *Giolla Faoil* (servant of *Faol*, "wolf")

.14	Reillys	Ó Raghailligh (ó rayelí)	des. of *Raghallach* ("[strong-]fore-armed")
.16	Midleinster	Midhe (mí)	Middle; anc. royal province, now co., N. & W. of Dublin, anglic. Meath
		Laighin (lein)	Lance; E. province, anglic. Leinster
.19	MacGuiney's	Mac Géibheannaigh (mok géení)	son of *Géibheannach* ("fettered")
		Mag Aonghusa (mogénġesi)	son of *Aonghus* ("single-choice" [god of love]); anglic. Guinness, McGuinness
.22	blurney	Blárna (blárne)	Little Field; Co. Cork, anglic. Blarney
.22	Cashelmagh	Caisealmagh (kashelmá)	Stone-fort Plain
.22	Clare	Clár (klár)	Level; frequent place-name element (but *not* Co. Clare)
.23	*todue*	indiu (iñú)	today
.23	*todie*	indé (iñé)	yesterday
.25	Roderick O'Conor	Ruaidhrí Ó Conchobhair	see 380.12
.25	arrah	ara (ore)	deprecatory interj.
.29	wishawishawish	mhuise (wishi)	well, indeed (interj.)
.30	sliggymaglooral	slíogach (slígokh)	smooth, sleek, fawning
		Mag Labhraidh (moglourí)	son of *Labhraidh* ("spokesman"); anglic. Magloory, etc.
382.03	Guiness's	Mag Aonghusa (mogénġesi)	son of *Aonghus* ("single-choice" [god of love]); anglic. Guinness
.05	O'Connell's	Ó Conaill (ó kunil)	des. of *Conall* ("high-powerful")

.11	Kaven's	Ó Caomháin (ó kéváñ)	des. of *Caomhán* (dim. of *caomh*, "comely"); anglic. Kevans, Cavan
		Caomhán (kéván)	dim. of *caomh*, ("comely"); n. of 15 I. sts.; anglic. Kevan
.12	MacMichael	Mac Giolla Mhichil (mok gilevikhil)	son of *Giolla Mhichil* ("servant of Michael")
.21	hone	ochón (ukhón)	alas
.22	Faugh MacHugh O'Bawlar	Fiach Mac Aodha Ó Broin (fíkh moké ó brin)	Raven son of Fire des. of Raven; anglic. Fiach Mac Hugh O Byrne, 16th c. chief of Wicklow O Byrnes who terrorized English-held Dublin
.22	Faugh . . . O'Bawlar	Fág an bealach (fág un byalokh)	Leave the way, clear the way
.22	O'Bawlar	Balor (boler)	chief of Fomorian pirates on Tory Is.
.27	Liff	Life (lifi)	*Liffey River
.30	Starloe	Ceatharlach (kaherlokh)	Quadruple-lake; S.E. co. & town, anglic. Carlow
383.18	kuss	cos (kus)	foot
384.04	-sucker-	socair (suker)	calm, steady, at rest
.05	Moykle	Magh Caol (mákíl)	Narrow Plain, Co. Fermanagh, anglic. Moykeel
		Sruth na Maoile (srune mwíle)	Sea-stream of the Bald-headland; sea between I. & Scotland, anglic. Moyle (poetic)
.06	four maaster waves	Tonn Chlíodhna, Rudhraighe, Scéine, Tuaithe	see 254.02

.06	Erin	Éirinn (érin), *dat.*	[to, for] Ireland
.08	Lyons	Ó Laighin (ó lein)	des. of *Laighean* ("lance")
.08	four waves		see 383.06, 254.02
.09	bausnabeatha	bás na beathadh (bás nu bahe)	the death of life
		bás ná beatha (bás ná bahe)	death nor life
.11	Tarpey	Ó Tarpaigh (ó *t*orpí)	des. of *Tarpach* ("sturdy")
.14	MacDougall	Mac Dubhghaill (mok *d*úġil)	son of *Dubhghall* ("black-foreigner," i.e., Dane)
.19	luistening	luis (lish)	quicken bush; letter L
.21	*colleen bawn	cailín bán (kolín bán)	"white" (pretty) girl
.22	oscar	Oscar (usker)	Champion; son of *Oisín*, grandson of *Fionn*
.23	Gaelic	Gaedhealach (gélokh)	Irish, native
.23	champion	*trans.* Oscar	see 384.22
.29	bulbubly	bolb (bulub)	caterpillar
.34	poghue	póg (póg)	kiss
.34	*Arrah-na-poghue	ara na bpóg (ore nu bóg)	one given to kissing
385.01	Cullen's	O Cuileáin (ó kwiláñ)	des. of *Cuileán* ("whelp")
		Ó Cuilinn (ó kwilin)	des. of *Cuileann* ("holly")
.01	Cullen's barn	cailín bán	see 384.21
.03–04	Arrah-na-pogue	ara na bpóg	see 384.34
.07	O'Clery	Ó Cléirigh (ó klérí)	des. of *Cléireach* ("clerk, cleric"); surname of 3 of the *"Four Masters"
.15	Boris O'Brien	Brian Bóroimhe (bríen bórivi)	Brian of the Tribute, anglic. *Brian Boru, high king killed defeat-

			ing Danes at Clontarf, 1014
		Ó Briain (ó bríin)	des. of *Brian [Boru]
.15	Clumpthump	Cluain Tarbh (klún torev)	Bull Meadow; N.E. Dublin district, site of *Brian Boru's defeat of Danes, 1014; anglic. Clontarf
.22	Arrah-na-poghue	ara na bpóg	see 384.34
.32	poghuing	póg (póg)	kiss
.36	Ossian	Oisín (ushín)	Fawn; son of *Fionn Mac Cumhail*; *Macpherson's version of the n.
386.06	MacDougall	Mac Dubhghaill	see 384.14
.20	O'Clery's	Ó Cléirigh	see 385.07
.22	Dana	Dana (done)	eponymous goddess of *Tuatha Dé Danann*, goddess of the dead; *Anna
.22	Dana O'Connell	Domhnall Ó Conaill (dónel ó kunil)	World-mighty des. of High-powerful; anglic. Daniel O Connell
.24	Bootersbay . . . Battersby	bóthar (bóher)	road; anglic. Booter- (Booterstown, Dublin), -batter (Stonybatter, Dublin)
.26	Hoggin	Ó hAodhagáin (ó hégáñ)	des. of *Aodhagán* (dim. of *aodh*, "fire")
.27	tailturn horseshow	Aonach Tailtean (énokh tolt'in)	*Tailte*'s Fair: annual August games in honor of *Tailte*, Firbolg chieftainess, foster-mother of *Lugh*; recently revived; site anglic. Teltown
.33	onasmuck	muc (muk)	pig, swine
387.01	the Curragh	Cuirreach Life	Moor/Racecourse of the *Liffey [Plain]

		(kwirokh lifi)	anglic. the Curragh of Kildare
.06	gallowglasses	gallóglach (goulóglokh)	"foreign-youth": heavy-armed I. foot soldier
.09	Strathlyffe	Srath-Life (sralifi)	*Liffey-Holm; *Dublin, *Anna
.14	Lyons	Ó Laighin	see 384.08
.18	Momonian	Muimhneach (mwínokh)	of Munster (S. province)
.19	Lally	Ó Maola-laidh (ó mwélalí)	des. of *Maolaladh* ("speckled chief")
.23	Casemate	Mac Ásmuint (mokás-mwint')	son of *Ásmund* (Norse *Asmundr*); anglic. Casemate
.28	Cornyngwham	Ó Cuinneag-áin (ó kunigáñ)	des. of *Cuinneagán* (dim. of *Conn*, "intelligence"); anglic. Cunningham
.29	Erin	Éirinn (érin), *dat.*	[to, for] Ireland
		Árann (árun), *g.*	[of a] Kidney; islands off Co. Galway, anglic. Aran Islands
.30	suir	Siuir (shúr)	River, Water; S. river, anglic. Suir; by folk confused with *síor*, "everlasting"
.31	Saman	Samhain (soun)	winter feast of the dead; November; All-hallows
		sámhán (sáwán)	doze, swoon
388.01	darras	doras (*d*urus)	door
.02	Kram	crom (krum)	bent, stooping; n. of anc. idol; *Humphrey
.06	Fin	Fionn (fin)	Fair
.14	Kevin	Caoimhghin (kívġin)	Comely-birth; fndr. of monastic settlement at *Gleann-dá-loch* ("Two-lake valley"), S. of Dublin; *Shaun

.15	Dona	dona (*d*une) Dana (*d*one)	wretched, miserable eponymous goddess of *Tuatha Dé Danann*, god- dess of the dead
.17	Clunkthurf	Cluain Tarbh (klún *t*orev)	Bull Meadow; N.E. Dublin district, site of *Brian Boru's defeat of Danes, 1014, anglic. Clontarf
.17	Cabinhogan	Ó hÓgáin (ó hógáñ)	des. of *Ógán* ("youth"): uncle of *Brian Boru
.23	poghuing	póg (póg)	kiss
.25–26	Arrah-na-Poghue	ara na bpóg	see 384.34
.27	Brian	Brian	*Brian Boru
.27	Bride	Brighid (bríd′)	fem. pers. n. (from *brigh*, "strength") god- dess of poetry; st., pa- troness of I.; anglic. Bridget
.33	Bockleyshuts	Ó Buachalla (ó búkheli) Ó Bachlaigh (ó bokhlí)	des. of *Buachaill* ("boy"); anglic. Buckley des. of *Bachlach* ("husbandman"); anglic. Bockley
.34	gerachknell	gearrach (gyarokh) gearrchaile (gyarekhili)	shortcut girl 8–16 yrs. old
.34	Lyons	Ó Laighin	see 384.08
389.04–05	Eringrowback	Éire go bráth (ére gu brá)	Ireland until Judg- ment
.05	Ulcer	Uladh (ule)	Ulster, N. province
.05	Moonster	Mumha[n] (mún)	Munster, S. province
.05	Leanstare	Laighin (lein)	Leinster, E. province
.05	Cannought	Connachta (kunukh*t*e)	Connacht, W. prov- ince
.06	Erryn	Éirinn (érin), *dat.*	[to, for] Ireland

.06–07	Killorcure . . . Killthemall . . . Killeachother . . .	Cill (kil)	Church; anglic. Kil-, *Kill- in about 2,700 place-names
	Killkelly	Coill (kíl)	Wood; anglic. Kil-, *Kill- in about 700 place-names
.07	Killkelly	Ó Ceallaigh (ó kyalí)	des. of *Ceallach* ("contention"); anglic. Kelly
.12	Bambam's	Banba (bonbe)	Ireland (poetic) [n. of *Tuatha Dé Danann* queen]
.18	MacDougall	Mac Dubhghaill	see 384.14
.27	dullokbloon	dallbhach (*d*oulwokh) dallóg (*d*oulóg)	puzzledness, crazedness blindman's buff
.27	rodolling	dall (*d*oul)	blind
.27–28	olosheen	oisín (ushín) Oisín (ushín)	fawn son of *Fionn Mac Cumhail*
.28	Anumque	anam (onem)	soul
.32	ag	ag (eg)	at, with, by
.34	Lally	Ó Maolalaigh	see 387.19
390.03	Lally	Ó Maolalaigh	see 387.19
.03	Gosterstown	gastaire (gos*t*ire) gasta (gos*t*e)	tricky person cunning
.04	Lagener	Lagán (logán)	dim. of *Lag*, "hollow"; N.E. river anglic. Lagan
.04	Locklane	Loch Léin (lokhlén)	*Léan*'s (masc. pers. n. of anc. artificer: "Loin") Lake; chief lake at Killarney, anglic. Lough Leane
		Lochlainn (lokhlin)	Scandinavia, Norway
.07	Skelly	Ó Scalaighe (ó skalí)	des. of *Scalaighe* ("crier")
,09	bohereen	bóthairín (bóhirín)	"little road": lane

.09	Mahmullagh	Magh-mullaigh (mámulí)	Plain of the hillock
.10	Mullarty	Ó Maoil Earca (ó mwél arke)	des. of *Maol Earca* ("servant of *Earc* ['animal']"); anglic. Mullarkey
		Ó Maoil Chárthaigh (ó mwél-khárhí)	des. of *Maol Chárthach* ("servant of *Cárthach* ['loving']")
.11	Duignan	Ó Duibh-geannáin (ó *d*úígyanáñ)	des. of *Dubhgeannán* (dim. of *Dubhceann*, "black-head"); one of the *"Four Masters" (see 349.24)
.13	Tarpey	Ó Tarpaigh	see 384.11
.24	foretolk	tolca (*t*ulke)	flood, torrent, wave
.25	Burrymecarott	Baile Mic Gearóid (bolye mic garód')	Town of the Son of Gerald [i.e., Fitzgerald], near Belfast, anglic. Ballymacarret
.29	Dalkymount	Dealg-inis (d'alginish)	Thorn Island; S.E. Dublin suburb; Norsified Dalkey
.31	Kunut	Connachta (kunukh*t*e)	Race of *Conn* (masc. pers. n., "intelligence"), W. province; anglic. Connacht, Connaught
.31	haryman	Eireamhán (erewán)	coleader of Celtic *colonization
.32	Koombe	Cúm (kúm)	Hollow; S. Dublin slum, anglic. the Coombe
.35	Carpery	Cairbre (karbri)	Charioteer; masc. pers. n. of many I. kings
.35	Fins	Fionn (fin)	Fair
391.03	Arrahnacuddle	ara na [cuddle] (ore nu [cuddle])	one given to [cuddling]

		ara na chodalta (ore nu khu*del*te)	one given to sleeping
.04	clan	clann (kloun)	progeny
.04	Dougals	Dubhghaill (*dúġil*)	of *Dubhghall* ("black-foreigner," i.e., Dane)
.04	Scuitsmand	scuit(skut')	excitement, fuss
.05	dinna	duine (*d*ini)	person
.15	nolandslan	Ó Nualláin (ó núláñ)	des. of *Nuallán* (dim. of *nuall*, "noble"); anglic. Nolan
.21	bronnanoleum	bron (bron) brón (brón)	raven grief, sorrow
.30	Rosse	rásaidhe (rásí)	wandering woman, jilt; gipsy
.33	Sweainey	Mac Suibhne (mok swíñi)	son of *Suibhne* ("well-going")
.33	Cailcainnin	cál ceann- fhionn (kál kyanin)	white-head cabbage: dish of cabbage & potatoes dressed with butter
392.04	Connachy	Mac Dhonnchaidh (mok onukhí) Connachtach (kunukh*t*ukh)	son of *Donnchadh* ("brown-warrior"), anglic. MacConnachie Connachtman
.08	MacCawley's	Mac Amhlaoibh (mokoulév)	son of *Amhlaoibh* (Norse *Ólafr*); *Humphrey; anglic. Macauley, MacCawley, etc.
.15	Achoch	eachach (akhokh)	horseman; abounding in horses
.17	Aran	Árann (árun), *g*.	[of a] Kidney; islands off Co. Galway, anglic. Aran
.19–20	perigrime	Cúchoig- críche (kúkh- igkríkhi)	Hound-of-the-border, masc. pers. n. latinized *Peregrinus* ("one-who-goes-around," i.e., "borders"), anglic. Peregrine; n. of one of *Four Masters

.24	geasa	geasa (gase)	magical injunctions (tabus)
.27	Iren	Éire (ére)	Ireland
.30	Duna	dúna (dúne)	forts; fort's
.30	Duna O'Cannell	Domhnall Ó Conaill (dónel ó kunil)	World-mighty des. of High-powerful; anglic. Daniel O Connell
.32	Lynch	Ó Loingsigh (ó liñshí)	des. of Loingseach ("having to do with a fleet")
.33	dilisk	duileasc (dilesk)	edible seaweed
393.05	Cunningham	Ó Cuinneagáin (ó kunegáñ)	des. of Cuinneagán (dim. of Conn, "intelligence")
.09	Hungerford	Áth Cliath (áklíe)	Hurdle Ford; *Dublin
.10	Finnan	Fionnán (finán)	dim. of Fionn ("fair")
.24	oves	ubh (uv)	egg
.27–28	Shandon	Sean-dún (shandún)	Old fort; townland, Co. Cork
.29	knockneeghs	Loch nEachach (lokh nakhokh) cnoc (knuk)	Eachach's ("horserich") Lake; largest lake in I.; anglic. Lough Neagh hill; anglic. Knock- in place-names
.32	oerkussens	cos, cosa (kus, kuse)	foot, feet
394.10	rathure's	Rath-úir (rá úr) [?]	Fort of slaughter
.11	bawneen	báinín (báñín)	flannel; white flannel smock worn by peasants
.15–16	Foehn again	Ó Fionnagáin (ó finegáñ)	des. of Fionnagán (dim. of Fionn, "fair")
.18	Lally	Ó Maolalaigh	see 387.19
.18	Roe	Ruadh (rúe)	red

.22	coolun dare	cúilfhionn deas (kúlin d'as)	pretty fair-hair[ed girl]
.26	Aithne	aithne (ani)	commandment; recognition, acquaintance with
		Eithne (eni)	Kernel; fem. pers. n. (of mother of *Colmcille); anglic. Annie; *Anna
.26	Meithne	Eithne meith- (me), *pfx.*	as above weak-, slight-, pliable-
.26	Aithne Meithne	*English spelled as I.* (ani meni)	any man he eeny meeny
.29	Huber	Éibhear (éver)	coleader of Celtic *colonists, king of S.I. until killed by his brother
.29	Harman	Eireamhón (erawón)	coleader of Celtic *colonists, king of N.I. until he killed his brother & became 1st high king of all I.
.34	Errin	Éirinn (érin), *dat.*	[to, for] Ireland
395.03	MacGolly	Mac Amhlaoibh (mokoulév)	son of *Amhlaoibh* (Norse *Ólafr*); *Humphrey
.15	shee shee	sidhe (shí)	fairy
.24	poghue	póg (póg)	kiss
.25	shee shee	sidhe	see 395.15
396.03	Alris!	Arís! (arísh)	Again!
397.02	owneirist	Éire (ére)	Ireland
.05	girleen bawn asthore	cailín bán a stór (kolín bán as*t*ór)	my precious pretty girl
.05	galore	go leór (gulór)	enough, plenty
.12	magrees	mo chroidhe (mukhrí)	[of] my heart
.21	Lyons	Ó Laighin	see 384.08

.22	ghosses	gas (gos)	stalk; boy
.25	magories	Mac Gothraidh (mok gorí)	son of Godfrey
.26	caschal	caiseal (kashel)	stone fort
		Cáisc (káshk)	Easter (Latin *pascha*; *P/K Split)
.26–27	caschal pandle	*P/K Split	paschal candle
.31	Senchus Mor	Seanchas Mór (shane-khus mór)	Great Register: corpus of early I. law
.34	Lally	Ó Maolalaigh	see 387.19
.36	Roe	Ruadh (rúe)	red
.36	O'Mulcnory	Ó Maol Chonaire (ó mwél khunere)	des. of *Maolchonaire* ("follower of *Conaire* ['high-care']"); anglic. O Mulconry; *Fear-feasa Ó Maolchonaire* was one of the *Four Masters
398.01	Conry	Mac Conraoi (mok konré)	son of *Cúraoi* ("hound of the plain")
.01	Conry ap Mul	*fake Welsh*: Mac Maol Chonaire	distortion of O Mulconry; see 397.36
.01–02	Mac Gregory	Mac Greagair (mok greger)	son of Gregory
.02	de Wyer	Ó Dubhuidhir (ó dwíyir)	des. of *Dubhodhar* ("black-pale"); anglic. Dwyer, etc.
.03	scullogues	scológ (skulóg)	male farm-servant; yoeman
.05	Eren	Éireann (érun), *g.*	[of] Ireland
.05	Gowan	Mac an Ghabhann (mokun ġouwen)	son of the smith
		Ó Ghabhann (ó ġouwen)	des. of a smith

.06	Gawin	Ó Gábhain (ó gáwin)	des. of *Gábhadhán* (dim. of *gábhadh*, "want, need, danger")
.15	Peregrine	Cúchoig-críche	n. of one of the *Four Masters: *Cúchoigcríche Ó Cléirigh*, anglic. Peregrine O Clery; see 392.19–20
.15	Farfassa	Fear-feasa (farfase)	Man of knowledge; sage; *Fearfeasa Ó Maolchonaire*, anglic. Farfassa O Mulconry, one of the *Four Masters; see 397.36 [*Mícheál* & *Conaire Ó Cléirigh* were the other two Masters]
.16	Fionnachan	Fionnachán (finekhán)	dim. of *Fionn* ("fair")
.21	thoh	toth (*to*)	female; female organs
.23	Senchus Mor	Seanchas Mór	see 397.31
.29	Lambeg	Leamh-beig (lavbeg)	Little Elm; town S. of Belfast
.30	Lombog	lom (loum) bog (bug)	bare soft
.34	*galore*	go leór (gulór)	enough, plenty
.34	*girleen*	-ín (ín), *dim. suffx.*	little, darling
399.03	*Dingle*	Daingean (*dañin*)	Stronghold; town, Co. Kerry
.05	*curragh*	curach (kurokh)	light boat made of canvas
.09	*Yerra*	a Dhia ara (yare)	O God well! (expostulation)
.09	*grogram grey*	gruagán gré (grúgán gré)	grey-hairdye hue; in saying: *gruagán gré dath ná tréigeann*, "grey-hairdye hue, a color that doesn't fade"
.13	*machree*	mo chroidhe (mukhrí)	[of] my heart

.14	*Balbriggan*	Baile Breag-áin (bolye bragáñ)	*Breacán*'s (dim. of *breac*, "spotted") Town, N. Co. Dublin (textile mills)
.15	*Wisha*	mhuise (wishi)	well, indeed (interj.)
.18	*acushla*	a chúisle (akhúshle)	my pulse (endearment)
.25	*Cong*	Conga (kuñge)	Strait; monastic retreat of *Ruaidhrí Ó Conchobhair*, last high king, anglic. Cong, Co. Mayo; jeweled processional cross is now in National Museum
.28	*Bohermore*	bóthar mór (bóher mór)	highway
403.02	kater	ceathair (kahir)	four
.16	dhove's	dubh (*d*uv)	black
.21	speckled church	*trans.* Coill Breac (kíl brak) *as if* Cill Breac (kil brak)	Speckled Wood Speckled Church; place-name: "Kilbracks (speckled woods or churches) in Armagh"—P. W. Joyce; *Kill
404.04	arrah	ara (ore)	deprecatory interj.
.07	Shaun! Shaun!	Seán (shán)	John; *Shaun
.12	moren	Ó Móráin (ó móráñ)	des. of *Mórán* (dim. of *mór*, "great")
.12	glaow	glaodh (glé)	howl, call
.17	mac	mac (mok)	son
.20	brogues	bróg (bróg)	shoe
.32	kersse	Mac Fhiarais (mokírish) *for* Mac Phiarais (mokfírish)	son of Piers [Healy]
405.02, 07, 09	Shaun	Seán	see 404.07
.04	Lyons	Ó Laighin (ó lein)	des. of *Laighean* ("lance")

.05	Tarpey's	Ó Tarpaigh (ó *torpí*)	des. of *Tarpach* ("sturdy")
.05–06	MacDougall's	Mac Dubh-ghaill (mok *dúġil*)	son of *Dubhghall* ("black-foreigner," i.e., Dane)
.20	Traroe	Trágh Ruadh (*trárúe*)	Red Strand
.24	of Toole's	Ó Tuathail (ó *túhil*)	des. of *Tuathal* ("people-mighty")
.27	Balrothery	Baile an Ridire (bolye un ridiri)	Knight's Town; near Dublin
406.02	Portarlington's	port (pur*t*)	[Lord] Arlington's Fortification; town, Co. Laoighis
.03	Corkshire	Corcaigh (kurkí)	Swamp; S. co. & town, anglic. Cork
.06	gaulusch	gall (goul)	foreigner
.07	bulby	bolb (bulub)	caterpillar
.11	praties	préataí (pré*tí*)	potatoes
.13	Boland's	Ó Beólláin (ó byóláñ)	des. of *Beóllán* ("active"[?])
.14	*avic*	a mhic (avik)	son; my boy
.21	dulse	duileasc (*d*ilesk)	edible seaweed
.27	Lynch	Ó Loingsigh (ó liñshí)	des. of *Loingseach* ("having to do with a fleet")
.28	Ayternitay	té (té)	tea
.33	guilby	Mac Giolla-buidhe (mok gilebwí)	son of *Giollabuidhe* ("yellow lad"); anglic. Guilbey, Gilbey, etc.
407.01	gormandising	[Maolmuire] Ó Gormáin	author of 12th c. calendar of sts. See 349.24
.02	deah smorregos	Dia's Muire dhuit (d'ís mwiri ġit')	God and Mary to you (greeting)
.04	ardilaun	Árd Oileán (ár*d*ilán)	High Island, Co. Galway; title of Arthur Guinness' baronage
.11	wish, O wish	thoist (hish*t*)	silence
.13, 28	Shaun	Seán (shán)	John; *Shaun

.16	Michaeleen	Míchilín (míhilín)	little Michael
.16	Kelly	Ó Ceallaigh (ó kyalí)	des. of *Ceallach* ("contention")
.16	Mara	Ó Meadhra (ó myare)	des. of *Meadhair* ("mirth")
.16	O'Mario	ó (ó)	descendant, grandson
.18	Inchigeela	Ínse Gialla (ínshigíle)	Islands/Water-meadows of the Hostages
.20	Clifden	Clochán (klukhán)	Stonehouse; town, W. Co. Galway
408.06	iosals	Íosa (íse) íos (ís) íosal, *correctly* íseal (ísel, íshel) íoth; íotach (í; í*t*okh)[?]	Jesus below low, lowly, humble corn, fat; greedy; etc.
.08	Erin	Éirinn (érin), *dat.*	[to, for] Ireland
.23	Tighe	Ó Taidhg (ó *t*eig)	des. of *Tadhg* ("poet")
.25	Macsorley	Mac Somhairle (mok sórle)	son of *Somhairle* (Norse masc. pers. n.)
.24	owelglass		see 101.29; 549.34 (*Loch Uair*)
.27	bladdhers	bladar (bla*d*er)	flattery, coaxing
.27	Guinness	Mag Aonghusa (mogénġesi)	son of *Aonghus* ("single-choice" [god of love])
.28	Badeniveagh	Uíbh-Eachach (ívakhokh)	descendants of *Eochaidh* ("horse-rich"), tribal area, Co. Down, home of Guinness family, baronage of Edward Cecil Guinness, anglic. Iveagh
.33–34	Shaunti . . . shaunti . . . shaunti	Seán (shán) sláinte (slánt'i)	John; *Shaun health
.34	coolinder	cúilfhionn (kúlin)	fair-hair[ed girl]

409.02	man Shee	bean-sidhe (banshí)	fairy-woman
.02	pantry	Beanntraighe (ban*t*rí)	Race of *Beann* ("peak" masc. pers. n.) tribal land, Co. Cork, anglic. Bantry
.06	the phost	an phoist (un fush*t*), *g.*	of the post, the post's
.08, 11, 33	Shaun	Seán (shán)	John; *Shaun
.23	MacBlacks . . . Mac Blakes	mac (mok) Mac Duibh (mok *d*iv)	son [of] son of Dubh ("black"); anglic. Mac Duff
.24	bcliek	Béal Leice (bél leki)	Mouth of the Flag-stone, Co. Fermanagh; anglic. Belleek
.28	Colleenkiller's	cailín (kolín)	girl; St. Kevin (*Shaun) is the only girl-killer among I. sts.
		Colmcille (kulumkili)	Dove of the Church; latinized Columba
410.14	ponteen	poitín (put′ín)	"little pot": illicit whiskey
.14	Morrissey's	Ó Muirgheasa (ó mwiryase)	des. of *Muirgheas* ("sea-choice")
.20, 24, 28, 31	Shaun	Seán (shán)	John; *Shaun
.21	limricked	Luimneach (limnokh)	Bare-spot; S.W. town & co., anglic. Limerick
.23	Emailia	Eamhain (aven)	Twin[?] (explained as "Neck-Brooch" by folk etymology); anc. capital of Ulster (N. province); latinized *Emania*
.28	beg	beig (beg)	little
.29	moreboy	mór (mór)	big
.33	eilish	Éire (ére)	Ireland; *L/R Interchange
.33–34	eilish mires	*L/R Interchange	eirish miles: Irish miles (6,000 ft.)
411.12	Eironesia	Éire (ére)	Ireland

.22	tarabred	Teamhar (t'our)	Prospective-hill; anc. royal capital; anglic. Tara
.23, 25	Shaun	Seán (shán)	John; *Shaun
.30	Saozon	Sasanach (sosenokh)	England, English ("Saxon")
.32	focoal . . . focoal	focal (fukel)	word
412.05	Moyhard's	Magh Árd (má árd)	High Plain; anglic. Moyard
.08	*Emenia*	Eamhain	see 410.23
.09	O phausdheen phewn	a pháistín fionn (a fásht'ín fin)	O fair-haired child
.10	Pontoffbellek	Béal Leice (bél leki)	Mouth of the Flagstone, Co. Fermanagh; anglic. Belleek
.13	Shaun	Seán (shán)	John; *Shaun
.18	teom	tiom (t'im)	lukewarm
.18	bihan	Ó Beacháin (ó byakháñ)	des. of *Beachán* (dim. of *beach*, "bee"), anglic. Behan
.21	mecback	Mac Beatha (mok bahe)	son of life; anglic. Macbeth
.25	in sthore	a stór (astór)	my precious
.36	Nolaner	Ó Nualláin (ó núláñ)	des. of *Nuallán* (dim. of *nuall*, "noble")
413.20	sophykussens	cos (kus)	foot, leg
.30, 32	Shaun	Seán (shán)	John
414.04	Clowntalkin	Cluain Dealgan (klún d'algen)	Thorn Meadow; W. of Dublin, anglic. Clondalkin
.07	culkilt	cúl (kúl) cuilt (kilt)	back of the head, back covering
.12	Goonness's	Mag Aonghusa (mogénġesi)	son of *Aonghus* ("single-choice" [god of love]); anglic. Guinness
.14, 16	Shaun	Seán (shán)	John; *Shaun
.19–20	-nacosaghcusagh-	na casachta (nu kosokhte) casacht, cas-achtach (kos-okht/okh)	of the cough cough

		cosach (kusokh)	footed
		Mac Íosóc (mokísók)	son of Isaac; anglic. Cusack
.20	-cashl-	caiseal (kashel)	stonefort
415.08	taon	aon (én)	one
.10	McCaper	Mac Cába (mok kábe)	son of *Cába* ("hood"); anglic. McCabe
.13	duffmatt	dubh (*d*uv)	black
.17	Sommboddy	bod (bu*d*)	penis
.19	Newbuddies	bod (bu*d*)	penis
.21	O'Cronione	Ó Cróinín (ó króñín)	des. of *Cróinín* (dim. of *crón*, "swarthy"); an- glic. O Cronin
.25	sahul	sabhall (sál)	barn, granary
.28	thothfully	toth (*to*)	female; female organs
.32	sloghard	slog (slug)	gulp, swallow
.32	khul	cúl (kúl)	back of the head
416.11	durrydunglecks	Doire (*d*iri)	Oakwood; N. city & co., anglic. Derry
		Dún Leicne (*d*ún lekni)	Fort of Flagstones; town, Co. Carlow an- glic. Dunleckny
.19	moy Bog	magh bog (má bug)	boggy plain
417.11	dhrone	dron (*d*ron) dronn (*d*roun)	upright hump on the back
.31	Dorsan	dorsán (*d*ursán)	grasshopper
.31	Dunshanagan	Dún Seangáin (*d*únshanegáñ) seangán (shanegán)	Ant's Fort ant
418.01	Artalone	Árt (árt) Parthalón (páralón) Áth Luain (álúñ)	Bear/Stone leader of 2nd prehis- toric *colonists *Luan*'s ("hero") Ford; town on Shannon, an- glic. Athlone
.17	*Moyhammlet*	Magh- Thaimhleachta (má houlokh*t*e)	Plain of a Plague-grave

.31	*Nolans*	Ó Nualláin (ó núláñ)	des. of *Nuallán* (dim. of *nuall*, "noble")
419.12	fokloire	foclóir (fuklór)	dictionary, vocabulary
.16	blarneyest	Blárna (blárne)	Little-field; Co. Cork, anglic. Blarney
.16	blather	bladar (blader)	flattery, coaxing
.17	Lettrechaun	leitreachán (let'rekhán) leipreachán *for* luchorpán (leprekhán; lukhurpán)	one frequenting wet hillsides (*nonce*) "active little body": sprite
.20	Shaun	Seán (shán)	John; *Shaun
.24	Oscan	Oscar (usker)	Champion
.36	Lucan's	Leamhcán (loukán)	Producing marshmallows; W. Dublin suburb on Liffey; anglic. Lucan
420.07	peep	píop (píp)	pipe
.10	Bauv	Badhbh (báv)	royston-crow, vulture; death-goddess of battle
.10	Betty	biadhtaigh (bítí)	food-productive (land, etc.); anglic. -betty in place-names
.17, 18, 19	Shaun	Seán (shán)	John; *Shaun
.18	Alp	alp (olp)	lump, heap; job; snarl
.20	Baile-Atha-Cliath	Baile Átha Cliath (bláklíe)	Hurdle Ford Town; *Dublin
.22	Guineys	Ó Geibheannaigh (ó géení)	des. of *Geibheannach* ("fettered")
.23	Nave	naomh (név)	saint
.25	Finn's	Ó Finn (ó fin)	des. of *Fionn* ("fair")
.28	Domnall O'Domnally	Domhnall Ó Domhnaill/ Donnghaile (dónel ó dónil/douneli)	World-mighty des. of World-mighty/Brownvalor; anglic. Daniel O Donnell/Donnelly

.30	Clontalk	Cluain Deal-gan/Toirc/Tairbh (klún d'algen/*t*urk/*t*orev)	Thorn/Boar/Bull Meadow; W./central/N.E. of Dublin; anglic. Clondalkin/Clonturk/Clontarf
.33–34	Traumcondraws	Drom Conaire (*d*rum kunire)	*Conaire's* (masc. pers. n.) Ridge; N. Dublin district, anglic. Drum-condra
.34	Laffey	Life (lifi)	*Liffey River
.36	Cabranke	Cabrach (kobrokh)	Bad-land; N. Dublin district, anglic. Cabra
421.04	Shellburn	Síol Broin (shíl brin)	Seed of *Bran* ("raven"); tribal land, Co. Wexford
.14	Aireen	Éire (ére) -ín (ín), *dim. suffx.*	Ireland little, darling
.15, 21	Shaun	Seán (shán)	John; *Shaun
.21	sheltar	seilte (shelte)	jargon, argot, secret language, slang
.21–22	broguish	barróg (beróg)	defect in speech
.25	O'Shem	Ó Séim (ó shém)	des. of Shem (biblical); *Shem
.26	dieoguinnsis	Mag Aonghusa (mogénġesi)	son of *Aonghus* ("single-choice" [god of love]); anglic. Guinness
.32	Gilligan's	Ó Giollagáin (ó gilegáñ)	des. of *Giollagán* (dim. of *giolla*, "lad, servant")
.35	far	fear (far)	man
422.03	Gach!	gach (gokh)	each, every
.13–14	Is he on whose-keeping	*trans. idiom:* ar a coimhead	"on his keeping": on the run, in flight (from authorities)
.14	are	ar (er)	on
.18	cuistha	coiste (kushte) cuisne (kishne)	jury frost, icc
.19, 24	Shaun	Seán (shán)	John; *Shaun
.28	agum	agam (agum)	"at-me"; I have
423.01	jameymock farceson	Mac an Phear-sain (mokun farsen)	son of the parson; *Macpherson

.25	coombe	Cúm (kúm)	Hollow; S. Dublin slum
.36	Cahlls	Ó Cathail (ó kahil)	des. of *Cathal* ("battle-powerful"); anglic. Cahill
424.14, 17, 24, 26	Shaun	Seán (shán)	John; *Shaun
.20	Ull-	ull- (ul), *pfx.*	great, huge, chief, many, very, monstrous, mighty, all-
.25	O'	ó (ó) ó (ó) *enclitic interj.*	descendant, grandson O, oh
.27	Sweeney's	Ó Suibhne (ó swíñi)	des. of *Suibhne* ("well-going")
.27	slug	slog (slug)	swallow
.35	Thaw!	Tá! (*tá*)	There is; It is so; Yes
425.02	shur	Siuir (shúr)	River, Water; S. river anglic. Suir; by folk confused with *síor*, "everlasting"
.06	Shamous	Séamus (shémus)	James; *Shem
.07, 09	Shaun	Seán (shán)	John; *Shaun
.08	Upu	abú (abú)	to victory
.18	arrah	ara (ore)	deprecatory interj.
.18	arrah go braz	Éire go bráth (ére gu brá)	Ireland until Judgment
.20	Lief	Life (lifi)	*Liffey River
.22	soamheis	somhaoin (sówín)	profit, advantage
.30–31	broather brooher	bráthair (bráhir) bruthmhar (brúher)	kinsman; friar ardent, furious; cosy
.34	hairyman	Eireamhón (erewón)	see 394.29
.36	piop	píop (píp)	pipe
426.01	Shaun	Seán (shán)	John; *Shaun
.08	mooherhead	mothar (moher)	clump, thicket; place, Co. Clare, anglic. Moher

.08	jerry	Diairmín (d'írmín)	dim. of *Diarmaid* ("freeman"); anglic. Jerry; *Shem
.10	semplgawn	gam (gom) gann (gon)	soft foolish person stunted
.11	slob	slab (slob)	soft lump; soft person
.12	harvey	Ó hAirmh- eadhaigh (ó harvahí)	des. of *Airmheadhach* ("having a herd of cat- tle")
.35	Rattigan's	Ó Reach- tagáin (ó rakhtegáñ)	des. of *Reachtagán* (dim. of *reacht*, "de- cree")
427.01	Killesther's	Cill Easra (kilasre)	*Easar*'s ("profusion": 8th c. st.) Church, N.E. Dublin district, anglic. Killester
.04	Mac Auliffe's	Mac Amhlaoibh (mokoulév)	son of *Amhlaoibh* (Norse *Ólafr*); *Humphrey
.06	uila	uile (ili)	all, whole
.11	pibrook	píobaireacht (píbrokh*t*)	playing on the [bag]- pipes
.17	dall	dall (*d*oul)	blind, dark
.19	Shaun	Seán (shán)	John; *Shaun
.25	myriamilia	[na] míre Míchil (nu míri míhil)	[of] St. Michael's por- tion (morsel of food set apart for the archan- gel)
		míle (míli)	thousand
.27	Sean	Seán (shán) sean (shan)	John; *Shaun old
.27	Sean Moy	Sean-Magh (shanmá)	Old Plain, Old Coun- try
.30	Fuinn	Fionn (fin) fuin (fwin)	Fair end, limit; sunset, late evening
.33	Musha	má 'seadh (másha)	if so, if it be, neverthe- less (interj.)
.35	Wisha	mhuise (wishi)	well, indeed (interj.)
428.02	Samoanesia	somhaoin (sówín)	profit, advantage
.08	mamourneen's	mo mhúirnín (muvúrñín)	my darling

.15	aruah	ara (ore)	deprecatory interj.
		athrughadh (arúa)	change, transformation
		ruadh (rúe)	red
.18	Don Leary	Dún Laogh-aire (dún líre)	Laoghaire's ("calf-keeper," n. of high king in Patrick's time) Fort; town & harbor just S.E. of Dublin, called Kingstown (for George IV) for 90 years
.20	Erin's	Éireann (érun), g.	[of] Ireland
.21	Moylendsea	Sruth na Maoile (sru nu mwíli)	Sea-stream of the Bald-headland; sea between I. & Scotland, anglic. Moyle (poetic)
.24	knockside	cnoc (knuk)	hill
.26	tussocks	Túsach (túsokh)	Beginning [?]; st. who attended Patrick's deathbed; anglic. Tussach
429.05	brogues	bróg (bróg)	shoe
.19	warden of the peace	trans. Gárda Síothchána	I. national policeman
430.02	Berched	Beircheart (berkhert)	masc. pers. n. (Anglo-Saxon Beorthere, "bright-army"); Anglo-Saxon st. settled in Co. Cork, d. 839
.24	Finfria's	Fionn (fin) fria (fríe)	Fair with its, with his
.34–35	dollybegs	beig (beg)	small, little
.36	columbillas	Colmcille (kulumkili) bile (bili)	Dove of the Church; st.; latinized Columba sacred tree (beside well)
.36	tubberbunnies	Tobar Bainne (tuber bonyi)	Milk Well, village Co. Dublin, anglic. Toberbunny
432.13	coppall	capall (kopel)	horse

.31	is in it	*lit. trans.* atá ann	that exists
433.05	O'Toole	Ó Tuathail (ó *t*úhil)	des. of *Tuathal* ("people-mighty")
.06	Gwenn du Lake	Gleann dá Loch (gloun *d*á lukh)	Two-lake Valley, monastic settlement Co. Wicklow, S. of Dublin, founded by St. Kevin (*Shaun); anglic. Glendalough
.10	couple in Myles	[Myles] na gCapaillín ([M.] nu gopelín)	[M.] of the Little Horses: "Myles na gCopaleen," pen n. of journalist & novelist; *The Colleen Bawn*
.13	Killiney	Cill na nInghin (kilne níñin)	Church of the Daughters [six virgins], town, S. Co. Dublin coast
.16	Dar	dair (*d*ar)	oak; letter D
.16	Bey	beith (be)	birch; letter B
.16	Coll	coll (kol)	hazel; letter C
.19	*Murry*	Ó Muireadhaigh (ó mwirayí)	des. of *Muireadhach* ("mariner")
.29	colleen	cailín (kolín)	girl
434.12	Hayes	Ó hAodha (ó hé)	des. of *Aodh* ("fire")
.12	Conyngham	Ó Cuinneagáin (ó kunegáñ)	des. of *Cuinneagán* (dim. of *Conn,* "intelligence")
.13	forglim	forgla (forgle)	choice, pick or cream of
.13	mick aye	Mac Aodha (moké)	son of *Aodh* ("fire"); anglic. McKay, etc.
.15	Mangain's	Ó Mongáin (ó mongáñ)	des. of *Mongán* (dim. of *mongach,* "hairy")
.21	limenick's	Luimneach (limnokh)	Bare-place; S.W. city & co., anglic. Limerick
.28	Doveyed	dubh (*d*uv)	black
.32	martimorphysed	Ó Murchadha (ó murukhu)	des. of *Murchadh* ("sea-warrior"); anglic. Murphy, Morphy

435.10	Buylan	Ó Baoigheall-láin (ó bwéláñ)	des. of *Baoigheallán* (dim. of *Baoigheall*, "vain-pledge")
.29	Sully van	Ó Súileabháin (ó súleváñ)	des. of *Súil-dubhán* ("black-eyed"); anglic. Sullivan
.29	van	bhean (van)	woman
.34–35	Tunnelly's	Ó Tonnaigh (ó *t*uní)	des. of *Tonnach* ("glittering"); anglic. Tunny
		Ó Donnghaile (ó *d*ouneli)	des. of *Donnghal* ("brown-valor"); anglic. Donnelly
436.09	kosenkissing	cos (kus)	foot
.12	barely	Béarla (bérle)	English language
.27	bally	baile (bolye)	town; homestead
.27	billing	bile (bili)	sacred tree
.28	meeth	Midhe (mí)	Middle; anc. royal province, now co. N. & W. of Dublin, anglic. Meath
.29	Navan	An Uaimh (unúiv) neamh (nyav)	The Hollow; town, co. seat of Meath heaven
.29	Kellsfrieclub	Ceannanus *altered to* Ceann-lios (kyanenus; kyanlis)	Head-residence, altered to Head-fort, anglic. Kenlis, then Kells; monastic settlement, Co. Meath, fndd. by Colmcille
.31	Kildare	Cill Dara (kil*d*ore)	Church of the Oak; town & co. W. & S.W. of Dublin
437.18	rawny	ránaidhe (rání)	thin lank person
.23	muck	muc (muk)	pig, swine
.33	MacShine MacShane	Mac Seagháin/Seáin (mok sháyin/ sháin)	son of *Jehan/Jean* (Norm.-Fr. John) anglic. MacShane, MacCheyne, etc.
438.13	Tubber	tobar (*t*uber)	well, spring

.16	talker-go-bragk	go bráth (gu brá)	until Judgment
.28	vicereeking	rí (rí)	king
.30–31	Lucalamplight	Leamhcán (loukán)	Producing marshmallows; W. Dublin suburb on Liffey; anglic. Lucan
.33	collion boys	cailín buidhe (kolín bwí)	yellow girl
.34	colleen bawns	cailín bán (kolín bán)	white girl: pretty girl
.35	duffs	Dubh (*d*uv)	Black
.36	lindsays	Ó Loingsigh/ Loinn (ó liñshí/lin)	des. of *Loingseach* ("having to do with a fleet")/*Flann* ("ruddy"); both anglic. Lindsay
439.09	Moore's	Ó Mórdha (ó mórye)	des. of *Mórdha* ("majestic")
.16	Glor galore	glór go leór (glór gulór)	plenty of noise
.19–20	Theo Dunnohoo's	Ó Donnchadha (ó *d*unukhu)	*The* des. of *Donnchadh* ("brown-warrior"); title of head of family of *O Donnchadha an Ghleanna* ("of the Valley"); *Brian Boru
.20	O'Dowd	Ó Dubhda (ó *d*úde)	des. of *Dubhda* ("black")
440.02	*An*	an (un)	the
.03	castle bar	Caisleán an Bhearraigh (kashlán un varí)	Castle of the Barry (prob. Norm. *de Barri*); co. seat of Co. Mayo; anglic. Castlebar
.05	labronry	leabhar (lyour)	book
		leabharlann (lyourlon)	library
		labhar (lour)	speak; talkative
		brón (brón)	grief, sorrow

.09	Cullen	Ó Cuilinn/ Cuileáin (ó kwilin/ kiláñ)	des. of Cuileann ("holly")/Cuileán ("whelp"); both anglic. Cullen
.10	Finn's	Ó Finn (ó fin)	des. of Fionn ("fair")
.14	Gill . . . Gill	Mac Giolla/ an Ghoill (mok gili/ unġil) gil (gil)	son of the servant of . . . [shortened form of a surname]/of the Foreigner [n. for dess. of 1st Anglo-Normans] bright, white, fair
.15	Gillydehooly's	Mac Giolla-ghuala (mok giliúli)	son of Giolla-ghuala ("servant of gluttony"); anglic. Gilhooly
.25	Contrabally	baile (bolye) ball (bol)	town; homestead limb, member
441.06	Whisht!	Thoist! (hisht)	Silence!
.11	Cantilene	Caitilín (kat'ilín)	fem. pers. n. from Gk. Katherine
.23	Shone	Seón (shón)	John; *Shaun
442.01	black fremdling	trans. Dubh-ghall (dú ġoul)	Black-foreigner, i.e., Dane; also n. Dugall, Doyle, etc.
.03	mucky	muc (muk)	pig, swine
.08	Baas	bás (bás)	death
.14	Brendan's	Breanndán (broundán)	Ill-odored[?]; n. of several sts. including reputed discoverer of America
.14	Kerribrasilian	Ciarraighe (kírí) Í Breasail (í brasil)	race of Ciar ("black": son of Queen Maev); S.W. co., anglic. Kerry Red Island[?]; legendary land to W. across Atlantic; anglic. Hy Brasil
.22	Shaun	Seán (shán)	John; *Shaun

.29	Leary	Ó Laoghaire (ó líri)	des. of *Laoghaire* ("calf-keeper")
		Laoghaire (líre)	Calf-keeper; high king at time of Patrick's arrival, 5th c.
.30	Leinsterface	Laighin (lein)	Lance; E. province; anglic. Leinster
.35	coombe	Cúm (kúm)	Hollow; S. Dublin slum
443.02	Mohomadhawn	amadán (omadán)	fool, dolt
.10	clonmellian	Cluain Meala (klún male)	Meadow of Honey; town, Co. Tipperary, anglic. Clonmel
.27	colman's	Colmán (kulumán)	Little Dove; n. of several sts.
.29	Rhoss's	rásaidhe (rásí)	wandering woman; jilt
.30	pubpal	pobal (pubel)	people, the public
.35	angeleens	-ín (ín), *dim. suffx.*	little, darling
.36	morvaloos	mór (mór)	big, great
444.05	loadenbrogued	bróg (bróg)	shoe
.36	Limerick	Luimneach (limnokh)	Bare-spot; S.W. co. & town
445.06	unbrodhel	bródh (bró) bród (bród)	dirt delight, pride
.07	skelp	sceilp (shkelp)	slap
.07	budd	bod (bud)	penis
.12	pud	bod (bud)	penis
.15	splitpuck	poc (puk)	sharp sudden blow
.34	Liffalidebankum	Life (lifi)	*Liffey River
446.04	in-you	indiu (iñú)	today
.21	Ealing	Éirinn (érin), *dat.*	[to, for] Ireland; *L/R Interchange
.24	Coppal	capall (kopel)	horse
.25	suirland	Siuir (shúr)	River, Water; S. river, anglic. Suir; by folk identified with *síor*, "everlasting"
.25	noreland	An Fheoir (unór)	Brim; S. River, anglic. Nore

.30	Murphy	Ó Murchadha (ó murukhu)	des. of *Murchadh* ("sea-warrior")
.31	O'Dwyer	Ó Dubhuidhir (ó *d*wír)	des. of *Dubh-odhar* ("black-pale")
447.10	mownself	mún (mún)	urine
.15–16	Castleknock	Cnuca (knuke)	Hill; W. of Phoenix Park, scene of battle in which *Goll Mac Mórna* killed *Cumhal, Fionn*'s father
.23	liffe	Life (lifi)	*Liffey River
.23	Dufblin	Dubh-linn (*d*uvlin)	Black Pool; *Dublin
.23	Egan	Mac Aodhagáin (mok égáñ)	son of *Aodhagán* (dim. of *Aodh*, "fire")
.23–24	Egan . . . Ralli	Aodhagán Ó Raithile (égán ó rahili)	Little-fire des. of Grace[?], poet, d. 1726; anglic. Egan O Rahilly
.23	baugh	beatha (bahe)	life, existence
.24	Baughkley	Baile Átha Cliath (bláklí)	Hurdle Ford Town; Dublin
		Ó Buachalla (ó búkheli)	des. of *Buachaill* ("boy"), anglic. Buckley
.24	Fino Ralli	Fionn Ó Raghailligh (fin ó rayelí)	Fair des. of *Raghallach* ("[strong-]fore-armed")
.30	town of the Fords in a huddle	Baile Átha Cliath (bláklíe)	Hurdle Ford Town; *Dublin
.32	Drumgondola	Drom Conaire (*d*rum kunire)	*Conaire*'s Ridge; N. Dublin district anglic. Drumcondra
448.03	Kane	Ó Catháin (ó kaháñ)	des. of *Cathán* (pet form of n. beginning *Cath-*, "battle-")
.03	Keogh's	Mac Eochadha (mokyókhu)	son of *Eochaidh* ("horseman")
.07	kakes	cac (kok)	excrement

.11	muckloved	muc (muk)	pig, swine
.11	d'lin	Dubh-linn (duvlin)	Black Pool; *Dublin
.18	Brayhowth	Brí (brí)	Hillside; resort, S. Co. Dublin coast anglic. Bray
.19	Bailey	Baile (bolye)	Homestead; lighthouse, Howth Head
.19	Lorcansby	Lorcán (lurkán)	dim. of *lorc*, "fierce"; masc. pers. n. anglic. Laurence; *Brian Boru
449.08	deerdrive	Deirdre (d'írd'ri)	fem. pers. n.; *Red Branch heroine
.08	conconey's	Conchobhar (kunukher)	High-will; masc. pers. n.; *Red Branch king
		Cú Chulainn (kúkhulin)	Hound of *Culann* (masc. pers. n.); *Red Branch hero
		con (kon), *g.* coinín (kuñín)	[of a] hound rabbit
.11	Lyons	Ó Laighin (ó lein)	des. of *Laighean* ("lance")
.13	tinny	teine (tini)	fire
.14	Jamas	Séamus (shémus)	James; *Shem
.14	Hanway	Ó hAinbheith (ó haneve)	des. of *Ainbhioth* ("storm")
.21	maurdering row	maidrín ruadh (moderín rúe)	"red little dog": fox
.26	Drumsally	Drom Salach (drum solokh)	Dirty Ridge; places in Cos. Limerick & Donegal; anglic. Dromsallagh
.09	Mac Courther	Mac Muircheartaigh (mok mwirkhartí)	son of *Muircheartach* ("navigator"); anglic. MacCourty
.19	livy	Life (lifi)	*Liffey River
.28	Erin	Éirinn (érin), *dat.*	[to, for] Ireland

.29	Lucan	Leamhcán (loukán)	Producing marshmallows; W. Dublin suburb on Liffey
.30	Aerial	Éireann (érun), *g.*	[of] Ireland
.33	grenoulls	Gráinne Ní Mháille (gráñí wályi)	Grain/Spearpoint daughter of a des. of *Máille* ("chief"): Grace *O Malley
.33	belleeks	Béal Leice (bél leki)	Ford-mouth of a Flagstone, Co. Fermanagh, anglic. Belleek
450.04	grannom	grean (gran)	sand or gravel at bottom of sea or lake
.06	MacEels	Mac Giolla/ an Ghoill (mok gili/ unġil)	son of the servant of . . ./son of the foreigner
.06	Gillaroo	giolla ruadh (gile rúe)	red fellow
.09	logansome	Ó Lógáin (ó lógáñ)	des. of *Lóchán* (pet form of n. beginning *Lóch-*, "chaff"), anglic. Logan
.14	griffeen	-ín (ín), *dim. suffx.*	little, darling
.18	blackbudds	bod (bu*d*)	penis
.25	whatyoumacormack	Mac Cormaic (mok kurmik)	son of *Cormac* ("chariot-son"); anglic. McCormack
.28	athlone	Áth Luain (álún)	*Luan*'s (masc. pers. n. "hero") Ford; central I. on Shannon River, home of John McCormack; anglic. Athlone
.29	killarnies	Cill Áirne (kilárñi)	Church of the Sloes, Co. Kerry, anglic. Killarney
.31	logans	Ó Lógáin	see 450.09
.32	Bryony O'Bryony	Brian Ó Briain (bríen ó bríin)	Brian des. of Brian; *Brian Boru

451.01	poteen	poitín (put′ín)	"little pot": illicit whiskey
.08	bragget	braicheas (brakhes)	pot-ale
.12	brogues	bróg (bróg)	shoe
.13	kishes	cis (kish)	wickerwork basket; *Dublin
.13	Ulster	Ulaidh (uli)	Monument; N. province
.13	Cork	Corcaigh (kurkí)	Swamp; S. city & co.
.13	Milice	milis (milish)	sweet, sugary
.14	Connacht	Connachta (kunukhte)	progeny of *Conn* ("intelligence"); W. province
.15	annyblack	eanaigh (aní), *g.*	[of a] marsh, fen; *Anna
.15	rann	rann (ron)	verse, stanza
.23	Sheila	Síle (shíle)	fem. pers. n. from Latin Cecilia
452.09	Tennis Flonnels Mac Courther	Donnchadh Finghin Mac Cárthaigh (*d*unukhu finyin mok kárhí)	Brown-warrior Fair-birth son of *Cárthach* ("loving"); anglic. Denis Florence Mac-Carthy
453.04	moriarty	Ó Muirch-eartaigh (ó mwirkhartí)	des. of *Muircheartach* ("navigator")
.06	blarney	Blárna (blárne)	Little Field; town, Co. Cork
.12	thay	té (*té*)	tea
.21	blatherumskite	bladar (bla*d*er)	flattery, coaxing
454.06	Ann Posht	An Phost (unfus*t*)	The Mail
.07	Shorn	Seán (shán)	John; *Shaun
.09	blossy	blas (blos) blasta (blos*t*e)	taste, flavor delicious

.14	spladher	splaid (splad′)	spark
.14	splodher	spleodar (shplo*d*er)	glee, joy
.15	magorios	Mac Gothraidh (mokgorí)	son of Godfrey; anglic. MacGorey, etc.
.21	Rizzies	rásaidhe (rásí)	wandering woman; jilt
.35	seanad	seanad (shane*d*)	senate, synod
.35	pobbel	pobal (pubel)	people, the public
455.01	apuckalips	poc (puk)	short sharp blow
.02	Byrns	Ó Birn (ó birn)	des. of *Bjorn* (Norse n.)
.04	shinner	sinn (shin)	we, us
.07	bonhams	banbh (bonev)	suckling pig
.09–10	Hogmanny di'yegut?	Go mbeannu- ighe Dia dhuit (gu maníyi d′íe ġit′)	May God bless you
.10	Hogmanny di'yesmellygut?	Go mbeannu- ighe Dia 's Muire dhuit (gu maníyi d′íes mwiri ġit′)	May God and Mary bless you
.10–11	hogmanny di'yes- mellyspatterygut?	Go mbeannu- ighe Dia 's Muire 's Pád- raig dhuit (gu maníyi d′íes mwiris pá*d*rig ġit′)	May God and Mary and Patrick bless you
.18	Moy	Magh (má)	Plain [of], Country [of]
456.07	kailkannonkabbis	cál ceann- fhionn (kál kyanin)	"white-head cab- bage": dish of cabbage & potatoes with butter

.20	curry and cinnamon, chutney and cloves	[*acrostic:*] cac (kok)	excrement, ordure
.22	naboc	ná bac (ná bok)	don't bother, leave alone
.22	erics	éiric (érik)	fine, ransom
.25	ryoull	ríoghamhail (ríúl)	kingly
.26	Killadown	Cill-dubh-dúin (kil*dúdúñ*)	Black-fort-church; village, Co. Sligo, anglic. Killadoon
.26	Letternoosh	Leitir nGiúis (let'ir ñúsh)	Hillside of a Firwood; village, Co. Galway
.26	Letterspeak	Leitir *Peak* (let'ir pík)	Hillside of the Peak (English word); village Co. Galway, anglic. Letterpeak
.27	Lettermuck	Leitir Muc (let'ir muk)	Hillside of Pigs; village Co. Derry
.27	Littorananima	Leitir an Anama (let'ir unoneme)	Hillside of the Soul; hill, Co. Donegal, anglic. Letterananima
.30	Thaddeus	Tadhg (*t*eig)	Poet; masc. pers. n. of typical rural laborer; anglic. Thady, Thaddeus
.30, 31	Kellyesque . . . Kelly-Cooks	Ó Ceallaigh (ó kyalí)	des. of *Ceallach* ("contention")
.35	machree	mo chroidhe (mukhrí)	[of] my heart
457.01	Con	Conn (kon)	Intelligence; masc. pers. n.
.01	Connolly's	Ó Conghalaigh (ó konġalí)	des. of *Conghalach* ("valorous")
.02	Collopys	colptha (kulupe)	calf of the leg
		Ó Colptha (ó kulupe)	des. of *Colptha* ("calf of the leg")
.15	drawhure deelish	dearbhráthair dílis (*d*ráher dílish)	dearest brother

.25	Meesh, meesh	mise (mishi)	I, me (emphatic)
.26	drawher	dearbhráthair (*dr*áher)	brother
.27	dove	dubh (*d*uv)	black
.27–28	dart eyes	*half-trans.* Dart-shúile (*dort* húle)	Heifer-eyes; *Mac- pherson's Darthula; see 329.17
458.09	galways	Gaillimh (goliv)	Foreign; W. co. & town; anglic. Galway
459.03	dovedoves	dubh (*d*uv)	black
.03	mouthbuds	bod (bu*d*)	penis
.03–04	msch! msch!	mise (mishi)	I, me (emphatic)
.18	Erne	[Loch] Éirne (érne)	*Éarna*'s ("knowledge," masc. pers. n.) [Lake]; anglic. [Lough] Erne; lake, Co. Fermanagh
.24	coss . . . cusses	cos, cosa (kus, kuse)	foot, feet
460.01	Arrah	ara (ore)	page, lackey; agent of an action
		aire (ari)	minister, overseer
.04	mearest	méar (mér)	finger
.15	Dargle	Deargail (d'argil)	Red; stream near Bray, Co. Wicklow
.17	asthone	a stór (astór) tón (*tó*n)	my precious bottom, backside, arse
.17	A'Mara	Ó Meadhra (ó myare)	des. of *Meadhair* ("mirth")
.18	O'Morum	Ó Móráin (ó móráñ)	des. of *Mórán* (dim. of *mór*, "great"); anglic. O Moran
461.13	stheal	staoil (s*tí*l)	style, mode, title, pride
.25	Shane	Seán (shán)	John; *Shaun
462.04	Erin go	Éire go (ére gu)	Ireland until
.07	dhouche on Doris	deoch an dorais (d'ukh un *d*urish)	"drink of the door": parting drink
.08	Shaunathaun	Seán (shán)	John; *Shaun

.32	mourn mountains	Mughdhorna (múyorne)	[territory of the] Progeny of *Mughdhorn* ("ankle"); tribal lands N.E.I., incl. mtn. range, anglic. Mourne
463.18	henesy	Ó hAonghusa (ó hénġesi)	des. of *Aonghus* ("single-choice" [god of love]); anglic. Hennessy
.22	O'Cormacan	Ó Cormacáin (ó kurmokáñ)	des. of *Cormacán* (dim. of *Cormac*, "chariot-son")
.22	MacArty	Mac Cárthaigh (mok kárhí)	son of *Cárthach* ("loving"); anglic. MacCarthy, etc.
.22	O'Cormacan MacArty	Cormac Mac Airt (kurmuk mok art')	Chariot-son son of *Art* ("bear/stone"), high king in *Fionn Mac Cumhail*'s time (3rd c.)
.24	Alba	Alba (olbe)	Scotland
.35	breans	bréan (brén)	fetid, rotten, putrid
464.01	annyone	eanaigh (aní), *g.*	[of a] fen, marsh; *Anna
.01	oweand	abhainn (ouwin)	river; anglic. Owen-
.07	O'Looniys	Ó Luanaigh (ó lúní)	des. of *Luanach* (from *luan*, "warrior")
.07	a Brazel	Ó Breasail (ó brasil)	des. of *Breasal* ("war"); anglic. O Brazil, Brazel
.07	aboo!	abú! (abú)	to victory!
.11	spatton	Ó Peatáin (ó patáñ)	des. of *Peatán* (dim. of *Pádraig*, "Patrick"); anglic. Patton
.14	paudeen	Páidín (pád'ín)	dim. of *Pádraig*: Paddy
.24	Claddagh	Cladach (klodokh)	Stony seashore; fishing community in Galway town
.31	Peadhar	Peadar (pader)	Peter
465.08	shamewaugh	Séam (shém) seamróg (shameróg)	Sant Iago; *Shem shamrock, trefoil, clover; *Shem

.10	buds	bod (bud)	penis
.18	shinners	sinn, sinn-ne (shin, shini)	we, us (& emphatic)
.30	racist . . . racy, rossy	rásaidhe (rásí)	wandering woman; jilt
.32	inish	inis (inish)	island
.32	offalia	Uí Fáilghe (í fályi)	dess. of [*Ros-*]*fáilghe*, ("[Horse] of the rings"), son of *Cathair Mór*, high king 120–123; tribal land now central co., anglic. Offaly
.33–34	cool . . . finish	Fionn Mac Cumhail (fin mok kúl)	Fair son of *Cumhal*, 3rd c. hero of saga cycle
.33	mackinamucks	mac (mok) muc (muk)	son pig, swine
466.02	Curlew	Ceatharlach (kaherlokh)	Quadruple-lake; S.E. town & co., anglic. Carlow
.11	darearing	dá réir (dárér) dá ríribh (dáríriv)	accordingly in earnest, serious
.23	deas	deas (d'as)	nice
.23	dockandoilish	deoch an dorais (d'ukh un durish) dáil (dál)	"drink of the door": parting drink assembly; *Dáil Éireann*, I. Legislative Assembly
		Ó Dubhghaill (ó dúġil)	des. of *Dubhghall* ("black-foreigner," i.e., Dane); anglic. Doyle
.29	Heenan	Ó hEidhneáin (ó hénáñ)	des. of *Eidhneán* (dim. of *eidhean*, "ivy")
.33	Meehan	Ó Miadhacháin (ó míakháñ)	des. of *Miadhachán* (dim. of *miadhach*, "honorable")
467.05	Areesh! Areesh!	Arís! (arísh)	Again!
.10	schamlooking	seamróg (shameróg)	shamrock, trefoil, clover; *L/R Interchange

.11	Areesh!	Arís! (arísh)	Again!
.12	faher's	athair (aher)	father
.15	stomebathred	*half-trans.* Bóthar na gCloch (bóhernu-glukh)	Road of the Stones; Dublin street, anglic. Stonybatter
.17	duff	dubh (*d*uv)	black
.25	beurlads	Beurla (bérle)	English language
.29	orileys	Ó Raghailligh (ó rayelí)	des. of *Raghallach* ("[strong-]fore-armed"); anglic. O Reilly, O Riley, etc.
.32	Erin's	Éireann (érun), *g.*	[of] Ireland
.36	tullying	Ó Taithligh (*ó* talí) Ó Maoltuile (ó mwél*t*uli)	des. of *Taithleach* ("peaceful") des. of *Maoltuile* ("devoted to the will [of God]"); both an-glic. Tully
468.03	brather	bráthair (bráher)	friar, brother-in-reli-gion
.09	Paltry	Pádraig (pá*d*rig)	Patrick
.27	moore	Ó Mórdha (ó mórġe)	des. of *Mórdha* ("ma-jestic"); anglic. Moore
.28	Toole	Ó Tuathail (ó *t*úhil)	des. of *Tuathal* ("people-mighty")
.29	fiacckles	fiacal, fiacla (fíkel, fíkle)	tooth, teeth
.33	Daniel's old collie	Domhnall Ó Conaill (*d*ónel ó kunil)	World-mighty des. of High-mighty; anglic. Daniel O Connell
.34	azores	a stór (as*t*ór)	my precious
.35	a chorines	a cháirde (a khárd′i)	friends, my friends
.36	'Bansheeba	bean-sidhe (banshí) bean (ban)	fairy-woman woman
469.01	muinnuit	muin (mwin)	neck-and-shoulders; affection, desire

.06–07	Banbashore	Banba (bonbe)	Ireland (poetic)
.11	moyne	maighin (mein)	little plain; places in Cos. Mayo & Tipperary
.15	Fingale	Fine-Gall (finigoul)	Foreign Kindred; N. Co. Dublin district, anglic. Fingal
		Fionn-Gall (fingoul)	Fair Foreigner; i.e., Norwegian
		Fionn-Gaedh-eal (fingél)	Fair Irishman/Scotsman
		Fionn-ghal (finġal)	Fair-fight; *Macpherson's n. for *Fionn Mac Cumhail*: Fingal
.18	Hazelridge	*trans.* Drom Coll- [Choille] (*d*rum kolkhíli)	Hazel[wood] Ridge; I. n. for Thomas St. Dublin; also place Co. Limerick, anglic. Dromcolliher
.20	Macadam	Mac Ádaim (mokád*i*m)	son of Adam
.21	Linduff	linn dubh (lin*d*uv)	black pool; *Dublin
		lionndubh (lin*d*uv)	porter, stout; black bile, melancholy
.21	Erynnana	Éireann (érun), *g.*	[of] Ireland; *Anna
.24	whished	thoist (hish*t*)	silence
.26	kerrycoys	Ciarraighe (kírí)	Progeny of *Ciar* ("black"); tribal land now S.W. co., anglic. Kerry
470.07	piopadey	píopa (pípe)	pipe
.07	solase	solas (sules)	light
.07	dorckaness	dorcha (*d*urukhe)	dark; darkness
471.01–02	Sososopky	sos (sus)	peace, respite
.15	kingscouriered	Ceann Coradh (kyoun kure)	Weir Head; *Brian Boru's residence on Shannon River; anglic. Kincora

.19	mear	méar (mér)	finger
		mear (myar)	rapid
.22	bouchal	buachaill	boy
		(búkhel)	
.33	*Harvey*	Ó hAirmh-	des. of *Airmheadhach*
		eadhaigh	("having a herd of cat-
		(ó harvaí)	tle")
.35	Haun	a Sheáin	John (vocative);
		(a hyáñ)	*Shaun
472.01–02	Shamrogueshire	seamróg	shamrock, trefoil,
		(shameróg)	clover; *Shem
.04	bawny	bán (bán)	white
.06	disdoon blarmey	Dún Bláirne	Little-field Fort:
		(*d*ún blárñi)	Blarney Castle, Co.
			Cork
		Lios Dún	Fort of Gap-Fort, Cu.
		Bheárna (lis	Clare; anglic. Lisdoon-
		*d*ún várne)	varna
.11	Hauneen	a Sheáinín	Johnny (vocative);
		(a hyáñín)	*Shaun
.14, 20	Haun	a Sheáin	see 471.35
.15	Chris-na-Murty	[Chris] na	[the Chris] of the des.
		Muircheart-	of *Muircheartach*
		aigh ([C.] nu	("navigator")
		mwirkhar*tí*)	
473.07	Molochy	Maelsheach-	Servant of [St.]
		lainn	Secundinus (disciple of
		(mélokhlin)	Patrick); n. of 2 kings;
			anglic. *Malachy
.21	Haun	a Sheáin	see 471.35
474.07	lucan	Leamhcán	Producing marshmal-
		(loukán)	lows; W. Dublin sub-
			urb on Liffey
.20	Brosna's	brosna	bundle of firewood; n.
		(brosne)	of 2 small rivers
475.02	aggala!!!!	eagla (ogle)	fear
.06	Conn's half	*trans.* Leath	*Conn Céadcathach*'s
		Cuinn	("Intelligence the
		(lakin)	Hundred-fighter")
			half (N.) of I.; *Conn*
			was high king 177–212,
			forced to yield S. half
			to *Eoghan Mór*

.07	Owenmore's	Eoghan Mór (ówen mór)	Wellborn the Great, surnamed *Mogh-Nuadhat* ("slave of *Nuadha*"), 2nd c. king of Munster, seized S. half of I. from *Conn Céadcathach*, whence still-recognized division *Leath Cuinn/Leath Mogha* (*Conn's* half/ *Mogh's* half)
.07	Owenmore's	Abhainn Mór (ouwin mór)	Great River; n. of several rivers, many anglic. Owenmore
.07	five quarters	Eoghanachta (ówenokhte)	Progeny of *Eoghan* [*Mór*]; *Eoghan* divided Munster among his five sons; collectively, Munster (S. province)
.12	Aran	Ára; *g.* Árann (áre, áren)	Kidney; n. of island group off Co. Galway
.13	Aggala!!!!	eagla (ogle)	fear
.22	esker	eiscir (eshkir)	ridge of mounds
.22	esker ridge	Eiscir Riada (eshkir ríede)	*Riada's* ("cunning [?]") Ridge; ridge of sandhills, E. to W. across I. from Dublin to Galway, border between *Leath Cuinn* and *Leath Mogha* (see 475.06–07)
.22	Mallinger	An Muileann Cearr (un mwilin kyar)	The Left-handed Mill; town, Co. Westmeath, central I., anglic. Mullingar
.23, 24	Shanator	Seanadóir (shanadór) sean (shan)	Senator old
.25	Lyons	Ó Laighin (ó lein)	des. of *Laighean* ("lance")
.27–28	Shunadure	Seanadóir	see 475.23, 24
.28	Tarpey	Ó Tarpaigh (ó torpí)	des. of *Tarpach* ("sturdy")

.29	Shunny MacShunny	Sionnach Mac Sionnaigh (shinokh mok shiní)	Fox son of Fox; anglic. Shunny
		Seanach Mac Sionaigh (shanokh mok shuní)	Old/Wise son of Old/Wise; anglic Shunny
.30	MacDougal	Mac Dubhghaill (mok*d*úġil)	son of *Dubhghall* ("black-foreigner," i.e., Dane)
.34	kuss yuss	cos dheas (kus yas)	right foot
.35	kuss cley	cos clé (kus klé)	left foot
476.06	Asnoch	asnach (asnokh)	ribbed; (in place-names) ploughed
.12	firrum	fir (fir)	men
.26	Lyons	Ó Laighin	see 475.25
.26	Tarpey	Ó Tarpaigh	see 475.28
.26	mack	mac (mok)	son
.27–28	na Hossaleen	na h-asailín (nu hoselín)	[of] the little asses; also allusion to "Myles na gCopaleen [*na gcapaillín*: 'of the little horses']"; *The Colleen Bawn
477.01–02	And it is what they began to say to him . . . what way was he	*lit. trans.* Agus 'sé a thosnuigh-eadar a rádh leis [ná] . . . cé'n caoi a bhí/raibh sé	And what they began to say to him was . . . how was he
.04	Yerra	a Dhia ara (ġeri)	O God well! (interj.)
.05	Wisha	mhuise (wishi)	well, indeed (interj.)
.05	alannah	a leanbh (a lanev)	child, my child

.10	Whisht	thoist (hisht)	silence
478.03	Throsends	rásaidhe (rásí)	wandering woman; jilt
.10	alpman	alp (olp)	lump, hump; job; Dublin
.12	tartallaght	Taimhleacht (talokht)	Plague-grave; village S.W. of Dublin, anglic. Tallaght; *colonists
.21	*Moy*	Magh (má)	Plain (= *champs*)
.28	Are you in your fatherick	*trans.* An bhfuil tú i do Phádraig/i d'athair?	Are you a Patrick/ father (i.e., by avoca-tion)?
.32	Is there cold on ye	*lit. trans.* An bhfhuil fuacht ort?	Are you cold?
.34	fogloot	fochla (fukhle)	den, cave
.35	Whisht	thoist (hisht)	silence
479.02	Tear-nan-Ogre	Tír na nÓg (tír nenóg)	Land of the Young
.03	Mayo	Magh-eó (máyó)	Yew-Plain; W. co.
.06	Tucurlugh	Ceatharlach (kaherlokh)	Quadruple-lake; S.E. co. & town; anglic. Carlow
		lugh (lú)	small
		Lugh (lú)	god of light & genius
.07	Conway	Ó Connmhaigh (ó konwaí)	des. of *Connmhach* ("intelligent")
.09	Meads	Midhe (mí)	Middle; anc. royal province; co. N. & W. of Dublin; anglic. Meath
.10	Dougal	Ó Dubhghaill (dúgel)	des. of *Dubhgall* ("black-foreigner," i.e., Dane)
.13	Fochlut	fochla (fokhle)	den, cave
.17	bloss	blas (blos)	flavor; accent in speech
.18	bleather	bladar (blader)	flattery, coaxing

.18	Dunlin	Dún-linn (dúnlin)	Fort pool; *Dublin
.24–25	plague-burrow	trans. Taimhleacht	see 478.12
.34	dungcairn	dún (dún) carn (karn)	fort heap, pile
.35	Allmaun	Almhain (alún)	Whitened; HQ of Fionn & Fianna, Co. Kildare; anglic. Hill of Allen
480.04	Wolfhound	lit. trans. faolchú	"wild [but also wolf]-hound": wolf
.04–05	Folchu! Folchu!	faolchú (fwélkhú) folchadh (folkhu)	"wild-hound": wolf burying
.18	Bailey	Baile (bolye)	Homestead; light-house, Howth Head
.21	Emania	Eamhain (ouwin, aven)	Twin[?] ("Neck-Brooch" by folk ety-mology) anc. capital of Ulster (N. province); latinized Emania; see 410.23
.23	acushla	a cúisle (a kúshle)	pulse (endearment)
.28	Dyb! Dyb!	dubh (duv)	black
.30	dob dob dobbling	Dubh-linn (duvlin)	Black pool; *Dublin
.31–32	vuk vuk . . . vuk vuk	mhuc (vuk)	pig, swine
.34	fingall	Fine Gall (finigoul)	Foreign Kindred; N. Co. Dublin district, an-glic. Fingal
481.05	*Eirae*	Éire (ére)	Ireland
.13	Finnsen . . . occeanyclived	Oisín Mac Finn (ushín mok fin)	Fawn son of Fair: Fionn Mac Cumhail's son, *Macpherson's Ossian
.13	Faynean	Fiannach (fínokh)	soldier; member of Fiann, 3rd c. standing army led by Fionn Mac Cumhail

.13	occeanyclived	claidheamh (klív)	sword
.26	Mushame, Mushame	muise (mwishi) Séam (shém)	well, indeed (interj.) Sant Iago; *Shem
.26	ahore	a chara (a khore)	my friend
.28	Huddlestown	Baile Átha Cliath (bláklíe)	Hurdle Ford Town; *Dublin
.32	faher	fear (far) athair (aher)	man father
.35	Ranelagh	Raghnallaigh (rañelí)	of the family of *Raghnall* (Norm.-Fr. Reynald); S. Dublin district
482.05	Pursyriley	Piaras Uí Raghailligh (píres í rayelí)	Piers des. of *Raghallach* ("[strong-]forearmed")
.07	Lucas	Leamhcán (loukán)	Producing marshmallows; W. Dublin suburb on Liffey; anglic. Lucan
.07	Dublinn	Dubh-linn (*d*uvlin)	Black-pool; *Dublin
.09	Macdougal	Mac Dubhghaill (mok *d*úġil)	son of *Dubhghall* ("black-foreigner," i.e., Dane)
.09	chuam	Tuaim (túm)	burial mound, tumulus; town, Co. Galway, anglic. Tuam
.10	coughan	Cabhán (kaván)	Hollow; N. central co., anglic. Cavan
.11	Maho	Magh-eo (máyó)	Yew-Plain; W. co., anglic. Mayo
.12	O'mulanchonry	Ó Maol Chonaire (ó mwél khunere)	des. of *Maol Chonaire* ("follower of *Conaire*"), anglic. O Mulconry; n. of one of *Four Masters, also of *Finghin O Maol Chonaire*, Archbishop of Tuam, fndr.

			of I. Franciscan convent at Louvain
		lionndubh (lin*d*uv)	black bile, melancholy; *Dublin
.18	Keven	Caoimhghin (kívġin) Caomhán (kíván)	Comely-birth; anglic. Kevin; *Shaun dim. of *caomh*, "comely," anglic. Kevan; *Shaun
.18	Vaughan	bhán (ván)	white
.19	Guiney	Ó Geibheannaigh (ó geiní)	des. of *Geibheannach* ("fettered")
.27	Armagh	Árd Macha (ár*d* mokhe)	*Macha*'s (fem. pers. n. of legendary queen) Height; N. co. & town; primatial see of I.
.33	kills	Ceannanus (kyanenus) *altered to* Ceann-lios (kyanlis)	Head Residence Head-fort; anglic. Kenlis then Kells; monastic settlement, Co. Meath, fndd. by Colmcille
		Cill (kil)	Church; anglic. *Kill- in place-names
483.03	Shaum	Seán (shán) Séam (shém)	John; *Shaun Sant Iago; *Shem
.04	Sameas	Séamus (shémus)	James; *Shem
.04	Shan	sean (shan) Seán (shán)	old John; *Shaun
.04–05	There is . . . on . . .	*lit. trans.* Tá . . . ar . . .	[Kevin] suspects
.05	Kevin	Caoimhghin (kívġin)	Comely-birth; *Shaun
.13	are you in your post?	*lit. trans.* an bhfhuil tú i do phost?	are you a post (by avocation)?
.16	blarneying	Blárna (blárne)	Little-field; town, Co. Cork, anglic. Blarney

.20	an	an (un)	the
.20	am	am (oum)	time
.26	O cashla	a chúisle (a khúshle)	my pulse (endearment)
		a chaiseal (a khashel)	O stonefort
484.23	Ailbey	Ailbhe (alve)	masc. pers. n., Latin *Albeus*, missionary to I., died 541
.23	Ciardeclan	ciar (kír)	black
		Ciarán (kírán)	dim. of *Ciar* ("black"); n. of 15 sts., anglic. Kieran
		Déaglán (déglán)	Capacity[?]; st., latinized Declanus, anglic. Declan
.29	leabhour	leabhar (lyour)	book
.32	Prestopher Palumbus	*P/K Split	Crestopher Calumbus
.32	Porvus Parrio	*P/K Split	Corvus Carrio
.33	Kelly	Ó Ceallaigh (ó kyalí)	des. of *Ceallach* ("contention")
.33	Derry	Doire (*d*iri)	Oakwood; N. city & co.
.35	Pappagallus	*P/K Split [?]	Cappagallus [?]
.35	Pumpusmugnus	*P/K Split	Cumpusmugnus (Campus Magnus)
485.01	Sagart	sagart (soger*t*)	priest
.01	Lowman	*L/R Interchange	Rowman (Roman)
.01	Catlick's	*P/K Split, *L/R Interchange	Patrick's
.06	Moy Bog's	Magh Bog (má bug)	Soft Plain
.07–08	Suck at!—Suck it	Succat (suko*t*)	supposed baptismal n. of Patrick
.08	Misha	mise (mishi) muise (mushi)	I, me (emphatic) well, indeed (interj.)

.16	wrily	Ó Raghailligh (ó rayelí)	des. of *Raghallach* ("[strong-]fore-armed"); anglic. Reilly, Riley, etc.
.16	Bullydamestough	Baile Shéamais Dhuibh (bolye hémish ġuv)	Black James's Town, Co. Cavan, anglic. Ballyjamesduff
.16	buddy	bod (bu*d*)	penis
.16	rowly	Ó Raghailligh	as above
.20	Doyne	Ó Dubhghaill (ó *d*úġil)	des. of *Dubhghall* ("black-foreigner," i.e., Dane); anglic. Doyle (+ Dane = Doyne)
.22	tangue	teanga (t'oñe)	tongue, language
.32	maam	madhm (moum)	high mountain pass; anglic. Maam in place-names
.36	Thot's	toth (*to*)	female; female organs
486.02	cawthrick	*L/R Inter-change Pádraig (pá*d*rig)	cawthlick Patrick; *P/K Split
.02–03	cawthrick . . . *Quadrigue*	*P/K Split	pawthrick . . . *Paudrigue*
.02–03	cawthrick . . . *Quadrique my yoke*	Cathraighe, Cothraighe (kahrí, kohrí) [Mogh] Ceathrair	O.I. form of *Patricius* (*P/K Split); later folk-etymologized as [Servant] of Fourmen; explained as circum-stance of Patrick's boy-hood slavery
.28	adze	*allusion to* Táilcenn	"Adze-head"; early n. for Patrick, from ton-sure or bishop's miter
.33	Fairshee	sidhe (shí)	fairy
487.07	thinking to	tuigeann tú	you understand
.20	craythur	créatúir (kréa*t*úr)	"creature": person to be pitied
.31	Lapac	capall (kopel)	horse

.32	Capalisoot	capall (kopel)	horse
		Séipéal Io-said (shépél isid')	*Iosada*'s (fem. pers. n.: Iseult, Isolda) Chapel; W. Dublin district on Liffey; anglic. Chap-elizod
488.14	Felin	Feidhlim (félim)	shortened *Feidhlimidh* ("ever-good"); masc. pers. n. anglic. Felim
.14	Felin make Call	Fionn Mac Cumhail (fin mok kúl)	Fair son of *Cumhal*, 3rd c. hero of saga cycle
.15	Nolans	Ó Nualláin (ó núláñ)	des. of *Nuallán* (dim. of *nuall*, "noble")
.24–25	High Brazil	Í Breasail (í brasil)	Red [?] Island; leg-endary country W. in Atlantic; anglic. Hy-Brasil
.25	Brandan's	Bréannáin (brénáñ)	Putrid[?], Moist[?], Sorrowful[?]; masc. pers. n. of several sts., including supposed dis-coverer of America; anglic. Brendan
.26	Dublire	dubh (*d*uv) Dún Laoghaire (*d*ún líri)	black; *Dublin Laoghaire*'s ("calf-keeper") Fort; town & harbor on S. Dublin Bay
.36	Graw McGree	grádh mo chroidhe (grá mu khrí)	love of my heart
489.11	fawngest	fánach (fánokh)	wanderer, exile, stray, itinerant
.13	Nolan	Ó Nualláin (ó núláñ)	des. of *Nuallán* (dim. of *nuall*, "noble")
.14	Jerrybuilt	Diairmín (d'írmín)	dim. of *Diarmaid* ("freeman"); anglic. Jerry; *Shem
.27	moonshane	Seán (shán)	John; *Shaun
.30	Devitt	Mac Daibh-éid (mok *d*avéd')	son of David

490.01	bostoons	bastún (bos*t*ún)	poltroon, blockhead
.06	Madonagh	Mac Donnchadha (mok *d*unukhu)	son of *Donnchadh* ("brown-warrior"); anglic. MacDonagh, etc.
.06, 07	Nolan	Ó Nualláin (ó núláñ)	des. of *Nuallán* (dim. of *nuall*, "noble")
.28	Tuwarceathay	Teamhar (t'our)	Prospective-hill; anc. royal capital, anglic. Tara
.32	Pegeen	Peigín (pegín)	dim. of *Peig* (fem. pers. n., from English)
491.11	Lismore	Lios Mór (lis mór)	Great Enclosure; town, Co. Waterford
.12	Brendan	Bréannáin	see 488.25 (Cape Brendan, if it existed, would be in Co. Kerry)
.26	Tara's	Teamhar (t'our)	see 490.28
.29	Maomi	maon (mwén)	dumb
.36	Iran	Éireann (érun), *g*.	[of] Ireland
492.05	Loonacied	Luan (lún) Lughnasa (lúnese)	Monday August (festival of *Lugh*, sun-god)
.05	Marterdyed	Dia Máirt (dé márt') Márta (már*t*e)	Tuesday March
.08	Dias domnas!	Dia Domhnaigh (dé*d*ounig) Dia's donas! (d'ís *d*unes)	Sunday God and evil!
.12	ara poog	ara na bpóg (ore nu bóg)	one given to kissing
.21	Dowling	Ó Dubhláin (ó *d*úláñ) Ó Dubhlainn (ó *d*úlin)	des. of *Dubhshlán* ("black-challenge") des. of *Dubhfhlann* ("black *Flann* ['ruddy']")

		Ó Dúnlaing (ó dúliñ)	des. of *Dúnlang* (masc. pers. n.); all anglic. Dowling
		Dubh-linn (dúlin)	Black-pool; *Dublin
.22	Borumborad	Brian Bóroimhe (bríen bórivi)	Brian of the Tribute, anglic. *Brian Boru, high king killed defeating Danes at Clontarf, 1014
.22	M.A.C.A.	maca (moke)	posterity
.28	Kavanagh	Caomhánach (kévánokh)	belonging to *Caomhán* (dim. of *caomh*, "comely"; *Shaun); agnomen replacing original surname of des. of *Domhnall Caomhánach* [fostered at the monastic settlement of St. *Caomhán*] *Mac Murchadha*, son of *Diarmaid Mac Murchadha*, (*Shem), Leinster king who invited Anglo-Norman invasion
.34	moor's	Ó Mórdha (ó mórge)	des. of *Mórdha* ("majestic"); anglic. Moore
493.03	vallad	*Aspiration*: bhallad	ballad
.27	Eivin	Éirinn (érin), *dat.*	[to, for] Ireland
		aoibhinn (ívin)	pleasant
.32	Ani	eanaigh (aní)	fens, fenny; *Anna
.35	coolun dearast	cúilfhionn deas (kúlin d'as)	pretty fair-head (song)
		cailín deas (kolín d'as)	pretty girl
494.26	Magraw	Mag Raith (mogra)	son of *Mac Raith* ("son of grace")
		mo ghrádh (muġrá)	my love

495.01	Sully	Ó Súiligh (ó súlí)	des. of *Súileach* ("quick-eyed")
.02	Shovellyvans	Ó Súileabhán (ó súleváñ)	des. of *Súil-dubhán* ("black-eyed"); anglic. Sullivan
.03	Magrath's	Mag Raith (mogra)	son of *Mac Raith* ("son of grace")
.11	Lynch	Ó Loingsigh (ó liñshí)	des. of *Loingseach* ("having to do with a fleet")
.12	Galway	Gaillimh (goliv)	Foreign; W. co. & town
.17	Riley	Ó Raghailligh (ó rayelí)	des. of *Raghallach* ("[strong-]fore-armed")
.20	Finnyking	Ó Fionnagáin (ó finegáñ)	des. of *Fionnagán* (dim. of *fionn*, "fair"); anglic. Finnegan
		Ó Fionn-mhacáin (ó finwokáñ)	des. of *Fionnmhacán* ("fair little son"); anglic. Finucane
.24	cherrywickerkisha-brack	cis (kish)	wickerwork basket; lighthouse, *Dublin Bay
		breac (brak)	speckled
.27	O'Neill	Ó Néill (ó nél)	des. of *Niall* ("champion"); *Uí Néill
.33	Anm.	ainm (anim)	name
496.11	ingen	inghean (inyin)	daughter; virgin
.13	bumgalowre	go leór (gulór)	enough, plenty
.15	Eire	Éire (ére)	Ireland
.18	fingall's	Fine-Gall (fini goul)	Foreign Kindred; N. Co. Dublin district, anglic. Fingal; *Macpherson
.23	ariring	éirghe (eirí)	rising
.27	Abha na Lifé	Abha na Life (ouwe nu lifi)	The River *Liffey
.36	*quinnigan*	Ó Cuinne-agáin (ó kwinegáñ)	des. of *Cuinneagán* (dim. of *Conn*, "intelligence")

		Ó Fionnagáin (ó finegáñ)	des. of *Fionnagán* (dim. of *Fionn*, "fair"); an- glic. Finnegan
497.01	*Quinnigan's*		see 496.36
.04	Arra	ara (ore)	deprecatory interj.
.04	irrara hirrara	a Dhia are (ayíore)	O God now (interj.)
.05	fogabawlers	fág an beal- ach (fág a byalokh)	leave the way, clear the way
.11	Rathgar	Ráth Garbh (rá gorev)	Rough Fort; S. Dub- lin district
.11	Rathanga	Ráth Iom- ghain (rá omġen)	*Iomghan's* ("very- small"[?]) Fort; town, Co. Kildare, an- glic. Rathangan
.11	Rush	Ros-eó (roshó)	Yew-tree Peninsula; village, N. Co. Dublin
.17	Merrionites	Muirbhthean (mwirvyan)	Seashore; S. Dublin suburb, anglic. Mer- rion
.17–18	Dumstdumb- drummers	Dún Droma (*dún d*rume)	Fort of a Ridge; S. Dublin suburb, an- glic. Dundrum
.18	Luccanicans	Leamhcán (loukán)	Producing marshmal- lows; W. Dublin sub- urb on Liffey; anglic. Lucan
.19	Krumlin	Croimghlinn (krumlin)	Crooked Valley; S. Dublin district, an- glic. Crumlin
.19	Cabraists	Cabrach (kobrokh)	Badland; N. Dublin district, anglic. Cabra
.19	Finglossies	Finn-glas (finglos)	Clear Stream; village & stream N. of Dub- lin, anglic. Finglas
.20	Ballymunites	Baile Munne (bolye mune)	*Munna's* [9th c. st.] Town; Dublin sub- urb, anglic. Ballymun
.20	Raheniacs	Ráth Éanna (rá éne)	Enda's (st.'s n.) Fort; N.E. Dublin suburb; anglic. Raheny

.20	Clontarf	Cluain Tarbh (klún *torev*)	Bull Meadow; N.E. Dublin district
.23	*Uisgye*	uisce (ishki)	water
.27	Magennis Mor	Mag Aonghuis Mór (mogényish mór)	Great son of *Aonghus* ("single-choice" [god of love])
.33	claddagh	Cladach (kla*d*okh)	Stony seashore; fishing settlement in Galway town: The Claddagh
498.09	Brehons	breitheamhain (brehún)	judges, lawgivers of anc. I.
.10	Flawhoolags	flaitheamhlach (flohúlokh)	"princely": generous
.11	Kong	Conga (kuñge)	Strait; town, Co. Mayo, anglic. Cong
.12	Athclee	Áth Cliath (áklíe)	Hurdle Ford; *Dublin
.12	Athlone	Áth Luain (álúñ)	*Luan*'s ("warrior") Ford; central town
.13	fain awan	féin amhain (fén awáñ)	self alone
.14	epheud	Uíbh Eachach (ívakhokh)	des. of *Eochaidh* ("horseman"); tribal land, Co. Down, anglic. Iveagh: baronage of Edward Cecil Guinness
.14	ordilawn	Árd Oileán (ár*d*ilán)	High Island, Co. Galway; anglic. Ardilaun, baronage of Arthur Guinness
.15–16	amok and amak	amuigh's amach (amwís amokh) mac (mok)	"out and out": altogether, completely son
.17	gougerotty	Mag Fhógartaigh (mogógor*t*í)	son of *Fógartach* ("banished"); anglic. Gogarty
.18	a'mona	móna (móne)	of a peat bog

.19	o'ryely	Ó Raghailligh (ó rayelí)	des. of *Raghallach* ("[strong-]fore-armed"); anglic. O Reilly, etc.
.19	annagolorum	eanach (anokh)	fen, marsh; *Anna
		go leór (gulór)	enough, plenty
.19	Kennedy's	Ó Cinnéide (ó kinéd'i)	des. of *Cinnéididh* ("helmeted-head") *Brian Boru
.23	Ogonoch	ógánach (ógánokh)	youth, bachelor
.26	tilly	tuile (*t*ili)	extra, addition (as 13th to dozen)
499.06	Bawse	bás (bás)	death
.07	Moutmaro	marbhadh (morú)	killing, murder
.11	donal	Domhnall (*d*ónel)	World-mighty; masc. pers. n.
.13–14	keyn . . . keying	caoin (kín)	bewail, lament
.17	saouls	sábhal (sál)	barn, granary
.18	dhaoul	diabhal (d'oul)	devil
.18	Finnk	Fionn (fin)	Fair
.21	tolkshap	tolc (*t*ulk) tolca (*t*ulke)	strong blow flood, torrent
.22	muck	muc (muk)	pig, swine
.22	Sorley boy	Somhairle Buidhe (sórli bwí)	Yellow *Sumerlide* (Norse, "summer-sailor"): *Somhairle Buidhe Mac Domhnaill*, anglic. Sorley Boy Mac Donnell, led Mac Donnells of Antrim in resistance to Elizabeth I
.24	Surly	Somhairle	see 499.22
.26	ollaves	ollamh (ulev)	sage, poet, professor
.29	Dingle	Daingean [Uí Chúis] (*da*ñin [í kúsh])	Stronghold [of the des. of *Cús*]; town, W. Kerry

.31–32	*Usque! Usque! Usque!*	uisce (ishki)	water
.33	Rawth of Gar	Ráth Garbh (rá gorev)	Rough Fort; S. Dublin district, anglic. Rathgar
.33	Donnerbruck	Domhnach/ Tamhnach Broc (*d*ounokh/ *t*ounokh brok)	Badger Church/ Green-field; S. Dublin district; anglic. Donnybrook
.35–36	Whoishe . . . whoishe	mhuise (wishi)	well, indeed (interj.)
500.02–03	Clan of the Gael	Clann na nGaedheal (klon nu ñél)	Children of the Irish: n. of an association
		Clanna Gaedheal (klone gél)	"Irish progenies": the Irish race
.04	Dovegall	Dubh-gall (*d*uvgoul)	Black-foreigner; i.e., Dane
.04	finshark	fionn (fin)	fair
.06	Crum	Crom (krum)	Crouching; anc. idol overthrown by St. Patrick
.06	abu!	abú! (abú)	to victory!
.17	Slog	slog (slug)	sudden swallow
.17	sluaghter	sluagh (slúe)	host, army
501.04	Ballymacarett	Baile Mic Gearóid (bolye mic garód')	Town of the son of Gerald (i.e., Fitzgerald), near Belfast
.14	Sybil Head	Ceann Sibéal (kyoun shibél)	Isabel's Head, promontory N.W. of Dingle, Co. Kerry
502.01	farranoch	fearthanach (farenokh)	rainy
		fearthanacht (farenokh*t*)	downpour of rain
.04	snaachtha	sneachta (snokh*te*)	snow

.04	snaachtha clocka	clocha sneachta (klukhe snokh*te*)	"snow-stones": hail-stones
		seacht a' chlog (shokh*t* akhlug)	seven o'clock
.04	clocka	clocha (klukhe)	stones
.09	Brr	Biorra (bire)	Watery, Marshy; town, Co. Westmeath, anglic. Birr
.09	Brr na brr	Biorra na biorra [?] (bire nu bire)	Watery of the Wateries
.09	ny	ní (ní)	not
.12	Muna	mún (mún) muna (mune)	urine unless
.14	geallachers	gealach (gyalokh)	moon
.35	Finglas	Fionn-glas (finglos)	Clear Stream; village & stream N. of Dublin
503.10	Fanagan	Ó Fionnagáin (ó finegáñ)	des. of *Fionnagán* (dim. of *Fionn*, "fair"); anglic. Fanagan, Finnegan, etc.
.13	Fingal	Fine-Gall (finigoul)	Foreign Kindred; N. Co. Dublin district; *Macpherson
.17	delville	Dealbhna (d'alvne)	Progeny of *Lughaidh Dealbhaodh* ("fire-shape"); tribal land; n. of river N. Co. Dublin anglic. Delvin
.17	tolkar	Tolca (*t*ulke)	Flood, Torrent; N.E. Dublin river, site of battle of Clontarf, 1014; anglic. Tolka
.23	grianblachk	grian (gríen) blacht (blokh*t*)	sun milk

.23	gan greyne	gan ghréin (gon ġrén)	without sun, sunless
.23	Eireann	Éireann (érun), g.	[of] Ireland
.23	gan greyne Eireann	gan ghrian Éireann (gon ġrín érun)	without the sun of Ireland
.31	Annar	An Dobhar (undówer)	The Water, river, Co. Tipperary, anglic. Anner
		eanach (anokh)	marsh, fen; *Anna
.32	Slivenamond	Sliabh na mBan (slív nu mon)	Mountain of the Women, Co. Tipperary, anglic. Slievenamon
.32	Oakley Ashe's elm	dair, nuin, ailm	oak, ash, elm: letters D, N, A
.33	beerchen	beith	birch: letter B
.35	Nolan's	Ó Nualláin (ó núláñ)	des. of *Nuallán* (dim. of *nuall*, "noble")
504.01–02	cran . . . cran . . . crans	crann (kroun)	tree
.20	Corcor	corcair (kurkir)	purple
.20	Corcor Andy	*P/K Split	Porpor Andy: purpurando (see 504.17)
.22	Idahore	Íde (íd′e)	Thirst; fem. pers. n.; anglic. Ita, Ida
.23	sweenyswinging	Mac Suibhne (mok swíni)	son of *Suibhne* ("well-going"); anglic. Sweeney, etc.
.25	fenians	Fianna (fíene)	members of 3rd c. standing army led by *Fionn Mac Cumhail*
.31	killmaimthem	Cill Maighnenn (kil meinen)	*Maighneann*'s Church; Dublin district (with former political prison) S. of Liffey; anglic. Kilmainham; *Brian Boru
505.20	Mushe, mushe	muise (mwishi)	well, indeed (interj.)
.24	Finight	fionn (fin)	fair

506.09	Finlay's	Ó Fionn-ghalaigh (ó finġalí)	des. of *Fionnghalach* ("fair-valorous") [a leader of *Brian Boru's forces at Clontarf]
.12	coombe	Cúm (kúm)	Hollow; S. Dublin slum, anglic. The Coombe
.13	grauws	grádh (grá)	love
.29	Finoglam	Fionn-óglach (finóglokh)	fair-haired young soldier
.34	Lynsha's	Ó Loingsigh (ó liñshí)	des. of *Loingseach* ("having to do with a fleet"); anglic. Lynch
507.02	Kimmage	Cam-ínse (komínshi)	Curving water-meadows; Dublin district
.06–07	rapparitions	rapaire (ropire)	robber, snatcher; 18th c. I. outlaw, anglic. rapparee
.11	tubbernuckles	tobar (*t*uber)	well, spring
.12	longarmed lugh	Lugh Lámhfhada (lú lávo*d*e)	n. of god of sun & genius: *Lugh* of the Long Arm
.22	sprogue	barróg (beróg)	defect in speech
.26	O'Connell	Ó Conaill (ó kunil)	des. of *Conall* ("high-powerful")
.29	Connor's	Ó Concho-bhair (ó konukher)	des. of *Conchobhar* ("high-will")
.35	Boaterstown	*half-trans.* Baile an Bhóthair (bolye un vóher)	Town of the Road, S. Dublin suburb, anglic. Booterstown
.36	crannock	crannóg (kranóg)	piece of wood; pulpit; box, chest, hamper; lake-dwelling
508.02	Eryen	Éireann (érun), *g.*	[of] Ireland
.15	Meagher	Ó Meachair (ó myakhir)	des. of *Meachar* ("hospitable")
.17	skib	scib (shkib)	skiff; boat-shaped basket

.23	Clopatrick's	cló (kló)	stamp, print, impression
		*L/R Interchange	Cro[agh] Patrick, mtn., Co. Mayo
.32	Collinses	Ó Coileáin (ó kuláñ)	des. of *Coileán* ("whelp"); anglic. Collins
		cailín (kolín)	girl
510.13	Guinness	Mag Aonghusa (mogénǵesi)	son of *Aonghus* ("single-choice" [god of love])
.15	Gaelers'	Gaedheal (gél)	Irishman, Scotsman
.16	Gall	gall (goul)	foreigner
.18	lairking o'tootlers	Lorcán Ó Tuathail (lurkán ó *t*úhil)	*Lorcán* (dim. of *lorc*, "fierce") des. of *Tuathal* ("people-mighty"); Abp. & patron st. of Dublin; anglic. Laurence O Toole
.24	ehren	Éirinn (érin), *dat.*	[to, for] Ireland
.24	Fyn's	Fionn (fin)	Fair
.32	Kerssfesstiydt	Mac Fhiarais (mokírish) for Mac Phiarais (mokfírish)	son of Piers [Healy]; anglic. Kersse
.33	Inishfeel	Inis Fáil (inish fál)	Island of *Fál* (n. of fetish stone at Tara): Ireland (poetic)
511.02, 07	Magraw	Mag Raith (mogra) mo ghrádh (muǵrá)	son of *Mac Raith* ("son of grace") my love
.12	divileen	-ín (ín), *dim. suffx.*	little, darling
.15	she laylylaw	Síol Élaigh (shíl élí)	Progeny of *Éalach* ("skillful" [?]), tribal land, Co. Wicklow, famous for oakwoods & blackthorns; anglic. Shillelagh

.24	burley	Béarla (bérle)	English language
.31	findring	fionndruine (findrini)	white bronze; silver-plated bronze
512.01	Lollgoll	goll (gol)	blind; *Goll Mac Mórna*, companion & rival of *Fionn Mac Cumhail*
.08	kished	cis (kish)	wickerwork basket; lighthouse, *Dublin Bay
.10	Annabella	Eanach-bile (anokh bili)	Marsh of the Sacred Tree; village, Co. Cork
.25	Suilful	súil (súl)	eye
.30	artained	Árd Aidhin (árd ein)	*Aidhin*'s ("ember" [?]: 9th c. st.) Height; N.E. Dublin suburb with industrial school for boys, anglic. Artane
.31	O'Ford . . . hurdley	Áth Cliath (áklíe)	Hurdle Ford; *Dublin
513.05	Corrig	Carraigidh (korigí)	Rocky-hills; anglic. Corriga, etc. in place-names
		corrach (korokh)	morass, marsh
.08	*lenonem*	Ó Lionnáin (ó lináñ)	des. of *Leannán* (dim. of *leann*, "cloak"); anglic. Lennon
.27	darm it	Diarmaid (d'írmid')	Freeman; hero of *Toraidheacht Dhiarmada agus Ghráinne*; *Shem
.28	graunt ye	Gráinne (gráñi)	Grain/Spearpoint; heroine of *Toraidheacht Dhiarmada agus Ghráinne*
.33	Kerry	Ciarraighe (kírí)	Race of *Ciar* ("black"); S.W. co.
.33	Listowel	Lios Tuathail (lis túhil)	*Tuathal*'s ("people-mighty") Fort; town Co. Kerry
514.02	Normand, Desmond, Osmund . . . Kenneth	four provinces: N., S. [*deas*, "south"], E., W.	Ulster, Munster, Leinster, Connacht

.02	Normand, Desmond, Osmund	Tuath-Mumhan, Deas-Mumhan, Thoir-Mumhan (*t*úemún, *d*'asmún, hirmún)	North Munster, South Munster, East Munster; anglic. Thomond, Desmond, Ormond
.02	Kenneth	Connachta (kunukh*t*e)	Progeny of *Conn* ("intelligence"); W. province, anglic. Connacht, Connaught
.18	.i..'. [Finn's]	Fionn (fin)	Fair
.19	shuler's	siubhlóir (shúlór)	traveler, wayfarer, vagrant
.25	Bonnybrook	Domhnach/Tamhnach Broc (*d*ounokh/*t*ounokh brok)	Badger Church/Green-field; S. Dublin district, anglic. Donnybrook
.33	Gaelicise	Gaedheal (gél)	Irishman, Scotsman
		Gaedhilg (gélg)	Irish language
.36	eirest . . . ourest . . . airest	Éire (ére)	Ireland
515.01	erestationed	Éire (ére)	Ireland
.07	gael	Gaedheal (gél)	Irishman, Scotsman
.07	galled	gall (goul)	foreigner
.24	kerryer	Ciarraighe (kírí)	Race of *Ciar* ("black"); S.W. co., anglic. Kerry
.30	foggus	fogas (foges)	near, close to
.35	pratey	préataí (prétí)	potatoes
516.05	MacSmashall Swingy of the Cattlelaxes	Mac Suibhne (mok swíñi)	son of *Suibhne* ("well-going"); *Mac Suibhne na dTuath Toraighe* ("of the districts of Towery [Island]") is sometimes called MacSweeney of the Battleaxes by mistake of *Tuath* for *Tuagha*, "Axes"

.06	Kildare	Cill Dara (kil*d*ore)	Church of the Oak-wood; town & co. W. of Dublin
.11	naas	Nás na Rí (nás nurí)	The King's Meeting Place; town, Co. Kildare, anglic. Naas
.13	coocoomb	cúm (kúm)	hollow; S. Dublin slum anglic. The Coombe
.20	Cogan	Mac Cogadháin (mok kugáñ)	son of *Cogadhán* (pet form of *Cúchogaidh*, "war-hound")
.31	O'Farrell	O Fearghail (ó faryil)	des. of *Fearghal* ("supervalor")
517.15	Black Pig's Dyke	*trans.* Cladh na Muice Duibhe	an earthen *vallum*, anc. border of Ulster
.27	higgins	Ó hUigín (ó higín)	des. of *Uige* ("skill")
.36	dath	dath (*d*o)	color
518.01	Dunsink	Dún Sinche (*d*ún shinkhi)	*Sinche*'s (fem. pers. n.) Fort; meteorological observatory W. of Dublin
.06	Drogheda	Droichead Átha (*d*rihe*d* áhe)	Bridge of the Ford; town between Cos. Meath & Louth N. of Dublin
.07	Milesian	Míleadh (míle)	Celtic *colonist
.09	Ghyllygully	an giolla goillín (un gilegulín)	the tormentor-lad: the devil
.11	Lorcans	Lorcán (lurkán)	dim. of *lorc*, "fierce"; masc. pers. n. anglic. Laurence; *Brian Boru
.25	Bucclis	Ó Buachalla (ó búkheli)	des. of *Buachaill* ("boy"); anglic. Buckley
.26	Dorans	Ó Deóráin (ó d'óráñ)	des. of *Deóradhán* (dim. of *deóradh*, "exile, stranger")
.26	finnish	fionn (fin)	fair

.27	Feeney's	Ó Fiannaidhe (ó fíní)	des. of *Fiannaidhe* ("soldier")
.29	Canniley	Ó Coingheall-laigh (ó kinyalí)	des. of *Coingheallach* ("serving under conditions")
		Ó Cinn-fhaolaidh (ó kinélí)	des. of *Ceannfhaoladh* ("wolf-head")
.30	Donnuley	Ó Donnghaile (ó *d*onyali)	des. of *Donnghal* ("brown-valor"); anglic. Donnelly
519.05	O'Huggins	Ó hAodhagáin (ó hégáñ)	des. of *Aodhagán* (dim. of *Aodh*, "fire")
.05	ormonde	Thoir-Mumhan (hirmún)	East Munster (S. province); anglic. Ormond
.06	O'Hefferns	O hIfearnáin (ó hifernáñ)	des. of *Ifearnán* ("infernal" [?])
.07	MacClouds	Mac Leóid (moklód′)	son of *Leód* (Norse *Ljotr*, "ugly")
.10	ri	rí (rí)	king
.14	Finny . . . finny	fionn (fin)	fair
.24	Corth	Corcaigh (kurkí)	Swamp; S. city & co., anglic. Cork
.24	reen	ríoghan (rín)	queen
.31	Tarpey	Ó Tarpaigh (ó *t*orpí)	des. of *Tarpach* ("sturdy")
.33	Lyons	Ó Laighin (ó lein)	des. of *Laighean* ("lance")
520.02	tarrable	Teamhar (t'our)	Prospective-hill; anc. royal capital, anglic. Tara
		tarbh (*t*orev)	bull
.02	Turk	torc (*t*urk)	boar, hog
.03	begalla	gall (goul)	foreigner
.03	Michael Clery	Mícheál Ó Cléirigh (míhál ó klérí)	Michael des. of *Cléireach* ("cleric"); n. of most prominent of *Four Masters
.04, 10	MacGregor	Mac Greagair (mok greger)	son of Gregory

.08	Tarpey	Ó Tarpaigh	see 519.31
.09	tumple	teampall (t'oumpul)	church, esp. Protestant
.13	Lyons	Ó Laighin	see 519.33
.15	Clery	Ó Cléirigh (ó klérí)	des. of *Cléireach* ("cleric"); n. of 3 of *Four Masters
.18	Anlone	Anluan (onlún)	Great-hero; masc. pers. n.
		an (un)	the
		Áth Luain (álún)	*Luan*'s ("hero") Ford; central town on Shannon; anglic. Athlone
.22	Nils	níl (níl)	is not
.23	Mugn	Mumha[n] (mún)	S. province; anglic. Munster
		mún (mún)	urine
.23	Cannut	Connachta (kunukh*t*e)	Progeny of *Conn* ("intelligence"); W. province, anglic. Connacht, Connaught
.24	bil	bile (bili)	sacred tree
.30	paddyflaherty	Páidín Ó Flaithbheartaigh (pád'ín ó flaher*t*í)	Paddy des. of *Flaithbheartach* ("bright-ruler")
.33	boolyhooly	Baile Átha Ubhla (bolye áhúle)	Appletree-Ford Town, Co. Cork; anglic. Ballyhooly ("ballyhooly/hooly": riotous celebration)
		buaile (búli)	byre, milking enclosure; in place-names anglic. Booly-
		bualadh (búle)	beating
.34	ulstar	Ulaidh (ule)	N. province, anglic. Ulster
.36	labrose	labhras (loures)	laurel
		labhartha (loure)	spoken, said

521.03	Rootha	rúta (rúte)	root, stock
.03	Rootha prootha	rúta práta (rúte práte)	potato root (see 521.06: potators)
.03	prootha	prútach (prútokh)	brute
.06	Lucan	Leamhcán (loukán)	Producing marshmallows; W. Dublin suburb on Liffey
.24	Annybody's	eanaigh, eanaighe (aní)	[of a] marsh, fen; marshes, fens
.28	leinconnmuns	Laighin (lein)	Lances; E. province, anglic. Leinster
		Connachta (kunukhte)	Progeny of Conn ("intelligence"); W. province, anglic. Connacht, Connaught
		Mumha[n] (mún)	S. province; anglic. Munster
		mún (mún)	urine
.30	hulstler	Ulaidh (ule)	Monument; N. province, anglic. Ulster
.32	Emania	Eamhain (ouwin, aven)	Twin [?]; anc. capital of Ulster, latinized Emania
.32	Raffaroo	Ó Rabhartaigh (ó ravertí)	des. of Robhartach ("given to fits"); anglic. Rafferty
		ruadh (rúe)	red
.33	Finnians	Finnián (finían)	dim. of Fionn ("fair"); n. of several sts.
		Fionn (fin)	Fair
		Fianna (fíene)	soldiers: members of 3rd c. standing army led by Fionn Mac Cumhail
.35	moll	mol (mul)	praise
.35	me roon	mo rún (mu rún)	my precious
522.19	nass	nás (nás)	omen
523.11	bally	baile (bolye)	town; homestead; anglic. Bally-

.18	MacMannigan's	Mac Mainchín/ Manacháin (mok manikhín/ monekháñ)	son of *Mainchín/ Manachán* (dim. of *manach*, "monk")
524.28	gillybrighteners	gile (gili) giolla (gili) gilidhe (gilí)	brightness; beloved servant, lad little trout
.29	gallockers	gealach (gyalokh) gall (goul)	brightness; moon foreigner
525.03	bracksullied	breac (brak)	speckled; trout; any fish caught by hook
.06	Errian	Éireann (érun), *g.*	[of] Ireland
.15	fenian	Fíannaidhe (fíení)	soldier; member of 3rd c. standing army led by *Fionn Mac Cumhail*
.17	monach	manach (monokh) monach (munokh)	monk guileful
.18	dans, oges and conals	Domhnall Ó Conaill (*dónel ó kunil*)	World-mighty des. of High-powerful; anglic. Daniel O Connell
.18	oges	óg (óg) óigh (óí)	young virgin
.18	conals	Conall (kunel)	High-powerful; masc. pers. n.
.29	Malin	Malainn (molin)	Hill-brow, Co. Donegal; N.-most point of I.
.31	fin may cumule	Fionn Mac Cumhail (fin mok kúil)	Fair son of *Cumhal*; 3rd c. hero of saga cycle
526.06	Rush	Ros-eó (rushó)	Yew-tree peninsula; seaside resort, N. Co. Dublin
.08	Toomey	Ó Tuama (ó *túme*)	des. of *Tuaim* ("mound")
.14	*Shaun*	Seán (shán)	John; *Shaun
.14	*shame*	Séam (shém)	Sant Iago; *Shem

.20	Naif	Naomh (név)	Saint
.20	Cruachan	Cruachán (krúkhán)	Little Hill; frequent place-name; anc. royal seat of Connacht, home of Queen *Maedhbh* ("Maeve") in *Red Branch sagas
		cruachán	dim. of *cruach* ("symmetrical heap"): little porpoise-shaped fish found in tidal rock pools; *Humphrey
		crúach (krúkh)	gory, clotted, as in *Crom Crúach* ("gory croucher"), anc. idol
.20	Daly	Ó Dálaigh (ó *dálí*)	des. of *Dálach* ("assemblist")
.24	MacGarry	Mac Fhearadhaigh (mokarí)	son of *Fearadhach* ("manly, virile")
.28	Corrack-on-Sharon	corrach (korokh)	morass, marsh
		curach (kurokh)	light canvas boat; anglic. curragh
		Cora Droma Rúisc (kore *d*rume rúshk)	Weir of Tree-bark Ridge; town, Co. Roscommon, irrationally anglic. Carrick-on-Shannon
.28	Rosecarmon	Roscomáin (roskumáñ)	*Cómán*'s (dim. of *cam*, "bent") Wood; W. central co., on Shannon, anglic. Roscommon
.30	Tarpeyan	Ó Tarpaigh (ó *torpí*)	des. of *Tarpach* ("sturdy"); anglic. Tarpey
.33	Lough Shieling's	Loch Inse Uí Fhlainn (lokh inshí lin)	Lake of a descendant of *Flann*'s ("ruddy") Island, Co. Derry, anglic. Lough Shillin
.34	shielsome	Síle (shíli)	fem. pers. n. from Latin *Cecilia*, anglic. Sheila

527.01	Iscappellas	uisce (ishki)	water
		Séipéal Iosaid (shépél isid′)	Iosada's (fem. pers. n., Iseult, Isolda) Chapel; W. Dublin district anglic. Chapelizod
.03	mearest	méar (mér)	finger
.03–04	finweeds	fionn (fin)	fair
528.04	Bansh	bean (ban) bean-sidhe (banshí)	woman, wife fairy-woman
.05	bloss	blas (blos)	taste, flavor
.06	Audiens	Aodhán (éán)	masc. pers. n., dim. of aodh ("fire"); n. of 23 sts.; anglic. Aidan, Aedan
.06	rosan	rosán (rosán)	shrubbery
.13	Tolka	Tolca (tulke)	Flood, Torrent; N. Dublin river, site of battle of Clontarf, 1014
.28	Moonster	Mumha[n] (mún) mún (mún)	S. province; anglic. Munster urine
.29	Connacht	Connachta (kunukhte)	Progeny of Conn ("intelligence"), W. province
.30, 32	lion's . . . leinstrel	Laighin (lein)	Lances; E. province, anglic. Leinster
.32	moreen	Móirín (mórín)	dim. of Mór (fem. pers. n.: "sun"; n. of typical peasant woman)
.32	astoreen	a stóirín (a stórín)	my little treasure (endearment)
.33	Monn	Mumha[n] (mún)	S. province, anglic. Munster
.33	Conn	Conn (kon)	Intelligence; masc. pers. n.
		Connachta (kunukhte)	Progeny of Conn, W. province, anglic. Connacht, Connaught
.36	skullabogue	scealbóg/ scolbóg (shkalebóg/ skulebóg)	splinter, slice, pinch, piece of kindling wood

529.15	anterim	Aontruim (éntrim)	One Elder tree (folk-etymologized *aontreabh*, "one tribe"), N.E. co., anglic. Antrim
.16	Tooley	Ó Tuathghaile (ó *tú*yelí)	des. of *Tuathal* ("people-mighty")
.16	O'Bejorumsen	ó (ó)	descendant, grandson, scion
.16	Mockmacmahonitch	Mac Mathghamhna (mok mahúne)	son of *Mathghamhain* ("bear"); anglic. Mac-Mahon
.19	the coombe	Cúm (kúm)	Hollow; S. Dublin slum anglic. The Coombe
.23	Glassthure	*L/R Inter-change Glas-Tuathail (glos*tú*hil)	Glasthule *Tuathal*'s ("people-mighty") Stream; village & stream near Dun Laoghaire, anglic. Glasthule
		túr (*tú*r)	tower
.25	O'Dyar	Ó Duibhidhir (ó *d*vír)	des. of *Dubh-odhar* ("black-dun"); anglic. Dyer
.26	glenagearries	Gleann na gCaoirigh (gloun nu gírí)	Valley of the Sheep; village near Dun Laoghaire, anglic. Glenagarey; village Co. Tyrone, anglic. Glennageeragh
		Gleann na gCaora (gloun nu gíre)	Valley of the Berries; villages Co. Cork, Co. Clare, anglic. Glennageare
.33	torc	torc (*t*ork)	torque (twisted neck decoration)
.34	Bar Ptolomei	Parthalón (paralón)	2nd legendary *colonist; anglic. Bartholomew
530.02	buckleybackers	Ó Buachalla (ó búkheli)	des. of *Buachaill* ("boy"); anglic. Buckley

.12	balbriggans	Baile Breacáin (bolye brekáñ)	*Breacán*'s (dim. of *breac*, "speckled") Town; N. Co. Dublin (textile mills); anglic. Balbriggan
.15	lagenloves	Lagán (logán)	dim. of *log* ("hollow"); Belfast's river anglic. Lagan
.16	Heliopolitan	Ó hÉilidhe (ó hélí)	des. of *Ealadhach* ("ingenious"); anglic. O Healy, Hely, etc.
.18	arianautic	Éireann (érun), *g.*	[of] Ireland
.21	Errick	Éiric (érik)	Fine, Ransom; n. of two townlands, Co. Roscommon
531.03	Pave Pannem	*P/K Split	Cave Cannem
.04	Log Laughty	Log an Lagh (lug un lá)	Hollow of the Hill; valley, Co. Wicklow, S. of Dublin, anglic. Luggelaw
		Loch Lachan (lokh lokhen)	Duck Lake, Co. Antrim, anglic. Loughloughan
.10	Abarm's brack	bairghean breac (boryen brak)	speckled cake: Halloween currant cake, anglic. barmbrack
.16	Lanner	leannán (lanán)	paramour
		leannóir (lanór)	brewer
.24	camcam	cam (koum)	crooked, curved, twisted
.28	Finnegan	Ó Fionnagáin (ó finegáñ)	des. of *Fionnagán* (dim. of *Fionn*, "fair")
.33	child of Coole	Mac Cumhail (mok kúl)	son of *Cumhal*; patronymic of *Fionn*
.33	Coole	Cúil (kúl)	Recess, Corner; frequent place-name
532.01	eirenarch's	Éire (ére) airchinneach (arkhinokh)	Ireland steward of church lands; anglic. erenagh
.02	Finn	Fionn (fin)	Fair

.05	Doff	dubh (*d*uv)	black
.08	Owllaugh	Amhlaoibh (oulév)	masc. pers. n. (Norse *Ólafr*, in I. since 9th c.); anglic. *Humphrey
.09	MacAuscullpth	Mac Amhlaoibh (mok oulév)	son of *Amhlaoibh* (*Ólafr*); anglic. Mac-Auliffe, Macauley; *Humphrey
		Mac Ascaill (mok oskil)	son of *Ascall* (Norse *Askell*); anglic. Mac-Askill
.12	Farnum's rath	Ráth Fearannain (rá farenin)	*Fearannan*'s (masc. pers. n., "landholder" [?]) Fort; S. Dublin district, anglic. Rathfarnham
.12–13	Condra's ridge	Drom Conaire (*d*rum kunire)	*Conaire*'s ("high-care") Ridge; N. Dublin district, anglic. Drumcondra
.13	meadows of Dalkin	Cluain Dealgáin (klún d'algáñ)	Meadow of a Bodkin (masc. pers. n.?); Dublin suburb, anglic. Clondalkin
533.08	Dolekey	Dealg-inis (d'alginish)	Thorn Island, on S.E. Dublin Bay, Norsified Dalkey
.19	cabinteeny	Cabán tSíle (kabán tíli) [*grammatically anomalous*]	Sheila's Hut (n. of 17th c. tavern); Co. Dublin village, anglic. Cabinteely
.33	Hiemlancollin	Ó Coileáin (ó kuláñ)	des. of *Coileán* ("whelp"); anglic. Collins
.34	Shaun	Seán (shán)	John; *Shaun
534.19	knockbrecky	Cnoc Breac (knuk brak)	Speckled Hill; widespread place-name, anglic. Knockbreck
		Cnoc Bhreacáin (knuk vrakáñ)	*Breacán*'s (dim. of *breac*, "speckled") Hill, Co. Down; anglic. Knockbrecan

		Cnoc Bréaga (knuk brége)	Hill of Falsehood, Co. Mayo, anglic. Knock-breaga
.19	bullfist	Béal Feirste (bél ferishti)	Sandbank River-mouth; N.E. city, anglic. Belfast
.26	caca	cac (kok)	excrement, ordure
.30	keshaned	Ó Casáin (ó kosáñ)	des. of *Casán* (dim. of *cas*, "bent, curly"); anglic. Kissane, Cashin, etc.
.31	lorking	Lorcán (lurkán)	masc. pers. n., dim. of *lorc*, "fierce" anglic. Laurence
.32, 33	Shames . . . Shamus	Séamus (shémus)	James; *Shem
535.08	Tara	Teamhar (t'our)	Prospective-hill; anc. royal capital
.20	shugon	siogán (shugán)	ant
.20	muckswinish	muc (muk) Mac Suibhne (mok swíñi)	pig, swine son of *Suibhne* ("well-going"); anglic. Mac-Sweeney, MacSwiney, etc.
536.10	ballyheart	baile (bolye)	town, homestead; anglic. Bally-
.10	krumlin	Crom-ghlinn (krumlin)	Curved Valley; S. Dublin district, anglic. Crumlin
.12	O Hone!	ochón! (ukhón)	alas!
.15	buckely	Ó Buachalla (ó búkheli)	des. of *Buachaill* ("boy"); anglic. Buckley
.21	Oscarshal's	Oscar (usker)	Champion; son of *Oisín*, grandson of *Fionn Mac Cumhail*
.34	Faagher	fághar (fáǵer)	favor
.36	O Shee	Ó Séaghdha (ó shéya) sidhe (shí)	des. of *Séaghdha* ("stately") fairy
537.10	*Ehren*	Éire (ére)	Ireland

.14	eric	éiric (érik)	fine, ransom
.34	Fanagan's	Ó Fionnagáin (ó finegáñ)	des. of *Fionnagán* (dim. of *Fionn*, "fair")
.34	bray	Brí (brí)	Hill-slope; town on border of Cos. Dublin & Wicklow, anglic. Bray
.35	clownsillies	Cluain Sailighe (klún salí)	Willow Meadow; an-glic. Clonsilla
.35	Donkeybrook	Domhnach/ Tamhnach Broc (*d*ounokh/ *t*ounokh brok)	Badger Church/ Green-field; S. Dublin district, anglic. Don-nybrook
.35	mackin	Ó Maicín (ó makín)	des. of *Maicín* (dim. of *mac*, "son")
538.04	talc	tolc (*t*ulk)	flood, torrent, overflow
.14	cansill	*P/K Split ceannsail (kyansil)	pansill ascendancy, ostenta-tion
.14	cassey	ceasaigh (kasí)	corduroy road (of hur-dles or wickerwork) over fenny ground; *Anna, *Dublin
.21	boyne	Bóinn (bóñ)	n. of a goddess (from *bó*, "cow"): River *Boyne
.29	Carlow's	Ceatharlach (kaherlokh)	Quadruple-lake; S.E. co. & town
.32	upann	ean- (an), *pfx.*	water-; *Anna
.32	Congan's	Conga (kuñge)	Strait; town, Co. Mayo, anglic. Cong
.35	ransom of beeves	*trans.* bóramha (bórúe) [?]	tribute; *Brian Boru
539.11–12	cramkrieged	Crom Crúach (krum krúkh)	Gory Crouching; anc. idol overthrown by Patrick
.17	Athacleeath	Áth Cliath (áklíe)	Hurdle Ford; *Dublin
.28	cleantarriffs	Cluain Tarbh (klún *t*orev)	Bull Meadow, N.E. Dublin district, site of

			*Brian Boru's defeat of Danes, 1014, anglic. Clontarf
.33	tenenure	Tír an Iubhair (tír un yúr)	Land of the Yew Tree; S. Dublin suburb, anglic. Terenure
540.09–12	*Drumcollogher*	Drom Coll-Choille (*d*rum kolkhíle)	Ridge of the Hazel-wood, Co. Limerick, anglic. Dromcolliher (*L/R Interchange); also I. n. of Thomas St., Dublin
.12	*Moonis*	mún (mún)	urine
		Mumha[n] (mún)	S. province, anglic. Munster
		Ó Muimhnigh (ó mwimní)	des. of *Muimhneach* ("Munsterman"); anglic. Mooney
.35	Firebugs	Fir Bolga (firbulge)	Bags Men; prehistoric *colonists
541.16	Bulafests	Béal Feirste (bél ferishti)	Sandbank River-mouth; N.E. city, anglic. Belfast
.17	Corkcuttas	Corcaigh (kurkí)	Swamp; S. city; anglic. Cork
.17	Brien Bereume	Brian Bóroimhe (bríen bórivi)	Brian of the Tribute, anglic. *Brian Boru; high king killed defeating Danes at Clontarf, 1014
.17	berow	bóramha (bórúe)	"cow-counting": tribute
.18	Loughlins	Lochlainn (lokhlin)	Scandinavia, Norway
		Lochlainnigh (lokhliní)	Scandinavians
		Ó Lochlainn (ó lokhlin)	des. of *Lochlainn* ("Scandinavia"); anglic. Loughlin
.18	tolkies	Tolca (*t*ulke)	Flood, Torrent, N.E. Dublin river, site of battle of Clontarf; anglic. Tolka

.18	Fugabollags!	Fág an bealach! (fág a' byalokh)	Leave the way! Clear the way!
		fág-an-bealach	worthless person
		bolg (bulug)	belly
.19	Lusqu'	losc (lusk)	lame; blind
		Lusc (lusk)	Cave, N. Co. Dublin town; anglic. Lusk
.26	slobodens	slab (slob)	mud, filled land
.26	rothgardes	Ráth Garbh (rá gorev)	Rough Fort; S. Dublin district; anglic. Rathgar
.26	wrathmindsers	Ráth Maoinis (rá mwénish)	Magnus' Fort; S. Dublin district; anglic. Rathmines
.34	ourangoontangues	teanga (t'oñe)	tongue, language
542.01	murphyplantz	Ó Murchadha (ó murukhu)	des. of *Murchadh* ("sea-warrior"); anglic. Murphy
.03	curraghcoombs	Cuirreach Life (kwirokh lifi)	Moor/Racecourse of the *Liffey [Plain]; anglic. The Curragh of Kildare
		Cúm (kúm)	Hollow; S. Dublin slum; anglic. The Coombe
.05	rainelag	Raghnallach (reinelokh)	[belonging to the family] *Raghnall* (Norm.-Fr. Reynald); S. Dublin district; anglic. Ranelagh
.13	meckamockame	mac (mok)	son
.18	pupuls	pobal (pubel)	people, the public
.20–21	maugher machrees	máthair mo chroidhe (máher mukhrí)	mother of my heart
543.03	slog	slog (slug)	swallow, gulp
.08	thingabolls	ball (bol)	limb, member, place, spot, thing
.09	feshest cheoilboys	Feis Cheoil (fesh khyól)	Festival of Music: annual competitive musical convention
.10	bi	bí (bí)	be

.17	Thomars	Tómhar (tór)	Thor; Cork Hill, Dublin, is *recte* Thor's Hill
.17	Thomars Sraid	Sráid Thomáis (srád' humásh)	Thomas' Street: Thomas Street, Dublin, formerly *Drom Coll-Choille* ("Hazelwood Ridge"); see 540.09–12
.17	Huggin	Ó hAodhagáin (ó hégáñ)	des. of *Aodhagán* (dim. of *Aodh*, "fire")
.19	oges	óg (óg) ó (ó)	young descendant, grandson, scion; person bearing Ó surname
.20	macks	mac (mok)	son; person bearing *Mac* surname
.19–20	oges . . . macks	idir ó agus mac	"between grandsons/ people-with-Ó-names and sons/people-with-Mac-names": everybody, *tout le monde*
.33	Roe's	Ruadh (rúe)	Red-haired: epithet replacing real surname; anglic. Roe
		Ó Ruaidh (ó rúí)	des. of *Ruadh* ("red-haired"); anglic. Roe
545.32	loy	láighe (láí)	mattock, spade; implement for digging peat
.32	lynch	Ó Loingsigh (ó liñshí)	des. of *Loingseach* ("having to do with a fleet"); anglic. Lynch
.32	lavgiver	lámh (láv)	hand
546.02	Morgh	morgadh (morgu)	putrefaction, decay
.02	soliven	Ó Súileabháin (ó súleváñ)	des. of *Súil-dubhán* ("black-eyed"); anglic. Sullivan
.18	roberoyed	Rob Ruadh (rob rúe)	Red-haired Rob[ert]; Scottish outlaw; anglic. Rob Roy
.18	faineans	Fianna (fíene)	3rd c. standing army led by *Fionn Mac Cumhail*
.27	Sree!	sraoth (srí)	sneeze

.33	Earalend	Éire (ére)	Ireland
547.18	portreeve	Port Ríogh (pur*tr*í)	Stronghold of the King; anglic. Portree
.18	Kevin's	Caoimhghin (kívġin)	Comely-birth; st., fndr. of monastic settlement at Glendalough
.18	Hurdlesford	Áth Cliath (áklíe)	Hurdle Ford; *Dublin
.20	Ringsend	Rinn (riñ)	Point of land; S. Dublin district near Liffey mouth
.22	Cowhowling	Cúchulainn (kúkhulin)	Hound of *Culann* (masc. pers. n.); 2nd c. hero of *Red Branch saga cycle
.25	os	os (us)	deer (n. of a god)
.33	Erin	Éirinn (érin), *dat.*	[to, for] Ireland
.34	iday	indé (iñé)	yesterday
.35	igone	indiu (iñú)	today
.35	imorgans	imbárach (imárokh)	tomorrow
		Í Mór (í mór)	Big Island; I-mor, according to *Macpherson in *Temora,* is one of the Hebrides (scc 548.03)
548.01	Livland	Life (lifi)	*Liffey River
.06	Pluviabilla	bile (bili)	sacred tree; *Anna
.27	Slyne's	Mac Sleimhne (mok sleini)	son of Stephen (i.e., FitzStephen)
.34	moyles	Sruth na Maoile (sru nu mwíle)	Sea-stream of the Bald[headland]; sea between I. & Scotland; anglic. Moyle (poetic)
549.02	Dunphy's	Ó Donnchadha (ó *d*unukhu)	des. of *Donnchadh* ("brown-warrior")
.04	mhuttons	*Aspiration	wuttons, vuttons
.10	tolvmaans	talamh (*t*olev)	soil, earth, ground

.13	duindleeng	duine (dini) -ín (ín), dim. suffx.	person little, darling
.17	Mourne	Mughdhorna (múyorne)	Progeny of Mughdhorn ("ankle"); N.E. tribal land, incl. mtn. range
.19	Hy Kinsella	Uí Cinn- sealaigh (í kinshalí)	Progeny of [Éanna] Cinnsealach ("ostenta- tious"), son of Diarmaid Mac Murchadh, Lein- ster king who invited Anglo-Norman inva- sion (*Shem); tribal land, Co. Wexford
.26	island of Breasil	Í Breasail (í brasil)	Ruddy Island, legend- ary land W. in Atlan- tic, anglic. Hy Brasil
.28	O'Connee	ochón (ukhón) Ó Conaill/ Conchobhair (ó kunil/ kunukher)	alas des. of Conall ("high- mighty")/Conchobhar ("high-will"); anglic. O Connell/O Connor
.28	Mahar	máthair (máher)	mother
.31	turlyhide	Mac Toir- dhealbhaigh (mok turyalví)	son of Toirdhealbhach ("shaped like Thor"); anglic. Turly
.33	Conn	Conn (kon)	Intelligence: Conn Céadchathach ("hun- dred-fighter"), high king defeated by Eoghan Mór, retained only N. half of I., since called Leath Cuinn ("Conn's Half")
		[Loch] Con (lokh kon)	Lake of a Hound, Co. Mayo; anglic. Lough Conn
		Cán (kán)	Cain
.34	Owel	Eoghan (ówen)	Wellborn; anglic. Owen; Eoghan Mór surnamed Mogh- Nuadhat seized from

			Conn Céadchathach S. half of I., since called *Leath Mogha* ("*Mogh*'s Half")
		[Loch] Uair (lokh úr)	Cold/Hour Lake, Co. Westmeath, where *Malachy I drowned Turgeis; anglic. Lough Owel (*L/R Interchange)
		Ábhail (áwil)	Abel
.34	Guinnass	Mag Aonghusa (mogénġesi)	son of *Aonghus* ("single-choice" [god of love]); anglic. Guinness
.36	gaelic	Gaedhealg (gélg)	Irish language; Irish, native
550.07	Paudraic's	Pádraic (pádrik)	Patrick
.08	barelean	Béarla (bérle)	English language
.08–09	linsteer	Laighin (lein)	Lances; E. province; anglic. Leinster
.11	dillisks	duileasc (dilesk)	edible seaweed
.18	Uliv's	ollamh (ulev)	sage, poet, professor
.20	carrycam	cam (koum)	curved, crooked, twisted
.21	duist	dúist (dúsht)	boor
.23	doveling	Dubh-linn (duvlin)	Black Pool; *Dublin
.24	fineglas	Fionn-glas (finglos)	Clear Stream; village & stream N. of Dublin; anglic. Finglas
.27	bray	Brí (brí)	Hill-slope; town on Dublin–Wicklow border; anglic. Bray
.31	O'Niell	Ó Néill (ó nél)	des. of *Niall* ("champion"); *Uí Néill
.32	Currens	Ó Corraidhín (ó kurahín)	des. of *Corraidhín* (dim. of *corradh*, "spear")
551.26	showne	Seón (shón)	John; *Shaun
.33	Ulitzas	Ulaidh (ule)	Monument; N. province, anglic. Ulster

552.06	shinners'	sinn, sinn-ne (shin, shini)	we, us (and emphatic)
.11	gowgow	gabha (gou)	smith
.11	Cassels	Ó Caisile (ó kashili)	des. of *Caiside* ("curled" [?])
.11	Redmond	Mac Réamoinn (mok rémin)	son of *Réamonn* (Norm.-Fr. *Raimond*)
.12	Foley	Ó Foghladha (ó fólu)	des. of *Foghlaidh* ("plunderer")
.12	Farrell	Ó Fearghail (ó faryel)	des. of *Fearghal* ("super-valor")
.13	Hogan	Ó hÓgáin (ó hógáñ)	des. of *Ógán* (dim. of *óg*, "young")
.22	coolocked	Cúlóg (kúlóg)	Little Corner; N.E. Dublin suburb, anglic. Coolock
.24	clashcloshant	clais (klash) cloisint (kloshint)	choir hearing, listening to
.27	oriel	Óirghialla (óryíli)	Golden Hostages; anc. N.E. principality, anglic. Oriel
.29	sass her nach	Sasanach (sosenokh)	Englishman
553.03	alderbirk	*imitation:* ailm, beith	elm, birch: letters A, B
.03	tannenyou	*imitation:* teithne, ur	furze, heath: letters T, U (last letters of Mod. I. 18-letter alphabet)
.03	myraw	mí-rath (míra)	misfortune, ill-luck
.03–04	dundrum	Dún Droma (*dún d*rume)	Fort of the Ridge; S. Dublin suburb; anglic. Dundrum
.04	Livvy	Life (lifi)	*Liffey River
.12	templeogues	Teampall Óighe (t'oumpul ógi)	Church of a Virgin; village near Dublin; anglic. Templeogue
.12–13	Pardonell	*P/K Split Domhnall (*dó*nel)	Cardonell [Cardinal] World-mighty; masc. pers. n.

.13	Maynooth	Magh Nuadhat (má nút)	*Nuadhat*'s (king of Leinster, foster-father of *Eoghan Mór Mogh-Nuadhat*) Plain, Co. Kildare
.14	Conall	Conall (kunel)	High-mighty; masc. pers. n.
.14	eiligh	Ó hÉilighe (ó hélí)	des. of *Ealadhach* ("ingenious"); anglic. Healy
		eirigh (eirí) *L/R Interchange	rise, arise
.22	feyrieglenn	gleann (gloun)	valley
.23	Finmark's	Fionn (fin)	Fair
.23	lickybudmonth	bod (bud)	penis
.27	lindub	lionn dubh (linduv)	"black ale": porter, stout; black bile, melancholy
		linn dubh (linduv)	black pool; *Dublin
.27–28	puss, puss	pus (pus)	lip, lips
.29	stony battered	*half-trans.* Bóthar na gCloch (bóher nuglukh)	Road of the Stones: Dublin street; anglic. Stonybatter
554.07	rink	rinnce (riñki)	dance
555.10	ballyhooric	Bealach Fheabhra (balokh youre)	*Feabhra*'s (n. of a weed; also "February") Pass; mtn. range, Co. Cork; anglic. Ballyhoura
.13, 15	esker	eiscir (eshkir)	ridge of mounds; village, Co. Galway; anglic. Esker
.13, 15	saggard	Teach Sacra (t'okh sokre)	*Sacra*'s (7th c. st.) House; village S.W. Co. Dublin, corruptly anglic. Saggart
		sagart (sogert)	priest
.13, 15	crumlin	Crom-ghlinn (krumlin)	Crooked Valley; S. Dublin district; anglic. Crumlin

.16	Kevin	Caoimhghin (kívġin)	Comely-birth; 7th c. st.; *Shaun
.20	Jerry	Díairmín (d'írmín)	dim. of *Diarmaid* ("freeman"); anglic. Jerry; *Shem
556.23	Havelook	Amhlaoibh (oulév)	masc. pers. n. (Norse *Ólafr*); I. form became Mid. E. *Havelok*; *Humphrey
.26	pubbel	pobal (pubel)	people, the public
.29	ogas	agus (ogus)	and
.32	Kothereen	Cáitrín (kát'rín)	fem. pers. n. from Gk. Katherine
.33	my veal asthore	mo mhíle stór (mu víle stór)	my thousand treasures (endearment)
.34, 35	dowanstairs . . . dowandshe	Ó Dubhchon (ó dúkhon)	des. of *Dubhchú* ("black-hound"); anglic. Dowan, etc.
.36	Shuhorn	Seán, Seón (shán, shón) Siobhán (shún)	John; *Shaun Joan
.36– 557.01	tillycramp	tuile (tili)	extra bit, addition (13th to dozen)
.03, 04	galorybit . . . galohery	go leór (gulór)	enough, plenty
.07	O'Toole	Ó Tuathail (ó túhil)	des. of *Tuathal* ("people-mighty")
.08	sliving	sliabh (slív)	mountain
.09	turruns	turainn (turin)	overthrow; stroke of misfortune
.11	whisht	thoist (hisht)	silence
558.01	Gilbey's	Ó Giollabuidhe (ó gilibwí)	des. of *Giollabuidhe* ("yellow lad")
.12, 14	Sully	Ó Súiligh (ó súlí)	des. of *Súileach* ("quick-eyed")
.18	Nolans	Ó Nualláin (ó núláñ)	des. of *Nuallán* (dim. of *nuall*, "noble")
.19	honeymeads	*trans.* Cluain Meala (klún male)	Meadow of Honey, Co. Tipperary; anglic. Clonmel (prison)

.20	hurlyburlygrowth	Béarla (bérle)	English language
.23	toppingshaun	Seán (shán)	John; *Shaun
.27–28	Nyanzer . . . Nyanza	ní h-annsa (níhounse)	not hard; formula for answering riddles
.29	moddereen	máthairín (máherín)	little mother
		maidrín (mod'rín)	little dog
.29–30	moddereen ru arue	maidrín ruadh (mod'erín rúe)	"red little dog": fox (*an maidrín ruadh ruadh ruadh ruadh ruadh* ["the red red red red red little dog" i.e., "the fox fox fox fox fox"]—refrain of children's song)
.31	dinny	duine (*d*ini)	person
.35	Fyon	fíon (fín)	wine
		Fionn (fin)	Fair
559.33	Finnuala	Fionnghuala (finúle)	Fair-shoulders; fem. pers. n.
.34	sallowlass	gallóglach (goulóglokh)	"foreign-youth": heavy-armed I. foot soldier; anglic. gallowglass
.34	nanny's	An Eanaigh (unaní)	The Fenny; *Anna; river, Co. Meath, where *Malachy I drowned prince of Bregia (604.04); anglic. Nanny
560.27	gaffneysaffron	Ó Gamhna (ó govne)	des. of *Gamhain* ("calf"); anglic. Gaffney
.30	bally	baile (bolye)	town, homestead
561.17	friendeen	-ín (ín), *dim. suffx.*	little, darling
562.13	brigidschool	Brighid (bríd')	fem. pers. n. (from *brigh*, "strength"); goddess of poetry; st. patroness of I.
.23	Kevin	Caoimhghin (kívġin)	Comely-birth; 7th c. st.; *Shaun

.25	buchel	buachaill (búkhel)	boy
.25	Iosa	Íosa (íse)	Jesus
.27	Quinn	Ó Cuinn (ó kwin)	des. of *Conn* ("intelligence")
563.07	Jerry	Díairmín (d'írmín)	dim. of *Diarmaid* ("freeman"); *Shem
.08	capers	*P/K Split	papers
.14	bannars	banna (bone)	censure, reproach
.24	portereens	-ín (ín), *dim. suffx.*	little, darling
.26	Donnybrook	Domhnach/ Tamhnach Broc (*d*ounokh/ *t*ounokh brok)	Badger Church/ Green-field; S. Dublin suburb
.27	Hoy's	Ó hEochaidh (ó hyókhí)	des. of *Eochaidh* ("possessing cattle")
.29–30	barmhearts . . . brackfest	bairghean breac (baryen brak)	"speckled loaf": currant cake eaten at Halloween; anglic. barmbrack
.30	brackfest	breac (brak)	"speckled": trout
.36	kerryjevin	Ciarraigh (kírí) Díairmín (d'írmín) Caoimhghin (kívġin)	Race of *Ciar* ("black"); S.W. co.; anglic. Kerry dim. of *Diarmaid* ("freeman"); *Shem; anglic. Jerry Comely-birth; anglic. Kevin; *Shaun
564.08	Finn	Fionn (fin)	Fair
.21	olave	ollamh (ulev)	poet, sage, professor
.22	firile	fir (fir)	men
.22	liveside	Life (lifi)	*Liffey River
.30	fionghalian	Fine-Gall (finigoul) Fionnghal (finġal)	Foreign Kindred; N. Co. Dublin district; anglic. Fingal; its inhabitants are Fingallians Fair-fight/Fair-valor; *Macpherson's Fingal
.32	Shamus	Séamus (shémus)	James

.33	Lucan's	Leamhcán (loukán)	Producing marshmallows; W. Dublin suburb; anglic. Lucan
.34	bodom	bod (bud)	penis
.35	gardeenen	gáirdín (gárd'ín)	garden
565.08	shayest	sé (shé)	he
.10	jerry	Díairmín (d'írmín)	dim. of Diarmaid ("freeman"); *Shem
.15	keve	caomh (kív)	comely; *Shaun
.17	eire	Éire (ére)	Ireland
.18	pawdrag	Pádraig (pádrig)	Patrick
.18	fawthrig	Phádraig (fádrig); *Asp.	Patrick
		fathach (fohokh)	giant; hairy man
.19	phantares	phantar (fanter); *Asp.	clumsy thing; thickset person
.19	avikkeen	a mhicín (a vikín)	my little son
.20	capallo	capall (kopel)	horse
.33	Lucalised	Leamhcán (loukán)	Producing marshmallows; W. Dublin suburb on Liffey, anglic. Lucan
		Iosaid (isid'), g.	[of] Iosada (fem. pers. n., Iseult, Isolda)
566.03	gallpitch	gall (goul)	foreigner
.11	duntalking	Dún Dealgan (dún d'algen)	Dealga's ("Thorn") Fort; town, Co. Louth, N. of Dublin, anglic. Dundalk
.11	dowan	Ó Dubhchon (ó dúkhon)	des. of Dubhchú ("black-hound"); anglic. Dowan
.11–12	droghedars	Droichead Átha (drihed áhe)	Bridge of a Ford; town N. of Dublin on *Boyne River; anglic. Drogheda
.20	deevlin	Duibh-linn (divlin)	Black Pool; *Dublin
.21, 24	duffgerent	dubh (duv)	black

.36– 567.01	dunleary	Dún Laoghaire (*dún* líri)	*Laoghaire*'s ("calf- keeper") Fort, town & harbor S. Dublin Bay
.06	big	beig (beg)	little
.06	bog	bog (bug)	soft
.22	aryan	Éireann (érun), *g.*	[of] Ireland
.22	Nolan	Ó Nualláin (ó núláñ)	des. of *Nuallán* (dim. of *nuall*, "noble")
.26	poblesse	pobal (pubel)	people, the public
568.17	thon	tón (*tón*)	bottom, arse
.18	Nanny's	An Eanaigh (un aní)	The Fenny; *Anna; river, Co. Meath, where *Malachy I drowned prince of Bregia (604.04); an- glic. Nanny
.28	Caubeenhauben	cáibín (kábín)	old hat
569.23	Finncoole	Fionn Mac Cumhail (fin mok kúil)	Fair, son of *Cumhal*; 3rd c. hero of saga cycle
.24	saoul	samhail (soul)	likeness, ghost
.35	tyronte	Tír Eoghain (tírówin)	*Eoghan*'s ("wellborn" *Shaun) Land; tribal land of N. *Uí Néill; co., anglic. Tyrone
570.03	Dalchi	dailcín (*d*alkín) dailce (*d*alki)	dim. of *dailc*, strong low-sized stout person moroseness
.13	toth's tother's place	toth-ball (*t*ovol)	"female-place": fe- male genitals
.21	Hurtleforth	Áth Cliath (áklíe)	Hurdle Ford; *Dublin
.22–23	mic . . . mac . . . mick . . . mack	mac; mic (mok; mik)	son; of a son
.32–33	ford . . . hurdley	Áth Cliath (áklíe)	Hurdle Ford; *Dublin
571.02–03	clear springwell . . . park	*trans.* Páirc an Fionnuisce (párk un finishki)	Clear-water Field; an- glic. Phoenix Park
.07	Elm	ailm (elim)	elm (pine); letter A

.08	bay	beith (be)	birch; letter B
.08	cull	coll (kol)	hazel tree; letter C
.08	dare	dair (*dor*)	oak; letter D
.08	tawny	teithne (tene)	furze; letter T
.08	runes	*imitation I.* *tree-letter*	letter R
.08	ilex	*imitation I.* *tree-letter*	letter I
.08	sallow	sail (sal)	willow; letter S
.09	pine	ailm (elim)	letter A
.24	saarasplace	saor (sér)	free
.26	Annshee	ean- (an), *pfx.* sidhe (shí) bean-sidhe (banshí)	water-; *Anna fairy fairy-woman
572.24, 25	Eugenius	*trans.* Caoimhghin (kívġin)	Comely-birth, anglic. Kevin; *Shaun
.24–25, 26, 35	Jeremias	Diairmín (d'írmín)	dim. of *Diarmaid* ("freeman"); anglic. Jerry; *Shem
.30, 33	Magravius	Mag Raith (mogra)	son of *Mac Raith* ("son of grace"); anglic. MacGrath, etc.
.33, 35	Gillia	gile (gili)	brightness (endearment)
573.02, 05, 15	Magravius	Mag Raith	see 572.30 ff.
.05, 11, 17	Eugenius	*trans.* Caoimhghin	see 572.24 ff.
.07, 13	Sullivani	Ó Súileabháin (ó súleváñ)	des. of *Súil-dubhán* ("black-eyed"); anglic. Sullivan
.08, 28	Macdugalius . . . Magdugalius	Mac Dubhghaill (mok *d*úġil)	son of *Dubhghall* ("black-foreigner," i.e., Dane)
.11, 18	Jeremias	Díairmín	see 572.24–25 ff.
.16	Gillia	gile	see 572.33 ff.
.33	bradaun	bradán (bra*d*án)	salmon

574.01	D'Oyly	Ó/Mac Dubhghaill (ó/mok dúģil)	des./son of *Dubhghall* ("black-foreigner," i.e., Dane); anglic. Doyle
.01, 04	Owens	Mac Eoghain (mok ówin)	son of *Eoghan* ("wellborn"); *Shaun
.02	Finn	Fionn (fin)	Fair
.09, 32	Doyle . . . doyles	Ó/Mac Dubhghaill dáil (dál)	see 574.01 assembly; *Dáil Éireann*, I. Legislative Assembly
575.06, 07	Doyle . . .	Ó/Mac	see 574.01
	Doyle's . . .	Dubhghaill	
09–10,	Doyle . . .	dáil	see 574.09 ff.
	doylish . . .		
32	Doyler		
.24	Mack	mac (mok)	son
.24	Dar	dair (dor)	oak
.25	jerrykin	Díairmín (d'írmín)	dim. of *Diarmaid* ("freeman"); anglic. Jerry
.25	jureens	-ín (ín), *dim. suffx.*	little, darling
576.03	Eaudelusk	duileasc (dilesk) Lusc (lusk)	edible seaweed Cave; town N. Co. Dublin, anglic. Lusk
.06	Kilbride	Cill Bhrighde (kilvríd'i)	*Brighid*'s Church; n. of 35 places; anglic. Kilbride
.06	Una	Úna (úne)	Famine; fem. pers. n.
.23	muck's	muc (muk)	pig, swine
.26	hungerford	Áth Cliath (áklíe)	Hurdle Ford; *Dublin
.28	Finnykin	Ó Fionnacáin (ó finekáñ)	des. of *Fionnacán* (dim. of *Fionn*, "fair"); anglic. Finnegan, etc.
.36	neoliffic	Life (lifi)	*Liffey River
577.01	mor	mór (mór)	big, great

.14	Urloughmoor	An Tulach Mór (un *t*ulokh mór)	The Great Assembly-Hill; co. seat of Co. Offaly (see 577.15); anglic. Tullamore
		Úr-loch mór (úrlokh mór)	great fresh lake
.15	leaks	Laoighis (lísh)	Progeny of *Lughaidh Laoighseach* ("calf-rich"); tribal land now central co., anglic. Laoighis, Leix [quondam "Queen's County," its seat, *Portlaoighse*, was called "Maryborough"]
.15	awfully	Uí Fáilghe (ffályi)	descendants of *Ros-Fuilgheach*; tribal land now central co. N. of Laoighis, anglic. Offaly
.21	Neaves	Neamh (nyav) naomh (név)	Heaven saint
.23	mala	mála (mále)	sack
.23	alptrack	alp (olp)	lump, heap; snarl; job of work; *Dublin
.25	cozenkerries	Ciarraigh (kírí)	Progeny of *Ciar* ("black"); S.W. co., anglic. Kerry
.29	coddlam	codladh (kule) codlaim (ku*d*lim)	sleep I sleep
.35	slogo	Sligeach (shligokh)	Shelly, Shell-mound; N.W. co. & town, anglic. Sligo
.35	slee	slighe (shlí)	way, road, route
578.06	Gill	Mac an Ghoill (mokunġil)	son of the foreigner; anglic. Gill
		Mac Giolla (mok gili)	shortened from n. beginning *Mac Giolla* . . . ("son of the servant of . . .")
.06	Macfinnan's	Mac Fionnáin (mokfináñ)	son of *Fionnán* (dim. of *Fionn*, "fair")

.06	Macfinnan's cool	Fionn Mac Cumhail (fin mok kúl)	Fair son of *Cumhal*, 3rd c. hero of saga cycle
.10	finnoc	fionnóg (finóg)	fair maiden
.10	cauwl	cála (kále)	cape
.10	finnoc in a cauwl	Fionn Mac Cumhail (fin mok kúl)	see 578.06
.11	O'Sorgmann	Ó (ó)	descendant
.16	bodikin	bod (bud)	penis
579.01	Dunmow's	Dún Mogha (dún móe)	*Mogh*'s Fort
.28	Thawland	tá (tá)	there is; yes
580.12	Multaferry	Muilte Farannain (mwilti farenin)	*Farannan*'s ("land-holder" [?]) Mills, Co. Westmeath, anglic. Multyfarnham
.15	durk	dorcha (durukhe)	dark
.18	Sheem	síom (shím)	trick, prank; *Shem
.18	Shaam	Séam (shém)	Sant Iago; *Shem
.19	Finnegan	Ó Fionnagáin (ó finegáñ)	des. of *Fionnagán* (dim. of *Fionn*, "fair")
.28	fenians	Fiannaidh (fíení)	member of 3rd c. standing army led by *Fionn Mac Cumhail*
.31	O'Connell	Ó Conaill (ó kunil)	des. of *Conall* ("high-powerful")
.32	O'Hara	Ó hEaghra (ó hyare)	des. of *Eaghra* ("fatal" [?])
.33	rann	rann (ron)	verse, stanza
.34	Eryan's	Éireann (érun), *g.*	[of] Ireland
.34	Malin	Malainn (malin), *g.*	[of a] Hillbrow, Co. Donegal, extreme N. point of I.
.34	Clear	Cléire (kléri)	Band, Company, Co. Cork, extreme S. point of I.

.34	Carnsore Point	Ceann an Chairn (kyoun un kharn)	Head of the Rock-heap, Co. Wexford, extreme S.E. point of I.; Norsified Carnsore [*Cairn* (I., "rock-heap") + s + *ör* (Danish, "rock-heap")]
.34–35	Slynagollow	Ceann Léime [na Gail-limhe] (kyoun lémi nugolivi)	Leap Head of Galway, promontory, Co. Galway, W. coast; anglic. Slyne Head [*léim* preceded by unaccountable s]
581.04	sullivan's	Ó Súileabháin (ó súleváñ)	des. of *Súil-dubhán* ("black-eyed")
.07	Reilly	Ó Raghailligh (ó rayelí)	des. of *Raghallach* ("[strong-]fore-armed")
.09	banishee's	bean-sidhe (banshí) bean a' tigh (banat'í)	fairy-woman woman of the house
.11	find me cool's	Fionn Mac Cumhail (fin mok kúl)	Fair son of *Cumhal*, 3rd c. hero of saga cycle
.16	thunderslog	slog (slug) log (log)	swallow, gulp place, locus
.16	sbrogue	barróg (beróg) bróg (bróg)	defect in speech shoe
582.07	clooshed	cluas (klús)	ear
.08	Taaffe	Táth (tá)	son of David
.09	Auliffe	Amhlaoibh (oulév)	Norse *Ólafr*; anglic. Auliffe, *Humphrey
.12	enver	inbhear (inver)	estuary
.21–22	Dyfflinsborg	Duibh-linn (divlin)	Black pool; *Dublin
.25	Iarland	iar- (ír), *pfx.*	west-, western-, remote-
.26	Youghal	Eochaill (yókhil)	Yew-wood; town, Co. Cork
.28	Derg	dearg (d'erig)	red

.28	Derg rudd face	[Loch] Dearg-dhearc	[Lake] Red-eye, on Shannon, anglic. Lough Derg; Lough Derg, Co. Donegal, site of St. Patrick's Purgatory (see 582.29), is *Loch Dearg*, "Red Lake"
.32	Thon's	tón (*tón*)	bottom, arse
.32	dullakey-	Dealg-inis (d'alginish)	Thorn Island, on S. Dublin Bay; Norsified Dalkey
.35	Leary, leary, twentytun	Dún Laoghaire (*dúnlíre*)	*Laoghaire*'s ("calf-keeper") Fort; town & harbor, S. Dublin Bay
583.04	bulloge	bollóg (bulóg)	bullock; loaf of bread
.11	garrymore	Garrdha Mór (gore mór)	Big Garden; place-name
.20	Irryland	Éire (*ére*)	Ireland
.21	malahide	Baile Átha Thíd (bolyá híd')	Town of the Ford of *Teud* (masc. pers. n.), seaside town, N. Co. Dublin, anglic. corruptly by *Eclipsis, Malahide
.21	Liv	Life (lifi)	*Liffey River
.21, 22	rosebuds	bod (bu*d*)	penis
.29	tarrant's	tarr (*t*or)	underpart, bottom, belly
		tarraint (*t*arint')	drawing, pulling, dragging
.33	shiminey	simné (shimné)	chimney
.34	duffed	dubh (*d*uv)	black
584.05	Magrath	Mag Raith (mogra)	son of *Mac Raith* ("son of grace"), anglic. Magrath, Magraw, etc.
		mo ghrádh (muġrá)	my love
.12	hooley	*from* Baile Átha Ubhla (bolyáhúle)	Appletree-Ford Town (anglic. Ballyhooly): riotous celebration

.20	keek	cíoc (kík)	peep
.21	doran's	Ó Deóráin (ó d'óráñ)	des. of *Deóradhán* (dim. of *deóradh*, "exile, stranger")
.21	shantyqueer	sean-tigh (shant'í)	old house
.31	Tubbernacul	Tobar na Cuill (*t*ubernu kwil)	Well of the Hazel Tree
.31	tipherairy	Tiobraid Árann (tibrid árun)	Well of *Ára* (district n.); town & co. S. central, anglic. Tipperary
585.28–29	Donnelly's	Ó Donnghaile (ó *d*onyelí)	des. of *Donnghal* ("brown-valor")
586.14	bawnee	bán (bán)	white
.29	crumlin	Crom ghlinn (krumlin)	Curved Valley, S. Dublin district
.29	mac	mac (mok)	son
.30	turkling	torcalach (*t*urkelokh)	well-fed
587.30	MacCawthelock	Mac Amhlaoibh[?] (mok oulév)	son of *Amhlaoibh* (Norse *Ólafr*); anglic. Mac-Auliffe, MacCawley, etc.; *Humphrey
		Mac Ádháimh[?] (mokáv)	son of Adam; anglic. MacCaw
.30	Cawthelock	*P/K Split, *L/R Interchange	Pawtherock [Patrick]
588.23	Timgle	timchill (timkhil, timpil)	circuit, circumference; long way round
.29	Arrah Pogue	ara na bpóg (ore nubóg)	one given to kissing
.29	Killdoughall	Cill/Coill Dubhghaill (kil/kíl *d*úġel)	*Dubhghall*'s ("black-foreigner," i.e., Dane) Church/Wood
.31	o'briertree	Ó Briain (ó bríin)	des. of *Brian Boru; anglic. O Brien
.31	rowantree	Ó Robhacháin (ó rowokháñ)	des. of *Robhacán* ("crafty"); anglic. Rowan

		Ó Ruadháin (ó rúáñ)	des. of *Ruadhán* (dim. of *ruadh*, "red"); anglic. Rowan
.31	o'corneltree	Ó Conaill (ó kunil)	des. of *Conall* ("high-mighty"); anglic. O Connell
.31	behanshrub	Ó Beacháin (ó bakháñ)	des. of *Beachán* (dim. of *beach*, "bee"); anglic. Behan
.32	magill	Mac an Ghoill (mok unġil) Mac Giolla (mok gili)	son of the foreigner; anglic. Gill short form of n. beginning *Mac Giolla* . . . ("son of a servant of . . ."); anglic. Gill
.32	o'dendron more	Ó [d.] Mór (ó [d.] mór)	Great des. of [d.]
589.07	mayom	Magh-eó (máyó)	Yew-Plain; W. co. & town, anglic. Mayo
.07	tuam	Tuaim (*t*úim)	Funeral Mound, Tumulus; town, Co. Galway, anglic. Tuam; "Mayo & Tuam": the archdiocese of Tuam
.11	Finner!	Fionn (fin) sinn-ne (shini)	Fair we, us (emphatic)
.18	Duffy's	Ó Dubhthaigh (ó *d*ufí)	des. of *Dubhthach* ("black")
.18	MacKenna's	Mac Cionaodha (mok kiné) cíonádh (kíná)	son of *Cionaodh* ("portion-fire") five at cards; see 589.19, 27–28
.30	smithereen	smiodairín (smi*d*erín)	small fragment
590.02	leareyed	Laoghaire (líre)	Calf-keeper; masc. pers. n. of high king at Patrick's arrival
.02	letterish	leitir (let′ir)	wet hillside; anglic. Letter- in place-names
.13	beacsate	beach (byakh) beac (byak)	bee mushroom
.14	conningnesses	coinín (koñín)	rabbit

.17	Nuah-Nuah	Nuadha (núa)	anc. Celtic god; king of *Tuatha Dé* Danann; surnamed *Airgead-Lámh* ("silver-hand")
		nua (núe)	new
.19	kek	cac (kok)	excrement
593.02	Array	éirghe (érí)	rising, ascending
.03	Eireweeker	Éire (ére)	Ireland
.03, 04	O rally	Ó Raghailligh (ó rayelí)	des. of *Raghallach* ("[strong-]fore-armed"); anglic. O Reilly, etc.
.05	Osseania	Oisín (ushín)	Fawn; son of *Fionn Mac Cumhail*, *Macpherson's Ossian
.08–09	Sonne feine, somme feelm avaunt!	Sinn féin, sinn féin amháin! (shin fén shin fén aváñ)	Ourselves, ourselves alone!
.12	culminwillth	Cúl-mín (kúl mín)	Smooth-head; masc. pers. n. in *Macpherson's *Temora*, explained as "soft-haired," an adequate trans.
.12–13	Foyn MacHooligan	Fionn Mac Cumhail (fin mok kúl)	Fair son of *Cumhal*, 3rd c. hero of saga cycle
.13	Hooligan	Ó hUallacháin (ó húlekháñ)	des. of *Uallachán* (dim. of *uallach*, "proud")
.13–14	Temoram	Teach/Tigh an mhóir-ríogh (t'okh/tí un vór rí)[?] Teamhar (t'our)	House of the great king; *Macpherson's strained etymology for his Temora Prospective-hill; anc. royal capital, anglic. Tara; true probable basis for Temora
.14	Clogan	clogán (klugán)	little bell, small clock
		Colgán (kulugán)	"pointed": swordfish, salmon; masc. pers. n. in *Macpherson's *Temora*

		Ó Colgan (ó kulgen)	des. of *Colga*: *Seán Ó Colgan*; anglic. John Colgan, first named the famous *Annals* "of the *Four Masters*"
.14	slogan	sluagh-ghairm (slúgorim)	"host-summons": call or proclamation of mobilization
.15	Feghin	Ó Feichín (ó fekhín)	des. of *Feichín* (dim. of *fiach*, "raven")
.17	pratyusers	préataí (prétí)	potatoes
.22	Nuahs	nuadhacht (núokht)	news
		Nuadhat (nút)	anc. Celtic god; king of *Tuatha Dé Danann*; surnamed *Airgead-Lámh* ("Silver-hand")
		Seán (shán)	John; *Shaun
594.04	Tirtangel	tír (tír)	land, country
.18	Ahlen	Almhain (alúñ)	Whitened; hill, Co. Kildare, HQ of the *Fianna* led by *Fionn Mac Cumhail*; anglic. Hill of Allen
.19	Lugh	Lugh (lú)	god of sun & genius; surnamed *Lámh-fhada* ("Long-Arm")
.20	Brathwacker	bráth (brá) brat (brot)	judgment, doom cloak, mantle
.21	teiney	teine (tini)	fire
.22	ath	áth (á)	ford
.23–24	Fangaluvu	Fine-Gall (finigoul)	Foreign Kindred; N. Co. Dublin district, anglic. Fingal
		Fionn-ghal (fingal)	Fair-fight: Fingal, *Macpherson's version of *Fionn Mac Cumhail*
		Fionn-gall (fingoul)	Fair-foreigner, i.e., Norwegian
		Gaillimh (goliv)	Foreign; W. co. & town, anglic. Galway

.28	Edar's	Beinn Éadair (ben édir)	*Éadar*'s (masc. pers. n.) Peak, I. n. for Howth Head
.29	duan	duan (dúen)	poem, stanza
.29–30	duan Gallus	Dún na nGall (dún nu ñoul)	Fort of the Foreigners; N.W. co., & town, anglic. Donegal
.36–595.01	Ceolleges	ceol (kyól)	music, singing
.03	knock and knock	cnoc (knuk)	hill
.03	nachasach	sasanach (sosenokh)	English
.05	Bryne	Ó Briain (ó bríin)	des. of *Brian [Boru]
.08	liv	Life (lifi)	*Liffey River
.12–16	limericks . . . sly	*names of I. cos.; I. meanings almost certainly irrelevant*	Limerick, Waterford, Wexford, Louth, Kildare, Leitrim, Kerry, Carlow, Laoighis, Offaly, Donegal, Clare, Galway [Clare & Galway are cos., Claregalway a town], Longford, Monaghan, Fermanagh, Cavan, Antrim, Armagh, Wicklow, Roscommon, Sligo (missing: Cork, Derry, Down, Dublin, Kilkenny, Mayo, Meath, Tipperary, Tyrone, Westmeath)
.17	larksmathes . . . homdsmeethes . . .	Midhe (mí)	Middle; anc. royal province; co. N. & W. of Dublin, anglic. Meath
	quailsmeathes	Íar-midhe (írmí)	West-Middle; central co., anglic. Westmeath
.17	kilalooly	Coill a'Dubhlaoich (kíl a dúlékh) Cill Dha-Lua (kilġolú)	Wood of the Black Hero, town Co. Laoighis, anglic. Killadooley Church of St. Dalue; towns in Cos. Clare &

			Derry, anglic. Killaloe, Killaloo
		Cill Choinnigh (kil khiní)	Church of *Cainneach* ("fair one"); S.E. co. & city, anglic. Kil- kenny (see 595.12–16); *Kill
.18	Tep!	Tiobraid Árann (tibrid'árun)	Well of *Ára* (district n.); S.-central co., & town; anglic. Tip- perary (see 595.12–16)
		teip (tep)	failure
.18	crom lech	crom-leac (krumlyak)	stooped stone: mono- lith or dolmen
.19	alpsulumply	alp (olp)	lump; job of work; *Dublin
.21	Amslu!	am (oum) sluagh (slú)	time host, army
.22	Arans	Árann (árun), *g.*	[of a] Kidney; islands off Co. Galway, anglic. Aran
.28	Deepereras	Tiobraid Árann	see 595.18, 12–16
596.02	dogdhis	Dághdha (*d*áǵe)	god or hero surnamed *Ollathair* ("All- father"), father of *Aonghus;* anglic. Dagda
.04	fincarnate	fionn (fin)	fair
.07	solas	solas (sulus)	light
.08	Banba	Banba (bonbe)	Ireland (poetic)
.12	rassias	rásaidh (rásí)	wandering woman, jilt
.12	leery subs of dub	Dún Laoghaire (*d*ún líri)	*Laoghaire*'s ("Calf- keeper") Fort; subur- ban town & harbor on S. Dublin Bay
		dubh-linn (*d*uvlin)	black pool; *Dublin
.14	angalach	aingeal (añel) aingealach (añelokh) an gealach (un gyalokh)	angel numbness the moon

.14	sousenugh	sasanach (sosenokh)	English(man)
.16	forefivest	ceathar cúige (kaher kúge)	"four-fifths": four provinces
		cúige (kúge)	"fifth": province; mod. **I.** has four provinces
.32–33	sure . . . swift	*adj. "run"*	see Additional Note, *Fionn Mac Cumhail*
.36	Fingal	Fine-Gall (finigoul)	Foreign Kindred; N. Co. Dublin district
		Fionn-ghal (finġal)	Fair-fight; *Macpherson's n. for *Fionn Mac Cumhail*
.36	Loughlin's	Ó Lochlainn (ó lokhlin)	des. of *Lochlainn* ("Scandinavia")
597.01	La!	lá (lá)	day
.01	Lamfadar's	Lámhfhada (lávo*d*e)	Long-Arm, surname of *Lugh*, god of sun & genius
.25	thots	toth (*t*o)	female; female organs
.33	mornal	Mórna (mórne)	lovable person (pers. n.)
598.06	neanzas . . . neantas	ní h-annsa (níhounse)	not hard; formula for answering riddles
.09	Endee	indé (iñé)	yesterday
.09	sendee	Séan Dé (shén d'é)	Omen/Happiness of God; n. of 9th c. hymn
.09	Diu!	diu (d'ú)	day
		indiu (iñú)	today
.18	vanvan	bhean (van)	woman
.19	Tamal	tamall (*t*omel)	time, period, while
599.03	Time-o'-Thay	té (té)	tea
.04	a clonk	a clog (a klug)	o'clock
.05	harruad	ruadh (rúe)	red
.05	bathar	bóthar (bóher)	road
.06	gow	gabha (gou)	smith
		gabhar (gour)	goat
.07	athar	athair (ahir)	father
.09	tolkan	tolca (*t*ulke)	flood, torrent

.18	Gam	gam (gom)	soft foolish person
600.05	Innalavia	linn (lin)	pool
.08	hiarwather	iar (ír)	west, western, remote
.08	lives	Life (lifi)	*Liffey River
.10	Funn and Nin	Fionn (fin)	Fair
.10	Cleethabala	Baile Átha Cliath (bláklíe)	Hurdle Ford Town; *Dublin
.10	kongdomain	conga (kuñge)	strait
.11	Libnud	Dubh-linn (*d*uvlin)	Black pool; *Dublin
.11–12	Moylamore	[Sruth na] Maoile (sru nu mwíli) mór (mór)	[Sea-stream of the] Bald-headland; sea between I. & Scotland, anglic. Moyle (poetic) big, great
.12–13	Neandser . . . Neeinsee	ní h-annsa (níhounse)	not hard; formula for answering riddles
.13	Linfian	Linn-fian (linfíen) Life (lifi) Fian (fíen)	Wild/Fierce pool; *Dublin *Liffey River band of soldiers; soldiers commanded by *Fionn Mac Cumhail*
.14	Caughterect	*P/K Split Cothraige (kuregi)	Paughterect [Patrick] early n. for Patrick because of *P/K Split; falsely etymologized as "of four"
.15	Fane	Ó Fiacháin (ó fíkháñ)	des. of *Fiachán* (dim. of *fiach*, "raven")
.18	Dweyr O'Michaels	Ó Dubhuidhir (ó *d*uwír) Ó Maoil-mhichil (ó mwélwikhil)	des. of *Dubh-odhar* ("black-wan"); anglic. Dwyer, etc. des. of *Maolmhichil* ("servant of St. Michael")
.20	alomdree	ailm (alim) draoi (*d*rí)	elm, pine; letter A druid
.26	slab slobs	slab (slob)	mud, mire, filled ground
.29	*Elochlannensis*	Lochlainn (lokhlin)	Scandinavia; Norway

.32	Paudheen	Páidín (pád'ín)	dim. of *Pádraig* (Patrick): Paddy
.32	Poghue	póg (póg)	kiss
.33	arrah	ara (ore)	deprecatory interj.
.34	feist	feis (fesh)	convention, celebration, festival
.35–36	Mainylands	Uí Maine (í mañi)	[territory of the] dess. of *Maine Mór*; tribal land along Shannon in Cos. Roscommon, Galway, Offaly, Clare
.36	glaum	glám (glám)	grasp, clutch
601.03	ewon . . . owen	abhainn (ouwin)	river; *Anna
		Eoghan (ówen)	Wellborn; masc. pers. n. anglic. Owen; *Shaun
.06	Erie	Éire (ére)	Ireland
.07	Lough	loch (lokh)	lake; anglic. lough
.08	dairmaidens	dair (*d*ar)	oak
		Diarmaid (d'írmid')	Freeman; hero of *Toraidheacht Dhiarmada agus Ghráinne*; *Shem
.08	Asthoreths	a stór (as*t*ór)	my precious (endearment)
.10	daughters of the cliffs	mac alla (mokole)	"son of a cliff": echo
.11	thoo . . . thoo	tú (*t*ú)	you (thou)
.13	clanagirls	clann (klon)	children of the same family
		Clann na nGaedheal (klon nu ñél)	"Children of the Irish": the I. race
.18, 19	Keavn!	Caoimhghin (kívġin)	Comely-birth; st., fndr. of Glendalough; anglic. Kevin; *Shaun
		Caomhán (kíván)	dim. of *caomh* ("comely"); masc. pers. n. anglic. Kevan
.24	Ruadagara's	ruadh (rúe)	red
		Ráth Garbh (rá gorev)	Rough Fort; S. Dublin district, anglic. Rathgar

.24	Driminicumtra's	Drom Conaire (*d*rum kunire)	*Conaire*'s ("high-care") Ridge; N. Dublin district, anglic. Drumcondra
.24	Una	Úna (úne)	Famine; fem. pers. n.
.25	Misha-La-Valse's	mise (mishi)	I, me (emphatic)
.25	Clouonaskieym's	Cluain Sceiche (klún shkehi)	Meadow of a Thornbush; S. Dublin district, anglic. Clonskeagh
.26	Ringsingsund's	Rinn [Uí bhFaoláin] (riñ [í véláñ])	Promontory [of a des. of Little-Wolf]; at Liffey-mouth; anglic. Ringsend
.27	Glacianivia's	Glas Naoidhean (glos nín)	*Naoidhe*'s (masc. pers. n.) Stream; N. Dublin district; anglic. Glasnevin
.28	Loellisotoelles	Lorcán Ó Tuathail (lurkán ó *t*úhil)	*Lorcán* (dim. of *lorc*, "fierce") des. of *Tuathal* ("people-mighty"); abp. & patron st. of Dublin; anglic. Laurence O Toole
.31	meidinogues	maighdin (meid′in) óg (óg) ógh (óġ)	virgin young maiden, virgin
.32	Kathlins	Caitlín (kat′lín) Ga-linn (golin)[?]	fem. pers. n. from Gk. Katherine Sea-ray; Cathlin, n. of a star in *Macpherson's *Temora*, explained as "beam of the wave"; Cathlin is fem. pers. n. in *Macpherson's *Cathlin of Clutha*; one or other is supposed n. of girl who pursued St. Kevin to a lakeside cave, whence he pushed her to death in the lake; "Kevin's Kitchen" is popular n. of chapel at Glendalough

.33	ma brone!	mo bhrón (muvrón)	my sorrow!
.33	Tolan	Ó Tuathaláin (ó *túh*eláñ)	des. of *Tuathalán* (dim. of *Tuathal*, "people-mighty")
.36	Milenesia	Míle (míli)	n. of leader of Celtic *colonists
602.09	Coemghen	*Old I. spelling of* Caoimhghin (kívġin)	Comely-birth; n. of st., fndr. of monastic settlement at Glenda-lough, 30 miles S. of Dublin; *Shaun
.10	moraltack	Móralltach (móroul*t*okh)	Very-wild, Fierce; n. of *Diarmaid*'s sword; *Toraidheacht Dhiar-mada agus Ghráinne
		móráltacht (mórál*t*okh*t*)	morality
.14	Croona	Crónán (krónán)	Murmuring; Crona is a stream in *Macpher-son, explained as "murmuring"
		Cróna (króne)	Dark, darkening (pos-sible correct etymology for *Macpherson's Crona)
.14	O'Dwyer	Ó Dubhuidh-ir (ó *d*uwír)	des. of *Dubh-odhar* ("black-wan")
.14–15	O'Dwyer of Grey-glens	[Seán] Ó Dubhuidhir á' Ghleanna ([shán] ó *d*uwír a ġlane)	[John] des. of *Dubh-odhar* of the Valley ("John O Dwyer of the Glen"); hero of 17th c. song
.16	burlehearted	Béarla (bérle)	English language
.18	gortan	gortán (gur*t*án)	miser
.23	Oscur	Oscar (usker)	Champion; son of *Oisín*, grandson of *Fionn Mac Cumhail*
.26	Sullivence	Ó Súileabh-áin (ó súleváñ)	des. of *Súil-dubhán* ("black-eyed"); an-glic. Sullivan

.27	buddhy	bod (bu*d*)	penis
.28	scuity	scuit (skit')	excitement, fuss
.28	Londan	lon (lon)	blackbird
.28	canavan	Ó Ceanndubh-áin (ó kyan*d*uváñ) ceanna-bhán (kyaneván)	des. of *Ceanndubhán* ("black-headed") anglic. Canavan "white-headed": bog-cotton, anglic. canavawn
.30	touthena	tonn-teine (*t*on t'ini)[?]	wave-fire; Tonthena, star in *Macpherson's *Temora*, is explained as "meteor of the waves"
		tuath-teine (*t*úet'ini)	magic-fire; people-fire
		Tuatha Dé (*t*úhe d'é)	"God's People": the Jews
603.01	smeoil	smól (smól)	smudge, candle-snuff
.04	Shoan	Seón (shón)	John; *Shaun
.04	Shoon	Siobhán (shún)	Joan
.05, 06	Tay . . . tay	té (té)	tea
.05	tanny	teine (t'ini)	fire
.12	shay	sé (shé)	he
.12	shee	sidhe (shí) sí (shí)	fairy she
.13	sloo	sluagh (slú)	host, army
.13	slee	slighe (shlí)	way, route
.13	butting	bod (bu*d*)	penis
.16	ahike	a mhic (awik)	son, my boy
.21	kinkles	*P/K Split	pinples
.34	Coemghem	(misprint?) Coemghen/ Caoimhghin	see 602.09
.34	tora	teora (t'óre)	border, boundary; Tora is a river in *Macpherson's *Carric-Thura*
604.02	Jerry	Diairmín (d'írmín)	dim. of *Diarmaid* ("freeman"); anglic. Jerry; *Shem

.03	soorkabatcha	Sorcha (surukhe)	Clear; fem. pers. n.
		suairce (súrki)	pleasantness, graciousness, wit
.04	Heremonheber	Eireamhón (erewón)	coleader of Celtic *colonists, ruled N.I., killed his brother & became 1st high king of all I.
		Éibhear (éver)	coleader of Celtic *colonists, ruled S.I. until killed by his brother
.04	Bregia's	Fir Breagh (fir braġ)	Fine [?] Men; tribal n. & land in Co. Meath; anglic. Bregia
.04	Teffia	Fir Teathbha (fir tafe)	Obscure [?] Men; tribal n. & land in Cos. Longford, Westmeath, Offaly (central I.)
.05	cublic	*P/K Split	public
.06	rincers'	rinnce (rinki)	dance
		rinnceóir (rinkór)	dancer
.06	Higgins	Ó hUiginn (ó higin)	des. of *Uige* ("skill")
.06	Cairns	Ó Céirín (ó kérín)/ Ciaráin (kíráñ)	des. of *Céirin/Ciarán* (dim of *ciar*, "black")
.06	Egen	Ó hAodhagáin (ó hégáñ)	des. of *Aodhagán* (dim. of *aodh*, "fire")
.08	theirinn	Éirinn (érin), *dat.*	[to, for] Ireland
.10	morries	Muire (mwiri)	[Virgin] Mary
		Ó Muirgheasa (ó mwiryasi)	des. of *Muirgheas* ("sea-choice"); anglic. Morris
.12	Reulthway	reul (rél)	silver sixpenny
.15	smooltroon	smual (smúl)	smudge
.18	Shamus	Séamus (shémus)	James; *Shem
.22	Gaulls	gall (goul)	foreigner

.23–24	free state on the air	*part trans.* Saorstát Éireann (sérstát érun)	Irish Free State
.24	Gael	Gaedheal (gél)	Irishman, Scotsman
.27	Kevin	Caoimhghin (kívġin)	Comely-birth; 7th c. st., fndr. of monastic settlement at Glendalough, 30 miles S. of Dublin; *Shaun
605.02	messy messy	muise (mwishi) mise (mishi)	well, indeed (interj.) I, me (emphatic)
	.07, 13, Kevin 18, 22, 25, 27, 34, 36	Caoimhghin	see 604.27
.11	Glendalough	Gleann dá Loch (gloun dá lukh)	Two Lake Valley; monastic settlement, Co. Wicklow, S. of Dublin
.12	Yssia	ise (ishi)	she (emphatic)
.12	Essia	eisin (eshin)	he (emphatic)
.19	Yshgafiena	uisce fian (ushki fíen) uisce fíon (ishki fín)	wild water wine water
.20	Yshgafiuna	uisce fionn (ishki fin) Fionn-uisce (finishki)	clear water Clear-water; anglic. Phoenix [Park]
606.03, 04	Kevin	Caoimhghin	see 604.27
.14	Benns	beinn (ben)	peak, headland
.23	*cupla*	cúpla (kúple)	couple, pair, twins
.32	claddaghs	Cladach (kladokh)	Stony-seashore; fishing settlement in Galway town
607.04–05	MacCowell	Mac Cathmhaoil (mok kowél) Mac Cumhail (mok kúl)	son of *Cathmhaol* ("battle-chief") son of *Cumhal*; patronymic of *Fionn*
.16	Finnegan's	Ó Fionnagáin (ó finegáñ)	des. of *Fionnagán* (dim. of *Fionn*, "fair")

.18	Ni	ní (ní)	not
.21	polog	pollóg (poulóg)	recess, pantry; kind of fish
.24	Dayagreening	grian (grín) deo-gréine (d'ogréne)	sun spark of the sun: De-grena, fem. pers. n. in *Macpherson's *Fingal* is explained as "sun-beam"; see 228.08
.25	durknass	dorcha (durukhe)	dark, darkness
.34	coppyl	capall (kopel)	horse
608.02	Brehons	breitheamh-ain (brehúñ)	judges, lawgivers in anc. I. legal system
.07	Arth	Árt (árt)	Bear/Stone, masc. pers. n.
.08	Billhealy	Ó hÉilidhe (ó hélí)	des. of *Ealadhach* ("ingenious"), anglic. Healy
.08–09	Ballyhooly	Baile Átha Ubhla (bolyáhúle)	Appletree Ford Town, Co. Cork
.15	baas	bás (bás)	death
.29–30	hindled firth . . . hundled furth	Áth Cliath (áklíe)	Hurdle Ford; *Dublin
.36	Ah diar, a diar!	a Dhia (a d'íe)	O God
609.02	pettyvaughan	bhán (ván)	white
.03	magnumoore	mór (mór) Ó Mórdha (ó mórġe)	big, great des. of *Mórdha* ("ma-jestic"); anglic. Moore
.04	boydskinned	buidhe (bwí)	yellow
.05	duffyeyed	dubh (duv) Ó Dubhthaigh (ó dufí)	black des. of *Dubhthach* ("black")
.10	Grogram Grays	gruagán gré (grúgán gré) glagram gré (glogrem gré)	grey-hairdye hue; see 399.09 rattling trinket: foolish prater
.12	Sallysill or Silly-sall	sail (sal)	willow

.20	oriel	Óirghialla (órǵíle)	Golden-hostages; anc. principality, N.E.I., anglic. Oriel
.34	cabrattlefield	Cabrach (kobrokh)	Badland; N. Dublin district, anglic. Cabra
.34	slaine	Sláine (sláñi)	Entireness; village N. of Boyne River, Co. Meath where Patrick lit Paschal Fire challenging druids at Tara; anglic. Slane
610.09	leary	Laoghaire (líre)	Calf-keeper; high king at Patrick's arrival
.19	Suc?	suc (suk)	call to a calf
.19	Suc . . . Wutt	Succat (sukot)	Patrick's supposed baptismal n.
.32	Erinmonker	Éirinn (érin), *dat.*	[to, for] Ireland
611.02	Paddrock	Pádraic (pádrik)	Patrick
.02	bookley	Ó Buachalla (ó búkheli)	des. of *Buachaill* ("boy"); anglic. Buckley
.05	Balkelly	Ó Ceallaigh (ó kyalí)	des. of *Ceallach* ("contention"), anglic. Kelly
.05	islish	*L/R Interchange	irish
.07	Patholic	*P/K Split *L/R Interchange	Catholic Pathoric
.27	Bilkilly	bile (bili) cill (kil) coill (kíl)	sacred-tree church wood
.27	Belkelly	Ó Ceallaigh	see 611.05
.33	Leary	Laoghaire (líre)	Calf-keeper; high king at Patrick's coming
612.02	twobreasttorc	torc (tork)	torque: twisted neck ornament
.04	Leary	Laoghaire	see 611.33

.06	Ardreetsar	Árd Rí (árdrí)	High King
.15	Ebblybally	baile (bolye)	town, homestead; anglic. Bally-
.15	Sukkot	Succat (sukot)	Patrick's supposed baptismal n.
.25	shammyrag	seamaróg (shameróg)	trefoil, clover, shamrock
.27, 28	Balenoarch	Balór (balór)	Fomorian king, grandfather of *Lugh*
.32	Bilkilly	bile/cill/coill	see 611.27
.32	Belkelly-Balkally	Ó Ceallaigh	see 611.05
.35	Ards	Árd (árd)	High
613.05	Taawhaar	Teamhar (t'our)	Prospective-hill; anc. royal capital; anglic Tara
.06	sogs	sagart (sogert)	priest
.09	Feist	feis (fesh)	convention, celebration, festival
.10	Shamwork	seamróg (shamróg)	shamrock; *Shem
.30	Murnane	múirnín (múrñín)	sweetheart
		Múirne/ Mórna	Lovable person: fem. pers. n., supposedly of *Fionn Mac Cumhail*'s mother
.30	Aveling	aoibhinn (évin)	delightful, pleasant
		áluinn (áliñ)	beautiful, lovely
.34	Aruna	a rún (arún)	my secret (endearment: darling)
614.03	Doon of the Drumes	Dún Droma (dún drume)	Fort of the Ridge; S. Dublin suburb anglic. Dundrum
.11	iorn	íorna (yorne)	hank
.14	Fennsense	*trans.* eanach (anokh)	fen, marsh; *Anna
.14	finnsonse	fionn (fin)	fair

.14	Fennsense, finn- sonse, aworn!	Sinn féin, sinn féin amhain (shin fén shin fén awáñ)	Ourselves, ourselves alone
615.02–03	Columcellas	*Colmcille (kulumkili)	Dove of the Church; st., Latinized Columba
.07	Finnius	Fionn (fin)	Fair
.30	me craws	Mag Raith (mogra)	son of *Mac Raith* ("son of grace"); an- glic. Magraw, Mc- Grath, etc.
		mo ghrádh (muġrá)	my love
		crádh (krá)	misery, torment
.34	keenin	caoineadh (kínu)	mourning, lamenting
		Ó Cianáin (ó kínáñ)	des. of *Cianán* (dim. of *cian*, "tedium"); an- glic. Keenan
		Mac Fhinghin (mokíñin)	son of *Finghin* ("fair- born"); anglic. Keenan
616.01	Mulloyd	Ó Maol- mhuaidh (ó mwélúí)	des. of *Maolmhuadh* ("noble-chief"); an- glic. Mulloy (heredi- tary bearers of English standard in I.)
.01	O'Reilly	Ó Raghail- ligh (ó rayelí)	des. of *Raghallach* ("[strong-]fore- armed")
.01	fann	fann (foun) fionn (fin)	weak, languid fair
.02	Coolock	Cúlóg (kúlóg)	Little Corner; N.E. Dublin suburb
.03	Eirinishmhan	Éire (ére) inis (inish) Inis Meadhoin (inishman) mhan (won) *English spelled as I.*	Ireland island Middle Island; one of Aran Islands, anglic. Inishmaan one

.11	Sulvans	Ó Súileabh-áin (ó súleváñ) súil (súl) bhean (van)	des. of *Súil-dubhán* ("black-eyed"); an-glic. Sullivan eye woman
.11	Dulkey	Dealg-inis (d'alginish)	Thorn Island, on S. Dublin Bay; Norsified Dalkey
.12	Monacheena	Móin a' chaointe (mónakhínte)	Peat bog of the lamen-tation
.21	Cloon's	Ó Cluain (ó klúñ)	shortened *Ó Cluanaigh*: des. of *Cluanach* ("de-ceitful")
.31	brad	brad (bro*d*)	thieving
617.06	Fintona	Fionn-tamhnach (fin*t*ounokh)	Fair Arable-land, town, Co. Tyrone
.10	pellow	peil (pel)	football
.11	funn make called Foon MacCrawl	Fionn Mac Cumhail (fin mok kúl)	Fair son of *Cumhal*, 3rd c. hero of saga cy-cle
.12	Lorcan	Lorcán (lurkán)	dim. of *lorc*, "fierce," anglic. Laurence; *Brian Boru
.14	Conan	Conán (konán)	masc. pers. n., dim. of *Conn* ("intelligence") or n. beginning *Con-*"high"): *Conán Maol* ("Bald C.")—compan-ion of *Fionn Mac Cum-hail*, buffoon of *Fianna*
.14	Boyles	Ó Baoighill (ó bwéĝil)	des. of *Baoigheall* ("vain-pledge")
.19	Gilly	giolla (gili)	lad, servant
.36	straith	sraith (sra)	swath; holm, fen; an-glic. Strath-
618.01	MacCrawls	Fionn Mac Cumhail	see 617.11
.04	Kinsella	Cinnsealach (kinshalokh)	Proud; des. of *Éanna Cinnsealach*, son of *Diarmaid Mac Murch-adha*, Leinster king who

			invited Anglo-Norman invasion; *Éanna*'s agnomen replaced true surname among his descendants
.08, 29	Sully	Ó Súiligh (ó súlí)	des. of *Súileach* ("quick-eyed")
.15	sympowdhericks	Pádraig (pá*d*rig)	Patrick
.23	Hillary Allen	Cnoc Almhain (knuk alúñ)	Whitened Hill, Co. Kildare; HQ of *Fianna* led by *Fionn Mac Cumhail*; anglic. Hill of Allen
619.03	Finnlater	Fionn (fin)	Fair
.06	Rathgarries	Ráth Garbh (rágorev)	Rough Fort; S. Dublin district anglic. Rathgar
.20, 29	leafy	Life (lifi)	*Liffey River
.20–21	Folty and folty	folt (ful*t*)	long head-hair; foliage (figurative)
		foltach (ful*t*okh)	long-haired
		fáilte (fált′i)	welcome
.30	life	Life (lifi)	*Liffey River
.35	brogues	bróg (bróg)	shoe
620.03	nill, Budd	Dubh-lin (*d*uvlin)	Black-pool; *Dublin
.03	Budd	bod (bu*d*)	penis
.04	buckly	Ó Buachalla (ó búkheli)	des. of *Buachaill* ("boy"): anglic. Buckley
.05	Alby	Alba (olbe)	Scotland
.05	pooraroon	a rún (arún)	"my secret": darling
.05–06	pooraroon Eireen	Eibhlín a rún (eilín a rún); *L/R Interchange	Helen (Eileen) my darling—a song
.06	Eireen	Éirín (érín) Éireann/ Éirinn (érun/ érin), *g./dat.*	Little Ireland (nonce) [of/to, for] Ireland

.08	Lucan	Leamhcán (loukán)	Producing marshmallows; W. Dublin suburb on Liffey; Patrick Sarsfield, I. hero of Williamite wars (c. 1690), was Earl of Lucan
.11	Rathgreany	Ráth Gréine (rágréñi)	Fort of the Sun
.13	Galliver	gall (goul)	foreigner
.14	Gellover	Gaedheal (gél)	Irishman, Scotsman
.24	jackeen	*half-trans.* Seóinín (shóñín)	Johnny: countryman's derisive n. for Dubliner
621.09	Ilma	iolmhaitheasa (ilwohese) ilmhianach (ilvínokh)	many benefits having many desires
.11	Finvara	Ceannmhara (kyanvore) Fionnmhara (finvore)	Head of the Sea, village, Co. Galway, on S. Galway Bay; anglic. Kinvarra Clarity of the Sea (nonce: analogous to above)
.13	Blugpuddels	*trans.* Dubh-linn	Black-pool; *Dublin
.14	tay	té (té)	tea
.14	Is't you fain	Is tú féin (is *t*ú fén)	It is/And yourself
.21	padder avilky	Peadar a mhic (pa*d*er avik)	Peter my son/boy
.24	glave	claidheamh (klív)	sword
.25	hugon	Aodhagán (égán)	dim. of *Aodh* ("fire"); masc. pers. n.
.34	timpul	teampal (t'oumpul)	church, esp. Protestant
622.01	cooshes	cúis (kúsh) cuas (kús)	cause, case, affair hollow, cavity
.01	Coole	Cumhal (kúl) cúl (kúl)	father of *Fionn* ingle, back of the head
.03	Kinsella	Cinnsealach	see 618.04

.04	MacGarath	Mag Raith (mogra)	son of *Mac Raith* ("son of grace"), anglic. MacGrath, etc.
		Mac Gearóid (mok garód')	son of Gerald (i.e., Fitzgerald); anglic. MacGarret
.04	O'Cullagh	Ó Cúlach[áin] (ó kúlekh[áñ])	des. of *Cúlach*[*án*] (dim. of *cúlach*, "fat")
.05	O'Muirk	Ó Muirch [eartaigh] (ó mwirkh[artí])	des. of *Muirch*[*eartach*] ("navigator")
.05	MacFewney	Mac Fiannaidhe (mok fíení)	son of *Fiannaidhe* ("soldier")
.06	Fjorn na Galla	Fionn na nGall (fin nu ̶g̶a̶l)	*Fionn* ("fair") of the Foreigners
		cp. Dún na nGall	Fort of the Foreigners; anglic. Donegal
		Fine-Gall (finigoul)	Foreign Kindred; N. Co. Dublin district, anglic. Fingal
		Fionn-ghal (finġal)	Fair-fight; *Macpherson's n. for *Fionn Mac Cumhail*
		na fionn-ghall (nu fingoul)	the fair foreigners, i.e., Norwegians
.07	Caubeen	cáibín (kábín)	old hat
.12	Buahbuah	buadh (búe)	victory
.22	Gilligan	Ó Giollagáin (ó gilegáñ)	des. of *Giollagán* (dim. of *giolla*, "servant, youth")
.22	Halligan	Ó hAilleagáin (ó halegáñ)	des. of *Ailleachán* (dim. of *áille*, "handsome")
.22	hooligan	Ó hUallacháin (ó húlekháñ)	des. of *Uallachán* (dim. of *uallach*, "proud")
.23	Sullygan	Ó Súileacháin (ó súlekháñ)	des. of *Súileachán* (dim. of *súileach*, "quick-eyed")
.24	theagues	Tadhg (teig)	Poet; masc. pers. n. of typical peasant; anglic. Teigue, etc.

.25	the Naul	An Áill (un ál)	The Cliff; village, N. Co. Dublin
.27	Tallyhaugh	Taimhleacht (talokht)	Plague-grave (place-name element)
.27	Ballyhuntus	Béal Átha hAmhnais (bél áhounish)	Ford-Mouth of Plundering; town, Co. Mayo, anglic. Ballyhaunis
.34	Knocks	Cnoc (knuk)	Hill; anglic. Knock- in place-names
.35	Fyne	Fionn (fin)	Fair
.35	Delvin	Deilbhín (d'elvín)	Little Warp; N. Co. Dublin river
623.01	Ericoricori	Éire (ére) éiric (érik)	Ireland fine, ransom
.22–23	Shaughnessy's	Ó Seachnasaigh (ó shokhnasí)	des. of Seachnasach ("elusive")
.25	heathery benn	Beinn Éadair (ben édir)	Éadar's (masc. pers. n.) Peak; I. n. for Howth Head
.26	Drumleek	Drom Leac (drum lek)	Flagstone Ridge; place on S. side of Howth Head, anglic. Drumleck
.28	Glinaduna	Gleann/ Glinn a' Dúna/na nDún (gloun/ glin adúne/ nanún)	Valley of the Fort/ Forts; valley, Co. Wicklow; anglic. Glen-of-the-Downs
.28	Lonu	lon (lon)	blackbird
.28	nula	Nuala (núle)	fem. pers. n., contraction of Fionnghuala ("Fair-shoulders")
.34	an an	an (un)	the
624.05	ruddery dunner	Ruaidhrí Ó Conchobhair [Donn] (rúrí ó kunukher [doun])	Ruaidhrí (Norse Rothrekr) des. of Conchobhar ("high-will"), the Brown; anglic. Roderick O Connor, last high king; Ruaidhrí's (the senior) branch of

			Ó *Conchobhair* family is called *Donn* ("the Brown"), 2nd branch is *Ruadh* ("the Red") [N.B. "ruddery"]
.08	Gowans	Ó/Mac an Gobhann (ó/mokun goun)	des. of a/son of the smith
.16	Donachie's	Ó/Mac Donnchaidh (ó/mok *d*unukhí)	des./son of *Donnchadh* ("brown-warrior")
.18	sinfintins	sinn féin (shin fén)	ourselves
		Fionntán (fin*t*án)	dim. of *Fionn* ("fair")
		teine (t'ini)	fire
.22	Leafiest	Life (lifi)	*Liffey River
.23	dowling	Ó Dubhsh-láin/Dubh-lainn/ Dún-laing (ó *d*úláñ/*d*úlin/ *d*úlañ)	des. of *Dubhshlán* ("black-challenge")/ *Dubhfhlann* ("black-*Flann* ['ruddy']")/ *Dunlang* ("fort-house/ ship"); anglic. Dowling
.28–29	Finsen makes cumhulments	Fionn Mac Cumhail (fin mok kúl)	Fair son of *Cumhal*; 3rd c. hero of saga cycle
.32	Bray	Brí (brí)	Hillside; town on Dublin-Wicklow border
.32	bes	*trans. of Habitual Present tense:* bíonn (bín)	habitually/usually is (Hiberno-English: does be)
625.04	Aeships	Aos-sidhe (és shí)	fairy-folk
.06	*Cadmillersfolly*	Céad Míle Fáilte (ké*d* míli fált'i)	A hundred thousand welcomes
.07	*Wellcrom*	crom (krum)	stooped, crooked
.08	murphies	Ó Murchadha (ó murukhu)	des. of *Murchadh* ("sea-warrior")

.09	Claffey's	Mac Fhlaitheamh (moklahiv)	son of *Flaitheamh* ("lord")
.12	Conal O'Daniel	Conall Ó Domhnaill (kunel ó *d*ónel)	High-mighty des. of *Domhnall* ("world-mighty")
		Domhnall Ó Conaill (*d*ónel ó kunil)	World-mighty des. of *Conall* ("high-mighty"); anglic. Daniel O Connell
.13	*Finglas*	Fionn-glas (finglos)	Clear-stream; stream & village N. of Dublin
.17–18	Clane turf . . . tarf	Cluain Tarbh (klún *t*orev)	Bull Meadow; N.E. Dublin district, site of *Brian Boru's defeat of Danes, 1014
.18	broin	brón (brón) broin (brin), *g*.	sorrow, grief [of a] raven
.18–19	broin burroow	Brian Bóroimhe (bríen bórivi)	Brian of the Tribute, anglic. *Brian Boru, high king killed defeating Danes at Clontarf, 1014
.24	cara	cara (kore)	friend
.36	Londub	lon dubh (lon *d*uv)	blackbird
		lionn dubh (lyon *d*uv)	porter, stout; black bile, melancholy
		linn dubh (lin *d*uv)	black pool; *Dublin
626.01–02	Annamores	Eanach Mór (anokh mór)	Great Fen; anglic. Annaghmore
.04	norewhere	An Fheoir (unyór)	The Stream; S.E. river, anglic. The Nore
.06	bogue and arrohs	ara na bpóg (ore nu bóg)	one given to kissing
.06	Lashlanns	Lochlainn (lokhlin)	Scandinavia, Norway
		Lochlannaigh (lokhlení)	Scandinavians

.17	*Find Me Colours*	Fionn Mac Cumhail (fin mok kúl)	Fair son of *Cumhal;* 3rd c. hero of saga cycle
.23	fan me coolly	Fionn Mac Cumhail	see 626.17
.26	thawe	tá (*tá*)	there is; yes
.31–33	dev . . . duv . . . div . . . linn	Dubh/Duibh-linn (*d*uv/*d*iv lin)	Black-pool; *Dublin
.33	Inn	inn (in)	we, us
.35	acoolsha	a chúisle (a khúshle) cúl (kúl)	my pulse (endearment) back of the head
627.03	Imlamaya	iomlán (imlán) iomlaoid (imleid)	whole, complete change, exchange
628.03	moyles and moyles	Sruth na Maoile (sru nu mwíle)	Sea-stream of the Bald-headland: sea between I. & Scotland; anglic. Moyle (poetic)
.03	moananoaning	Manannán (monanán)	*Tuatha Dé Danann* magician & minor sea-deity, eponymous owner of Isle of Man, son of *Lear*, the sea-god
.06	moremens	Muir Meann (mwir myon)	Limpid Sea: the Irish Sea
.06	Avelaval	abha (ouwa, ova)	river
.07	Lff	Life (lifi)	*Liffey River
.13	Whish!	thuis! (hish)	shush!
.14	Finn	Fionn (fin)	Fair

Glossary for Joyce's Other Works

THE GAELIC WORDS AND PHRASES IN *Dubliners, A Portrait of the Artist as a Young Man, Pomes Penyeach, Exiles,* AND *Ulysses*

Because of the relative sparsity of Gaelic in these works, and still more because of the multiplicity and variation of editions of these works, I have cited the instances by page number only, making no attempt to locate by line numbers. For both *A Portrait of the Artist* and *Ulysses* I have cited two representative editions for each entry. The two citations for *Exiles* I identify by place. The entries for *Dubliners*, additionally, are listed successively after the title of the story in which they occur, and the entries for *Ulysses* after an identification of the pertinent episode.

The following are the relevant editions used:

Dubliners. Modern Library (1926, 1954).

A Portrait of the Artist as a Young Man. Modern Library (1928). Cited as M.

A Portrait of the Artist as a Young Man. Viking: Compass Books (1956). Cited as C.

Ulysses. Modern Library, new ed., corrected and reset (1961). (Previous ed. varies by about three pages at times.) Cited as M.

Ulysses. Shakespeare & Co., Paris (1922–1930). Cited as P.

Dubliners

"The Sisters"

p. 16	he was in it	*lit. trans.* bhí sé ann	he existed, he was [alive]

"Eveline"

p. 47	Derevaun Seraun	*probably gibberish but phonetically like Irish:*	

		deirbh (d'erev)	true-, real-, genuine- (pfx.)
		dearbhán (d'areván)	small genuine thing [nonce]
		seireán (shcrán)	little sea-anemone
		soireán (sirán)	laughingstock
		sarán (serán)	louse

"A Little Cloud"

| p. 98 | deoc an doruis | deoch an dorais (d'ukh un durish) | "drink of the door": parting drink |
| p. 105 | Lambabaun | bábán (bábán) bán (bán) leanbh (lanev) | child, baby [macaronic "lamb-child"] white, pretty child |

"Counterparts"

| p. 119 | gab | gab (gob) | beak, snout |
| p. 119 | smahan | smeathán (smahán) | taste or small quantity, esp. of liquid |

"Clay"

| pp. 123, 125 | barmbracks | bairghean breac (baryen brak) | "speckled loaf": currant cake used at Halloween |

"Ivy Day in the Committee Room"

p. 152	shoneens	Seóinín (shónín)	"Little John [Bull]": aper of English ways; *Shaun
p. 153	Musha	muise (mwishi)	well, indeed (interj.)
pp. 154, 156	'Usha	mhuise (wishi)	well, indeed (interj.)
p. 155	moya!	mar bh'eadh (mor ya)	as if it were (ironic interj.)
p. 159	goster	gasrán (gosrán) gastaire (gosteri)	conversation tricky person
p. 160	Yerra	A Dhia ara (ġere)	O God well!
p. 161	Wisha! wisha ... Wisha!	mhuise (wishi)	well, indeed (interj.)

"A Mother"

p. 171	*Eire Abu*	Éire Abú (ére abú)	Ireland to victory!
p. 180	Feis Ceoil	Feis Ceoil (fesh kyól)	Music Festival; annual competitive musical convention

"Grace"

p. 192	Sha	'seadh (sha)[?]	it is, yes; interj. indicating satisfaction, or interrogative expressing surprise
p. 200	banshee	bean sidhe (ban shí)	fairy woman
p. 204	bostooms [misprint: bostoons?]	bastún (bostún)	poltroon, blockhead, bounder
p. 204	omadhauns	amadán (omadán)	fool
p. 217	blathering	bladar (blader)	coaxing, flattery

"The Dead"

p. 251	*Beannacht libh*	beannacht libh (banokht liv)	a blessing with you: goodbye

Pomes Penyeach

"Tilly"	tuile (tili)	extra, addition, little added bit (the collection contains thirteen poems, to be sold for a shilling—twelve at a penny each and this "Tilly" extra)

A Portrait of the Artist as a Young Man

Chapter I

M44, C43 smugging	*of possible Irish etymology:* smug, smuga (smug, smuge) snot, nose drip, slime

Chapter II

M99, C89	drisheens	drisín (drishín)	stuffed sheep intestine cooked as pudding
M103, C91	maneens	-ín (ín), *dim. suffx.*	little (contempt or affection)
M105, C93	lob	lab (lob)	considerable lump, as of money (often ironic)
M105, C93	jackeen	*half-trans.* Seáinín, Seóinín (shánín, shónín)	Little Jack: countryman's derogatory term for Dubliner; *Shaun
M106, C94	Yerra	A Dhia ara (ġere)	O God well!
M204, C176	sloblands	slab (slob)	mud, mire, filled land
M209, C180	Firbolg	Fear Bolg (far bulug)	"Bags Man": member of pre-Celtic subject race; *colonists
M209, C180	Milesian	Míleadh (mílú)	soldier; des. of *Míle*, legendary ancestor of Celtic *colonists
M210, C180	Gael	Gaedheal (ġél)	Irishman, Scotsman
M211, C182	cool	cúl (kúl)	goal in ball games
M212, C182	caman	camán (komán)	crook: stick used in playing hurley
M236, C201	fianna . . . fianna . . . Fianna	fianna (fíene)	soldiers (see Additional Note on *Fionn Mac Cumhail*)
M264, C225	Thoth . . . the god's name . . . was like an Irish oath	tat (tot)	call to sheep about to take wrong turn (possibly interpreted by Stephen-Joyce as drover's oath)
		tot (tut)	clamor, noise
M270, C230	Clanbrassil	Clann Bhreasail (klon vrasil)	Children of *Breasal* ("red"): clan-name of the MacCanns of Armagh
M278, C236	sugan	súgán (súgán)	hay- or straw-rope

Exiles

Act I

Brigid's sixth speech	he does be	*trans.* bíonn sé	he usually or normally is (present habitual verb-form)
Robert Hand, accepting cigar	dark foreigners	*trans.* Dubh-ghaill	popular n. for "Danes" —first wave of Norsemen

Ulysses

"Telemachus" (Martello Tower)

M4, P5	scutter	scaid (skod′) [?] scodal (sku*d*el) [?]	refuse, waste jellyfish
M9, P9	Sassenach	Sasanach (sosenokh)	Englishman (Saxon)
M13, P14	tilly	tuile (*t*ili)	extra, addition, little added bit
M14, P14	Silk of the kine	*trans.* Síoda na mbó	Ireland (poetic)
M14, P14	poor old woman	*trans.* Sean bhean bhocht	Ireland (poetic)
M14, P14	Is there Gaelic on you?	*incorrect trans.* An bhfhuil Gaedhealg agat?	"Is there Irish at-you?": Do you know Irish?
M23, P23	Horn of a bull, hoof of a horse, smile of a Saxon	Cheithre nithe nách tugtha d'Éireannach ionntaoibh leó—adharc bhó, crúb chapaill, dranna madra, agus gáire Sag-sanaigh	Four things which an Irishman ought not to trust—a cow's horn, a horse's hoof, a dog's snarl, and an Englishman's laugh (*although I find this as a tetrad, Joyce's triadic form is more typical of such aphorisms*)

"Nestor" (Mr. Deasy's School)

M31, P31 brogues	bróg (bróg)	shoe
M31, P31 fillibegs	filleadh beig (filu beg)	"little fold": kilt
M31, P31 Ards	árd (árd)	height

"Proteus" (Sandymount Strand)

M38, P38 Mananaan	Manannán Mac Lir (monenán mok lir)	*M*. son of *Lear* ("Ocean"); *Tuatha Dè Danann* enchanter, son of seagod
M43, P43 *slainte*!	sláinte (sláñt'e)	health! (toast)
M43, P43 Dalcassians	Dál gCais (*d*ál gash)	Race of *Cas* ("Twist"); clan of which *Brian Boru was chief
M43, P43 gossoon	garsún (gorsún)	boy, lad
M43, P43 tanist	tánaiste (*t*ánishte)	second-in-command; heir presumptive
M45, P45 Lochlanns	Lochlann (lokhlon) Lochlannaigh (lokhloní)	"Lake-place": Scandinavia Scandinavians

"Calypso" (Bloom's Breakfast)

M58, P56 Inishturk	Inis Tuirc (inish*t*irk)	Boar's Island
M58, P56 Inishark	Inis Eirc (inisherk)	Ox's Island
M58, P56 Inishboffin	Inis Bó Finn (inish bófin)	White Cow's Island (N.B. *all edible beasts*)
M58, P56 Slieve Bloom	Sliabh Bladhma (shlív bláme)	*Bladhm*'s ("Flame") Mountain; but P. W. Joyce gives as *Bládh*'s ("Bloom, Flower")

"Lotus-Eaters" (Toward the Bath)

M74, P71 fostering	fostughadh (fos*t*ú)	being employed, being engaged

"Hades" (The Funeral)

M99, P95 *Bugabu*	abú (abú)	to victory!
M99, P95 Brian Boroimhe	Brian Bóroimhe (bríen bórive)	Brian of the Tribute, anglic. *Brian Boru

M108, P104	grig	griog (grig)	excite desire or envy, tantalize

"Aeolus" (Newspaper Office)

M129, P125	spaugs	spág (spág)	paw; long flat foot; clubfoot
M132, P128	Tirconnel	Tír Chonaill (tír khunil)	Conall's ("High-mighty") Land; tribal land of O Donnell, modern Co. Donegal; *Uí Néill
M135, P130	on the shaughraun	part trans. ar seachrán (er shokhrán)	astray, out of work
M145, P140	crubeen	crúibín (krúbín)	dim. of crúb, "hoof": pig's or sheep's trotter

"Lestrygonians" (Lunch)

M163, P156	Sinn Fein	Sinn Féin (shin fén)	Ourselves
M170, P162	Gobstuff	gab (gob)	beak, snout
M175, P167	kish	cis (kish)	wickerwork, hamper
M175, P167	brogues	bróg	see M31, P31
M176, P167	Ben Howth	Beinn (ben)	peak

"Scylla and Charybdis" (National Library)

M184, P177	ollav	ollamh (ulev)	sage, poet, professor
M189, P181	Mananaan, Mananaan Mac Lir	Manannán Mac Lir	see M38, P38
M190, P183	Sinn Fein	Sinn Féin	see M163, P156
M192, P184	caubeen	cáibín (kábín)	old hat
M192, P185	Lir's	Lear, g. Lir (lar, lir)	Ocean; anc. I. sea-god; *Children of Lir
M194, P186	Ta an bad ar an tir	Tá an bád ar an tír (tá un bád er un tír)	The boat is on the land
M194, P186	Taim imo shagart	Táim i mo shagart (tám imu hogert)	I am a (lit., "in my") priest

M194, P186	Put beurla on it	*lit. trans.*Chuir Béarla air	Translate it into English
M194, P186	beurla	Beurla, Béarla (bérle)	English (language)
M194, P187	He is in my father	*burlesque of* "Táim i mo shagart" *idiom*: Tá sé i n-a athair	He is a (lit., "in his") father
M194, P187	I am in his son	*as above:* Táim i mo mhac	I am a (lit., "in my") son
M195, P187	*Tir na n-og*	Tír na nÓg (tír nunóg)	Land of the Young; legendary elysium
M199, P190	usquebaugh	uisce beatha (ishki bahe)	"water of life": whiskey
M199, P191	keened	caoin (kín)	wail, lament
M199, P191	brogue	barróg (beróg)	defect in speech
M199, P191	mavrone	mo bhrón (mu vrón)	my sorrow
M199, P191	pussful	pus (pus)	lip, lips, mouth
M200, P191	pampooties	pampúta/-í (pampú*te*/*tí*)	primitive shoe/s or moccasin/s worn in Aran Islands
M200, P192	Oisin	Oisín (ushín)	Fawn; son of *Fionn Mac Cumhail*; *Macpherson's Ossian
M201, P193	gombeen	gaimbín (gombín)	usury
M205, P197	*Pogue mahone!*	Póg mo thón (póg mu hón)	Kiss my arse
M205, P197	*Acushla machree!*	A chúisle mo chroidhe (a khúshle mu khrí)	O pulse of my heart
M206, P198	Magee Mor	Mag Aodha Mór (mogé mór)	Great Son of *Aodh* ("Fire"); Magee the Great
M207, P198	kern	ceatharn[ach] (kahern[okh])	mercenary foot soldier

M207, P198	clauber	clábar (kláber)	filth, dirt, mud
M211, P202	Father Dineen	*probably* An t-Athair Pádraig Ua Duinnín	Father Patrick S. Dinneen, compiler of Irish dictionary
M215, P206	priesteen	-ín (ín), *dim. suffx.*	little (contempt or affection); Joyce perhaps understood Dinneen ("Dineen") as *duinín*, dim. of *duine*, "person": Fr. Dinneen was a quite small man
M216, P207	*fillibeg*	filleadh beig	see M31, P31
M217, P208	mulberrycoloured, multicoloured, multitudinous	*"run" of adjectives*	*Toraidheacht Dhiarmada agus Ghráinne*

"Wandering Rocks" (Streets of Dublin)

M229, P220	gillies	giolla (gili)	lad, servant
M231, P222	the Fitzgerald Mor	Mac Gearailt Mór	Great Son of Gerald; title of head of Fitzgeralds, earls of Kildare, dukes of Leinster
M240, P231	bosthoon	bastún (bostún)	poltroon, blockhead (see *Dubliners*, "Grace," p. 204)
M244, P234	gombeen	gaimbín	see M201, P193
M244, P234	bockedy	bacach (bokokh) bacaideach (bokedokh)	lame, halt undulating, going up and down
M245, P235	Ford of Hurdles	*trans.* Áth Cliath (áklíe)	*Dublin
M245, P235	Lobengula	Lab an Guala (lobungúle)[?] Lab na Gualann (lob nu gúlen)[?]	Lump of the Vat[?] Lump of the Shoulder, Humpback[?]
M245, P235	Lynchehaun	Loingseachán (liñshekhán)	dim. of *Loingseach* ("having [to do with] a fleet")

| M245, P235 | shraums | sream (shram) | corrupt matter, rheumy droppings |

"Sirens" (Ormond Hotel)

M271, P260	Ben Howth	Beinn	see M176, P167
M272, P261	banshee	bean-sidhe (banshí)	fairy-woman (see *Dubliners*, "Grace," p. 200)
M274, P263	brogue	barróg	see M199, P191
M287, P275	machree	mo chroidhe (mu khrí)	[of] my heart
M288, P276	Ben Howth	Beinn	see M176, P167

"Cyclops" (Barney Kiernan's Pub)

M292, P281	mavourneen's	mo mhúirnín (mu vúrñín)	my darling
M293, P282	Inisfail	Inis Fáil (inish fál)	Island of *Fál* (fetish stone at Tara): Ireland (poetic)
M294, P282	crans	crann (kron)	wooden vessel
M294, P282	Cruachan's	Crúachán (krúkhán)	Little Hill; n. of several places, incl. capital of Medhbh, queen of Connacht in *Red Branch; *Humphrey
M295, P283	Thomond	Tuath-Mumhan (*tú*emún)	North Munster
M295, P283	place of the race of Kiar	Ciarraidhe (kírí)	[territory of the] des. of *Ciar* ("swarthy"): S.W. co., anglic. Kerry
M295, P283	crannocks	crannóg (kronóg)	(wooden) box, vessel, chest
M295, P283	cruiskeen lawn	crúiscín lán (krúshkín lán)	full little jug
M295, P283	rapparee	rapaire (ropiri)	robber; 17th c. outlaw
M295, P283	Arrah	ara (ore)	well, indeed (interj.) (deprecatory)

M296, P284	*a chara*	a chara (akhore)	friend, my friend
M296, P284	broadshouldered . . . sinewyarmed	*adjective "run"*	see M217, P208
M296, P284	brogues	bróg	see M31, P31
M296, P284	Ardri Malachi	Árd Rí Maelsheach-lainn (árd rí mélokhlin)	High King *Malachy
M296, P284	Soggarth	sagart (sogert)	priest
M297, P285	Savourneen Deelish	's a mhúirnín dílis(sa vúrñín dílish)	and, my precious dar-ling
M297, P285	*Arrah na Pogue	ara na bpóg (ore nu bóg)	one given to kissing
M297, P285	*Colleen Bawn	cailín bán (kolín bán)	"white" (pretty) girl
M297, P285	Angus the Culdee	Aonghus Céile Dé (énġus kyéli dé)	Single-choice, Servant (Companion) of God
M297, P285	Ben Howth	Beinn	see M176, P167
M297, P285	O'Bloom	Ó Bladhma (ó bláme)	des. of *Bladhm* ("Flame"), *but as if* of *Bládh* ("bloom, flower"); see M58, P56
M298, P286	honourable person	*trans.* a dhuine uasal	sir, gentleman (ordi-nary polite form of ad-dress)
M299, P287	*Bi i dho husht*	Bí i do thost (bí i *du* hus*t*)	Be quiet
M302, P290	Banba	Banba (bonbe)	Ireland (poetic)
M303, P290	skeezing	scíosachtach (shkísokh*t*okh)	wagging
M305, P293	Arrah!	ara	see M295, P283
M305, P293	loodheramaun	ludramán (lu*d*eremán)	lazy idle fellow

M306, P293	*Sinn Fein! . . . Sinn fein amhain!*	Sinn féin! Sinn féin amhain! (shin fén, shin fén awáñ)	Ourselves! Ourselves alone!
M310, P297	shoneens	Seóinín (shónín)	Little John [Bull]; aper of English ways; see *Dubliners*, "Ivy Day in the Committee Room," p. 152; *Shaun
M311, P298	Maureen Lay	Máirín léighe (márín lé)	affectionate *Máirín* (dim. of *Máire*, "Mary")
M311, P298	colleen bawns	cailín bán (kolín bán)	"white" (pretty) girl
M311, P298	flahoolagh	flaitheamh- lach (flahúlokh)	princely; generous, hospitable
M311, P298	What's on you . . . ?	*lit. trans.* Cad tá ort?	What ails you? What is the matter with you?
M312, P299	ranns	rann (ron)	verse, stanza
M312, P299	the Little Sweet Branch	An Craoibhín Aoibhinn (un krévín íviñ)	"The Sweet Little Branch," pen name of Douglas Hyde, translator of *Love Songs of Connacht*, later (1938–45) President of Ireland
M312, P299	*a chara*	a chara	see M296, P284
M314, P301	shebeen	síbín (shíbín)	illicit tavern
M314, P301	*slan leat*	slán leat (slán la*t*)	"safe with you": goodbye
M315, P302	*Sluagh na h-Eireann*	Sluagh na hÉireann (slúe nu hérun)	The Host (army) of Ireland
M316, P303	*Na bacleis*	Ná bac leis (ná bok lesh)	Don't bother with it; Let it alone
M316, P303	shoneen	Seóinín	see M310, P297

M316, P303	*Brian O'Ciarnain's*	*as if* Brian Ó Cíarnáin (bríen ó kírnáñ)	*Brian* des. of *Ciarnán* (pseudodim. of *Ciar*, "swarthy")
		properly Mac Thighearnáin (mok írnáñ)	Son of *Tighearnán* (dim. of *tighearna*, "lord"); anglic. Kiernan
M316, P303	*Sraid na Bretaine Bheag*	Sráid na Breataine Bheag (srád' nu bra*t*ini vyug)	Little Britain (i.e., Brittany or Wales) Street
M316, P303	*Sluagh na h-Eireann*	Sluagh na hÉireann	see M315, P302
M318, P305	puck	poc (puk)	short sharp blow
M319, P306	Caddereesh	Cad arís? (ko*d* arísh)	What again?
M321, P307	pishogue	piseog (pishog)	superstitious practice, charm, spell; talisman
M322, P308	badhachs	bodach (bu*d*okh)	lout, churl, bumpkin
M323, P309	brehons	breitheamh-ain, *pl.* (brehúñ)	judges, lawgivers in anc. I. legal system
M323, P309	Iar	iar (ír) Ír (ír)	remote-, west- one of three sons of *Míle*, Celtic *colonists of I.
M324, P311	Sassenachs	Sasanach	see M9, P9
M325, P311	medher	meadar (mya*d*er)	one-piece quadrangular wooden cup
M325, P311	*Lamh Dearg Abu*	Lámh Dearg Abú (láv d'areg abú)	Red Hand (heraldic symbol of Ulster & O Neill) to Victory!
M326, P312	*Raimeis*	ráiméis (rámésh)	"romance": nonsense, rubbish
M326, P312	yellowjohns	*trans.* Seón Buidhe	Yellow (derogatory epithet: "filthy") John: John Bull; *Shaun

M326, P313	Eire	Éire (ére)	Ireland
M328, P314	Lynches	Ó Loingsigh (ó liñshí)	des. of *Loingseach* ("having [to do with] a fleet")
M328, P314	Desmond	Deas-Mumhan (d'asmún)	South Munster
M328, P314	Thomond	Tuath-Mumhan	see M295, P283
M328, P314	Moya	mar bh'eadh (mor ya)	as if it were (ironic interj.)
M329, P315	meila murder	*half trans.* míle marbhadh (míle morú)	"a thousand killings": great commotion
M330, P316	Sassenach	Sasanach	see M9, P9
M330, P316	Granuaile	Gráinne Ní Mháille (gráñíwályi)	Spearpoint [?] daughter of a des. of *Máille* ("chief"); anglic. Grace *O Malley
M330, P316	Kathleen ni Houlihan	Caitlín Ní hÚallacháin (kat'lín ní húlekháñ)	Katherine, daughter of a des. of *Úallachán* (dim. of *uallach*, "proud"): Ireland (poetic)
M330, P316	poor old woman	Sean Bhean Bhocht	see M14, P14
M331, P317	Manus Tomaltach og MacDonough	Maghnus Tomaltach Óg Mac Donnchadha (mañus *t*umol*t*okh óg mok *d*unukhu)	Magnus Bulky the Young, son of *Donnchadh* ("brown-warrior")
M332, P318	duns	dún (*d*ún)	fort
M332, P318	raths	ráth (rá)	ring-fort
M332, P318	cromlechs	crom-leac (krum lyak)	stooped-flagstone: popular n. for dolmen

M332, P318	grianauns	gríanán (grínán)	solar, soller (of medieval castle), sunroom
M332, P318	Kilballymacshonakill	Cill/Coill Baile mhic Seóin a' Chill (kil/kíl bolye vik shón a khil)	Church/Wood of the Town of the son of John of the Church
M333, P319	Moya!	mar bh'eadh	see M328, P314
M334, P320	usquebaugh	uisce beatha	see M199, P190
M334, P320	Shanganagh	Seangánach (shangánokh) Sean-gaineamh (shangañiv)	Ant-full; sometimes understood as Old-sand; on S. Co. Dublin coast
M335, P321	Sinn Fein	Sinn Féin	see M306, P293
M336, P321	argol bargal	argáil (orgál)	argument, discussion
M342, P327	leprechaun	leipreachán *for* lúchorpán *Metathesis* (leprekhán, lúkhurpán)	"little body": a kind of sprite
M342, P327	Arrah	ara	see M295, P283
M342, P327	whisht	thoist (hisht), *Asp.*	silence
M343, P328	*agus*	agus (ogus)	and
M343, P328	Slieve	sliabh (shlív)	mountain

"Nausicaa" (Sandymount Strand)

M346, P331	plucks	pluc (pluk)	cheek
M360, P344	brack	breac (brak)	speck, speckle
M360, P344	streel	sraoille (sríle) sraoilleog (srílog)	loose-hanging rag or garment slut, slattern

M365, P349	rossies	rásaidhe (rásí)	jilt, wandering woman
M378, P360	*Faugh a ballagh*	Fág a' bealach (fág a byalokh)	Leave the way! Clear the way!
M379, P361	smithereens	smiodairín (smi*d*erín)	small fragment

"Oxen of the Sun" (Holles Street Hospital)

M383, P366	Deshil . . . Deshil . . . Deshil	deiseal (d'eshil)	turning to the right; sunwise
M384, P367	O'Shiels	Ó Siadhail (ó shíl)	des. of *Siadhail* ("sloth"); family of physicians; *Eoghan Ó Siadhail*, "the Eagle of Doctors" was physician-in-chief to armies of the Kilkenny Confederation (1642–50)
M384, P367	O'Hickeys	Ó hÍceadha (ó híkú)	des. of *Íceadh* ("healer"); family of hereditary physicians to O Briens
M384, P367	O'Lees	Ó Laoidhigh (ó líyí)	des. of *Laoidheach* ("poetic"); family of hereditary physicians to O Flaherty produced complete medical *cursus* in Latin & Irish (15th c.)
M388, P371	Alba Longa	Alba (olbe)	Scotland
M393, P375	Clan Milly	Clann Mílidh (klon mílí)	Race of *Míleadh* (legendary ancestor of Celtic *colonists of I.): the I. race
M395, P375	Milesian	míleadh (mílu)	soldier; des of *Míleadh*; I. Celt
M399, P381	galore	go leór (gu lyór)	enough, sufficient
M412, P392	This is the appearance is on me	*lit. trans.* 'Seo é an chuma atá orm	This is the condition I am in

M412, P392	with my share of songs	*lit. trans.* lem' chuid amhrán	with that number of songs that I know, with such songs as I know
M412, P392	soulth	samhailt (soult')	apparition, ghost, likeness
M412, P392	bullawurrus	boladh a' mharbhadha[?] (bula woru) *cf.* boladh na húire (bula nahúrye)	the smell of murder the smell of earth (presage of death)
M412 P393	Mananaan Mannanaun	Manannán	see M38, P38
M413, P393	Clambrassil (misprint for Clanbrassil?)	Clann Breasail	see *Portrait* M270, C230
M417, P393	brogues	bróg	see M31, P31
M424, P403	bonnyclaber	bainne clabair (boñi klobir)	sour thick milk
M425, P404	at me	*lit. trans.* agam	with verb "to be": I have
M426, P405	Machree, Macruiskeen	[grádh] mo chroidhe mo chrúiscín ([grá] mukhrí mu khrúshkín)	[the love] of my heart [is] my little jug (a song)
M426, P405	colleen bawn	cailín bán	see M311, P298
M426, P405	coppaleen	capaillín (kopelín)	little horse
M427, P406	inyah!	an eadh? (un ya)	is it so? is that so?
	"Circe" (Nighttown)		
M429, P408	Kithogue	ciotóg (kitóg)	left-handed person
M429, P409	*Gobbing*	gab (gob)	beak, snout
M434, P413	*crubeen*	crúibín	see M145, P140

M436, P415	*Sraid Mabbot*	Sráid M. (srád′)	Mabbot Street
M436, P415	*Slan leath*	Slán leat	see M314, P301
M437, P416	*crubeen*	crúibín	see M145, P140
M439, P418	*crubeens*	crúibín	see M145, P140
M447, P425	deluthering	lútáil (lútál) [?]; *L/R Interchange	fawning, cringing, making up to
M448, P426	*brogues*	bróg	see M31, P31
M448, P426	shanderadan	seanandaire (shanandere) [?]	old[est] inhabitant
M450, P428	*shebeenkeeper*	síbín	see M314, P301
M451, P428	SHEBEEN-KEEPER	síbín	see M314, P301
M453, P430	*crubeen*	crúibín	see M145, P140
M462, P438	*boreens*	bóthairín (bóherín)	"little road": lane
M462, P438	*colleens*	cailín (kolín)	girl
M479 P453	Cead Mille Failte Cead Mile Failte	Céad Míle Fáilte (kéd míle fált′i)	A Hundred Thousand Welcomes
M492, P465	*sgenl inn ban bata coisde gan capall*	*garbled:* sgeul/ sgéal i mbarr bata cóisde gan capall (shkél i már bote kóshde gon kopul)	a pointless tale (lit., "tale in the top of a stick") is a horseless coach
M499, P471	*caubeen*	cáibín	see M192, P184
M499, P471	*brogues*	bróg	see M31, P31
M499, P471	*sugaun*	súgán (súgán)	hay- or straw-rope; see *Portrait* M278, C236

M507, P478	*gillie*'s	giolla	see M229, P220
M507, P478	*filibegs*	filleadh beig	see M31, P31
M510, P480	*ollave*	ollamh	see M184, P177
M510	*Mananaan MacLir* MANANAAN MACLIR	Manannán Mac Lir	see M38, P38
P480	*Mananaun MacLir*		
P481	MANANAUN MAC LIR		
M510, P481	Mor!	mór (mór)	big, great
M522, P491	MacChree	mo chroidhe (mu khrí)	[of] my heart
M533, P502	*brogues*	bróg	see M31, P31
M550, P516	*Ben Howth*	Beinn	see M176, P167
M554, P519	*keen*	caoin	see M199, P191
M556, P530	pishogue	piseog	see M321, P307
M595, P557	alanna	a leanbh (a lanev)	child, my child
M595, P557	*keens*	caoin	see M199, P191
M595, P557	*banshee*	bean sidhe	see M272, P261
M595, P557	Ochone! Ochone!	ochón (ukhón)	alas
M595, P557	Silk of the kine	Síoda na mbó	see M14, P14
M595, P557	Soggarth Aroon	sagart a rún (sogert a rún)	priest, my dear; my beloved priest
M596, P557	*Erin go bragh!*	Éire go bráth (ére gu brá)	Ireland until Judgment[-Day]!
M600, P561	acushla	a chúisle (a khúshle)	O pulse (endearment)

"Eumaeus" (Cabmen's Shelter)

M624, P584	Caoc	caoch (kéukh)	one-eyed [person]
M646, P604	pick	pioc (pik)	bit, jot
M650, P608	shebeen	síbín	see M314, P301
M658, P615	potheen	poitín (put'in)	"little pot": illicit whiskey
M662, P620	potheen	poitín	see M658, P615

"Ithaca" (Bloom's House)

M688, P644	*suil, suil, suil arun, suil go siocair agus suil go cuin*	siubhal/siúl, siúl, siúl a rún, siúl go socair agus siúl go ciúin (shúl shúl shúl arún shúl gu sukir ogus shúl gu kyúñ)	walk, walk, walk my dear, walk safely and walk calmly (a song)
M688, P644	gee, eh, dee, em, simple and modified	ᵹ, e, ᴅ, m, ᵹ̇, é, ᴅ̇, ṁ (g, e, *d*/d', m, ġ/y, é, ġ/y, w/v)	g, e, d, m, gh, é, dh, mh
M688, P645	culdees	Céile Dé (kyéle d'é)	Companion of God (anc. I. ecclesiastic)
M689, P645	ogham	ogham (oyem)	anc. I. writing by notches
M689, P646	his signature in Irish	Steafán Ó Deadaluis (sht'efán ó d'aᴅelish) [Seumas Seóigh (shémus shóí); *but perhaps should be* Seoghas (shós)	Stephen, des. of *Deadalus* (n. does not actually occur in I.) James [son] of *Joie* (Norman pers. n.); what James Joyce probably took to be the I. form of his n.; but Cork "Joyce" is [son] of *Josse* (Breton pers. n.)]

"Penelope" (Molly)

M743, P699	plabbery	plabar (plober) plabaire (ploberi)	anything pasty, viscous, or slushy fleshy-faced person with thick indistinct speech
M743, P699	glauming	glám (glám)	grasp, clutch
M743, P699	grigged	griog (grig)	see M108, P104
M748, P704	Sinner Fein	Sinn Féin	see M306, P293
M756, P711	bawn	bán (bán)	white, pretty
M764, P718	pluck	pluc	see M346, P331
M771, P724	blather	bladar (blader)	coaxing, flattery
M771, P724	strool	srúill (srúl) struille (strile)	stream, channel anything untidy or confused
M772, P725	Sinner Fein	Sinn Féin	see M306, P293
M779, P731	arrah	ara	see M295, P283

Supplementary Notes

ANNA[1]
(See also *Dublin, *Humphrey, *Liffey River)

The received impression of the Irish origin of the name *Anna* seems to be that "Anna Liffey" is a rendition of the phrase *Abha na Life*, "the River Liffey." [2] This derivation is improbable.

The word *abha* (ouwe), "river," in the names of actual Irish rivers has been anglicised variously Au-, Aw-, Ou-, Ov-, and Ow-. The more frequent alternate *abhainn* (ouwin) occurs sometimes as Avon- or Aven-, but usually as Owen-.[3] Various genitive forms give rise to such anglicised suffixes as -nahown, -nahone, -nahowna, -nahivnia. An adjectival form, *abhnach* (ounokh), "rivery, marshy," yields Ounagh and Onagh. But no form of *abha/abhainn* appears to have been anglicised Ann, Anna, or Anny.

Yet literally hundreds of anglicised Irish place-names contain the syllables *ann* and *anna* as prominent elements. Places exist with such names as Anna, Annagh, Annah, Anny, Annees, as well as Annabella, Annaduff, Annaghbeg, Annaghmore, Annakisha, Annalong, Annamoe, and Annaroe. Countless other place-names end with the suffix *-anny*. None of these place-names derive from *abha/abhainn;* none of those here listed, and probably very few, if any at all, derive from the feminine names Ann or Anna. The vast majority of these names, in fact, must be referred to some form of the noun *eanach* (anokh); most of the remainder to the phrase *áth na* (ánu).

Eanach—genitive singular *eanaigh*, nominative plural *eanaighe* (both pronounced aní)—comes from the compounding root *ean* (an), meaning "water-." An *eanach* is a watery place—pond or lake sometimes, but generally marsh, swamp, or fen. In place-names, therefore, the element *anna* or *annagh* means "marsh" or "fen," and the terminal *-anny*, "of a fen" or "fenny." The villages Anna, Annagh, and Annah are all named "Fen"; Anny and Annees are *Eanaigh* (aní), "Fens"—the latter with a duplicate English plural *s*. Annaghbeg is "Little Fen," Annaghmore

"Great Fen," Annaduff and Annaghduff "Black Fen," and Annabella, Co. Cork, is *Eanach-Bile*, "Fen of a Sacred Tree."

Áth na . . . ("the ford of . . ."), the less frequent source of the prefix *Anna-* in anglicised place-names, accounts for the names of Annaslee, Annacarrig, Annaglogh, and Annalecky ("Ford of the Way," "of the Rocks," "of the Stones," "of the Flagstones") among others. Annakisha is *Áth na Cise* (ánekishe), "Ford of the Wickerwork Causeway"—a name functionally identical with the Irish name for *Dublin: *Áth Cliath*, "Ford of Hurdles."

Analogy consequently suggests that the name of "Anna Liffey" must derive either from *Eanach-Life* ("Liffey-Fen") or *Áth na Life* ("Liffey-Ford"). And the second of these alternatives immediately identifies the river with the city of *Dublin. On the other hand, "Liffey-Fen" would also serve to identify the muddy or fenny place through which the river flows—Mudlin (136.02). Both possibilities are combined in Mudford (086.11) and Hurdlebury Fenn (297.20). The justness of thus compounding or crossing the names of Dublin City and of Dublin's river is made clearer under the notes for *Dublin and *Liffey River.

Joyce's acceptance of *eanach* as the phonetic basis of Anna is readily shown by recalling that "Fennyana" (055.05), that "fenemine" (093.14) person, is a "Fenny poor hex" (208.31) who is "just as fenny as he is fulgar" (242.28–29). This association with her husband also produces "Fenegans Wick" (358.23) and "fenland" (589.22), as well as the "Hurdlebury Fenn" already mentioned. The final consonant of *eanach* is preserved in "annacrwatter" (135.06), a word that also enshrines the basic meaning of the prefix *ean-*, "water." That prefix occurs alone in "Annushka" (207.08), reducible to *ean-uisce* (anishki), "water-water." "Lutetiavich," that pseudo-Russian lady's masculine patronymic, through Lutetia, the mud-goddess of Paris, also brings to mind the muddy *Eanach-Life*, and serves to remind us that Anna's "muddied name was Missisliffi" (159.12–13). The Irish place-names Annah (104.01), Annesley (130.21: "annesleyg"), Annabella (512.01), and Annamores (626.01), all perforce embody the word *eanach*, but the context in each case is insufficiently muddy or fenny to assert incontrovertibly that Joyce on the occasion is actively making use of the sense. On the other hand not one of these instances will comfortably accommodate the interpretation *abha na* . . . , "the river . . ."

A negative argument against Joyce's having construed Anna as meaning "the river" may be erected by examining the indubitable instances in which he has anglicised or otherwise made use of the word *abha/abhainn*. The explicit occurrence of "Abha-na-Lifè" (496.27) proves nothing phonetically, of course, but shows at least beyond cavil that Joyce knew at least one of the Irish words for "river" (the correct one, incidentally, in the name of the *Liffey). But his phonetic renditions of *abha* and *abhainn*, when they are not conventional anglicisations, are phonetically superior to the conventions. *Atha*, for instance, appears in conventional dress as "Ow" (203.14), but more faithfully as "Awa-" in "Awabeg" (248.34). *Abha Beag* (ouwe byug), "Little River"—a common name—is variously anglicised Awbeg and Owbeg; Joyce's "Awabeg" is a more accurate transcription of the sound. For *abhainn* (ouwin) he uses the conventional "owen" most convincingly in "a flewmen of her owen" (202.05–06)—equating Latin *flunen* with Irish *abhainn*. "Owen K." (066.24) is *Abhainn Coach*, "Blind River," conventionally anglicised Owenkeagh; "Owen-more" (206.27; 475.07) is the conventional rendition of *Abhainn Mór*, "Great River"—although in *Finnegans Wake* compounded with King *Eoghan Mór*: Owen the Great (see *Shaun). *Abhainn* likewise makes a separate conventional appearance as "owen" (601.03). But "Awaindhoo" (371.33) is a phonetically superior transcription of *Abhainn Dubh* (ouwin *dú*), "Black River." The conventional "Avon-" (209.06) and "Aven-" (242.28) also occur, but these are more ambiguous instances than the former because of the equal frequency of these elements in British (from Brythonic *afen*, "river") as in Irish river names.

The most illuminating use of *abhainn* in *Finnegans Wake*, however, occurs when we are told that Anna Livia is "still believing in her owenglass" (101.29). The first part of "owenglass" is of course *abhainn*, but the last syllable represents a word—*glas* (glos)—of piquant ambivalence. As an adjective *glas* in Irish signifies "green" as well as "raw, crude"; sometimes it takes the form *glais* (glash). But *glais* is a noun meaning "rivulet, stream," and sometimes takes the form *glas*. Joyce's "owenglass," therefore, means either "green [raw, crude] river" or "river-stream" (*abhainn glas; abhainn-glais*). But a few lines later the delicate equilibrium of this word is upset by the parallel compound "anngreen" (101.36). Since "-glass" (*glas*) would translate "-green," a deceptive logic here might suggest a similar relationship between "owen-" and "ann-"—that is, despite what has been argued here, that "ann-," like "owen-," represents *abhainn*, or perhaps even *abha na*, "the river . . ." Nevertheless, despite any byplays Joyce may be allowing himself, "ann-" is no other than *ean-*, "water-," the root word of *eanach*, and "anngreen" is a perverted half-translation of the Irish word *eanglais* (anglash), which Dinneen's dictionary defines as "milk and water; diluted liquid; unsatisfactory drink." The components of the word are, of course, *ean-*, "water-," and *glais*, "raw, crude," but Joyce—typically—has elected to translate the second element as "green." The alimentary-colorful-emotional context—"the hungray and anngreen"—nonetheless supports the identification of *eanglais*. And so in parallel instances, within the same page, the Irish word for "river" is rendered "owen," whereas the syllable "ann" almost as certainly comes from the *ean/eanach* family of Irish words, meaning "water-, watery-place, fen."

As for the less common basis of the anglicisation "Anna" in Irish topographical names—*áth na*, "the ford of"—its presence is difficult to establish in *Finnegans Wake* beyond cavil. Surprising indeed, in view of its functional identity with the Irish name for Dublin on which Joyce rings infinite changes, is the apparent absence of the name Annakisha, *Áth na Cise*, "Wickerwork Ford." Anna is everywhere, kishes abound; if you will take the view of wickerwork, it is at hand. Yet in at least one place there appears what looks like a translation of Annakisha: "at Wicker-works, still hold ford" (288.28—289.01). Here even "at" may reflect *áth*. Additionally, Annakisha may have a ghostly macaronic existence as *Ann-na-Cise*, "Ann of the Wickerwork": "a crone that hadde a wickered Kish" (13.36—14.01). The implications of this possibility are more fully explored in the note on *Dublin.

The syllable "ann" in *Finnegans Wake*, then, will almost always stand for "water," and "anna," "anni," "annie," "anny," and so forth, for "marsh/fen," *not* "river." At times "anna" may also signify "ford" or "causeway." Furthermore, through associations of these words and their translations, HCE and ALP are inextricably interwoven: "fen" and "finn" merge, Mudville melts into Anna's marshes, the crone with her kish becomes indistinguishable from the Hurdle Ford.

Two other possible Irish contributors to the name Anna must be mentioned. The first is the goddess Ana (or Dana, the same name with prosthetic *d*), tutelary deity of the Tuatha Dé Danann (see *Colonists). That mysterious people gives evidence of having really been the host of the dead, and Ana, therefore, is really Goddess of the Dead. But still another goddess has probably contributed to Anna—Eithne the mother of Lugh the sun-god. *Eithne* (ehini), meaning "kernel," has been a widely used feminine name in Ireland since antiquity, and is again returning to popularity, but during the nineteenth-century period of snobbish abjection before all things English the name was usually anglicised *Annie*. If *Eithne* is included in "Aithne meithne" (394.26), its contribution to Anna is beyond dispute. *Aithne* (ahini) sounds sufficiently like Anna although it represents two independent Irish words, meaning respectively "commandment" and "acquaintance."

Yet whatever accretions, Irish or otherwise, have grown about her name, Anna began as simple Anna Liffey, and as such *Eanach Life* or *Áth na Life*, not *Abha na Life*, must be the substratum upon which all else is erected.

1. The substance of this note has been argued in greater detail in my article, "Anna Livia Plurabelle's Gaelic Ancestry," *James Joyce Quarterly*, II (1965), pp. 158–166. I am greatly indebted to the editors of that periodical for their kind permission to reprint this material.

2. For a representative—if muddled—statement of this view, see Adaline Glasheen's valuable *A Second Census of Finnegans Wake* (Evanston, 1963), p. 9.

3. Even the apparently promising Anner River in Tipperary ("Annar" in *Finnegans Wake* [503.31]) has nothing to do with *abha*. The Irish form of its name is given both as *An Dobhar* and *An Úr* (the latter likely a corruption of the former), but meaning in either case "The Water."

ARRAH-NA-POGUE

Arrah-na-Pogue is one of several plays by the Irish actor and playwright, Dion Boucicault (1822–1890), which, together with their author's name, appear persistently throughout *Finnegans Wake*. (Of some eighty all told of Boucicault's plays, five besides Arrah-na-Pogue are easily spotted in *Finnegans Wake: *The Colleen Bawn, The O'Dowd, The Octoroon, The Corsican Brothers,* and *The Shaughraun.*)

Arragh-na-Pogue (first produced 1865) was perhaps Boucicault's greatest success, being not only received with acclaim in London (and previously in Dublin), but translated and acted in French and other languages. The play is a melodramatic comedy, peopled with japing stage-Irishmen rather oddly mixed with idealised representatives of surviving Irish nobility. Amidst the "bulls," the comedy, the elaborate stage effects, and the melodramatic perils are mingled pedagogic expositions of Gaelic custom—at times quite accurate, as on the tradition of fosterage and the use of the unadorned surname as an honorific (it is remarkable that Boucicault in this play eschews the usual anglicisation with a prefixed "The"—but in *The O'Dowd* succumbs to the unwarranted addition).

Boucicault's sporadic accuracy forsakes him, however, in accounting for his title character, who is one of the play's two chief contributions to *Finnegans Wake*. Arrah-na-Pogue is the lower-class heroine, foster-sister of the upper-class hero, and her name is explained as meaning Arrah of the Kiss (referring to an episode of the plot), and Arrah is proposed as a feminine name equivalent to Nora. But Arrah has no legitimate status as a version of Nora. Nora—*Nóra*—is merely a shortened form of *Onóra*, the Irish form of Latin Honoria. Anglicised forms are numerous and range from Honora to Nanno and Hannah, but include no Arrah that I have been able to discover. Nor does Arrah otherwise correspond to any usual feminine name (*aire* [ari], "guardian," constitutes an element of several Irish masculine names).

In the other direction, "na-Pogue" makes bad Irish for "of the Kiss." *Póg* (póg) means "kiss"; the genitive form "of the kiss" is *na póige* (nu pógyi). Genitive plural, "of the kisses," is *na bpóg* (nu bóg): a form "*na póg*" has no recognized existence. More to the point, however, a compound does exist which is the probable basis of Boucicault's confection. Several Irish words take the form *ara* (ore), but the pertinent one is a masculine noun defined as meaning: "a page, a lackey; a charioteer; the agent of an action, one given to a certain line of action." To illustrate the last sense, Dinneen's dictionary offers two examples: "*ara na bpóg*" and "*ara an óil*." The latter phrase means "habitual drinker," the former, "one given to kissing." Undoubtedly, therefore, some misunderstanding of the phrase *ara na bpóg* lies behind Arrah-na-Pogue, and accordingly the present Lexicon glosses "Arrah-na-Pogue" as "one given to kissing," disregarding Boucicault's play, which is in any case a locus outside the strictly lexical confines of this work.

A second contribution to *Finnegans Wake* of this play is the character Shaun the Post (that is, driver of the post-cart). He is a humorous character, the lower-class hero, who eventually marries Arrah-na-Pogue. Beyond his name, however, the character Shaun the Post contributes very little distinctive to the chuffy young champion of *Finnegans Wake*. But in the initial run of *Arrah-na-Pogue* in Dublin and London, the part of Shaun was played by Dion Boucicault himself, and the career of Boucicault is one that remarkably resembles that of Shaun in *Finnegans Wake*.

Born in Ireland as Dion Bourcicault in 1820 or 1822, he was educated in Ireland and England, and began his career as a young actor in London in 1838, under the name of Lee Morton. In 1841, under that alias, and at the age either of nineteen or twenty, he produced his first play, *London Assurance*. In February 1842 he brought out *The Irish Heiress*, this as Dion Boucicault, the slightly modified form of his original name which he was to retain for life. In the next ten years—that is, before 1852—he wrote, translated, or collaborated on no fewer than fourteen plays. Between that date and 1860 he produced on his own a further seven plays. But this prolific production was essentially Shaunlike: his dramas, though often models of construction, show little originality; when the plots are not derivative the plays are little more than adaptations of older or of foreign plays, dramatizations of novels, and so forth. As a typical example, his *The Dublin Boy*, of February 1862, is a translation and adaptation of something called *Le Gamin de Paris*. In other words, as a playwright Boucicault was a highly successful purveyor of other men's creations.

A second Shaunlike aspect of Boucicault emerged in 1853, with his first tour to New York. In America his success equaled or surpassed that in London, and since he was no subscriber to the rigorous sexual code of his Victorian contemporaries, it was probably about this time that he took up a certain amount of "canoodling"—a first step on the road to divorce.

In 1860 Boucicault brought out his first sensational success, **The Colleen Bawn*, starring himself and his wife. He brought out eight further plays before his all-time greatest success, *Arrah-na-Pogue*, in 1865. In the meantime, in January 1863, he had become manager of Astley's Theatre in London (see 214.14). Thereafter some fifteen plays followed before 1876, including in 1872 *Babil and Bijou* which created something of a scandal in London from the expensiveness of its production, and *The Shaughraun* in 1875. In 1876 Boucicault emigrated permanently to the United States, where he went into semiretirement, producing only five new plays before his death in 1890. In the United States he repudiated his first wife and remarried. There is some indication that the possibility of so doing was one of the attractions of the United States.

Boucicault had no artistic pretensions; he was an entrepreneur of the stage, a type born too soon to become a Hollywood tycoon, yet amply successful within the scope of the Victorian theater. For all that, his heroes are often engaging and alive, his characterization in general effective and convincing. His forte was scenic effects, and he took fuller advantage than perhaps anyone else of the new technical virtuosity of the physical Victorian stage: mechanical props and elaborate movable scenery. The exaggeratedly detailed stage directions in *Finnegans Wake* (558–560 and elsewhere) understate rather than inflate the typical Boucicault stage directions they parody.

For inquisitive readers who may wish to comb *Finnegans Wake*, the following is a list of Boucicault's plays, from 1841 to 1886 in approximate chronological order: *London Assurance; The Irish Heiress; Alma Mater, or a Cure for Coquettes; Woman; Old Heads and Young Hearts; A Lover by Proxy; Curiosities of Literature; Used Up; The Fox and the Goose; Caesar de Bazan; A School for Scheming; Confidence; The Knight of Arva; The Broken Vow; The Willow Copse; The Queen of Spades; The Vampire; The Corsican Brothers; Louis XI; Faust and Marguerite; Prima Donna; Janet Pride; Genevieve; The Colleen Bawn; The Octoroon; The Dublin Boy; The Life of an Actress; Dot (The Cricket on the Hearth); The Relief of Lucknow; The Trial of Effie Deans; Fox Chase; The Streets of London; Arrah-na-Pogue; The Parish Clerk; The Long Strike; The Flying Scud; Hunted Down; After Dark; Presumptive Evidence; Formosa; Paul Lafarge; A Dark Night's Work; The Rapparee; Jezebel; Night and Morning; Babil and Bijou; Led Astray; The Shaughraun; A Bridal Tour; Forbidden Fruit; The O'Dowd; Mimi; The Jilt.*

ASPIRATION

Aspiration is the conventional if inaccurate term used in Irish grammar books to denote one of the regular kinds of changes to which the consonants of Irish words are subject. The changes take place according to specific syntactic and phonetic laws upon which it is unnecessary to discourse here. The changes are limited, not random, and affect nine (spelling) consonants only: b, c, d, f, g, m, p, s, t. Under "aspiration" these consonants mutate in the following ways (see "Pronunciation"): b becomes v (or w); c [k] becomes kh; *d* becomes ġ; d′ becomes y (or ġ);

f becomes h (or mute); g becomes ġ (or y); m becomes w (or v); p becomes f; s, t, *t*, and t′ become h.

Irish spelling strives to retain so far as possible the unaspirated appearance of a word (unlike, for instance, Welsh, where the parallel phenomenon is treated by simply substituting the new consonant for the old). To facilitate this, the traditional and comely Irish form of the alphabet developed a system of placing a dot over the affected consonant to indicate its aspiration. Romanized Irish, however, has adopted the lunatic device of indicating aspiration by placing an h after every affected consonant (see 121.16 and such parodies as that at 310.11). The result is to pepper any page of romanized Irish with h's, and to support the popular belief that Irish spelling has little relationship to Irish sounds. Yet a quite rational convention determines that Ó Dubhthaigh, for instance, should be pronounced O Duffy, and the insular Irish spelling would appear somewhat less cumbrous: Ó Dubtaig.

Nevertheless the discrepancy between the appearance and the sound of Irish words allows at least a double option to an imitator or parodist such as Joyce in *Finnegans Wake,* and additionally complicates the task of the compiler of a Gaelic lexicon to the work. This may be illustrated from the independent case of the name of the ancient royal capital of Ireland: *Teamhar,* genitive *Teamhra* (t′our, t′oure). From the *sound* of the name undoubtedly came the conventional modern anglicisation, Tara; while from the *spelling* (despite his assertions and *ad hoc* etymologizing) almost as certainly arose *Macpherson's Temora. On occasion even Joyce's maneuverability is inhibited by the dichotomies thus set up: between insular and romanized spelling, between appearance and pronunciation; yet he can rise triumphantly over the obstacles. An instance occurs at 590.13, in the word "beacsate." Context confirms that he is using here the Irish word *beach* (bakh), "bee"—a word impossible to use in full roman spelling because of its identity in appearance to English "beach" (or in sound to German *Bach*). But "beac-" corresponds to the insular spelling of the word, and the overtones of the compound ("backseat," "backside") insure a reasonable approximation of the pronunciation.

Since phenomena similar to Irish "aspiration" have taken place in other languages—notably in the development of Modern from Ancient Greek—not all possible instances of aspiration in *Finnegans Wake* are glossed in this Lexicon. The words "vivle" (110.17) and "vivlical"

(183.13), for instance, are assumed to be of Greek rather than of Irish relevance. Withal, the reader of *Finnegans Wake* may perhaps profitably amuse himself by experimentally replacing b's and m's with v's and w's, and vice versa; d's with y's or g's, and vice versa; g's with y's; p's with f's; and f's, s's, and t's with h's—and also vice versa. As a general note it should be remarked that *Fionn* under aspiration is pronounced *hin* or *in*— a fact which accounts for Joyce's delight with the Chinese word *Hin* or *Fin* (letter to Miss Weaver, 2nd of March 1927).

BOYNE RIVER

The Boyne River (in Irish *An Bóinn*—a name derived from that of a goddess, itself probably having something to do with *bó*, "cow") is a river that figures largely in Irish history. It rises in the Bog of Allen, Co. Kildare, near Carbury, west of Dublin (and not far from the Hill of Allen, in *Fionn Mac Cumhail's* time chief depot of the *Fianna*), and flows north and east for seventy miles to reach the Irish Sea at Drogheda. Its course lies chiefly in Co. Meath, formerly the high king's royal province, and glimpses of it may be seen from the hill of Tara, the ancient royal capital. A part of the Valley of the Boyne was for millenia the cemetery of the kings of Tara, and the great Bronze Age burial tumuli at Knowth, Newgrange, and Dowth remain of the extremest archaeological interest and value. At Slane on the Boyne St. Patrick lit his challenging Paschal Fire, and from Slane he initiated the conquest of Tara, and of all Ireland, by Christianity. The Boyne Valley is the setting of several stories in both the *Red Branch and the *Fianna* cycles of sagas, and after Christianity it became equally famous as a setting for the exploits of saintly monks. The sixth-century monastic settlement of Monasterboice and the twelfth-century abbey at Mellifont are among the chief ecclesiastical remains still present in the valley.

For Irishmen a darker chapter in the history of the Boyne was commenced in 1649 with Cromwell's massacre of the women and children along with the defenders of Drogheda when that town fell to him. But the date that the name "Boyne" conjures up for all Irishmen, of whatever persuasion, is July 12, 1690. Perhaps not surprisingly, that date is erroneous, for it was on July 11 (July 1, Old Style) that the forces of William III and James II clashed in the battle that in Irish is known as *Briseadh na*

Bóinne, "The Breaking of the Boyne." Again, not surprisingly, the title is erroneous, for the Irish were not broken at the Boyne, but held intact to carry on the losing war for a further year.

Shortly after King James II fled from England to France in 1688 upon the advance of Dutch William, the Protestant champion, he attempted to resume the contest, chiefly with Irish troops and French support, in the Lowlands and in Ireland. With typical inefficiency he dissipated his best Irish regiments in England and France, and attempted therefore to hold Ireland with French auxiliaries and half-trained and raw Irish recruits. Sieges of Derry and Enniskillen, both held by Scotch Presbyterian settlers, the ancestors of today's Orangemen and America's so-called Scotch-Irish, were beaten off through the staunch obduracy of the Calvinist defenders and James's mismanagement, so that upon the retirement of the Jacobite forces William had a protected bridgehead in Ulster. Upon landing, William proceeded south in command of a heterogeneous army of Dutch Guards, two volunteer regiments of French Huguenots, a leavening of English, and units of Danish, Prussian, Finnish, and Swiss mercenaries, altogether about 35,000 men.

To face William, James concentrated his smaller and rawer army in a defensive position on the south side of the Boyne, near Oldbridge. He had 7,000 good French infantry, some well-trained regular Irish cavalry, and largely untrained Irish dragoons and infantry, amounting in all to about 21,000 men, numerically three-fifths the size of William's seasoned army. The French–Irish forces fought stubbornly and well, sparked particularly by the valorous leadership of Patrick Sarsfield, the Jacobite Earl of Lucan (see 452.29 et passim), but Williamite cavalry succeeded in crossing the river both at Rosnaree (the ancient royal burial place) on the left and at Oldbridge on the right. Fearful of encirclement, James himself fled precipitately from the battlefield and from the country. Despite the default of its king, the Jacobite army retreated intact, to fight subsequently the heroic defenses of Athlone and Limerick and the truly calamitous battle of Aughrim. But although the Irish army was not broken at the Boyne, in a very real sense that battle was the decisive battle of the Jacobite–Williamite War. With the defection of its pusillanimous king (known since to the Irish as *Séamas an Chaca*—James of the Shit) the Jacobite army had no cause to fight for but its own survival and the still but dimly apprehended notion of national independence, and little prospect of further French aid.

The surviving French forces remained, but it was Lord Lucan (holding the rank of brigadier) who held the army together, and after the death at Aughrim of the French General Saint-Ruth he assumed complete command. He defended the "indefensible" walls of Limerick against William and ultimately negotiated the Treaty of Limerick which ended the war. The terms of that treaty safeguarded the rights of the Irish and the Catholics, and if its terms were dishonored before the ink was dry, the fault was neither Sarsfield's nor, entirely, King William's. Thereafter Sarsfield, with 11,000 of his adoring men, sailed for France to form the Irish Brigade of the French army, and to die at last on the field of Landen, murmuring "If only it was for Ireland."

The Orangemen of Ulster celebrate the Protestant victory of the Boyne, which saved them from popery, every 12th of July. That date is actually the Old Style date of the Battle of Aughrim, mistakenly taken for the New Style anniversary of the Boyne. Yet they are not incorrect in so doing, for it was at Aughrim that the Irish Jacobite army was largely destroyed. After the Treaty of Limerick Catholic and Gaelic Ireland was completely prostrate—the country depicted in Jonathan Swift's *Modest Proposal*. Ireland was incapable of mounting even an insurrection against English rule until 1798, more than a century later. The Irish army that Sarsfield led into exile was the last formally organized, trained, and uniformed military force that Ireland put into battle before the handful of men in green uniforms seized the center of Dublin in Easter Week, 1916.

BRIAN BORU

Brian mac Ceinnéidigh, known in English as Brian Boru, was born at *Cill Dálua* (Killaloe), on the banks of the Shannon in the present Co. Clare, either in the year 926 or in 941. He was the third son of *Ceinnéidigh Mac Lorcáin* (or *Ceinnéididh*) head of the clan of *Uí Toirdealbhaigh* and thereby chief of the great and increasingly powerful North Munster tribe called *Dál gCais* (in English, Dalcassians) and ruler of the tribal state. For two centuries past Ireland had been harassed by the incursions of the Vikings, who had a stronghold at Limerick only a few miles from Brian's birth-place. But relatively successful resistance to the Northmen had been the basis of a rapid growth in the power of *Dál gCais* around the time of

Brian's birth and boyhood. The ancient royal family of Munster, the *Eoghanachta*—descendants of *Eoghan Mór Mogh Nuadhat* (*Shaun)—had been progressively weakened by Viking attacks on their tribal territories, so that *Dál gCais* was able to claim successfully the right of alternate succession to the provincial kingdom of Munster. (Alternate succession was a common arrangement in Irish kingships, extending to the high kingship itself, the legitimate succession to which alternated between the Northern and the Southern **Uí Néill*.)

Ceinnéididh was succeeded by his eldest son, Brian's half-brother, *Mathghamhain* (a name that means "Bear," and is anglicised Mahon). In 964 *Mathghamhain* seized the Rock of Cashel (in the present Co. Tipperary), royal acropolis of the kingship of Munster, and assumed the provincial kingship. In 968 the Danes of Limerick marched against Cashel, but Brian (at this time either forty-two or twenty-seven years of age), in command of his brother's forces, defeated them at Sulcoit and went on to sack Danish Limerick—his first major blow at the Danes. Some years later, in 976, King *Mathghamhain* was murdered in mysterious circumstances, apparently by collusion between jealous *Eoghanachta* chieftains and Ivar, Danish king of Limerick. *Maolmuadh*, one of the *Eoghanacht* conspirators, became king of Munster, while Brian succeeded *Mathghamhain* as chief of *Dál gCais*. Two years later Brian avenged *Mathghamhain* by killing *Maolmuadh* in the battle of *Belach Lechta*, and in 978 he was himself proclaimed king of Cashel—a succession which had the color of legitimacy since he was succeeding, in alternation, one of the *Eoghanachta*. But although Brian, at the age either of fifty-two or thirty-seven, was at the threshold of a brilliant regal career, that was his last legitimate succession to any crown.

By 984 Brian had made himself by force king of the eastern province of Leinster, and overran shortly thereafter Connacht, the western province, the northern principality of Breifne, and the royal province of Meath. Upon *Maelsheachlainn mac Domhnaill* (*Malachy), the high king, Brian forced an alliance in which, despite the nominal preservation of the high king's position, *Maelsheachlainn* was distinctly the junior partner. In the year 1000 the province of Leinster, in alliance with the Danish kingdom of Dublin, rose against Brian's rule, but the united forces of Brian and *Maelsheachlainn* crushed them at Glenmama, and Brian for the first time marched into Dublin to receive the submission of the Danish king.

Within less than a year Brian's urge to power led him covertly to incite the Dublin Danes—now in theory his allies or vassals—to seize the royal hill of Tara. Tara at the time was much the same as it is now—a grass-grown mound over the ruins of the old royal citadel—for it had been abandoned as a residence centuries before, and now retained only a ritualistic significance. *Maelsheachlainn*, however, was able to defeat the Danes, and so force Brian into the open. Brian advanced with a mixed force of Munstermen, Leinstermen, Ossorymen, and Dublin Danes against *Maelsheachlainn*'s stronghold of *Dún na Sciath* and forced the high king to capitulate. *Maelsheachlainn* remained as King of Meath, but Brian was thenceforth *de facto* high king. *Tighearnach*, the annalist of *Clonmacnoise, at the end of the year 1001 added the entry "Brian Borama regnat," recognizing the fact.

Brian then attacked Connacht, the western province, and received the submission of its king, and by 1004 he had conquered even the remote northern principalities of *Ailech* (west and central Ulster) and *Dál Riada* and *Dál Araidhe* (present Co. Antrim). In the same year he issued a charter (still extant) acknowledging Armagh (which he had occupied) as the primatial episcopal see of Ireland, and describing himself as *Imperator Scottorum*, "Emperor of the Irish." He followed this conquest by a circuit of Ireland, accepting submissions and hostages from the lesser kings and chiefs, following the precedent of *Muircheartach na gCóchall Croicionn* who in 941 had made a similar tour to assure his succession (more legitimate than Brian's) to the high kingship. *Muircheartach* had stayed for a night at *Ceann Coradh*, the castle of Brian's family, on that circuit, which was either in the year of Brian's birth or when he was fifteen years old. Brian's subjugation of all Ireland was followed by almost a decade of unusual tranquillity under his strong and enlightened rule, a brief revival of the pre-Viking golden age, an interval of peace and freedom Ireland would not experience again until the twentieth century.

Brian, however, had sowed too many winds not to reap a whirlwind. His cast-off wife, *Gormfhlaith*, sister of the king of Leinster (and formerly wife both of the Danish king Olaf [*Humphrey] and of *Maelsheachlainn*), stirred up against Brian both her brother and her son by Olaf, Sitric, king of Dublin (348.18). In 1013 fighting broke out between the Dublin Danes with their Leinster allies and King *Maelsheachlainn*, who sent to *Ceann Coradh* for help. Brian moved east and north, ravaging Leinster, and joined *Maelsheachlainn* at Kilmainham outside the walls of Dublin in September. The two kings beset Dublin until Christmas, when campaigning ceased for the winter. In the spring of 1014 Brian once more marched with *Maelsheachlainn* against the Dublin Danes, who meanwhile had received substantial aid from their kinsmen of Scotland, Man, the Orkneys, Scandinavia, and even Iceland, together with what forces *Maolmuire*, king of Leinster, could muster from his province which Brian once more was wasting. Brian's forces moved down toward Dublin Bay over the plains to the northeast of the town, and came to pitched battle with the Danes at the Bull Meadow—*Cluain-tarbh*—near the mouth of the Tolka River, on Good Friday, 23rd of April 1014.

The Irish king himself, whether his age be accounted seventy-three or eighty-eight, was too old and infirm to fight, and his armies were led by his sons *Murchadh* and *Donnchadh*, and his grandson *Toirdealbhach*. During the twelve-hour struggle, the king remained in his tent to pray. Slaughter was great on both sides, both *Murchadh* and *Toirdealbhach* falling in battle, but the Danes in the end were butchered and broken in a carnage that neither side ever forgot. After the battle a small band of fleeing Danes stumbled on Brian's tent, cut down the bodyguard, and hacked the old king to death. According to tradition a Dane named Brodar or Brodir (153.31, 312.13, 022.02, 481.33) was the actual killer.

The battle itself, known in English as the battle of Clontarf, despite its cost to the Irish was an undoubted and decisive victory. Thereafter the Danes were never again powerful in Ireland beyond the walls of their boroughs. Legends, anecdotes, songs, and poems about the battle grew and spread not only among the Irish but also among the Scandinavians. One of the most stirring accounts of the battle extant occurs toward the end of the famous Icelandic saga of the Burning of Njal, told of course from the Northmen's point of view.

Brian's body was buried in the cathedral church at Armagh, the Primatial See, but the location of his tomb has been forgotten. His sons *Tadhg* and *Donnchadh* returned to the rule of *Dál gCais* and Munster, but *Maelsheachlainn mac Domhnaill* resumed the high kingship and held it until his death in 1022. With his own death Brian's imperium collapsed, the only permanent result of his rule—aside from the taming of the Danes—being the overthrow of all dynastic principles of legitimacy. After 1022 no king could truthfully claim to be king *de facto* of all Ireland before James VI of Scotland, I of England, in the seventeenth century. Brian diminished the force of hereditary right, replacing it with the principle of submission only to him who could enforce submission. It was this latter principle, in effect, which justified the claims of the rulers of England from Henry II to George V to be also the lawful rulers of Ireland.

The prestige of Brian was nevertheless so great that his descendants adopted the surname *Ó Briain* (O Brien), "descendant of Brian," and have even to the present been prominent in Irish history. From 1022 until 1103 the high kingship was held by O Briens, although "with opposition," until they in turn were overthrown by a new dynasty *Ó Conchobhair* of Connacht. The O Briens in later times seem to have been regarded, not merely by themselves but by the English kings, as a "royal" family. Whatever "royalty" means, it will be seen that the O Brien claim on the defunct crown of Ireland is of a similar order to that of the Bonapartes to the throne of France.

Brian's agnomen, "Boroma" in the Latin of *Tighearnach*, is usually explained as *Bóroimhe*, genitive of *Bóramha*, "tribute, levy." The literal sense of the word is "a counting of cows." Numerous stories have sought to account for the agnomen, many ignoring the well-attested fact that Brian throughout his career was a determined collector of tributes and levies. It is possible, however, that his name derives from the word, *Béal Bóramha* ("Tribute-Mouth," or "Cow-counting Mouth") on the River Shannon near *Cill Dálua*, beside which he was born. In that case the name would reflect nothing of his career, but correspond to such a name as John of Gaunt.

A seventeenth-century descendant of Brian seems also to make an occasional appearance in *Finnegans Wake*. That is *Murchadh na dTóiteán Ó Briain*, Earl of Inchiquin. *Murchadh*'s father, chief of the O Briens, managed to avoid fatal implication in the wars against Queen Elizabeth, and, unlike other Irish leaders, had his submission accepted by James I, who created him Earl of Inchiquin. In compensation, James removed to his own fosterage the young *Murchadh*, heir to the old chieftainship and new earldom. His name anglicised to Morrough, the child was raised as a Protestant with James's aversion to popery, and upon succession to the title and estates, around the time of the opening of the English Civil Wars, he became notorious as a terrorist and incendiary against his native countrymen. So effective and impressive were his activities that, beyond acquiring his agnomen *na dTóiteán*, "of the Burnings," *Murchadh*'s name has entered the Irish language as a word meaning a severe fright or a bad thrashing. "To see *Murchadh*" means to be overtaken by calamity; when someone has had a fright people say ironically, "He has seen

Murchadh or the nearest bush." *Murchadh*'s evil name has not in the least been eradicated by the almost unknown latter half of his career: solidarity with his fellow Irishmen in the opposition to Cromwell's conquest, and reversion to his ancestral Catholicism.

For a brief discussion of the *Ó Conchobhair* successors to *Ó Briain* in the high kingship, see the separate Additional Note on *Ruaidhrí Ó Conchobhair*.

CHILDREN OF LIR

The story of the Children of Lir is a medieval fairy tale extant only in some late manuscripts, although references to it occur earlier. The tale combines pre-Christian magic elements with one of the miracle legends associated with the coming of St. Patrick. Joyce may have been attracted to this story by its Patrician relevance, but more probably by Thomas Moore's use of it for his *The Song of Fionnuala*, that begins "Silent, O Moyle, be the roar of thy waters." [1] The story has also been popularly edited by Joyce's namesake, P. W. Joyce, in *Old Celtic Romances* (1879, 1894, and innumerable reprints).

The story may be narrated in brief: *Aoife*, a wicked stepmother, by black magic turns into swans the four children of her husband, *Lir*. *Aoife*'s evil spell had its limitations, however, and although the children were compelled to spend three hundred years' durance severally on a lake, on the "Moyle" (the North Channel between Ireland and Scotland), and on the Western Ocean, they were eventually to be released. The principal condition of their freeing would be the advent of a hitherto unknown benevolent power to Ireland—the coming of Christianity. The stay of the swans on the Western Ocean nevertheless extends into the seventh century, until one day they hear from shore the unfamiliar tinkling of a bell: it is the matins bell of a hermit saint on a nearby island. The swans feel the spell breaking, come ashore, resume human shape, but as persons of immense age and decrepitude in place of the children who had been enchanted. They accept baptism, relate their history, die, and their spirits are seen entering Heaven in the form of four radiant children. Their bodies are buried together in consecrated ground according to the pattern in which they had floated together as swans on the stormy waters: the daughter *Fionnghuala* with her brother *Conn* at her right hand, her brother *Fiachra* at her left, and her brother *Aedh* before her face.

Probably all of the "Moyle" references in *Finnegans Wake* are allusions to this story in general and Moore's song in particular, since the name Moyle for the North Channel has only a literary currency in English. Perhaps also the four swans have had some influence on the four seagulls in the Mark of Cornwall chapter.

1. For a brief analysis of this poem, see my note on it in *Explicator* XV (1957), item 23.

CLONMACNOISE

Clonmacnoise, Co. Offaly, is a place of varied and disjunct interest to the reader of *Finnegans Wake*. The site at present is one of extensive ecclesiastical ruins on the left bank of the Shannon River. There are two Round Towers, remains of five High Crosses, nine churches, and more than five hundred early gravestones, many with inscriptions. The ruins are of a great monastic settlement and school, founded in the sixth century by St. *Ciarán* (516–549). Its history is intimately entwined with the medieval history of Ireland; seven high kings were buried there, including *Ruaidhri Ó Conchobhair*, the last Irish high king, whose body was removed from Cong, the place of his death and first interment.

The earliest Irish form of the name Clonmacnoise is *Cluain-maccu-Nóis*, "Meadow of the sons of *Nóis* ('noble')." The Four Masters in one place alter this to *Cluain-muice-Nóis*, "Meadow of *Nóis*'s pig," and later the form arose *Cluain-mic-Nóis*, "Meadow of *Nóis*'s son." In Modern Irish the name is restored to *Cluain-mac-Nóis*, equivalent to the older *Cluain-maccu-Nóis*, "Meadow of *Nóis*'s sons." For a long time, however, the sense of the name was mistakenly construed as "Meadow of the sons of the nobles" (which would require *maccu/mac Nós/Nósa*) and understood as alluding to "the warriors of Erin in their famous generations/[Who] slumber there" (T. W. Rolleston's translation of the poem "Clonmacnoise" by *Aonghus Ó Giolláin*).

The Golden Age of Clonmacnoise as a center of learning second only to Armagh, and hardly to be rivaled on the barbarian-ravaged continent, lasted from its founding until the beginning of the ninth century. In 795 the Vikings made their first raid on Ireland, and by 830 Torgeis, a Norse chief, not content with plundering Armagh, proclaimed himself its abbot

—not merely without benefit of Holy Orders, but without accepting Christianity. By 841 his wife, Ota, a pagan seeress, was uttering her oracles sitting on the high altar at Clonmacnoise (493.19 ff.). When Clonmacnoise was restored to Irish hands, its sanctity was broken, and a succession of Irish chieftains plundered its wealth with a ferocity equal to that of the Danes.

The reign of *Brian Boru, however, restored something of the tranquillity and prestige of Clonmacnoise, and in the eleventh century the *Annals of Clonmacnoise*, one of the most important source books for medieval Irish history, was commenced at Clonmacnoise, traditionally by *Tighearnach Ó Braoin* (d. 1088). The annalist's name is anglicisable as Tierney O Breen (see 056.32, 091.08, 091.09). Although the matter is scarcely susceptible of ready proof, it is my personal opinion that Joyce's imitations of and allusions to early Irish annals more distinctly reflect the *Annals of Clonmacnoise* than they do the *Annals of the Four Masters* (which draw heavily upon *Tighearnach's* work), despite the constant overt allusions to the latter. The date 1132 is, of course, later than *Tighearnach's* death, but the *Annals of Clonmacnoise* continue far beyond that date.

Perhaps the final matter of the significance of Clonmacnoise for *Finnegans Wake* has already been mentioned. Although upon his death in 1198 King *Ruaidhrí Ó Conchobhair* was buried at Cong the place of his monastic retirement in old age, nine years later, in 1207, his bones were removed solemnly to Clonmacnoise and there interred to await the Resurrection.

Finally, Rolleston's version of the poem on "Clonmacnoise" is much too well known among Irishmen, it would surely seem, to escape echoing somewhere in *Finnegans Wake*.

THE COLLEEN BAWN

Next in immediate success only to *Arragh-na-Pogue* among the plays of Dion Boucicault, and of perhaps more extensive fame, is *The Colleen Bawn*. First produced in London in 1860, it played initially for 360 nights, at the time an astounding success. Like so many of Boucicault's productions, this was an adaptation of another writer's original: Gerald Griffin's novel, *The Collegians*. Also, as usual with Boucicault, the adaptation is rather free; episodes only of the novel are dramatized, characters are drastically altered, and the setting of the action is transferred to Killarney. Doubtless a sufficient number of readers have been put off reading Griffin's rather good novel by the notion that it is "merely" *The Colleen Bawn*.

Boucicault's play was so immensely successful that the process of adaptation was carried one step further by Sir Julius Benedict, who converted the play into the formerly widely popular opera, *The Lily of Killarney*.

During the first run of *The Colleen Bawn* Boucicault himself played the comic role of Myles-na-Coppaleen, while his wife played the heroine, Eily O'Connor. The title of the play is reasonably good Irish: *an cailín bán*, "the white girl," idiomatically means "the pretty girl." The name of Myles-na-Coppaleen, however, leads immediately to difficulties of grammar reminiscent of those attendant upon the name Arrah-na-Pogue. The soubriquet is supposed to mean "of the little horses," but that would be properly *na gcapaillín*, which should yield "na-Goppaleen." The singular genitive, "of the little horse," would be even worse: *an chapaillín*, which at best would yield "an-Coppaleen." The grammatical difficulties associated with Myles's name may have been disregarded or bypassed by Joyce, but they have obviously been apparent to the late contemporary Irish writer who adopted the corrected *nom-de-plume* of Myles na gCopaleen. Brian Nolan (his true name), a man of many pseudonyms, published in 1939 under the name of Flann O'Brien a novel called *At Swim-Two-Birds*. A recent English edition of that book prints on its cover an undocumented attribution to James Joyce of the judgment: "That's a real writer with the true comic spirit. . . . A really funny book." If this quotation has any basis in fact, Nolan–O'Brien–Myles na gCopaleen may be the direct object of some of the apparent references to Boucicault's character in *Finnegans Wake*.

COLMCILLE

Colm-cille ("Dove of the Church") in the panhagion of Irish saints ranks with St. *Brighid* of Kildare—"the Mary of Ireland"—next below only St. Patrick. John Colgan (*Four Masters), in devoting to these three an entire volume (*Trias Thaumaturga* [1647]) of his projected six-volume complete hagiography of Ireland, reflected the general sentiment of his countrymen. And of the three, *Colmcille*, as both a male and a native Irishman, of recognizably Irish character, and of princely blood, is probably the real, if covert, favorite.

The saint was born in Gartan in the present Co. Donegal in 521, the son of a chieftain named *Feidhlimidh* and his wife *Eithne*. *Feidhlimidh* was the grandson of *Conall Gulban*, the prince for whom the present territory of the Co. Donegal is named in Irish (*Tír Conaill*, "*Conall's* Land"), and for whom, incidentally, Yeats's Benbulben (corrupt from *Beinn Gulbain*) is also named. *Conall's* father, and therefore *Colmcille's* great-great-grandfather, was *Niall Naoighiallach* (Niall Nine-Hostager: *Uí Néill), high king of Ireland (379–405). On his mother's side the saint was more remotely descended (twelfth in descent) from *Cathair Mór*, king of Leinster. He was baptized by the priest *Cruithneachan mac Ceallacháin*, receiving the name of *Colm* ("dove").

As a child, in accordance with chiefly custom, *Colm* was fostered by the family *Ó Firghil* at *Doire Eithne* (the name means "Acorn Oakwood," and has only an accidental connection with his mother's name). So soon as he was old enough he went to study under St. *Finghin* on the eastern coast of Ulster, and there he took orders as a deacon. Thereafter, however, he revealed another side to his complex nature, and undertook for a period the study of classical Irish poetry under the chief poet of Leinster. Thereafter he received ordination as a priest and retired with three companions to monastic seclusion at Glasnevin, on the banks of the stream called *Fionn-glas*, a place now well within the northern city limits of Dublin. In 544 an epidemic broke up the little community, and *Colmcille* returned to his own quarter of the country, to found at *Doire* (modern Derry) a new community, to be known for a thousand years as *Doire Cholmcille*. Thereafter he embarked on a career of founding monastic settlements which by the time of his death, according to his successor and biographer, amounted all told to thirty-eight in number, in Ireland alone.

By far his most influential foundation, however, was the monastic settlement *Colmcille* created for his own voluntary exile. In 563, two years after a war of which he was the instigator, he settled on the little island between Irish and Scottish *Dál Riada* which had up to that time borne the stark name *Í* ("isle"), but which thereafter in Irish has usually been called *Í-Cholmcille*, and has otherwise been Anglo-Latinized Iona. The war had been an unpriestly attempt to avenge blood with blood, when *Colmcille* roused his own tribe against King *Diarmaid* to requite the slaying of a cleric, and had led to a bitter battle near the present Drumcliff, beneath the slopes of Benbulben.

Colmcille's exile was apparently a self-imposed penance, but later Irish writers have often assumed it to have been the result of judicial sentence. Furthermore an intriguing and often-repeated story was invented to account for the war as arising from a breach of copyright. According to this legend, *Colmcille* surreptitiously copied a Gospel or Psalter which belonged to St. *Finghin*, and which *Finghin* had forbidden him to copy. In a subsequent lawsuit the decision was awarded to *Finghin*, the judgment being based on the laws regarding cattle ownership: "To each cow her calf, and to each book its son (*mac-leabhair*, 'son-of-a-book,' is Irish for 'copy')." *Colmcille* refused to surrender his book, and his clansmen rallied to his defense against the king. Such is the apocryphal tale.

Nevertheless the association of *Colmcille*'s name with book-copying is essentially correct. It is notable that two of the most famous illuminated manuscripts of medieval Ireland—the Book of Durrow and the Book of Kells—both emanated from monasteries which he had founded. (James Joyce, in *Finnegans Wake*, one scarcely needs reminding, is only the first of many commentators to suggest parallels between *Finnegans Wake* and the Book of Kells.) For centuries, also, the O Donnels, *Colmcille*'s people, carried into battle a Psalter they called *Cathach* ("Battler"), reputed to have been transcribed by *Colmcille*'s own hand; it is now in the library of the Royal Irish Academy.

Colmcille revisited Ireland twice, in 575 and in 585. On the first visit he acted as intermediary on the one hand between the Gaels of Scottish Dalriada and the high king, *Aodh mac Ainmire*, and on the other hand between the bardic order and the generality of the princes who, exasperated by the exactions of the bards, planned to extirpate their order. From the high king he extracted a guarantee of the autonomy of the overseas Gaels, and between princes and poets he effected a compromise which assured the survival of the bardic order even for a brief while past the extinction of the princely order in the seventeenth century.

In 597 *Colmcille* died and was buried on *Í;* three centuries later, in 878, his remains were brought back to Ireland. Still later, in 1127, the Danes of Dublin carried off the bones, but later restored them. Thereafter they became lost completely.

Outside of Ireland and Scotland *Colmcille* is usually known by the Latinized form of his name, Columba—sometimes also rendered Columbanus. But many later Irish saints—*Colms* and *Colmáns*, named after their great predecessor—also share the names Columba and Columbanus, whereas there is only one *Colmcille*.

If St. Kevin of Glendalough is in *Finnegans Wake*—as seems beyond question—one of the avatars of *Shaun, I suggest that *Colmcille* ("Calomnequiller"—050.09) is a type of *Shem. Certainly his career bears many marks of resemblance to that of James Joyce, who is sometimes presumed to be a prototype for Shem. Both men were voluntary exiles from Ireland, and each revisited the homeland twice. Both men are the progenitors of weird and wonderful books, and both have been involved in passionate lawsuits about copyrights. Each man has been, finally, proud, fierce, contentious, vain of his ancestry, concerned with the status of poets and authors, aloof from the generality of his countrymen, yet in himself ultimately an acme and epitome of the Irish race.

COLONIES, COLONISTS, COLONIZATIONS

Ireland is an island which has been subject to innumerable invasions, and since she is an island it is evident that all of her human inhabitants must be either themselves invaders or the descendants of invaders. The identity of the historical invaders is known, that of the prehistoric settlers has always been a matter for fascinated speculation. Modern archaeology finds little to distinguish the prehistoric cultures of Ireland from those of continental Europe, in this regard agreeing fundamentally with ancient and medieval Irish legend, which attributes a continental homeland to most of the legendary colonists (fixing, however, with a disconcerting specificity exclusively on Spain and Greece). The old Irish no doubt retained a certain admixture of remembered fact with their legendary accounts of their own origins—the stories permit extrapolation of the correct information that the Celtic invaders of Ireland were Iron Age intruders upon Bronze Age predecessors. But their legends to account for the presence of their predecessors even on internal evidence appear to be cut from whole cloth. Nevertheless these legends were accepted as sober history by the annalists, while less-inhibited storytellers wove around their cores webs of fanciful fairy tales.

According to the annalists, the first settlement in Ireland was made by a lady named Ceasair accompanied by fifty women and only three men.

One version of this story makes the event occur before the Flood, in which calamity the colony perished. A fanciful variation on this has one of the three men, *Fionntán Mac Bochra*, surviving the flood in the form of a salmon. *Finnegans Wake* seems to make some play with this story which, despite a certain implausibility, is yet somewhat more plausible than the soberer version which merely has the followers of Ceasair perish—for how else could their story have been transmitted to posterity? The second version of this story places the colony after the Flood, and represents Ceasair as the granddaughter of Noah. The colony simply died out—perhaps of sexual imbalance?

The second settlement is represented unanimously as having taken place some time subsequent to the Flood. This was led by one *Parthalón* (paralón, porelón) whose name is sometimes anglicised Bartholomew. The settlement was restricted to the seaside plain now largely occupied by the city of Dublin, stretching from Howth Head in the northeast to Tallaght in the southwest. After three hundred years the colony numbered 5,000 men and 4,000 women, when it was suddenly and completely wiped out by plague. According to the *Four Masters the victims were buried (by one another?) in a mound called *Taimhleacht Mhuintire Parthalóin*, "Plague-grave of *Parthalón*'s People"—reduced and anglicised to Tallaght, the name of a now suburban village southwest of Dublin. How their story survived is not clear.

The third colony was led by one Nemed, about thirty years after the extinction of the Parthalonians. The Nemedians, however, abandoned their settlement under the attacks of the Fomorians, a race of savage and magical pirates who inhabited the coastal islands of the northwest. The origin of the Fomorians is apparently never accounted for. Later, however, a more massive Nemedian invasion succeeded in occupying the entire country in the face of Fomorian opposition. The Nemedians of this second wave are known traditionally as *Fir Bolga* ("Bags Men"), and numerous tales seek to account for the name, which is usually anglicised Firbolgs. The *Fir Bolga* recur frequently throughout *Finnegans Wake*. Anthropologists tentatively identify the *Fir Bolga* with a short dark people of Mediterranean origin who are known to have inhabited ancient Ireland, and are the chief contributors to the present Irish people of the bloodstock which produces the typical "black" Irishman of rather Spanish appearance.

Only thirty-six years after the successful *Fir Bolga* colonization, they themselves were overwhelmed in turn by a race who are represented as fellow Nemedians, yet who in every trait contrast markedly with the *Fir Bolga*. These were the *Tuatha Dé Danann*, "Folk of the Goddess Dana," who crushed the *Fir Bolga* in a battle at *Magh Tuireadh* ("Plain of Towers") in the present Co. Sligo; they subjugated the *Fir Bolga*, who remained a subject helot race for the rest of their distinct existence. The *Tuatha Dé Danann* were also beset by Fomorians under their savage king *Balór*, surnamed "of the strong blows" and also "of the evil eye," and his equally fierce wife, *Cethlenn*. A second battle of *Magh Tuireadh* between Fomorians and *Tuatha Dé Danann* preceded a decline and ultimate dissolution of the Fomorian race. The legends speak of intermarriage between the rulers of the two races, so it may be assumed that in time they simply merged.

Of all the legendary pre-Celtic colonists of Ireland the *Tuatha Dé Danann* are the most enigmatic and fascinating. They are represented as possessing magical powers, and their leading personalities are impossible to distinguish from the gods of the pagan Gaels—gods who are known to have been shared with their continental Celtic cousins, the Gauls and others. *Lugh*, most widely worshipped Celtic god, is represented as of mixed *Tuatha Dé* and Fomorian ancestry; *Nuadha* (the continental *Noudons*) was also one of the *Tuatha*. Other *Tuatha Dé Danann* personalities who are also gods are the *Daghdha*—who nonetheless was mortally wounded at the second battle of *Magh Tuireadh*—and his son, *Aonghus an Bhrogha; Lear* ("Sea"), the sea-god, and his son, *Manannan Mac Lir*, after whom the Isle of Man is named. Both *Eriu* and *Banba*, whose names are interchangeably used for Ireland, are represented as princesses of the *Tuatha Dé*, but not as goddesses. Anthropologists have pointed out that the tutelary goddess of this folk, *Dana* (that is, *Ana* with prosthetic *D* [*Anna]), appears to be in fact the goddess of the dead, and the *Tuatha Dé* are described in *Dinnsenchus* as "na tréna dian treb thói"—"the strong ones who dwell in silence." In other words, the *Tuatha Dé Danann* may be in reality the host of the dead, and their later history as presented in the legends lends confirmation to this supposition. But their later history is also conflicting.

The crisis for the *Tuatha Dé Danann* came in the fourth or perhaps the sixth century B.C., with a new race of invaders. These were tall men, with reddish-brown hair and ruddy complexions, and warlike dispositions. They called themselves *Gaedheal*, a name which suggests their probable continental place of origin as either Gaul or Spanish Galicia. According to themselves they came from Spain, and arrived in Ireland under the leadership of three sons of a chief named *Miledh: Eireamhón, Eibhear,* and *Ir.* The initial invaders are referred to as *Mileadha,* after *Miledh,* and that name is rendered in English as "Milesians." The *Tuatha Dé Danann* sought to stave off the Milesians with magical storms, but in a series of battles Milesian iron decisively overcame *Tuatha Dé Danann* magic and bronze. The *Fir Bolga* helots passed from *Tuatha Dé Danann* to Milesian overlord-ship, but what happened to the *Tuatha Dé* is obscure. Some sources lump them thereafter with the *Fir Bolga* as *aitheach tuatha,* "plebeian races," but that is not the prevalent view.

Generally the *Tuatha Dé Danann* are taken to have retired, literally underground, to magic palaces. Ireland is full of peculiar grass-grown mounds, the word for one of which is *síodh,* plural *síodha.* These *síodha* came to be identified with the underground homes of the *Tuatha Dé,* who thence came to be known as *Aos Sidhe,* "people of the *síodh.*" But these *síodha* are in fact, generally speaking, Bronze Age burial tumuli, so that, if the Gaels had some inkling of the true nature of those mounds, *Aos Sidhe* really means "tomb people"—that is, the dead. In course of time the adjective *sidhe* has come to have the sense almost of a noun, and in Modern Irish is freely translated as "fairy," both adjective and noun. The *Tuatha Dé Danann,* therefore, continue a remnant of their "half-life" in the Irish countryside, where peasants still seek to propitiate the "good people," and protect their doorways with horseshoes made of the iron which gave their ancestors victory over the Folk of the Goddess Dana.

Their obliteration of the *Tuatha Dé Danann* and subjugation of the *Fir Bolga* did not give peace to the Milesian conquerors. At first the brothers *Eireamhón* (anglicised Heremon) and *Eibhear* (Heber) divided the rule of the country between them, *Eireamhón* taking the North and *Eibhear* the South. Subsequently they quarreled, came to battle in which *Eireamhón* slew *Eibhear,* and *Eireamhón* became the first high king of all Ireland. The battling brothers occur of course in *Finnegans Wake* among the many other pairs of fratricidal twins, and *Eireamhón* has the distinction of being first in the long series of high kings of which poor old *Ruaidhrí Ó Conchobhair,* Rex, was the last.

In the first century the Milesian kingship was interrupted briefly for the first time by an uprising of the *aitheach tuatha,* including *Tuatha Dé Danann* or not. Exasperated by oppression, the *Fir Bolga* revolted and succeeded in placing one of their own race, *Cairbre Cinn-cait* ("Charioteer Cathead"), on the throne of Tara. Upon *Cairbre*'s death his son *Mórán*, who might have succeeded him, instead restored the high kingship to the Milesians, in return for an alleviation of his people's lot.

These then—Ceasair, *Parthalón*, Nemed, the *Fir Bolga*, the Fomorians, the *Tuatha Dé Danann*, the Milesians—are the legendary colonists of Ireland with whom this note deals. After the Milesian or Gaelic conquest, despite an interval of a thousand years or more, there has been no cessation of further invasions and colonizations: of Danes from the ninth to the eleventh centuries; Normans in the twelfth century; English and Welsh almost as soon, and continuing to the present; Scotch in the seventeenth century; and in the twentieth century, German and Japanese electronics engineers.

DUBLIN

The name under which Dublin has become known to the wide world was given to the city by the Danes, but the name is Irish, not Norse. The name is compounded of the words *dubh* (*d*uv, *d*ú), "black, dark," and *linn* (lin), "pool." In the annals it is often spelled *Duibhlinn* (*d*ivlin), and this appears to represent the pronunciation not only of the Danes but of the earlier English settlers as well. Coins minted by Sitric, eleventh-century Danish king of Dublin and contemporary of *Brian Boru, bear the inscription "Dyflin," and early English records spell the name Divlin. Other places in Ireland of an identical original name have been anglicised Devlin, Dowling, and Doolin (all of these names occur in *Finnegans Wake*), but only in the modern pronunciation of Dublin has the *aspirated "b" been restored. The name originally applied to that part of the *Liffey River upon which the city now stands, and referred to the deep pool at the river mouth which in the times before artificial dredging made Dublin always feasible as a seaport even at lowest tides. It would naturally have been that characteristic that caught the attention of the seafaring Northmen, but the name *Dubh-linn* is obviously ancient, for it clearly lies behind the name Eblana reported in Ptolemy's second-century geography.

A smaller pool in the Liffey estuary outside the large dark pool which gave its name to the city was called, with little imagination, *Poll Beag*, "Little Hole." That name has been anglicised to Poolbeg, and gives its name to a lighthouse, frequently mentioned in *Finnegans Wake*, just at the bar of Dublin Harbor.

Although *Dubh-linn* is an Irish name, the name traditionally used for Dublin by speakers of Irish is *Baile Átha Cliath*, "Settlement of the Hurdle Ford." This name also associates the city with a feature of the *Liffey River, but this one of appeal to the landsman. In ancient times a causeway built of woven boughs, or hurdles, crossed the river at a point within the present city, and in Irish the town takes its name from the ford or crossing place thus constructed. Another Irish name for such a wickerwork causeway is *ciseach* or *ceasach* (kishokh, kasokh), and one of the wickerwork "hurdles" out of which it is constructed is a *cis* (kish). A *cis*, anglicised kish, is also a basket or hamper such as countrypeople strap on a donkey's back to carry turves of peat home from the bog. Many Irish place-names of a parallel structure with *Baile Átha Cliath* substitute the word *Cis* or one of its derivatives for *Cliath*, and so the possibility must have been latent in the naming of Dublin for it to have become *Baile Átha Cise*. At any rate, a light station, or lightship, in Dublin Bay is called The Kish; perhaps at one time a light was supported on a pontoon of hurdles or wickerwork. The relevance of all this to *Finnegans Wake* scarcely needs stressing.

One passage in *Finnegans Wake*, however, perhaps can be elucidated through these considerations. *Baile Átha Cliath*, though ostensibly composed of six syllables (bolye áhe klíe), in common pronunciation is reduced to two or three (bláklí, bláklíe). P. W. Joyce renders this pronunciation "Blaa-clee" (*Irish Names of Places*, I, 363). The potential name *Baile Átha Cise*, therefore, would presumably have been pronounced "Blaakish." As a consequence it seems more than probable that the phrase "the blay of her Kish" (014.02) represents a name for Dublin, especially since "of her" in Irish is *a*: "blay *a* kish" phonetically represents "blaakish," *Baile Átha Cise*, "Town of a Wickerwork Ford." [1]

1. For an elaboration of this discussion, see *Anna and also my article, "Anna Livia Plurabelle's Gaelic Ancestry," *James Joyce Quarterly*, II (1965), pp. 158–166, especially pp. 162–164.

ECLIPSIS

Eclipsis is the grammar-book name for a relatively simple kind of sound change to which the initial letters of Irish words are subject. It is a form of inflection, and takes place by substitution: unvoiced consonants become voiced, voiced consonants become nasals, and vowels are prefixed by n-. Seven consonants only are subject to eclipsis: b, c [k], d, f, g, p, t; these become, respectively, m, g, n, v, ñ, b, d.

It is in orthography that eclipsis becomes of most interest for *Finnegans Wake*. In order to retain the visible shape of the affected word, the eclipsed consonant is retained in spelling, but preceded by the eclipsing consonant which replaces it. Thus initial b becomes mb, pronounced m; c becomes gc, pronounced g; d becomes nd, pronounced n; f becomes bhf (*Aspiration), pronounced v; g becomes ng, pronounced ñ; p becomes bp, pronounced b; and d becomes nd, pronounced n. Where Joyce appears to be playing with eclipsis (089.17–18, etc.) the rule to remember is that only the first consonant is pronounced; the second is absolutely silent.

THE FOUR MASTERS
(See *Four Waves)

In *Finnegans Wake* the "Four Masters" appear frequently as one of the avatars of the Four, and so tend to merge with several other Irish foursomes as well as any number of non-Irish ones: the four provinces, the four alleged masters of Patrick the boy slave, the *Four Waves, the "Four Bloods" (*Uí Néill). But they have a distinct historical identity of their own, although their "fourness" is a rather ex post facto attribute conferred upon them by *Seán Ó Colgáin* (John Colgan), who in the Preface to his *Acta Sanctorum Hiberniae* (about 1645) referred to their work as "Annales Quatuor Magistrorum"—*The Annals of the Four Masters*. The Masters themselves, or more precisely, the chief of them, *Mícheál Ó Cléirigh* (1575–1643), had called the great work *Annales Dungallenses*—"The Annals of Donegal"—or *Annála Ríoghachta Éireann,* "Annals of the Kingdom of Ireland."

The moving spirit and chief compiler of these Annals was the Franciscan monk whose religious name was *Mícheál* or Michael, but who had been born *Tadhg Ó Cléirigh*, at Kilbarron, Co. Donegal, the fourth son of *Donnchadh Ó Cléirigh*, member of an illustrious family of scribes, poets, and historians; he was third cousin of *Lughaidh Ó Cléirigh* (fl. 1609), chief of the family and himself a distinguished historian. *Tadhg* ("poet"), known

in his family as *Tadhg-an-tsléibhe* (*Tadhg* of the mountain), following his
elder brother *Maolmuire*, entered the Franciscan monastery at Louvain.
In 1620 his superiors there, recognizing his great abilities, despatched him
to Ireland with the task of collecting and editing Irish manuscripts, a task
which occupied him for the next fifteen years. Between 1624 and 1630
he compiled a "Royal List," the manuscript of which is now in Brussels.
Between 1627 and 1631 he completed a revision of the *Leabhar Gabhála*
("Book of Invasions"), a copy of which, in the hand of his collaborator
and kinsman, *Cúchoigcríche Ó Cléirigh* (son of *Lughaidh*), is now in the Royal
Irish Academy. Next, in the Franciscan convent of Donegal, on 22nd of
January 1632, he began the great compilation and digest of previous
annals which is known as the "Annals of the Four Masters." The work
was finished there on 10th of August 1636.

Just exactly who the "Four Masters" were in Colgan's estimation is
difficult to make out. The book itself is signed (in theological approbation)
by the superior of the convent, *Bernardin Ó Cléirigh*, who was no other
than Michael's brother *Maolmuire* under his religious name. The dedica-
tion is signed by Michael, but the Preface lists six men as having had a
hand in the production: *Mícheál Ó Cléirigh*, *Fearfasa Ó Maolchonaire*,
Muiris Ó Maolchonaire, *Cúchoigcríche Ó Cléirigh*, *Cúchoigcríche Ó Duibhgeannáin*,
and *Conaire Ó Cléirigh*. *Muiris Ó Maolchonaire* is believed to have worked
on the book for only one month, so he may perhaps be eliminated from
the reckoning. Even so, five "Four Masters" are left, a fact which may
have attracted Joyce as a complement to the four "fifths" which constitute
the number of Irish provinces (*cúige*, "fifth," is the word for province, of
which there are, however, only four).

The names of these Masters are anglicised respectively, Michael O
Clery, Farfassa O Mulconry, Morris O Mulconry, Peregrine (this a fanciful extension hardly worth pursuing) O Clery, Peregrine O Duignan, and
Conary O Clery. Of these, *Finnegans Wake* alludes unmistakably to
Michael O Clery, Farfassa O Mulconry, Peregrine O Duignan; "Conry"
(398.01) may allude either to Conary O Clery or to one of the O Mul-
conrys; the list "Peregrine and Michael and Farfassa and Peregrine"
(389.15) names two Peregrines, and so may be taken to cover both
Peregrine O Clery and Peregrine O Duignan. "Mr. Martin Clery"
(520.15) does not clearly refer to any of the Masters, but might take in
any one of the three O Clerys. It has not been commented on, so far as I
am aware, that this embarrassing superfluity in attempting to enumerate

the Four Masters may be not unconnected with the ass in *Finnegans Wake*, always dragging along behind the four old men.

Despite Michael O Clery's Franciscan orders and the locus of the *Annals'* production in the convent of Donegal, not all of the Four Masters were clerics. *Cúchoigcríche* (Peregrine) *Ó Cléirigh* was a married layman, who had succeeded his father *Lughaidh* as chief of his family. In 1632 he was dispossessed of his lands as a "meere Irishman," and thereafter migrated to Co. Mayo where he ended his days in material poverty but in tenacious retention of his most precious possession, his library. At his death in 1664 he bequeathed his books, in a will which is still extant, to his two sons, *Diarmaid* (see *Shem) and *Seán* (see *Shaun). Can these coheirs have contributed anything to the invention or naming of the battling twins in *Finnegans Wake*?

FOUR WAVES
(See *Four Masters)

In *Finnegans Wake* Joyce mentions innumerable times "four waves" which he identifies closely with the *Four Masters. Yet on the one occasion when he gives names for the waves, he supplies only three: "Rurie, Thoath and Cleaver" (254.02). Moreover, behind this list stands a note in Joyce's "Scribbledehobble" notebook: "3 waves of I = Thoth, Ruri, Cleeva," and that note seems to have as its source an assertion by AE that the three great waves are "the wave of Toth, the wave of Rury, and the long, slow, white-foaming wave of Cluna." [1] Comparison of these lists will reveal immediately one discrepancy: for AE's "Cluna" Joyce gives "Cleeva [Cleaver]." Since the Irish name for the wave in question is *Tonn Chlíodhna* (khlíne), it is evident that neither is quite correct, but that AE is closer than Joyce.

At once then, with the urge to account for the discrepancy a probable explanation simultaneously comes to mind: Joyce's "Cleeva" is almost certainly a transcription error of a common sort—either Joyce or someone else has mistaken an n for v, and turned a "Cleena" to "Cleeva." The former, of course, would be a rendition of *Chlíodhna* superior to AE's "Cluna." It would therefore appear that "Cleaver" unwittingly perpetuates the mistake which brought the ghost word "Cleeva" into existence. But having decided so much we are just entering upon the central mystery, which propounds itself in the form of two questions: (1) did Joyce ever discover the error? and (2) why did he (and AE) think there were only three "Waves," and did he ever find out that there are in fact four?

For the first question we can arrive at no clear-cut answer. For the second we may speculate. Since Joyce in *Finnegans Wake* deals endlessly in foursomes, and since he repeatedly (373.08, 384.06,08, 385.35, 390.15–16, 424.29) speaks of "four waves," it surpasses credibility that he could for long have remained in ignorance of the actual existence of Four Waves of Ireland. (Indeed it strains probability to think that the "Waves" should come to any number other than four.) The Four Waves in fact may be found named in such an obvious and available source as Dinneen's dictionary: *Tonn Chlíodhna*, *Tonn Scéine*, *Tonn Rudhraighe*, and *Tonn Tuaithe*. Of these four *Tonn Scéine* is the one missing from both Joyce's and AE's lists, but the possibility that Joyce had never heard of it becomes slim indeed when it is recalled that all the annalists agree that it was at *Tonn Scéine*, the present Kenmare Bay between Co. Kerry and Co. Cork, that Eibhear the Milesian landed in Ireland (*Colonists).

Furthermore, whatever the true etymology of the name *Tonn Scéine*, it may plausibly be translated "Wave of a Knife (or Dagger)." Did Joyce perhaps discover the transcription error which produced "Cleeva" and also the existence of "Dagger Wave," but then, instead of correcting the first and adding the second to his list, combine both into a single cutting instrument, a "Cleaver"? Did he wish his fours always to be asymmetrical (see *Four Masters)?

The "Four Waves" in the order listed above are respectively represented in the modern geography of Ireland by Glandore Bay (on the south coast of Co. Cork; the "Wave" of the South), Kenmare Bay (chiefly in southwestern Co. Kerry; the "Wave" of the West), Dundrum Bay (in Co. Down, the "Wave" of the East), and the mouth of the Bann river (Co. Derry, the "Wave" of the North). If *Clíodhna* and *Scéine* are combined in "Cleaver," that represents a fusion of South and West (and in fact the two bays are only a few miles apart).

1. This information is encapsulated in Adaline Glasheen's *A Second Census of Finnegans Wake*, p. 226, entry "Rurie."

HUMPHREY[1]

Permutations of the name and personality of Humphrey in *Finnegans Wake* are beaded on tangled threads, but it is possible to unravel at least a few sequences of them. The place to begin is with the Old Norse masculine personal name *Ólafr*, which is more familiar in the modified form Olaf. The name means an ancestral or family relic, and so has an amusing pertinence to Humphrey Chimpden Earwicker, but our present concern is more strictly with onomastics than with personalities. Several Danes prominent in the medieval history of Ireland were named Olaf or Ólafr, including the father of Sitric of Dublin and first husband of the notorious *Gormflaith* (*Brian Boru). The name in fact was introduced into Ireland so early and so prominently that relatively quickly it was adopted and used by the Irish themselves. The sound the name assumed on Irish tongues was (oulév), which in writing was represented as *Amhlaoibh* (*Aspiration), whether in reference to a Danish Olaf or a native Irishman of the same name. The patronymic *Mac Amhlaoibh* soon became a permanent surname, and its wide distribution throughout the Gaelic-speaking world of Ireland and Scotland is attested by the numerous and varied anglicisations to which it gave rise: MacAuliffe, MacAuley, Macauley, MacCauliffe, MacCauley, MacCawley, Cawley, Cowley, etc.

Since at the time of early contact between the Irish and the Vikings the latter were a barbarian outlaw people and the former a literate people in close contact with the Latin culture of western Europe, it is not surprising that Viking names, for instance, were Latinized not directly but through the intermediary of Irish. Irish writers, writing in Latin about Viking persons, naturally Latinized the Irish forms of the names to which they were accustomed rather than seeking to go back to the original Norse as a basis. Thus it came about that the name Olaf entered Latin through an adaptation of the Irish form *Amhlaoibh*, so that when in the twelfth century Saxo Grammaticus wrote his Latin *Historica Danica* he wrote the name of a certain Danish Prince Olaf as "Amlethus." In the sixteenth century when Belleforest retold the story in his *Histoires Tragiques* he gave the name Amlethus a French form, "Hamlet," and it was under the name of Hamlet, Prince of Denmark, that the former Olaf soon became widely known in England. The sequence, therefore, was Ólafr–Olaf–Amhlaoibh–Amlethus–Hamlet.

For another, briefer sequence we must return to *Amhlaoibh*. A weakness of the Irish orthographic system (which doesn't much matter in Irish, where phonemic pronunciation is remarkably fluid) is that, whereas *Amhlaoibh* is undoubtedly a very accurate spelling of the sound (oulév), the spelling is also susceptible of pronunciation as (ovlév) (*Aspiration). Now in the thirteenth century a narrative poem was composed in the North Midlands of England, called *Havelok the Dane*. This poem narrates the struggles of a Danish prince, Havelok, to regain the throne of Denmark from a usurper who displaced the child Havelok upon the death of Havelok's father. Havelok is sent away with a man deputed to murder him, who takes him to England; Havelok survives to return to Denmark and overthrow the usurper. The resemblance of the gross outlines of this story to the story of Hamlet is obvious, and it is equally obvious that the name Havelok is no more a genuine Danish name than Hamlet is. But Havelok could rather readily have been derived, directly or indirectly, from *Amhlaoibh* (ovlév). Therefore to the previous chain another term may be added: Ólafr–Olaf–Amhlaoibh–Havelok in parallel to Ólafr–Olaf–Amhlaoibh–Amlethus–Hamlet. Furthermore, in *Finnegans Wake*, variants of Havelok/Havelock may be legitimately associated with the cluster of Olaf names.

How the name Humphrey comes to be identified with this cluster may be shown succinctly by quoting verbatim from the Reverend Patrick Woulfe's authoritative work on Irish names: "AMHLAOIBH . . . Auliffe, Olave (Humphrey); Norse, Ólafr, ancestral relic; also written Onlaf and Anlaf; a name introduced by the Norsemen and adopted by the Irish; it first occurs in the Annals at the year 851; still common in West Munster, but absurdly angl. Humphrey." [2]

Before proceeding to follow up another line of Humphrey–Olaf connections, it may be well to state clearly that the name Amhlaoibh in Irish does *not* mean "curled" as asserted by Mrs. Glasheen. [3] The name has no meaning whatsoever in Irish, being simply an attempted phonetic rendition of the Norse name Olaf. The word Mrs. Glasheen or her informant no doubt has in mind is *amalach* (omolokh), "curled," but to identify this word with *Amhlaoibh* on the basis, presumably, of the identity of a few letters in the spelling, is a mistake as silly as to assert the identity of the name *Hamlet* with the English word *hemlock*. Another loose end which may be considered here is that the *aspirated form of the Irish word for "plague-grave" (see *Colonists), *thaimhleacht*, in place-names is frequently anglicised -hamlet-.

Another sequence of names has its beginning outside Ireland but trends in time both into Ireland and into *Finnegans Wake*. Parties of the same Northmen who harried Ireland also, it is well known, harried the Atlantic coasts of France, ultimately settled there, adopted the French language, and became the Normans who in 1066 conquered England and the following century began the conquest of Ireland. The Northman settlers in Normandy brought with them the common Norse name Ólafr, but when they adopted French speech they altered that name to Oliver. With the Norman Conquest the name Oliver entered England, where it has since become extremely common. But of all the Englishmen who have borne the name Oliver, one alone is so preeminent as to overshadow all others: Cromwell, The Lord Protector Oliver. And of all the Ólafrs who at one time or another ravaged Ireland, none exceeded the devastation wrought by Oliver Cromwell. Now other Cromwells had come to Ireland centuries before Oliver's time, and their name had already received an Irish form, *Cromail*. As it happens, *cromail* in Irish can be interpreted as meaning something like "stooping cliff" or "crouching hill," but I find no clear-cut evidence in *Finnegans Wake* that Joyce made use of the fact (although "Crommalhill" occurs at 132.22). But he did very certainly seize upon the identity of the first syllable of "Cromwell" and the name of an ancient Irish idol overthrown by St. Patrick: *Crom*, also called *Crom Crúach* ("croucher"; "gory croucher"). So, by a long and tenuous chain, Humphrey is associated both with Cromwell and *Crom Crúach:* "cromcruwell" (022.14). The chain runs Humphrey–Amhlaoibh–Olaf–Ólafr–Oliver–Oliver Cromwell–Crom Crúach. Yet still it does not end. For the word *crúach*, "gory," is a homonym of *crúach*, "conical heap," and reminds one at once of *Cruach Phádraig*, the mountain of St. Patrick, opponent and overthrower of *Crom Crúach*. To enforce this reminiscence Joyce has invented "Naif Cruachan" (526.20) which may be regarded as *Naomh Cruachán*, "Saint Cruachán," and the latter name may be interpreted as "one who has to do with a *crúach*," that is, St. Patrick, whether it be *Crom Crúach* or *Cruach Phádraig* that is in question. But in fact a *cruachán* is a little heap, or hump, and is also the name of a little humpbacked fish; and of course both a hump and a fish return us directly to Humphrey, HCE. The chain therefore closes in something of the following fashion: Humphrey–Amhlaoibh–Olaf–Ólafr–Oliver–Oliver Crom-well–Crom Crúach–Cruachán (Patrick; fish; hump)–Humphrey. A great number of these themes coagulate together in "The Ballad of Persse O'Reilly" (044.24—047.29).

Two tag ends may conclude this note. One of the less frequent anglicisa-tions of the surname *Mac Amhlaoibh* is MacCooley, and the resemblance of this form to MacCool makes a point of connection between Humphrey and *Fionn Mac Cumhail*. The other is that the Irish word *alp* (olp) means, among other things, a hump. HCE and ALP, therefore, share a certain identity. The word *alp* actually means a short, thick, heavy bit of almost anything: a material substance, solid or liquid; speech; sound; action; work. Therefore, depending on its use, it may be translated "hump," "lump," "mouthful," "bite," "snarl," "bark," "section," "job," and so forth. In the stonemason's jargon known as *Béarlagair na Saor*, *"Alp Uí Laoghaire,"* which possibly should be interpreted "O Leary's *Job*, or *Piece of Work*," is the name for Dublin (243.29). At any rate it is clear that ALP is merely another name for HCE—at least some of the time.

Despite the peculiar Irish identification of Humphrey with *Amhlaoibh*, the name Humphrey has a legitimate independent existence in Irish. The name is of Teutonic origin (*Hunfrith*, "Hun-peace"), and was brought to Ireland by the Anglo-Normans. There it became Gaelicised *Unfraidh* (unfrí) and *Unfradh* (unfru). A phonetic version of the latter form appears in *Finnegans Wake* as the pseudo-Egyptian or Akkadian or whatever "Unfru" (024.07).

1. The substance of this note has previously appeared as "The Name of Humphrey," *A Wake Newslitter*, III (October, 1966), pp. 93–96; I am indebted to the editor of the *Newslitter* for his kind permission to reprint.
2. *Sloinnte Gaedheal is Gall: Irish Names and Surnames* (Dublin, 1923), pp. 169–170.
3. *A Second Census of Finnegans Wake*, p. 192, entry "Olaf."

KILL

The prefix "Kill," extremely frequent in Irish place-names, and propor-tionately frequent among the real and false names Joyce uses in *Finnegans Wake*, is of relatively uncomplicated etymology. To appreciate fully

Joyce's use of the element, however, it is necessary to go beyond a mere succinct explanation, and turn instead to the somewhat prolix work of his namesake, P. W. Joyce, author of *Irish Names of Places*. In Volume I of that book P. W. Joyce writes: "*Cill* (kill), also written *cell* and *ceall*, is the Latin *cella*, and next to *baile*, it is the most prolific root in Irish names. Its most usual anglicised form is *kill* or *kil*, but it is also made *kyle*, *keel*, and *cal;* there are about 3,400 names beginning with these syllables, and if we estimate that a fifth of them represent *coill*, a wood, there remain about 2,700 whose first syllable is derived from *cill* ['church']. Of these the greater number are formed by placing the name of the founder or patron after this word . . ." (p. 314).

What P. W. Joyce fails to distinguish is that, of his 3,400 names beginning *kill*, *kil*, *kyle*, *keel*, and *cal*, virtually all of those beginning *kyle* and *keel* may be ascribed to *coill*, and all of those beginning *cal* to *ceall*, a variant of *cill*, so that ambiguity really continues to reside only in the names beginning *kill* and *kil*. Of these the overwhelming majority—much greater than four-fifths—represent *cill*, though a certain crucial few do represent *coill*. Of all this P. W. Joyce has an unformulated awareness, and his instinctive feeling that *kill* or *kil* has a very much better than 80 per cent likelihood of standing for *cill* rather than *coill* comes to the surface in an almost comic manner when next he deals with these name elements: "At A.D. 1601, the Four Masters mention a place in Galway called *Coill-bhreac*, speckled wood—speckled, I suppose, from a mixture of various coloured trees; it is now called Kylebrack . . . With a slight difference of form we have Kilbrack in Cork and Waterford, and Kilbracks (speckled woods or churches) in Armagh" (Vol. II, 288).

Common sense, I think, would insist that Kilbrack and Kilbracks stand for speckled woods, not speckled churches, but P. W. Joyce has obviously intruded his saving alternative under pressure of his sense that Kil-*usually* means a church. Kylebrack and Brackyle, which he also gives, illustrate the real existence of speckled woods, of which Kilbrack and Kilbracks are mere variants, whereas speckled churches are absurd. There-fore, I suggest, *Finnegans Wake*'s "cute old speckled church" (403.21) is merely James Joyce having a laugh at the expense of Patrick Weston Joyce.

LIFFEY
(See *Anna, *Dublin)

Whereas the city of Dublin takes both its alternate names—Hurdle Ford and Black Pool—from features of the River Liffey upon which it is built, the River Liffey contrarily takes its name from the territory through which it flows: *Magh Life*, "*Life* Plain." Although it is certain that the name *Life* applies primarily to the plain, and only secondarily to the river, the precise meaning of that name is completely obscure. A very plausible hypothesis, however, would derive the word *Life* from *lubh*, *luibh* (luv, liv), "herb." The latter word is cognate with English *leaf*, and in place-names it is usually anglicised -liff-, testifying to its phonetic resemblance to *Life*, anglicised Liffey. Therefore it is quite likely that *Magh Life* is a form of *Magh Luibhe*, "Plain of Herbs," and the Liffey River accordingly would be the "Herb" (or "Leaf") River.

Whatever about the accuracy of this etymology, it seems clearly evident that James Joyce accepted it. Such forms as "leafy" (619.20) and "leafiest" (624.22) support this assumption, and recognition of this probable derivation will serve to gloss informatively a brief selection from Anna Livia Plurabelle's final sentences: "My leaves have drifted from me. All. But one clings still. I'll bear it on me. To remind me of. Lff!" (628.06–07).

Leaves: from the *Magh Life*, Leafy Plain, through which the river flows.
one clings still: the name *Life*, which the river retains from the plain.
Lff!: Life–Liffey–leaves–Life.

A problem for the Gaelic glossator of *Finnegans Wake* is that the river name *Life* is orthographically identical with the English word "Life." Joyce can scarcely be suspected of having failed to make use of this coincidence, but specific instances are not easy to document. As a general rule, therefore, the present Lexicon has made no attempt to gloss the bulk of occurrences of the English word "life" as instances of the Irish name of the Liffey River. It should nevertheless be always suspected that when Joyce uses the word he may be invoking both English and Irish meanings.

L/R INTERCHANGE

The mutual interchange in words of the sounds of l and r is by no means an exclusively Irish characteristic, but a linguistic phenomenon of world-

wide occurrence. Nevertheless it is an extremely frequent form of altera-
tion in Irish words, as may be endlessly demonstrated. For example the
borrowed word "orange" enters Irish as *óráiste* and is then corrupted to
láiste; such doublets are commonplace as *biorar/biolar, mairc/mailc,
aibghidir/aibidil,* and *goile/goire;* such a word as *sruthair,* "stream" is frequently pronounced in such fashion as to give rise to anglicisation in
place-names as Shrule, Shruel, Struell, and Sroohill. But these instances
are not particularly illuminative of *Finnegans Wake.*

All things considered, however, it has been thought best to gloss all
important occurrences of L/R Interchange in *Finnegans Wake,* not even
primarily because of the frequency of the phenomenon in Irish, but because of the frequency with which Joyce makes use of it in Irish contexts,
and especially in conjunction with the much more distinctive *P/K Split.
Reference to the *P/K Split, for instance, permits the restoration of
"roman pathoricks" (027.02) to "roman cathoricks"; but only further
invocation of the L/R Interchange permits us the full reconstruction
"roman catholicks."

MACPHERSON[1]
(See Additional Note on *Fionn Mac Cumhail*)

At the outset the temptation must be avoided of entering deeply into the
great Macpherson controversy. For aid in reading *Finnegans Wake* it will
be profitable only to sketch the less controvertible details of the matter.
In 1757, James Macpherson, a young man who had been born in a
Gaelic-speaking district of Scotland, as a result of some fragments he had
produced as translations of ancient Gaelic poetry, was despatched by a
group of Edinburgh gentlemen on an expedition to the Highlands and
Western Islands of Scotland to collect manuscripts and traditional Gaelic
literature. At the time the English-speaking world knew virtually nothing
about Scots-Gaelic literature and still less, if less were possible, about
Irish literature. Macpherson collected an undetermined number of manuscripts, of which one at least—*The Book of the Dean of Lismore* (made 1512–
1526)—is a national treasure of Scotland. He also had more skilled companions transcribe poems and stories from recitation. As a consequence
he published in 1760 *Fragments of Ancient Poetry Collected in the Highlands
of Scotland and Translated from the Galic or Erse Language.* The fifteen

Fragments are written in a cadenced prose, but despite Macpherson's collecting, they have only the slightest connection with any Gaelic originals. Nevertheless Macpherson was announcing that some of the fragments constituted passages from a single great epic poem, and that he had sufficient material to reconstruct the work entire. Good as his word, in 1762 he published *Fingal, an Ancient Epic Poem*, in six books, and added fifteen shorter pieces to round out the publication. For *Fingal*, scholarship has revealed, he made use of about nine genuine Gaelic ballads, to which he added much material of his own, invented and borrowed. There never has been any genuine Gaelic epic of *Fingal*.

Macpherson's abilities as a collector of Gaelic epics were not fully displayed, however, prior to *Temora*, an epic in eight books, which he published in 1763, together with a shorter work called *Cath-Loda*. This production contained elaborate explanatory notes, together with the seventh book of *Temora* printed in Gaelic as a specimen of the whole and a confutation of the skeptics. Despite this overwhelming parade, *Temora* appears to have been expanded from a single Gaelic ballad, and needless to say no genuine epic of *Temora* ever existed. In 1765 Macpherson republished all this material as *The Works of Ossian*, but produced no further Gaelic translations during the remaining thirty-one years of his life. He became very touchy of skeptical criticism, but steadfastly refused to publish the Gaelic originals which he still insisted he had. Politics rather than poetry made him rich, and his will provided £1,000 to publish finally the long controverted originals. The Gaelic version of Macpherson at last was published in 1807, eleven years after his death.

Macpherson's epics on their appearance in the eighteenth century were on the whole well received, but critical reaction ranged from complete acceptance of Macpherson's every assertion about them to outright rejection of the lot as a total fabrication. The poems themselves purport to be the work of a third-century poet named Ossian, and consequently the poems, if absolutely genuine, would perforce date from the third century. In them Ossian celebrates the exploits of his father, Fingal, his own son, Oscar, various followers of Fingal's, and heroes named Cairbar, Cuchullin (or Cuthullin or Cuchulaid), and Ferda, among others. Fingal is represented as king of a kingdom called Morven, extending over the Western Isles and Highlands of Scotland, which he rules from his castle of Selma; his father was named Comhal, and his mother was Morna, daughter of Thaddu. Temora is the name of a royal capital.

Among the results of the Macpherson controversy was a great stimulation of scholarly Gaelic studies, and the first facts to be incontrovertibly settled about the Ossianic productions were that the chief persons named in them were indeed familiar to the Highland storytellers, and that Ossianic ballads really existed, of which Macpherson had made use. The nineteenth-century advance in Celtic studies revealed the existence in Ireland of a saga cycle, attested in manuscripts as early as the eleventh century, dealing with a hero named *Fionn* son of *Cumhal* (see Additional Notes), his son *Oisín*, his grandson *Oscar*, and various companions who could be identified with persons mentioned by Macpherson. A quite distinct saga cycle also came to light, the Ulster or *Red Branch Cycle, which features a hero named *Cú Chulainn* with a friend named *Fer Diad*— Macpherson's Cuchullin and Ferda. A final evaluation of Macpherson became possible, which may be summarized as follows:

1. Most of his characters have a real traditional existence.

2. He used genuine Gaelic ballads as a basis for his epics.

3. Most of the material in the poems is his own.

4. His claim to have translated third-century originals is absurd: a) third-century Gaelic was far removed from the eighteenth-century Scottish Gaelic he knew; b) Gaelic was not introduced into Scotland until later than the third century; c) the earliest known written Gaelic dates only from the sixth century (in Ireland); d) the earliest Ossianic ballads can be dated only to the eleventh century (in Ireland), although the basic legends are earlier.

5. He confuses material from the quite distinct Ulster and Ferian (*Fionn Mac Cumhail*—see Additional Note) Cycles.

6. The purported Gaelic originals of the Ossian poems published in 1807 represent only half of the total of poems published as translations.

7. The Gaelic of *Temora*, Book VII published in 1807 is very different from the Gaelic of *Temora*, Book VII published as an illustration in 1763.

8. The manuscripts from which the 1807 edition was printed have never come to light, which is not surprising in view of the fact that

9. The 1807 Gaelic version is a translation of Macpherson's English into Gaelic.

10. Macpherson's Gaelic, whenever he produces it, offends against idiom and unnaturally strains the language.

11. Morven and Selma are entirely of his own invention, both as names and as places.

12. His Ossian, in style, diction, and turns of language, demonstrably owes a great deal to Homer, the Hebrew prophets, and—most extraordinary—John Milton.

13. Sometimes his translations are close to their originals, where they really exist, but more often he misunderstands the originals and completely alters their mood to romanticize them.[2]

In the Irish stories *Fionn Mac Cumhail*, although his status in society markedly advances through the historical development of the cycle, is at best a general, never a king. The kingdom of Morven which Macpherson invented for him is, however, but an extension of a general Scottish misunderstanding which has altered Fionn's name to Fingal. The form in which Macpherson gives his Gaelic version of the name Fingal— *Fiön gal*—leaves unclear just how he construed its etymology. The open possibilities are the pleonastic *Fionn geal*, "bright Fionn" (but *Fionn* itself means "fair"), or the dithemetic *Fionnghal* ("Fair-valor"). In any case the name Fingal really arises from a misunderstanding of a different order—one to delight the author of *Finnegans Wake*. Among the titles affected by the Scottish Lord of the Isles (whose domains roughly coincide with Macpherson's Morven) was that of *Rí Fionnghaill*, "King of Norwegians." *Fionn-gall*, "Fair-foreigner," was a term used in Gaelic to distinguish Norwegians from Danes, the *Dubh-ghaill* or "Dark-foreigners." But in time the Scots apparently mistook the title for a name, "King Fingal," and identified this nonexistent monarch with *Fionn*. For Macpherson then to provide him with the kingdom of Morven was not only an act of justice but, in creating it out of the territory of the Lord of the Isles, by a sort of *Finnegans Wake* logic, perfectly accurate.

James Joyce could hardly fail to avail himself of an identification which made *Fionn Mac Cumhail* into a King of Norwegians, but to him, as to any other Dubliner, the name "Fingal" had an immediate relevance quite unrelated to James Macpherson. The northern part of Co. Dublin, an almost featureless plain outside the city limits, is named Fingal, and it is of that neighboring district that the name primarily reminds any Dubliner. "Fingal" in this case is *Fine-Gall*, "Foreign Kindred" or "Foreign Tribe,ʼ a designation which indicates that the plain north of Dublin was regarded as the tribal land of the Dublin Danes. So for Joyce his own local Fingal also carried the Scandinavian connotations which pervade his book. It seems probable, therefore, that his uses of the name Fingal in *Finnegans Wake* refer primarily to the Dublin district, and then to

Macpherson's hero. This may be illustrated by such a passage as: "And Dub did glow that night. In Fingal of victories" (329.14). The context is heavily Macphersonian, and the phrase "Fingal of victories" is taken directly from *Temora*. But "Dub" in the first sentence returns us to Dublin, and the preposition "In" forces the recognition of Fingal as a place rather than a person—namely, the outlying North Dublin district.

As all history and legend conspires to create *Finnegans Wake*, the equation Joyce finds to hand makes a Dublin district be Fingal, a Viking territory, which is *Rí Fionnghaill*, King of Norwegians, who is King Fingal of Morven, who is really *Fionn Mac Cumhail* (who may really be a Viking; see Additional Note), who is HCE, who is Dublin, a Dano-Irish city.

1. For a conspectus of references in *Finnegans Wake* to Macpherson's Ossianic works, see Atherton, *Books at the Wake*, and Glasheen, *A Second Census of Finnegans Wake*, both *passim*, and especially Fritz Senn, "Ossianic Echoes," *A Wake Newslitter*, New Series, III (April, 1966), pp. 25–36.
2. For a full scholarly analysis of the Macpherson question, see D. S. Thomson, *The Gaelic Sources of Macpherson's Ossian* (1952).

MALACHY
(See *Brian Boru, and Additional Note on *Ruaidhrí Ó Conchobhair*)

Malachy is a fanciful anglicisation of the name *Maelsheachlainn* (mélokhlin) borne by two Irish high kings: *Maelsheachlainn* I *mac Maolruanaigh* (c. 800–863; king 846–863), and *Maelsheachlainn* II *mac Domhnaill* (949–1022; king 980–1002, 1014–1022). Although *Maelsheachlainn* II, "the Great," was by far the more prominent of these, both seem to be included in *Finnegans Wake* Malachy references, so the careers of both will be sketched here.

Maelsheachlainn I was a member of the ancient royal dynasty of the Southern *Uí Néill;* his father *Maolruanach* was king of *Midhe* (Meath), and his father's father, *Donnchadh*, was high king 770–797; his father's elder brother *Conchobhar* was high king 820–834. In 840 *Diarmaid*, son of *Conchobhar*, defeated *Maelsheachlainn*'s father in a skirmish, which *Maelsheachlainn* avenged the next day by killing *Diarmaid*, thus promoting his father to the position of paramount chief of the Southern *Uí Néill*, and himself to the second position. In 842 *Maolruanach* died, and *Maelsheach-*

lainn succeeded him in the provincial kingship and as chief of the Southern *Uí Néill*. Two years later *Maelsheachlainn* performed his first notable exploit against the Danes by capturing Turges or Turgeis, the pillager and self-proclaimed Abbot of Armagh, whose wife Ota had been uttering oracles from the high altar at *Clonmacnoise. *Maelsheachlainn* dealt with Turgeis by drowning him in *Loch Uair* (Lough Owel: see 408.24, 549.34; *L/R Interchange), Co. Westmeath.

Upon the death of *Niall Caille* in 846 it became the turn of the Southern *Uí Néill* to succeed to the high kingship, and *Maelsheachlainn* was inaugurated to the office. Within the year he defeated the Danes in two major battles, and in 847 took and plundered Dublin. Thereafter *Cinaedh*, chief of *Ciannachta Breagh* ("Bregia": 604.04), in alliance with the Danes ravaged *Maelsheachlainn*'s hereditary province of Meath, an error he expiated in 849 when *Maelsheachlainn* captured *Cinaedh* and publicly drowned him in the river Nanny in his own territory of *Ciannachta Breagh*. *Maelsheachlainn* obviously thought highly of water as a means of disposing of enemies.

Between 853 and 856, culminating with a winter campaign in the latter year, he brought the southern province of Munster under his domination, and in 859 he once more defeated the Dublin Danes at the battle of *Druimdamhaighe*. On November 30, 863 he died, to be succeeded as high king by an enemy, *Aedh Finnliath*, chief of the Northern *Uí Néill*, who had been pressing *Maelsheachlainn* in his final years. In 879, however, upon the death of *Aedh*, *Maelsheachlainn*'s son, *Flann Sionna*, succeeded as high king.

Maelsheachlainn II was a member of the same Southern *Uí Néill* dynasty, being in fact the great-great-grandson of *Maelsheachlainn* I. He was born in *Midhe*, the son of *Domhnall*, provincial king and chief of the Southern *Uí Néill*, who was the son of *Donnchadh* (high king 919–944), son of *Flann Sionna* (high king 879–916). His mother was *Donnfhlaith*, daughter of the Northern *Uí Néill* high king, *Muircheartach na gCóiceall Croicinn* (Murtagh of the Leather Cloaks: 289.19–20, etc.; see *Brian Boru), reigning at the time of *Maelsheachlainn*'s birth, 949.

In 979 *Maelsheachlainn* succeeded his father as ruler of *Midhe*, and celebrated his accession by defeating a Danish army led by *Raghnall mac Amhlaoibh* (Rognvaldr son of Amlaff or Olaf: see *Humphrey) at Tara, nominal (though long since abandoned) capital of the high king. The following year, upon the death of the High King *Domhnall*, of the Northern

Uí Néill, *Maelsheachlainn*, as the head of the Southern *Uí Néill*, succeeded to the throne. Thereupon he allied himself with *Eochaidh*, king of *Ulaidh* (the east-central portion of the modern province of Ulster), besieged Dublin, seized plunder from the Danes, and compelled them to release all their Irish captives.

*Brian Boru meanwhile had already established himself as the dominant power in the southern province of Munster, and was beginning to extend himself eastwards into Ossory and Leinster. To check Brian, *Maelsheachlainn* in 982 invaded *Dál gCais*, defeated the local defenders (Brian himself, with his main army, being in Ossory at the time), and cut down the *Bile* or sacred tree under which the *Dál gCais* chiefs were inaugurated. Brian returned, but *Maelsheachlainn* passed behind him to attack the Danish city of Waterford, and on the way home invaded Leinster. In 984 he also invaded Connacht, seeking probably to forestall Brian. In 986 he invaded Leinster once more, and in 989 defeated the Dublin Danes, besieged the city for three weeks, cutting off its water supply, and compelling the Danes to agree to an annual tribute of one ounce of gold for each family in the city, payable every Christmas eve. The following year he attacked North Munster, and on the way home captured *Donnchadh*, the king of Leinster who had become Brian's vassal in 984.

Two years later, in 992, Brian attempted to counter by invading Meath, but retreated without significant success. *Maelsheachlainn* in retaliation burned Nenagh, Tipperary, near Brian's nominal capital of Cashel, ravaged East Munster; and then, on the way back, to remain in practice he sacked Dublin, carrying off two notable trophies, the Ring of Tomar and the Sword of Karl. It is obscurely to this episode that Thomas Moore is alluding (in *Let Erin Remember*) in the words: "When Malachy wore the collar of gold that he won from the proud invader."

After five years of relative quiet *Maelsheachlainn* in 997 had to repel an incursion on *Midhe* of the *Óirghialla*, and slew their chief. The same year, in alliance with his rival Brian, he attacked the Danes once more. Brian's growth in strength was signalized the next year when the two kings concluded a formal pact on Loch Ree by the terms of which Brian was to refrain from plundering *Leath Chuinn*, the northern half of Ireland; by implication he was to be unopposed in *Leath Mogha*, his own southern half. Two years later, in 1000, the allied kings defeated a large Danish army at Glen Mama in Wicklow, then proceeded to burn Dublin, whence they carried off plunder and slaves.

The same year, in a more peaceful effort, *Maelsheachlainn* joined with *Cathal Ó Conchobhair* (see **Uí Néill* and Additional Note: *Ruaidhrí Ó Conchobhair*), king of Connacht, to make artificial fords across the Shannon —the border between their domains—at Athliag and Athlone.

By 1001 *Maelsheachlainn* was growing uneasy in his alliance with Brian, and called upon *Aedh Ó Néill*, king of *Ailech*, his coeval chief of the Northern *Uí Néill*, and *Eochaidh*, king of *Ulaidh*, to join him against Brian and the forces of *Leath Mogha*. *Aedh* superciliously responded that the Northern *Uí Néill* would not defend Tara for *Maelsheachlainn*, since whenever they held Tara they held it alone. In 1002, therefore, *Maelsheachlainn* was forced to give tribute to Brian and acknowledge his suzerainty. For the first time in six centuries the high kingship passed out of the hands of the *Uí Néill* into those of a usurper. In 1003 *Maelsheachlainn* accompanied Brian on an ineffective raid into North Connacht, but thereafter until 1011 he remained quietly in his own diminished domain, roughly equivalent to modern Co. Westmeath.

In 1011 *Maelsheachlainn* went to war again, this time against his Northern *Uí Néill* kinsmen, when he ravaged Tyrone. The next year he lost his son *Donnchadh* in battle, marched to Howth and fought the Dublin Danes; at a second battle, at Drinan, Co. Dublin, another son, *Flann*, was slain. *Maelsheachlainn* retreated to Meath, only to face an incursion of the Northern *Uí Néill*. Brian Boru came to his succor.

On 23rd of April 1014 *Maelsheachlainn* and Brian together once more fought the Danes, at the decisive and bloody battle of Clontarf; Brian was killed, and *Maelsheachlainn*, without dispute, resumed the high kingship, which he retained until his death. During the rest of 1014 he fought several smaller fights with the Danes; in 1016 he invaded *Ulaidh*, invaded Ossory twice, and Leinster once. In 1017 he fought the Danes again, and in 1018 went to war once more against the Northern *Uí Néill*. In 1021 he fought both Danes and Northern *Uí Néill*. On September 2, 1022, he died on the fortified island of *Cró-inis*, on Loch Ennell in Co. Westmeath; probably his last illness was spent on the island for security against attack.

Maelsheachlainn II was the last formally inaugurated king of all Ireland, and with him the alternate succession of northern and southern **Uí Néill*, after lasting six hundred years, came to an end.

METATHESIS

Metathesis—the transposition of consonants in pronouncing a word—is a widespread linguistic phenomenon and one of Joyce's regular methods of deranging words in *Finnegans Wake*. Accordingly, therefore, to gloss every instance of metathesis in *Finnegans Wake* as a specimen of Gaelic would be a task not only mindless but endless. Nevertheless metathesis is such a marked feature of Irish phonetics that in a small number of cases, where some other attribute strongly suggests the influence of Irish, instances of metathesis have been recorded in this Lexicon, and noted as such.

To display the operation of metathesis in Irish, particularly in the borrowing and in the inflection of words, would require an extensive treatise that would in the end shed little light on *Finnegans Wake*. The examples of two fairly commonplace Irish words will sufficiently show the working of the phenomenon. From the noun *mil*, "honey," comes the adjective *milis* (milish), "sweet," and from the adjective in turn comes the noun *milseán*, "sweet, confection, candy." *Milseán* is generally pronounced (milshán) but in Munster, by metathesis, the *l* and *s* of *milis* are reversed, and the word becomes (míshlán). That is an example of metathesis in inflection. Metathesis in borrowing can be illustrated by the Irish word for "bishop."

Behind both the Irish and the English word lies the Latin form *episcopus* of the Greek *episkopos*. Old English clipped off both beginning and end of the word to yield *biscop*, which has since become *bishop*. Irish clipped off only the termination, but by metathesis has scrambled the k and p (b; see *P/K Split) sounds, losing one of the p's in the process, to produce *easbog* (asbug). Without metathesis, the result should have been something more like *easgob*.

For English speakers, however, by far the most familiar product of Irish metathesis is the word "leprechaun"—in Irish *leipreachán*. The original of this word is *lúchorpán* (lúkhurpán), "little body," but the internal consonants have become so thoroughly scrambled by metathesis as to effect even a mutation of the vowels.

O MALLEY (GRACE)

Gráinne Ní Mhaille (gráñí wolyi), whose name occurs in the State Papers in almost as many forms as it does in *Finnegans Wake*—Grany O'Mayle, Grainne O'Mailey, Grany Ne Male, Grany Ny Mayle, Grayn Ny Vayle, Grany Ne Malley—unfortunately never accomplished the deeds which legend ascribes to her.

Grace O Malley, as she is now known in English, was born about 1530 somewhere in the southwestern part of the present Co. Mayo, near Clew Bay, in the district called *Umhaill Uachtarach Uí Mhaille*, now the barony and peninsula of Murrisk. By her own later testimony, she was the daughter of *Dubhdara Ó Maille*, chief of the district, and his wife Margaret, daughter of *Conchobhar Ó Maille*. The *Uí Maille* were sea rovers, and *Gráinne* spent her girlhood in Murrisk and among the countless islands off the Mayo coast.

Her first husband was *Domhnall-an-chogaidh* ("of the war") *Ó Flaithbheartaigh mac Giolla Dubh*, chief of *Baile na hInse* (Ballynahinch) in Galway. By him she had two sons, *Eoghan* and *Murchadh Ó Flaithbheartaigh*, known as *na dtuagha*, "of the axes." Her second husband was *Risteárd-an-iarain* ("of the iron") *Mac Oileverius de Búrca*, who in 1582 became chief of *Mac Uilliam Íochtar*. To him she bore a son, *Tibot na long* (Theobald of the ships). She also had as "son-in-law" (which I take to mean stepson) *Risteárd Deamhan-an-Chorráin* ("Demon of the Sickle") *de Búrca*, known in English, by a free rendering of his agnomen, as "The Devil's Hook." *Risteárd Deamhan-an-Chorráin* I take to have been the son of *Risteárd-an-iarain*.

In 1577 *Gráinne* was taken prisoner by the Earl of Desmond, who in 1578 brought her to Dublin. Released, she was suspected of seditious conspiracy in 1582, but no action was taken. In 1586 she was seized by Sir Richard Bingham, an official of Queen Elizabeth's, on accusation of having plundered Aran, and a gallows was built for her execution. On a pledge from *Deamhan-an-Chorráin* she was freed. Very soon, however, he himself rebelled, so she became again liable to death and fled for refuge to the O Neills and O Donnells of Ulster; Elizabeth notwithstanding pardoned her, and enabled her to return home.

Nevertheless in 1593 her old foe, Sir Richard Bingham, was writing that she was a "notable traitress and nurse of all rebellions in the province [of Connacht] for forty years." The property of her second husband, *Risteárd-an-iarain*, who died before 1586, had been forfeited, and in 1595 *Gráinne* petitioned Burghley for restoration of her widow's third. A few years later, about 1600, she died in great poverty and was buried, according to local tradition, in the Cistercian church of St. Bridget on Clare Island, at the mouth of Clew Bay.

Undoubtedly *Gráinne Ní Mhaille* was a turbulent and active woman, but the official records fail to confirm the truth of her most famous legendary exploit. That is the story that, upon returning from a visit to Queen Elizabeth (a visit of which there is no historical record), she landed her ships at Howth, her first landfall in Ireland, and demanded hospitality of the St. Lawrence family, holders of Howth Castle. The hospitality was refused, and in revenge *Gráinne* kidnapped the heir of the house, and returned him only on the condition that thenceforward the doors of Howth Castle must always stand open at mealtimes. Oddly, despite the lack of documentary proof that *Gráinne* really so collided with the family of the Earls of Howth, that family has retained the tradition, and the doors of Howth Castle always stood open at mealtimes until just a few years ago, when the hordes of gaping tourists forced a cessation of the custom. This story and its consequences, of course, form the basis for the prankquean episodes in *Finnegans Wake*.

P/K SPLIT

The P/K Split is a way of describing an important phenomenon in the development of the Irish language, or rather of the Celtic languages, from primitive Indo-European. It is also a widespread Indo-European event, characterized by the contrast in separate daughter languages of p-initial and k-(q-, c-)initial words derived from a single common ancestor, as Greek *pente, pempe*, "five," and Latin *quinque* both developed from Indo-European *penqe*. Nonetheless the Split has marked Irish with particular emphasis: where from Indo-European *pod*, "foot," for instance, Latin has derived *pes* and Greek *pous*—avoiding contrast—Irish has *cos*. (Notice that in both *five* and *foot* English has the characteristic Germanic f-alternative to both p and k.)

Neither Irish nor Welsh in becoming distinct languages retained from Indo-European any occurrences whatsoever of the sound *p*, but Welsh fairly early began a reverse process of developing p-initials from the Celtic q, so partly nullifying the primitive movement which had lost the original p. Irish, on the other hand, developed c-(k-)initials out of the general Celtic q, and so gave rise to a P/K split in the Celtic languages, exemplified by Welsh *pen*, Irish *ceann*, "head." This split remains typical of the differences between so-called Brythonic or P-Celtic and Goidelic or C-Celtic. Although Modern Irish has added to its vocabulary a considerable number of p-initial words, none are p-initials retained from Indo-European through Old Irish. Some have developed out of native Irish b- and f-initials, most are borrowed from other languages—Latin, Welsh, English.

A time of particularly heavy borrowing from Latin into Irish was, naturally, the time of the christianization of Ireland, but at first Irish resisted the initial p even of loan words, and assimilated such words to the native k-initial pattern. Thus Latin *pascha* became *Cáisc*, still the Irish name for Easter, *purpura* became *corcra*, which remains the word for "purple," and so on. Among the very earliest Latin p-words Irish was called upon to absorb was *Patricius*—the name of the apostle, St. Patrick himself. That name, in Irish *Pádraig*, may have been one of the very first p-words successfully naturalized, but even it went through a quarantine period as *Catraige* or *Cotraige*. Later, when the form *Pádraig* had become fully established, the recorded evidence that the saint had once been called *Cotraige* was misunderstood, and efforts were made to rationalize the apparent anomaly. Therefore one further name was added to the list of those St. Patrick was supposed to have answered to at one time or another, and the name *Cotraige* was assigned in legend to the period of his youthful bondage in Ireland. The name itself was ingeniously derived from *ceithre*, *ceathair*, "four," or *ceathrar*, "four persons," and in the forms *Cothraige* and *Cathraige* was interpreted to mean "belonging to four." This etymology then led to the thesis that the young British slave had been conjointly owned by four masters, in order to account for the name.

The P/K Split is exploited in every possible way in *Finnegans Wake*, and both the correct and the fanciful explanations of *Cotraige* are equally accepted. Therefore while the "Cottericks' donkey" (024.22) presumably belongs *chiefly* to The Four, the "roman pathoricks" (027.02) can convert or be converted into Irish Catholics. Additionally, since the K-side of the split is also represented by q, in *Finnegans Wake* the operations of the split often entail watching p's and q's, those mirror twins in print. Most of the important instances of the P/K Split in *Finnegans Wake* are perhaps recorded in this Lexicon, but the reader is advised to try on his own at any time the substitution of initial p for initial c, k, or q in *Finnegans Wake*, and of c, k, or q for any initial p.

RED BRANCH
(See *Macpherson; Additional Note on *Fionn Mac Cumhail*)

The Red Branch or Ulster Cycle of ancient Irish sagas and poems is, from a literary point of view, the most significant of the ancient Irish story cycles. In the form in which most of the Red Branch tales survive they are also of considerably greater antiquity than the stories concerning *Fionn Mac Cumhail*. As for the origins of the two cycles it may be truthfully if broadly stated that the Red Branch stories arose and were appreciated chiefly in courtly circles, while the stories of *Fionn* had a more lowly and popular origin. Concomitantly, the Red Branch stories came to be more and more restricted to books, while stories of *Fionn* continue to live in local traditions even to the present. It is perhaps not insignificant that the only native approach to an epic extant in Irish is a Red Branch tale— *Táin Bó Cúailgne* (*The Cattle-Raid of Cooley*).

This cycle was apparently produced by the *Ulaidh*, the people who have given their name to the modern province of Ulster, although in modern times Ulster is a good deal more extensive than the territory of the *Ulaidh*. Their capital was at *Eamhain Macha*, near Armagh, and their stories—although they were retold at princely courts throughout Ireland —all center in *Eamhain Macha* during the reign of King *Conchobhar Mac Neasa*, who may perhaps have lived about the second century A.D. The outstanding characters are clear-cut and unforgettable: the boy hero *Setanta* whose name is changed to *Cú Chulainn*, "Hound of *Culann*"; *Medhbh*, the Amazon queen of Connacht; *Naoise* and *Déirdre*, the tragic lovers. These persons make fitful appearances in *Finnegans Wake*.

Táin Bó Cúailgne, though it has fine parts, makes an incoherent whole. Its interest for scholars, however, is that it was reworked many times during centuries in which the more plebeian *Fionn* stories were advancing in popularity and Irish literary style was degenerating, so that the text of *Táin Bó Cúailgne* is a sort of palimpsest of attitudes and styles. The finest and most dramatic episode is that in which the Ulidian Fergus, in exile at the court of *Medhbh* (Maev, etc., in English) and her passive husband, *Aillil*, recounts the youth of *Cú Chulainn*. But as the style degenerates bare prose is replaced by bombastic alliterative runs, complex emotive verse by loose and clumsy ballad measures, ruthless humor by sentimentality. It is hardly surprising that it should be the sentimental episode of *Cú Chulainn*'s duel to the death with his boyhood friend, *Fer Diad*—each trapped by honor—that should have been assimilated by Macpherson for his *Fingal*, when he makes a love triangle the occasion for Cuthullin's killing of Ferda his boyhood friend.

In some sense the degeneration of tone which is notable in an extensive survey of the Red Branch material may have influenced the alterations and (usually) degenerations of personality which are so marked a characteristic of *Finnegans Wake*. The *Fionn Mac Cumhail* cycle, however, evidences the same phenomenon in an even more emphatic fashion (see Additional Note).

SHAUN[1]
(See *Anna, *Humphrey, *Shem)

"Shaun" is a direct phonetic representation of *Seán*, the commonest Irish version of the name John. Likewise, "Haun," "Hauneen," and "Yawn" are legitimate variations of *Seán*: "Haun" and "Yawn" of *Sheán* and *Sheáin* (*Aspiration), "Hauneen" of *Sheáinín*, Johnny.

Seán is not an old Irish name, but a derivative of the Norman-French *Jehan* (modern *Jean*) introduced in the twelfth century. Despite its widespread use as a name, its connotations are mainly derogatory: *Seán Saor*, "Cheap Jack"; *Seán Báidhte*, "Drowned John": anything—like a drink—destroyed by too much water. A variant, *Seón*, taken directly from English "John," has connotations even more derogatory. *Seón* alone is an English soldier; *Seón Buidhe*, "Yellow John," is John Bull or any other bully. An Irish toady to the English is a *Seóinín*, "Little John." Since Shaun in *Finnegans Wake* appears under forms recognizable as both *Seán* and *Seón*, he must be presumed to share the attributes of both.

The name *Seán* appears to occur in Irish spelling three times in *Finnegans Wake* (093.29, 220.11, 427.27), but the last, it will be noticed, is more convincingly interpreted as *sean* (shan), "old."

Before the introduction to Ireland of the name *Seán* a form of the name John had of course existed in the context of the Bible and hagiographical literature, although not as a name in popular use. That form was *Eóin* (óin). Later *Eóin* came into occasional use as a personal name, but it has always tended to become assimilated to the phonetically very similar name *Eoghan* (óen). Both names are frequently anglicised Owen, a form of frequent appearance in *Finnegans Wake*.

Therefore it must be recognized that the name "Owen" in *Finnegans Wake* may at any time stand for *Eóin*, John, and so represent Shaun. And, in *Finnegans Wake*, if Owen *may* stand for Shaun, then it always *does* stand for Shaun. But outside *Finnegans Wake* the name Owen more frequently represents *Eoghan* than *Eóin*, and in *Finnegans Wake* it often refers explicitly to *Eoghan Mór* ("Owen the Great"), third-century king of Munster who wrested the southern half of Ireland from *Conn Céadcathach*, the high king. In *Finnegans Wake* Shaun/Abel and Shem/Cain appear doubly disguised as "Conn and Owel" (549.33–34)—also incidentally the names of two Irish lakes. Elsewhere Shaun is also identified with Owen: "the whole of him . . . in Owenmore's five quarters" (475.06–07). The allusion here is to *Eoghan Mór*'s division of Munster among his five sons. In other instances, however, such as "beamy owen and calmy hugh" (223.13), "owen" more probably stands for *Eoghan Ruadh Ó Néill* (1590–1649), military leader of the Kilkenny Confederation who died just prior to Cromwell's invasion of Ireland (see **Uí Néill*). Additionally, "owen" in *Finnegans Wake* almost always also represents *abhainn*, "river" (see **Anna*). Even "Owenmore" is a real river—*Abhainn Mór*, "Great River," —as well as *Eoghan Mór*.

Although the name *Eoghan* is usually anglicised in the simple phonetic form Owen, sometimes it is more pretentiously rendered "Eugene," and conversely Eugene is always rendered *Eoghan* in Irish. The basis of this equation is the assertion (which cannot be substantiated) that *Eoghan* means "wellborn" and so corresponds exactly to the Greek *Eugenios*. Therefore it is no surprise to find Shaun appearing as "Eugenius" (572.24–573.17), or to behold the Mookse turning "eugenious" (154.20): the connection is established through *Eoghan/Eóin*. Other Shaun figures have the same characteristic: Taff is "wellbred" (352.17) and Primas, at least in the *First-Draft* (of 014.13), "was a gentleman and came of decent people"[2]—that is to say, they are both "eugenious."

In addition to the dubious equation of *Eoghan* with Eugenios, Irish has a name of clear etymology which matches Eugenios directly. *Caoimhghin*, anglicised Kevin, is a compound of *caomh*—"gentle, mild, fair; noble,

precious, beautiful" (the present Lexicon compromises with "comely")—
and *gein*—"conception, birth." *Caomh*, in short, corresponds to Greek *eu*,
and *gein* is a direct cognate of *genos*. The sequence of the equations of
Shaun's names, therefore, runs this way: Shaun = *Seán* = Jehan/Jean =
Seón = John = *Eóin* = *Eoghan* = Eugenius = Wellborn = Comely-
Birth = *Caoimhghin* = Kevin = Kev.

A more tenuous addition to this sequence may be possible if Shaun is,
as Mrs. Glasheen suggests, to be equated with *Goll Mac Mórna*. If he is
Goll he must be blind or one-eyed, for that is what *goll* means, and if he is
blind or one-eyed he shares an attribute with "Owen K." (066.24).
Owen K. is really *Abhainn Caoch*, "Blind River"—the Owen-keagh (see
*Anna)—but of course he could equally well be *Eoghan/Eóin Caoch*, and
so effectively hitch *Goll* onto the chain. An even further extension can be
made by shifting from *Goll* to *Gall*, "foreigner"—a word infinitely re-
peated in *Finnegans Wake* in conjunction with its correlative, *Gaedheal*
(gél), "Irishman." This will be supported by the quite independent connection of "Irishman" with the Shemese correlative of *Goll Mac Mórna*,
Diarmaid Ó Duibhne (see *Shem).

Still other names of Shaun can be illuminated through Irish, although
not all can be securely affixed to the equational chain. If he is Shakespeare's MacDuff, for example, then his name—*Mac Duibh*, "Son of
Black"—may equate him also with the "dooley boy," since Dooley is
Ó Dubhlaoigh, "descendant of a Black-Warrior" (and "boy" may be the
same opprobrious epithet *buidhe* [bwí], "yellow" as in *Seón Buidhe*).
Finally, "Chuff" and "Chuffy" are Anglo-Irish words meaning "full"
(from eating). Possibly they derive from the verb *tiomhlaim* (t'uvlim),
"I eat," or its participle *tiomhailt* (t'uvilt'), "eating."

> 1. The substance of this note has already appeared at somewhat
> greater length as "The Names of Shem and Shaun: 1. The Names
> of Shaun," *A Wake Newslitter*, New Series, I (October, 1964), pp.
> 1–6.
> 2. See David Hayman, *A First-Draft Version of Finnegans Wake*
> (Austin, 1963), p. 53.

SHEM[1]

(See *Shaun, *Anna, *Humphrey; also *Colmcille and *Toraidheacht
Dhiarmada agus Ghráinne; and Additional Note on *Fionn Mac Cumhail*.)

The onomastic career of Shem is both more complex and more discontinuous than that of his brother Shaun. Often Shem's particular identity depends more upon his antithesis to Shaun than to any easily traceable connection with other Shem identities. Some brief Shem chains may however be postulated.

First thing to acknowledge is that "Shem," unlike "Shaun," is not per se an Irish name. To assert its derivation from *Séamus/Seumas* (shémus —both spellings are legitimate), the Irish form of "James," is really a kind of ignoratio elenchi. In English, Shem primarily is the name of the son of Noah who became the ancestor of the Chosen People. From Shem, however, it is possible to move through a series of equations in Irish to reach *Séamus*. First, the Irish form of the name "Shem" is *Séim* (shém), which in turn is a homophone of the name *Séam* (shém). This last is usually reserved specifically as the name of Sant Iago—St. James of Compostella, the national patron of Spain—but is occasionally used more generally for "James." Since *Séim* and *Séam* are homophonic with the English "shame," it has not always been possible to distinguish occasions when the Irish name is mixed up with the English noun; when judged probable, such mixtures are glossed in this Lexicon. The case of "shaym" (092.28) is obviously unambiguous. From *Séam*, of course, it is a short step to *Séamus/Seumas* (211.04, 219.22; 425.06; 169.01, 211.31; 483.04; and numerous less obvious instances).

An interesting divagation from the main chain of Shem–*Séamus* equations, however, begins very early in *Finnegans Wake*. If, at the Battle of Waterloose, Shaun is the dark "dooley boy," then Shem must be the "hinnessy" (010.04 ff.). If so, he must be fair, in contrast to "dooley," for the first element in his name is undoubtedly *fionn* (fin), "fair" (*Aspiration). The contrasting elements in their names are conjoined to produce the "hinndoo" ("fair-dark"), whose name, Shimar Shin, is a compound of Shem and Shaun, as is revealed particularly clearly in the First Draft and Joyce's diagram of the battle.[2] "Shimar" is Shem's contribution to the name, and that is an exact phonetic transcription of the Irish word *siomar* (shimer), the designation of several low-growing wild ground plants, including trefoil and clover. A variant of this word is *seamar* (shamer), and with the diminutive suffix *-óg* these two words become respectively the more specific plant names *simearóg* (shimeróg) and *seamróg* (shamróg), both of which in English are rendered as "shamrock." The name "Shimar," then, which in the *First-Draft* was simply "Shim," by augmentation has come to mean "shamrock"—the emblem of Ireland and St. Patrick's symbol of the Trinity.[3]

Elsewhere in *Finnegans Wake* Shem continues to remain equatable with the shamrock. The statement, for instance, "amaid her rocking grasses the herb trinity shams lowliness" (014.33–34), invites a question to which at least three answers are available. Why does the herb trinity sham lowliness? The "herb trinity" is the shamrock ("rocking . . . shams"), which is a low-growing herb. But one answer is that it shams lowliness because it is really the Trinity, and therefore lofty, not lowly. A second answer may be obtained by treating the question as a riddle: Why does the herb sham? Because it is a *shammer*. Here the answer is a pun on "shammer"/*seamar*—Irish for one of the trefoils identified as shamrock. A third answer views the question morally: Why does the herb sham lowliness? Because it is a low sham. This answer directly equates the shamrock with Shem, for "Shem was a sham and a low sham" (170.25). That this identification is not fortuitous is shown by the fact that this statement about Shem derives from the answer to another riddle: "when is a man not a man?" (170.05)—"when he is a—yours till the rending of the *rocks,—Sham*" (170.23–24). Shem and the shamrock are once more inseparable in the *"Deal Lil Shemlockup Yellin"* (180.05–06) which, among other things, is the "Dear Little Shamrock of Ireland."

Whether identification with the shamrock also serves to identify Shem with St. Patrick, or not, is a matter that cannot be settled lexicographically. But there can be no question that identification with the shamrock is identification with Ireland and with the Irish. And in the Irish language, just as the name *Seón* denotes John Bull or the English in general, the personal name that denotes a typical Irishman or the Irish in general is *Diarmaid*. Dinneen's dictionary, for example, translates the sentence *"Tá Diarmaid dá chiapadh"* as "The Irish are being tortured." And Shem certainly appears in the character of *Diarmaid* quite frequently in *Finnegans Wake*, although he also expands in the rôle somewhat beyond the dimensions of the typical Irishman.

There are two significant Irish *Diarmaids* that Shem impersonates, in fact, who yet have some traits in common. *Diarmaid Ó Duibhne* was a close friend and companion of *Fionn Mac Cumhail*—unlike his Shaun opposite, *Goll Mac Mórna*, who was as much a rival as a friend (see Additional Note, *Fionn Mac Cumhail*). Yet *Diarmaid* became much more bitter a rival than *Goll* when he eloped with *Fionn's* betrothed, *Gráinne*, daughter of King *Cormac Mac Airt* (see **Toraidheacht Dhiarmada agus Ghráinne*). The second *Diarmaid* of note was *Diarmaid Mac Murchadha*, twelfth-century king of Leinster who, to settle a rivalry between the high king, *Ruaidhrí Ó Conchobhair* (see Additional Note) and himself, invited to his aid some of the Norman barons who had completed the conquest of England, and thus precipitated the agonized nightmare of later Irish history. *Diarmaid* may have been a typical enough Irishman, but he is certainly not one whose memory has been kept dear.

The name *Diarmaid*, like most other Irish names, was subjected in the nineteenth century and even earlier to a procrustean anglicisation and, because of a similarity in the sound (d'írmid'; becoming in the West jírmij), was converted to Jeremiah and Jerome. It is this that turns Shem into Jeremias (572.24—573.18) and also permits the identification of the "Jeremy" who occurs four times in *Finnegans Wake* with Shem. The diminutive form of *Diarmaid* is *Diairmín* (d'írmín; jírmín), and this, by the same process of anglicisation, yields Jerry, the naughty brother of nice-child Kevin. The common noun *diairmín* also exists, meaning "any small creature *(contemptuous)*; a finch; a curse-word." What, if any, employment this word finds in *Finnegans Wake* I cannot say. At any rate, the full extent of a chain of equations for Shem might go something like this: Shem = *Séim* = *Séam* = *Séamus*/*Seumas* = *siomar*/*seamar* = shamrock = Ireland = typical Irishman = *Diarmaid*/*Diairmín* = Jeremias/Jeremy/Jerry.

Additional Irish identities for Shem are disjunct. He is *Conn Céadcathach*, ruler of the northern half of Ireland, apparently largely because Shaun is *Eoghan Mór*, ruler of the south. If he is MacBeth, the opposite of Mac-Duff, he is *Mac an Beatha*, "Son of Life." As an opposite to St. Kevin he may be St. *Colmcille. As the opposite to Chuff, "full," he is Glugg, "empty." That is, Glugg is Irish *gliogar*, "gurgle, rattle; a child's rattle"; Glugger is *gliogaire*, "rattler; addled egg; vain empty foolish boaster."

1. The substance of this note has already appeared in "The Names of Shem and Shaun: 2. The Names of Shem," *A Wake Newslitter*, New Series, III (October, 1966), pp. 91–93.

2. See David Hayman, *A First-Draft Version of Finnegans Wake* (Austin, 1963), pp. 50–51.

3. Much of the material in this paragraph has appeared in "The Names of Shem and Shaun: 1. The Names of Shaun," *A Wake Newslitter*, New Series, I (October, 1964), pp. 4–6.

TORAIDHEACHT DHIARMADA AGUS GHRÁINNE
(See Additional Note on *Fionn Mac Cumhail*; and *Shem)

Toraidheacht Dhiarmada agus Ghráinne—the Pursuit (or Flight) of *Diarmaid* and *Gráinne*—is one of the longest and most fully developed of the prose tales in the *Fionn Mac Cumhail* cycle. The story is mentioned in the Book of Leinster (early twelfth century), a fact which proves the story to be at least that old, but the chief manuscript in which it is preserved (Royal Irish Academy 23 L 39) is a copy made between 1775 and 1778 by *Seaghán Ó Domhaill* (John Dowell). The story has been popularly translated by P. W. Joyce in his *Old Celtic Romances*, and made very accessible in Irish by "*An Seabhach*" in an edition published by *Comhlucht Oideachais na hÉireann* (The Irish Educational Company, Dublin).

The story is fairly long, naming about a hundred persons, not counting the duplicates of those who occur in multiples (this is an unattractive mannerism of the *Fionn*-cycle stories—see Additional Note—*Diarmaid*, for instance, kills nine different men in sequence, all of whom are named *Garbh*). *Seaghán Ó Domhaill*'s text contains much digressive material, and almost every one of the subsidiary manuscripts adds an incident or an episode not found elsewhere. It is difficult therefore to summarize the tale briefly, but the outline is about as follows:

Fionn Mac Cumhail, leader of the *Fianna*, comes to a feast at Tara with his chief followers, to celebrate his betrothal to *Gráinne*, daughter of the high king, *Cormac Mac Airt*. *Fionn* elects as *fear coimeádtha* of *Gráinne*—that is best man and guardian of the bride—his dearest friend, *Diarmaid Ó Duibhne*, a handsome and virile young Kerryman. At the feast *Gráinne* drugs the elderly *Fionn*, and places upon *Diarmaid* a *geas*—a magical injunction the breach of which would involve forfeit of honor—to elope with her and marry her. With misgivings *Diarmaid* accedes, and the lovers flee. (The general resemblance of this to the story of Tristan and Iseult was by no means lost upon the author of *Finnegans Wake*.)

Thereafter follow some years of flight and pursuit across Ireland, with *Diarmaid* and *Gráinne* perpetually falling into *Fionn*'s hands only to be rescued by the magic of *Aonghus an Bhrogha*, son of *Manannán Mac Lir* the sea-god. Since *Aonghus* is something of a love-god, these rescues are reminiscent of the rescues of Paris by Aphrodite in the *Iliad*. Finally *Fionn* recalls his old nurse from the Promised Land and incites her to encompass

Diarmaid's downfall by witchcraft. Baffled in this, he consents to peace, and *Diarmaid* and *Gráinne* settle down in isolation to rear the four sons and a daughter they have produced.

After some time, in an attempt at reconciliation, *Fionn* and the *Fianna* are invited to be houseguests of *Diarmaid* and *Gráinne*. They stay for a year, until in the middle of one night the *Fianna* go out to hunt a boar that has been reported nearby. Awakened by the noise of hounds, *Diarmaid* goes out to investigate and encounters *Fionn* on a hilltop. He proposes to join the hunt, but *Fionn* reveals to him that *Diarmaid*'s life is magically joined to that of a certain boar, and that he has really been under *geas* since childhood never to hunt a boar. The boar then breaks cover, rushes, and gores *Diarmaid*, who kills it, but lies himself bleeding to death. *Fionn* cannot refrain from gloating at *Diarmaid*'s plight and casts up to him his faithlessness at Tara. *Diarmaid* places the blame on *Gráinne* and begs *Fionn* to save his life. *Fionn* pretends not to know how to do this, but *Diarmaid* reminds him of his power to save the life of any dying man to whom he will bring a drink of water in his cupped hands. *Fionn* then asserts that no water is to hand, but *Diarmaid* points out a hidden spring nearby. *Fionn* thereupon starts to bring a handful of water, but while carrying it his anger against *Diarmaid* revives and he lets the water drop. *Diarmaid* then reminds him of their former friendship and of the numerous occasions upon which *Diarmaid* saved *Fionn*'s life. *Fionn* fetches a second handful of water but the same thing happens. *Fionn* pretends it was an accident but meanwhile his grandson *Oscar* has come upon the scene, who accuses *Fionn* of deliberately dropping the water and threatens to kill him if he does it again. A third time *Fionn* carries water, and under *Oscar*'s menaces retains it carefully. Before he can reach *Diarmaid*, however, *Diarmaid* dies.

A number of epilogues are given by the manuscripts—*Gráinne*'s adventures in raising her sons, *Gráinne*'s return to *Fionn*, and so forth, but these are both of dubious authenticity and distinctly anticlimactic.

A sidelight on *Toraidheacht Dhiarmada agus Ghráinne* is that—although the traditions have no support in the actual story—in many parts of Ireland the dolmens or "cromlechs"—usually a gigantic slab of stone supported on three smaller stones—are reputed to be the "beds" where *Diarmaid* and *Gráinne* rested during their flight from *Fionn*. Dolmens and cromlechs occur in *Finnegans Wake*, but whether or not associated with *Diarmaid* and *Gráinne* I am not prepared to say.

UÍ NÉILL
(See *Brian Boru, *Malachy; and Additional Note on *Ruaidhrí Ó Conchobhair*)

As a preliminary something needs to be said about the Irish system of clans. In the native Gaelic structure of society every free man belonged to a kinship group, an extended family, and indeed the individual scarcely had any real existence apart from that of his kindred. Society was built upward from lineages, septs, clans, tribes, all based on the principle of near or remote common ancestry. Old Irish district names are all the names of tribes, clans, or families, and political distinctions were in no way separable from kinship distinctions. *Brian Boru, for instance, had at the basis of his power the fact that he was chief of *Dál gCais*, which some writers describe as a "principality." But *Dál gCais* means "Race of *Cas*," who was sixth in descent from *Cormac Cas*, son of *Oilioll Olum*, king of Munster in the third century, and is the name properly of a group of kinsmen, a large number of families descended from a common ancestor. The basic unit of all society was the *fine*, usually consisting of four generations, the descendants of one man. All land was held by such *finte*, never by individual persons. The word *clann* (from Latin *planta*, "stock, grafting," by *P/K Split) is used strictly as a group noun meaning "all the children of a given parent," but more loosely may denote a kinship group of any degree of consanguinity. As a *clann* grew numerous it required more land, as one dwindled it could hold less; the requisite adjustments were effected by means of the petty warfare which was a constant and dismal feature of earlier Irish history. A stronger *clann* could usually become paramount in a local district, accept tribute from weaker *clanna* and arbitrate their disputes, thus bringing local peace. In this way petty chieftainships arose, and then on a larger and larger scale the greater chieftainships, the "principalities," the provincial kingships, culminating in the high kingship of all Ireland.

Since individuals had no proper existence outside their *finte* or clans, in which alone they lived and moved and had their being, loyalty to one's own clan was as spontaneous as self-interest. Reciprocally, the clan valued its members, since on their strength and numbers depended the life of the clan. Consequently it is not surprising that no one felt the least unreasonableness in an entire clan's paying the fine levied to requite the wrongdoing of one of its members, and conversely every member of a clan felt that a wrong done to any other member was a wrong done to himself. Among the more benevolent products of this social system was an intense family loyalty which even today is characteristic among the Irish. And a result of family loyalty was that as kinship groups expanded through the generations, as the multiple sons of a patriarch became patriarchs in their own right, family ties were not forgotten. Descendants of brothers, then of cousins, then of second cousins, remembered their common origin and so formed the greater clans which persisted over the centuries. Thus some stability in society was attained. If every man's hand was restrained from his neighbor because his neighbor was his clansman, large groups of family clans lived as amicable neighbors and as allies because they were all members of a greater clan.

It is not easy to estimate how many of these great clans existed contemporaneously at any time, and any attempted catalogue would have difficulty separating the greatest clans from their subclans, many of which might be more powerful than other completely independent clans. Unlike the Scottish clans of the popular notion, the Irish clans did not share a surname, for the clan system in Ireland arose "back in the presurnames period" (030.03–04). But the great clans did have names, names which recur incessantly in Irish history. Most of these names consist of the name of the common ancestor (in the genitive) preceded by *Cineal, Clann, Corca, Dál, Muintear, Síol, Sliocht, Teallach,* or *Uí*—all words meaning, with fine distinctions, kindred, race, progeny, tribe, family, people, seed, or household. And of all the great clans none whatsoever was greater, or great for longer, than the clan called *Uí Néill:* the descendants, or grandsons, of *Niall.*

Niall Naoighiallach ("Nine-Hostager") was high king of Ireland 379–406 A.D. Moreover he is the first high king who is, undisputedly, a real historical figure. From his time until 1002, with few and minor interruptions, the high kingship was held by his descendants, the *Uí Néill*, which is a measure of their power and importance. *Niall* had eight sons, of whom four settled in their ancestral lands in the north and northwest of Ireland— covering the present Counties Derry, Tyrone, and Donegal, and Sligo as far southwest as Ben Bulben. The other four settled closer to their father's royal seat of Tara, chiefly over the present Counties Meath and Westmeath. Of each group three clans became prominent: in the North, *Cineal Eoghain* (occupying *Tír Eoghain*, "Tyrone"), *Cineal Conaill* (occupying *Tír Chonaill*, modern Donegal), and *Cineal Cairbre*—known collectively as the "Northern *Uí Néill*"; in the north midlands, *Clann Cholmáin*, *Cineal Fiachach*, and *Fir Teathbha*—forming the "Southern *Uí Néill*." (For readers unfamiliar with Irish geography it may be needful to stress that both branches of *Uí Néill* inhabited the northern half of Ireland; the "Southern *Uí Néill*" were southern only relatively to their more hyperborean cousins.) Over the centuries the *Uí Néill* grew far enough apart to allow for mutual warfare, and an early bone of contention was the high kingship. Very quickly a compromise was attained, by which the high kingship was to pass in alternate reigns between the Northern and the Southern *Uí Néill*. In practice this came to mean that alternate high kings of Ireland for six centuries were provided by *Cineal Eoghain* and *Clann Cholmáin*.

A source of confusion in poorly informed discussions of the *Uí Néill* is that, understandably, the given name *Niall* was not rare among them. *Niall Glúndubh* ("Blackknee"), a member of *Cineal Eoghain*, high king of Ireland, was killed fighting the Danes in 919 (by one *Amhlaoibh* [see *Humphrey], on the site of Phoenix Park). His grandson, *Domhnall*, king of *Ailech* (the *Cineal Eoghain* subkingdom), called himself *Domhnall Ó Néill* —grandson of *Niall*—and the name became thereafter one of the earliest hereditary surnames in modern Europe. Many have written of the illustrious family *Ó Néill* as if it encompassed the entire double dynastic clan of *Uí Néill*, and constituted therefore the genuine original Irish "royal family." It is instead only one of the two leading families of the leading subclan of the Northern *Uí Néill* (the other being *Ó* or *Mac Lochlainn*). Nevertheless the O Neills represent effectively the northern partners in the alternating monarchy, and postdynastic O Neills gathered such effulgence about themselves that the title of leading Irish family cannot reasonably be denied them.

Yet after the death of *Niall Glúndubh* a sort of lassitude overtook the O Neills while a certain weakness is also evident in the two great Southern *Uí Néill* kings, *Maelsheachlainn* I and II. *Maelsheachlainn* II, for all his title of "the Great," lost the high kingship to the usurper *Brian Boru, and until the extinction of the high kingship only two *Uí Néill* rulers held it, neither of them securely, and neither of them an *Ó Néill*. (See Additional Note on *Ruaidhrí Ó Conchobhair*).

After *Ruaidhrí Ó Conchobhair* the history of the *Uí Néill*, however, largely reduces itself to a history of the O Neills. In 1395 Richard II on his expedition to Ireland knighted the "four kings of Ireland"—one to each province—and for Ulster knighted the chief Ó Néill. The advance of Normans and English elsewhere hardly affected the O Neill territory, and four English reigns later Edward IV acknowledged Henry Ó Néill as "chief of the Irish kings." Throughout this time their only serious opposition came from their kinsmen of *Cineal Conaill*, the leading family of which had acquired the surname of Ó *Domhnaill*—O Donnell—and with whom they were perpetually at war. Some O Neills had meanwhile moved eastward into Antrim to form the new *Clann Aodha Buidhe* ("Children of Yellow *Aodh* [Hugh Boy O Neill]"), rather roughly anglicised Clandeboy.

In the sixteenth century the history of the O Neills begins to become quite complex. *Con Bacach* Ó *Néill* (1484–1559), grandson of Henry, after fighting off an English invasion submitted to Henry VIII who created him Earl of Tyrone for his own life, nominating his illegitimate son Matthew as his successor. This was resented by Con's legitimate son, *Seán* ("Shane"), who had Matthew murdered in 1558. After much fighting and negotiating *Seán* in 1562 went to London, where Elizabeth acknowledged his claim to the chieftainship, repudiating Matthew's son Brian, and leaving the Earldom in abeyance. Two later English expeditions against *Seán* failed so dismally that Elizabeth conceded him complete local autonomy. O Neill then got caught in a trap of his own construction: in 1565 he attacked and defeated the Scottish MacDonnells of Antrim, taking prisoner their chief *Somhairle Buidhe* ("Sorley Boy"); in 1567 he was himself disastrously defeated by his western neighbors and kinsmen, the O Donnells, and fled for refuge to the MacDonnells, who murdered him in revenge for his maltreatment of *Somhairle*.

Seán was succeeded as Ó *Néill* by *Toirdealbhach* ("Turlough"), who fought and temporized with the English for about eighteen years, when he handed over the chieftainship to *Aodh* Ó *Néill*, son of Brian son of Matthew. *Aodh* ("Hugh") Ó *Néill* (1540–1616) was raised in England, out of reach of his uncle *Seán*, but returned in 1567. He was allowed to assume *Con Bacach*'s Earldom as Second Earl, and is known in Irish history as "the great earl." Inaugurated Ó *Néill* in 1593, he was supreme throughout the North; by 1595 his English youth had sufficiently passed for him to be proclaimed traitor to the Crown. He allied himself with his hereditary enemy, *Aodh Ruadh* Ó *Domhnaill* ("Red Hugh O Donnell"), and together they opened negotiations with Philip II of Spain for succor. Nonetheless by soft words he held off the English wrath and in 1598 received a formal pardon from the Queen. Almost immediately he had an army in the field against the English, coincident with a Fitzgerald insurrection in the South. For the first time in history a dawning national consciousness led to a really concerted general opposition to the English presence. The "War of the Earls" lasted for three and a half years, but the O Neills and O Donnells came to grief at Kinsale, where they were attempting to help the breakout of a Spanish beachhead, in December 1601. *Aodh Ó Domhnaill* immediately fled to Spain, while *Ó Néill* returned to the North and submitted.

James I upon his accession confirmed *Ó Néill*'s title of Earl, but by 1607 James's provocations forced *Ó Néill* to lead what is called the "flight of the earls." He and *Ruaidhrí Ó Domhnaill, Aodh Ruadh*'s successor, boarded ship on Lough Swilly, with their wives and children, and sailed for Spain. Winds carried them to the Netherlands instead, whence they crossed the continent to Rome, where *Aodh Ó Néill* lived until his death in 1616. *Aodh*'s successor as chief of *Ó Néill* was *Feidhlim* ("Phelim"), who died in 1653. A greater man, however, was *Eoghan Ruadh* (Own Roe) *Ó Néill* (1590–1649), who was both the leading spirit and the military genius of the Kilkenny Confederation, the native Irish government set up after the Rebellion of 1641. He defeated with great skill the efforts of the British forces—distracted by Civil War at home—sent to suppress the Confederation. But just before he would have had to test his mettle against Cromwell, he died suddenly, near the end of 1649. A kinsman, however, *Aodh Mac Airt Ó Néill*, had the honor of inflicting on Cromwell the only major defeat he suffered in Ireland, at Clonmel in 1650.

O Neill refugees attained great distinction in the military service of various continental powers, and they are still members of the nobility of Spain. The present chief of the name is a national of Portugal.

Additional Notes

FIONN MAC CUMHAIL
(See *Macpherson, *Toraidheacht Dhiarmada agus Ghráinne)

Fionn Mac Cumhail is the hero of the later Irish cycle of heroic tales (see *Red Branch). From the stories and from the Annals (see *Four Masters) a great deal of information can be derived about *Fionn*—almost everything, in fact, but evidence of his actual historical existence. He was the leader in his own time of the *Fian* or *Fianna*, a kind of standing army drawn from all parts of Ireland, and from men who either were, or had to become (this is obscure), alienated from their clans (see *Uí Néill). *Fionn*'s father had led the *Fianna* before him, and a contradictory picture is presented of rival clans within the *Fianna*. *Cumhal* (*Macpherson's Comhal) *Mac Tréanmór* carried off *Múirne Muin-chaomh* (*Macpherson's Morna), daughter of *Tadhg Mac Nuadhat* (*Macpherson's Thaddu), and made her his wife. This occasioned the battle of *Cnuca* (Castleknock, west of Phoenix Park, Dublin), at which *Cumhal* was slain by *Goll Mac Mórna* (*Macpherson's Gaul son of Morni), leader of the rival *Clanna Mórna*, in 174 A.D. *Fionn* was subsequently born and named *Demni* ("Assurance"), which was later changed to *Fionn* ("Fair"). During *Fionn*'s childhood *Goll* retained leadership of the *Fianna*, but yielded it upon *Fionn*'s maturity and became a follower, though a hostile one.

Fianna headquarters were at *Almhu* (Hill of Allen, Co. Kildare) where *Fionn* himself resided with some forces most of the year, while the remainder of the *Fianna* were scattered throughout the country. In times of invasion the *Fianna* were assembled to repel the foe and pursue him back to Scotland or Scandinavia or wherever he had appeared from. Among the heroes of the *Fianna* are those of *Fionn*'s clan, *Clanna Baoiscne*: the four generations of *Cumhal*, *Fionn*, *Oisín* (*Macpherson's Ossian), and *Oscar*, the Galahad of the cycle, as well as *Feargus Finnbhéil* and *Aodh Beag Mac Finn*, and perhaps *Caoilte Mac Rónáin*, the swift runner of the *Fian*. The rival clan included, beside others, *Goll Mac Mórna* and *Conán Maol*, the buffoon of the tales. In addition there are those of no clear affiliation, such as *Diarmaid Ó Duibhne*, whose surname indicates his relationship to

the West Kerry clan of *Corca Dhuibhne*. *Fionn*'s death is placed by the
Annalists either in 252 or 283, making him, presumably, either an improbable seventy-eight or an impossible one hundred and nine at the
time. The king of Ireland during *Fionn*'s leadership of the *Fianna* is represented to have been *Cormac Mac Airt*.

Following the deaths both of *Cormac* and of *Fionn*, the *Fianna* became
intolerable to *Cairbre Lifeachair Mac Cormaic mic Airt*, *Cormac*'s son and
successor, who, with aid from *Clanna Mórna*, fought and destroyed the
Fianna at *Gabhra* in the present Co. Limerick. Most of the heroes were
killed, but according to the earliest surviving *Fianna* stories, both *Oisín*
and *Caoilte* survived the battle and managed to live until the coming of
St. Patrick to Ireland in 432.

Although the true origin of the *Fionn* saga is hotly disputed, it is certain
that in its present form it is not ancient, and in details not accurate. Older
sagas narrate supposed events of the reigns of *Conn Céadcathach*, *Art mac
Cuinn* (166–196), *Lughaidh mac Con* (196–227), and *Cormac mac Airt* (227–
266), but are void of any allusion to *Fionn* or the *Fianna*. Moreover, as
they now stand, the tales are not all of equal age, nor is the personality
of *Fionn*, nor even his status, constant or consistent. He is believed to have
been a figure in local Leinster–Munster tradition prior to the Viking age,
although no documents exist to witness the hypothesis directly. And
originally he appears to have been a poet and magician, only promoted
to petty chief in the evolution of the saga. His quality as a magician clung
to him until the end (although he sometimes forgot about it—see **Toraidheacht Dhiarmada agus Ghráinne*) and his rôle of poet was never quite lost,
although it was his son *Oisín* who came to be regarded as premier poet
of the *Fianna*. In one of *Fionn*'s earliest personal documentary appearances,
in the early twelfth-century Book of Leinster, he is merely a local Leinster
chief who assists *Breasail*, his provincial king, against *Cairbre Lifeachair*.
In general, however, by about the year 1000 *Fionn* had become fixed in
the reign of *Cormac Mac Airt*, as leader of the *Fianna*, though how this came
about is utterly obscure.

The development of the stories and poems about *Fionn* may be considered under three separate aspects: the evolution of *Fionn* from poet-
magician to generalissimo (and in **Macpherson* to king); the origin and
growth in relative popularity of the tales; and the changes in the tone
and style of successive tales and redactions of tales. Naturally these
several aspects are not always easy to keep apart. The first is very obscure,

but obviously has some relation to the second. The most extreme theory of the origin of *Fionn* is that proposed in 1891 by the German scholar, Zimmer, who held that *Fionn* really was developed out of the personality and exploits of a Viking, Ketill Hviti (*Caitil Fionn* in Irish—Ketill the White). This thesis has found no acceptance (unless, indeed, by the totally catholic author of *Finnegans Wake*, who rejects no theories—see 099.15). A more convincing notion is that advanced by John MacNeill in his edition of *Duanaire Finn* (London, 1908), to the effect that *Fionn* was originally a hero of the Firbolg subject race. This would account for the slow acceptance of the stories in the courtly circles of the Milesian conquerors (*Colonists). While the Ulster *Red Branch epic was fashionable at court, the subject people told stories of *Fionn*. A corollary theory links the growth in acceptance of the *Fionn* saga, of a Munster–Leinster provenance, together with the concurrent relative decline of the Ulster cycle, to the rise in power of the southerner *Brian Boru and the O Briens and the waning of the northern dynasties of *Uí Néill*.

The plebeian origin of *Fionn* would also account for the initial relative stylistic inferiority of the *Fionn* to the Red Branch cycle, and to some extent for its further drastic deterioration. Despite sentimental appraisals, genuinely popular literature is usually defective in style, characterization, and psychology, and for a thousand years now *Fionn Mac Cumhail* has been the popular hero of the Gaelic-speaking peoples of Ireland, Scotland, and the Isle of Man. Accretions to the cycle have been developing throughout that time, and in few of the tales is there anything approaching the subtle nuances of character and motive evidenced in the best of the *Red Branch pieces. *Fionn* and his companions are stock characters, strong men, wallopers, and performers of muscular feats, rather than real persons. Only in *Toraidheacht Dhiarmada agus Ghráinne* do persons really come alive, and that tale is not free of stylistic extravagance. Typical mannerisms of the *Fionn* stories, designed to delight audiences which have come to expect them, but easy for a storyteller to acquire the knack of, and therefore, as Dr. Johnson might put it, cheap and vulgar, are the occurrences of names and events in groups of three or nine, and "runs" of adjectives, alliterating in groups of three. *Toraidheacht Dhiarmada agus Ghráinne*, for instance (which is one of the least-marred stories), seeks to gratify with nine persons named *Garbh*, three named *Garbh Sléibhe Mis*, and ten other instances of single names shared by exactly three persons each; it also groups foreign rulers in threes: three kings of Iceland, etc.

Opinion in general holds, however, that the most tediously bad of all the
Fionn stories is *Cath Fionntrágha* ("The Battle of Ventry"), which attains
the record "run" of twenty-seven (nine times three) alliterating adjectives
piled up on a single substantive. This is the bombastic degenerate style
that Joyce parodies (if it can be parodied) in the Cyclops episode of
Ulysses and, with surprising grace, in *Finnegans Wake* (596.32–33): "sure,
straight, slim, sturdy, serene, synthetical, swift."

The *Fionn* stories first make their appearance in medieval manuscript
collections in which they are far outnumbered by *Red Branch and non-
cyclic stories. With time, the proportion of *Fionn* stories rises, the proportion of *Red Branch stories declines, and the style of both deteriorates.
But another peculiarity of the *Fionn* stories is that they are intimately
connected with the person of St. Patrick, who lived three centuries after
the ostensible time of the *Fianna*, and that as the cycle develops the personality of Patrick suffers a deterioration even more marked than that
of the style. The earliest of these stories is *Agallamh na Seanórach* ("Inter-
rogation of the Old Men"), in which *Oisín mac Finn* and *Caoilte mac
Rónáin*, having escaped the destruction of the *Fianna* at *Gabhra*, are represented as surviving to meet St. Patrick. *Caoilte* and Patrick become
constant companions, and travel Ireland together while *Caoilte* elucidates
place-names and local history; this provides a framework for tales of the
exploits of the *Fianna* which *Caoilte* narrates as the companions reach the
locus of each. In later developments of the cycle Patrick still appears, but
he is represented more and more as a malevolent and vicious figure,
starving and bullying the decrepit survivors of a more glorious and spa-
cious age of warlike paganism. A tone of nostalgia infuses the later tales,
reflecting either Firbolg resentment of Milesian oppression and reminiscence of former freedom, or Irish peasant resentment of English material and political oppression and the Church's spiritual oppression. Even
in extraliterary Irish tradition, *"Oisín after the Fianna"* is the type of
nostalgic longing for lost youth and the past. In many stories *Oisín* is
preeminent as a laudator temporis acti in opposition to St. Patrick,
scornfully refusing baptism and its requisite repudiation of his past, and
deliberately electing to rejoin *Fionn* and the *Fianna* in hell. It is a contention difficult to put beyond controversy, but I believe the deterioration
of Patrick as he is shown in the *Fionn* cycle, and the more and more sullen
opposition to what he is made to stand for, are both major structural
contributions to *Finnegans Wake*.